'The authors offer a fresh, invigorating, and much-needed psychoanalytic treatise on race, race relations, and racism. The contributors that they have gathered represent multiple perspectives, diverse ethnocultural backgrounds, and different nationalities. Together these highly informed and somber voices create a moving chorus of cultural anthropology, psychoanalytic metapsychology, developmental studies, community politics, and, above all, clinical praxis.'

Salman Akhtar, *Professor of Psychiatry, Jefferson Medical College, Training and Supervising Analyst, Psychoanalytic Center of Philadelphia*

'This remarkable new book is a long-overdue treatment of a subject that has historically been neglected in psychotherapeutic and psychoanalytic discourse. I was enlightened by the brilliant insights from colleagues who provided new ways of understanding racism and the challenges we face. Readers will learn a great deal of practical and clinical information, as well as becoming more familiar with the tragic history of racism.'

Glen O. Gabbard, *Clinical Professor of Psychiatry, Baylor College of Medicine*

'This book is an important and thoughtful guide to one of the more urgent questions facing psychotherapeutic practice today—how to address the individual psychological implications and effects of larger structural biases, inequities, and prejudices. The book deftly connects psychological frameworks with historical and cultural ones. It is a vital resource for clinicians and citizens seeking to understand and address legacies of historical trauma.'

Jonathan M. Metzl, *Director, Center for Medicine, Health, and Society, and Frederick B. Rentschler II Endowed Professor, Vanderbilt University School of Medicine*

'Psychoanalysis gave us multiple lenses for illuminating complex human behavior through its metapsychology of the individual. In addition, Freud, as a social and cultural theorist, gave us a quintessentially powerful means of coming face to face with the *tragic* view of how humans are eminently capable of treating one another. These two projects of psychoanalysis converge in *The Trauma of Racism: Lessons from the Therapeutic Encounter.* Here, Beverly Stoute and Michael Slevin provide a masterfully designed and edited catalogue of accounts of the trauma of distorting the individual ego and endangering generations of collective and degraded human lives in our fractured world ripped by racism and its manifold systemic pathways of racialization. All scholars committed to understanding and transforming the inner world and its external fields of reference to the outside, and in reverse, how psychologically charged external fields of reference activate inner world drama, will benefit immensely from this tome. Now, hopefully, we can teach and study race in *earnest* without the facile charge of being polemic.'

Maurice Apprey, *Professor of Psychiatry, Member of the Academy of Distinguished Educators, School of Medicine, and Dean of African American Affairs, University of Virginia*

'This collection by Beverly Stoute and Michael Slevin is required reading for everyone practicing, supervising, or teaching the psychodynamic tradition. The authors provide the deep, subtle clinical thinking and practice wisdom on racism that until now has been lacking. But the reach of the book goes beyond clinical practice. Racism is searing. Its history shapes each of us regardless of racial identity. Its impact on the psyches of everyone in the U.S. is profound and traumatic. Anyone willing to look inward at themselves or outward at our society through the lens of racism could profit from this book. The authors' authenticity as they share critical reflections gained through work in the therapeutic encounter is a strength of a book that is a joy to read.'

Joanne Corbin, *Associate Dean for Academic Affairs, University of Connecticut School of Social Work, Former Director, Smith College School for Social Work Doctoral Program*

The Trauma of Racism

The Trauma of Racism: Lessons from the Therapeutic Encounter is a pioneering reflection on the psychology of racism and its impact on us all. With the intimacy of personal experience and depth of analytic exposition, the authors expose racism's searing effects on personal, clinical, and community interactions while providing pathways for change.

This book asserts that the insights and practice of psychoanalysis, applied behind the couch and in the community, create unique opportunities for change. Essayists address racially derived mental health inequities, including distortions, projections, stereotypes, and historical tropes. *The Trauma of Racism* invites personal and clinical exploration of how people learn, confront, and re-learn views on race. Narratives of the loss and grief and the burdens of slavery that crisscross the African American community are present. They are complemented by those of the psychological burdens and inspired acts of personal responsibility that respond to unequal access to wealth and opportunity along racial lines. In moving accounts portraying experiences of racism and access to privilege, the authors grapple with the possibilities of mutual understanding.

Readers concerned about racism will find themselves challenged and engaged. This book is intended for the general reader and for clinicians at any career stage. Likewise, scholars in the humanities, law, education, or public policy will find new opportunities to reflect and to act.

Beverly J. Stoute, M.D., is a child, adolescent, and adult psychiatrist and psychoanalyst, a training and supervising analyst at the Emory University Psychoanalytic Institute, and a child and adolescent supervising analyst at the New York Psychoanalytic Society & Institute. She teaches on the faculty of multiple training programs and is an internationally recognized author, speaker, educator, clinician and organizational consultant in private practice in Atlanta, Georgia.

Michael Slevin, MSW, a member of the Washington Baltimore Center for Psychoanalysis, is in private practice in Baltimore, Maryland. He is a writer and editor on psychoanalytic issues. He has been active in bringing psychoanalytic ideas and practice into contexts outside the consulting room, to less privileged communities, and into political decision making.

Psychoanalysis in a New Key Book Series
DONNEL STERN
Series Editor

When music is played in a new key, the melody does not change, but the notes that make up the composition do: change in the context of continuity, continuity that perseveres through change. Psychoanalysis in a New Key publishes books that share the aims psychoanalysts have always had, but that approach them differently. The books in the series are not expected to advance any particular theoretical agenda, although to this date most have been written by analysts from the Interpersonal and Relational orientations.

The most important contribution of a psychoanalytic book is the communication of something that nudges the reader's grasp of clinical theory and practice in an unexpected direction. Psychoanalysis in a New Key creates a deliberate focus on innovative and unsettling clinical thinking. Because that kind of thinking is encouraged by exploration of the sometimes surprising contributions to psychoanalysis of ideas and findings from other fields, Psychoanalysis in a New Key particularly encourages interdisciplinary studies. Books in the series have married psychoanalysis with dissociation, trauma theory, sociology, and criminology. The series is open to the consideration of studies examining the relationship between psychoanalysis and any other field—for instance, biology, literary and art criticism, philosophy, systems theory, anthropology, and political theory.

But innovation also takes place within the boundaries of psychoanalysis, and Psychoanalysis in a New Key therefore also presents work that reformulates thought and practice without leaving the precincts of the field. Books in the series focus, for example, on the significance of personal values in psychoanalytic practice, on the complex interrelationship between the analyst's clinical work and personal life, on the consequences for the clinical situation when patient and analyst are from different cultures, and on the need for psychoanalysts to accept the degree to which they knowingly satisfy their own wishes during treatment hours, often to the patient's detriment. A full list of all titles in this series is available at: https://www.routledge.com/Psychoanalysis-in-a-New-Key-Book-Series/book-series/LEAPNKBS

The Trauma of Racism

Lessons from the Therapeutic Encounter

Edited by Beverly J. Stoute and
Michael Slevin

LONDON AND NEW YORK

Cover image: Lightspring; Shutterstock.com

First published 2023
by Routledge
4 Park Square, Milton Park, Abingdon, Oxon OX14 4RN

and by Routledge
605 Third Avenue, New York, NY 10158

Routledge is an imprint of the Taylor & Francis Group, an informa business

© 2023 selection and editorial matter, Beverly J. Stoute and Michael Slevin; individual chapters, the contributors

The right of Beverly J. Stoute and Michael Slevin to be identified as the authors of the editorial material, and of the authors for their individual chapters, has been asserted in accordance with sections 77 and 78 of the Copyright, Designs and Patents Act 1988.

All rights reserved. No part of this book may be reprinted or reproduced or utilized in any form or by any electronic, mechanical, or other means, now known or hereafter invented, including photocopying and recording, or in any information storage or retrieval system, without permission in writing from the publishers.

Trademark notice: Product or corporate names may be trademarks or registered trademarks and are used only for identification and explanation without intent to infringe.

British Library Cataloguing-in-Publication Data
A catalogue record for this book is available from the British Library

Library of Congress Cataloging-in-Publication Data
Names: Stoute, Beverly J., 1964- editor.
Title: The trauma of racism : lessons from the therapeutic encounter / Beverly J. Stoute and Michael Slevin.
Description: Abingdon, Oxon ; New York, NY : Routledge, 2022. | Includes bibliographical references and index. |
Identifiers: LCCN 2022017018 (print) | LCCN 2022017019 (ebook) | ISBN 9781032247656 (hbk) | ISBN 9781032247472 (pbk) | ISBN 9781003280002 (ebk)
Subjects: LCSH: Racism--Psychological aspects. | Race relations. | Equality.
Classification: LCC HT1521 .T57 2022 (print) | LCC HT1521 (ebook) | DDC 305.8--dc23/eng/20220516
LC record available at https://lccn.loc.gov/2022017018
LC ebook record available at https://lccn.loc.gov/2022017019

Every effort has been made to contact copyright-holders. Please advise the publisher of any errors or omissions, and these will be corrected in subsequent editions.

ISBN: 978-1-032-24765-6 (hbk)
ISBN: 978-1-032-24747-2 (pbk)
ISBN: 978-1-003-28000-2 (ebk)

DOI: 10.4324/9781003280002

Typeset in Times New Roman
by KnowledgeWorks Global Ltd.

Michael Slevin

To Marilyn

Beverly J. Stoute

To Dexter, Spencer, and Ashley

And in loving memory of Argyle Stoute

Contents

List of Contributors	xiv
Acknowledgments	xvii
Credits List	xxiii
Introduction	1

PART I
Historical Perspectives — 5

1 Racism and Health Equity: A Challenge for the Therapeutic Dyad — 7
BEVERLY J. STOUTE

2 Race and Racism in Psychoanalytic Thought: The Ghosts in Our Nursery, 2nd Edition — 13
BEVERLY J. STOUTE

3 Race, African Americans, and Psychoanalysis: Collective Silence in the Therapeutic Situation — 42
DIONNE R. POWELL

PART II
Living with the Trauma of Racism — 73

4 African American Boys: Adolescents under the Shadow of Slavery's Legacy — 75
KIRKLAND C. VAUGHANS

5   Loss, Grief, and Fear in Everyday Lives of African
    American Women   80
    ANNIE LEE JONES

6   Everyday Racism: Psychological Effects   89
    IVAN WARD

7   Thinking Clinically About Post-Traumatic Reactions
    to Racial Trauma   105
    ANTON HART

8   From the Racially Provocative to the Evocative: Shaping
    the Destiny of the Racist Moment   125
    NARENDRA KEVAL

9   "And How Are the Children?" Intergenerational Trauma
    and the Development of Black Children in America   137
    KIRKLAND C. VAUGHANS

10 Black Rage: The Psychic Adaptation to the Trauma
    of Oppression   159
    BEVERLY J. STOUTE

11 Observations on the Use of the N-Word   192
    JYOTI M. RAO

PART III
Learning and Re-Learning Race   **219**

12 Racial Socialization and Thwarted Mentalization:
    Psychoanalytic Reflections from the Lived Experience
    of James Baldwin's America   221
    BEVERLY J. STOUTE

13 From Multicultural Competence to Radical Openness:
    A Psychoanalytic Engagement of Otherness   244
    ANTON HART

14 On Psychoanalysis, Race, and Class in an Urban ER   251
    MICHAEL SLEVIN

PART IV
Being Aware of White Privilege   271

15 How I Came to Understand White Privilege   273
     MICHAEL MOSKOWITZ

16 On Racism and Being White: The Journey to Henry's Restaurant   278
     RICHARD REICHBART

17 "Am I the Only Black Kid That Comes Here?"   283
     WARREN SPIELBERG

18 White Privilege and Its Fissures: A Personal Perspective   288
     ALEXANDRA WOODS

19 "It Takes One to Know One"   299
     MATTHEW VON UNWERTH

20 Psychoanalysis by Surprise: An Ad Hoc Experiment
     in Community Psychoanalysis on a South African Wine Farm   311
     MARK SOLMS

PART V
Interpreting Racism in Jordan Peele's *Get Out*   325

21 Get Out of My Head: Experiencing Cultural Paranoia
     in Jordan Peele's *Get Out*   327
     GRANT SHREVE

22 From *Guess Who's Coming to Dinner* to *Get Out*: Attaining
     Psychic Freedom and Emancipation across the Racial Divide   339
     DIONNE R. POWELL

Index   356

Contributors

Anton Hart, Ph.D., a clinical psychologist and a training and supervising analyst on the faculty of the William Alanson White Institute, holds leadership positions and teaches at multiple institutes and training programs nationally. He has a full-time private practice in psychoanalysis and psychotherapy, psychotherapy supervision, and organizational consultation in New York City.

Annie Lee Jones, Ph.D., a training and supervising analyst at the Institute for Psychoanalytic Training and Research, is a clinical psychologist and psychoanalyst in private practice in Queens, New York, and a founding member of Black Psychoanalysts Speak. She teaches on multiple faculties in New York City and Knoxville, Tennessee.

Narendra Keval, Ph.D., a clinical psychologist and psychoanalyst, is a member of the British Psychoanalytical Society and the Tavistock Society of Psychotherapists. He is known for his book *Racist States of Mind: Understanding the Perversion of Curiosity and Concern* (2016). He works in a range of settings, including in the National Health Service in the UK and in private practice.

Michael Moskowitz, Ph.D., a training and supervising analyst and former president of the Institute for Psychoanalytic Training and Research, has written about psychoanalytic theory, organizational dynamics, race, ethnicity, and neuroscience, and is co-producer of the film *Black Psychoanalysts Speak* and an associate producer of *Psychoanalysis in El Barrio.* He is in private practice in New York City.

Dionne R. Powell, M.D., a training and supervising psychoanalyst at the Columbia University Center for Psychoanalytic Training and Research and at the Psychoanalytic Association of New York (NYU affiliate), has held national leadership positions and has spoken and written extensively about race, racism, and gender issues. She is in private practice in New York City.

Richard Reichbart, Ph.D., a training and supervising analyst and president of the Institute for Psychoanalytic Training and Research, executive producer of the film *Black Psychoanalysts Speak,* executive co-producer of the film *Psychoanalysis in El Barrio,* and is in private practice treating adults and children in Ridgewood, New Jersey.

Jyoti M. Rao, LMFT, is an associate faculty member and psychoanalytic candidate at the San Francisco Center for Psychoanalysis. Formerly on the faculty of the department of integral counseling psychology at the California Institute of Integral Studies, she has taught a range of topics, including a course on multicultural counseling utilizing an experiential–psychodynamic approach to diversity education.

Grant Shreve, Ph.D., is a writer and scholar specializing in American literature and culture. His work has appeared in a variety of popular and academic publications. He is based in Baltimore, Maryland.

Michael Slevin, MSW, a member of the Washington Baltimore Center for Psychoanalysis, is in private practice in Baltimore, Maryland. He is a writer and editor on psychoanalytic issues. He has been active in bringing psychoanalytic ideas and practice into contexts outside the consulting room, to less privileged communities, and into political decision making.

Warren Spielberg, Ph.D., a psychologist, psychoanalyst, and Fulbright scholar, is an associate teaching professor at The New School and co-editor of *The Psychology of Black Boys and Adolescents* (2014). An authority on the psychology of masculinity, he served on the American Psychological Association's Task Force on the Guidelines for the Psychological Practice for Boys and Men.

Mark Solms, Ph.D., is a professor at the Neuroscience Institute at the University of Cape Town. He is a member of the South African and American psychoanalytic associations and the British Psychoanalytical Society. He has published over 350 articles and book chapters, and eight books. He has received numerous honors and awards internationally.

Beverly J. Stoute, M.D., is a child, adolescent, and adult psychiatrist and psychoanalyst, a training and supervising analyst at the Emory University Psychoanalytic Institute, and a child and adolescent supervising analyst at the New York Psychoanalytic Society & Institute. She teaches on the faculty of multiple training programs and is an internationally recognized speaker, educator, clinician, and organizational consultant in private practice in Atlanta, Georgia.

Matthew von Unwerth, Ph.D., a faculty member at the Institute for Psychoanalytic Training and Research, is in private practice in New York City and Reading, Vermont. He is on the faculty of the program in narrative medicine at Columbia University and is director of the Abraham A. Brill Library of the New York Psychoanalytic Society & Institute.

Kirkland C. Vaughans, Ph.D., a clinical psychologist, training and supervising analyst at the Institute for Psychoanalytic Training and Research, and co-editor of *The Psychology of Black Boys and Adolescents* (2014), has taught in and directed numerous training programs. He is an authority on child development and transgenerational trauma and is in private practice in New York.

Ivan Ward, BA, MA (Cantab), is the former Deputy Director and Head of Learning at the Freud Museum London, where he worked for 33 years. Born in Hackney, London, he is of mixed-race. The author of several books and papers on psychoanalytic theory and the applications of psychoanalysis to social and cultural issues, including race and racism, he is an honorary research associate at University College London's Psychoanalysis Unit.

Alexandra Woods, Ph.D., a clinical psychologist and psychoanalyst trained in couples and family therapy, has taught in the New York University Postdoctoral Program, where she has served with Dr. Annie Lee Jones on the Committee on Ethnicity, Race, Culture, Class and Language. She is a founding member of Black Psychoanalysts Speak and is in private practice in New York City.

Acknowledgments

Michel Slevin
This book for me began in 1949, when at two-and-a-half I fell from a second-story window. I must have been conscious, because, somehow, I got from the back of our townhouse to the front door. My grandmother, who rose early, heard my cries and said, I am told, "Michael, how did you get outside?" A day of consternation and anxiety followed. I was taken from the suburbs into the city and left at a hospital for overnight observation. Trauma had entered my life.

I was alone and terrified, in the care of unknown nurses. In the morning, cleared by doctors and leaving the hospital, I refused to be held. In that early-morning moment, I found my voice of protest and walked out on my own. My beloved Texas grandmother, Zillah Kate Price Day, with straight back and upright integrity, had come with my father to pick me up. To some concern of mine she had said, "You are good." Internally I rebelled. I heard her to mean, "You are a good person." But I knew I had done something terribly wrong to have caused such an abandonment.

Yet Mon, as the grandchildren called Zillah, was my rock until her death in the summer of 1964. She was the first to recognize me as a writer.

I met both Boyd Burris and Astere Claeyssens in 1967. In different ways, they were the mentors I needed. Claey taught literature, life, and writing as facets of one prism. Without Boyd Burris and later, Jay Phillips, this book would never have come to fruition.

I found an intellectual and professional home in 2001 at the Baltimore Washington Institute for Psychoanalysis, where I first studied as a scholar candidate. My teachers and my fellow candidates were sustaining. That community was the springboard to the American Psychoanalytic Association (APsaA). Prudy Gourguechon was responsible for my being named editor of *The American Psychoanalyst (TAP)*, a responsibility I held for three years, from 2004 to 2007. I returned in 2009 as special projects editor, a position I left only in 2021. I was welcomed by APsaA, where I served and learned variously, and by each of its presidents, notably Lynne Moritz, Harriet Wolfe, Bill Glover, and president-elect Kerry Sulkowicz. As I sought and edited manuscripts for the magazine, they gave me free rein. I had the rare opportunity to meet, know, and work with psychoanalysts from Boston to Birmingham, San Francisco to Atlanta. So many were dedicated to healing human suffering.

After the 2015 Charleston, South Carolina, murders of African Americans worshipping peacefully at Bible study, I knew I had to organize a special section of *TAP* on psychoanalysis and race. At that same mark in time, Beverly Stoute posted about the murders on the APsaA listserve. I knew immediately I wanted to edit the section with her.

That was seven years ago. Seven dedicated, emotional years of deepening friendship, hard work, thinking, writing, and editing. Over three issues, from September 2016 to March 2017, eight articles, titled "Conversations on Psychoanalysis and Race," were published in *TAP* by its editor, Doug Chavez. Several of those essays are reprinted in this book. The response to the articles was strong and helped open up a conversation about race that was already brewing in APsaA. The intensity of the response caused us to embark on this book.

The book has taken several forms. As events unfolded rapidly, two papers, Beverly's on Black Rage and mine on work in the emergency room of an urban hospital, although written with the book in mind, were first published elsewhere, Beverly's in the *Journal of the American Psychoanalytic Association,* mine in *The Psychoanalytic Study of the Child.* For that, and for permission to reprint them, we are grateful. A number of authors worked hard on essays that we could not include. But for their efforts and commitment to the project, I am also deeply grateful. From them and from those who appear in these pages, I have learned much. In the face of their efforts, I am humbled.

Lauren Purcell, the meticulous and insightful copy editor we have worked with, has been dedicated to this project almost from its inception. The American Psychoanalytic Foundation came through with a grant to help pay for her services. Donnel Stern, the series editor, Kate Hawes, our editor at Routledge, and Hannah Wright and Georgina Clutterbuck, her editorial assistants, have patiently supported a project that stretched long past its original deadline. Eva Herscowitz, through careful research of census data and other sources, helped me with my personal journey.

My father, Joseph R. Slevin, a newspaperman, had, framed on his wall, a clip taken from a news story and enlarged, with the subhead in bold black type: "Truth in News Vital." Through all the intellectual and political permutations of the late twentieth and twenty-first centuries, through my deepened understanding of psychological memory, I still believe it.

As I think about mornings listening to the voice of my mother, Zillah Katherine Day Slevin, in the last decade of her life, feelings well up similar to those I had when, at two-and-a-half, I climbed from her blanket box to the window ledge and there beyond saw a vista gray with morning, expansive, unknown, and waiting—feelings that, though after the fall forever at risk, had, I realized late in life, been a song for my journey.

Mostly, though, I am grateful to my wife, Marilyn Martin, M.D.—for her steadfast commitment to the African American community, her unshakable integrity and kindness, her psychological insight and unwillingness to judge. She has encouraged, sustained, and taught me.

Beverly J. Stoute

I am not sure when this book began. Its roots go back generations to a time I cannot name. In the 1600s, I believe half of my ancestors were enslaved in the Americas. The other half became Quakers in England, migrating from England in the late 1600s to the country of Sudan in Africa, a century or so later to the Caribbean, and in the early 1900s to North America as immigrants who had no transgenerational history of slavery. The link in the generations on one side of my family was my maternal great-grandmother, who died at the age of 104 when I was in college, having been born right after Reconstruction. Somehow, in ways that were not spoken, she kept her land in the South with a staunch fortitude and determination. I experienced and internalized her strength before I had words to express it. The strength, the fortitude, the determination were passed down. Then there were the stories I learned as a child, thinking, at the time, they were myths told to me by my father, a civil rights activist, of demonstrations and struggle, but after his death, I found the historical documents to verify that the stories were really true—some history-making—events. This was a long line of demonstrations waged, notable figures involved, demonstrations of Black Rage, and struggle—his struggle, our struggle. There was also the silence I knew from my mother and other family members, of the painful racism endured growing up in the South, for reasons we did not speak, as they struggled in the migration North. There were the family gatherings I remember from my childhood, when family and friends spoke of struggle in the Movement, and I came to understand what that meant, about the hard-won victories that paved my way by those ancestors to whom I had an obligation. So, first and foremost, I acknowledge that I am grateful for the strength of my ancestors and the generations of freedom fighters before me. In the words of Barack Obama who said, on November 4, 2008, as he stood in Grant Park in Chicago after his victory was announced, "Thank you to the giants on whose shoulders I stand."

I acknowledge my family for the generations of struggle and triumph, a family that taught me to fight, to overcome, to endure as we all carried the pain from the assault of racism and colonialism as descendants of slaves and immigrants. Racism, I learned, could be fought in the streets, in the classrooms, in the courtroom, and in our minds, but it must be fought if we are to survive it and if we are ever to recover our shared humanity in the world. In writing, I learned to give expression to the experience, to metabolize the impact. As far back as I can remember, I was told that one must have a voice, take a stand, and be unyielding in the fight for the cause of justice, freedom, and humanity, but fight with compassion and dignity. Always take a stand, and write to evoke a human response, a connection, to compel the reader to understand and to feel; that is what I learned from my father and from the generations in my family. For me, this book is part of converting that struggle into understanding.

The coming to reality of the book began in 2015. That year, after the murders in a South Carolina church, I asked myself what could I do with my psychoanalytic mind that had meaning and purpose that could be enduring in our world. At the same time, Michael Slevin approached me and asked me to write about racism. As Michael and I worked together on the series in *The American Psychoanalyst,* on this book, working together, editing together, challenging each other, learning from each other, changing each other in ways we did not even realize, I became a writer, and we became friends. We meet so many people in our lives, but only a few will change us in ways we did not expect. I thank Michael for this and for the opportunity to produce something together of which we are truly proud. We wrote at a time of unprecedented social upheaval across the globe. In it, through it, in the writing of this book, we developed our cooperative ability to talk together about, to debate, to question, to disagree, to endure, to come together in our reflections and experiences on the traumas of racism, and to be changed together for the better.

I thank all of the Black psychoanalysts before me, who paved the way so that I might have opportunities they only dreamed of.

I thank Marilyn Martin for her patience in reading our drafts and being our sounding board and whose authoritative humility was grounding for Michael and me in our most trying moments.

I thank my colleagues, some of whom may not even know how I have appreciated them and been sustained by them: Ruth Karush, Kirkland Vaughans, Dorothy Holmes, Dionne Powell, Anton Hart, Milton Hollar, Ronda Shaw, Steve Wein, Ted Becker, Ted Shapiro, Phil Herschenfeld, Lisa Korman, Alexander Kalogerakis, Naemi Stilman, Chris Lovett, and Sidney Phillips.

I thank my high school twentieth-century social studies teacher, Mr. Joseph Borlo, who challenged me to think critically in ways I have always treasured.

I thank my pediatrician, whose example inspired me: Dr. Muriel Petioni, one of the first Black women to train in her medical school class, who later taught at Harlem Hospital and practiced in the same Harlem office as had her father, a physician before her.

I thank my patients, whose openness to change, despite the work of it, allow me the privilege of finding purpose and renews my hope in the possibility of a better world.

I thank with a full heart our authors for their enduring commitment, patience, and extraordinary contributions to this volume. I stand in awe of you all.

I deeply appreciate our editors: first and foremost, Donnel Stern, our series editor, who encouraged and supported us throughout; and our meticulous and dedicated copy editor, Lauren Purcell, whose patience, understanding, and commitment were exceptional. I appreciate and thank Kate Hawes, our editor at Routledge, and Hannah Wright and Georgina Clutterbuck, her editorial assistants, who have been responsive throughout, and the American Psychoanalytic Foundation committee, which gave us a grant to help pay for copy editing services.

And mostly, and above all, I thank, again, my family. I thank my family in the generations before me, most notably the examples of those who have passed: Ella Kinchen, Dr. Argyle Stoute, Dr. Harvey J. Whitfield, and Raymond Fitzgerald Stoute, Helen Stoute whose strength and examples inspired me and encouraged me to dream. I thank my family, those who are with me: my husband, Dexter, and my children, Spencer and Ashley, for their support, their sacrifice that allowed me to make this work possible, and their love that sustains me, renews me, and gives me hope.

In closing, I thank my father, Dr. Argyle Stoute, who taught me that while racism must be fought, it can also be endured, metabolized, and understood if we keep our hearts open as we challenge our minds to learn and apply the radical tools that psychoanalysis has to offer. As one of the first African American psychoanalysts and a contemporary of Margaret Morgan-Lawrence, his example of compassion, insightfulness, love, and adaptive management of his Black Rage as a civil rights activist not only inspired me, but protected me from the destructive assault of racism as a child. Becoming a psychoanalyst, for me, has become the truest testament to the mobilizing and transformative power of operationalizing one's personal and transgenerational store of Black Rage, which I have drawn on to forge the reality of this book.

Credits List

The authors gratefully acknowledge permission to republish the following material:

Powell, D.R. (2018). Race, African Americans, and psychoanalysis: Collective silence in the therapeutic conversation. *Journal of the American Psychoanalytic Association* 66(6):1021–1049.

Rao, J.M. (2021). Observations on the use of the N-word during psychoanalytic conferences. *Journal of the American Psychoanalytic Association* 69(2):315–336.

Slevin, M. (2021). Of being and becoming: Psychoanalysis, race, and class in an urban ER. *Psychoanalytic Study of the Child* 74(1):77–89.

Stoute, B.J. (2019). Racial socialization and thwarted mentalization: Psychoanalytic reflections from the lived experience of James Baldwin's America. *American Imago* 76(3):335–357. *Copyright © 2019. Reprinted with permission of Johns Hopkins University Press. All Rights Reserved.*

Stoute, B.J. (2020). Racism: A challenge to the therapeutic dyad. *American Journal of Psychotherapy* 73(3):69–71. https://psychotherapy.psychiatryonline.org/doi/full/10.1176/appi.psychotherapy.20200043. *Copyright ©2020. Reprinted with permission from the American Journal of Psychotherapy. American Psychiatric Association. All Rights Reserved.*

Stoute, B.J. (2021). Black rage: The psychic adaptation to the trauma of oppression. *Journal of the American Psychoanalytic Association* 69(2):259–290

The authors also gratefully acknowledge permission to reprint excerpts from the following:

Baldwin, James, excerpt from 1961 radio interview, Rights held by WBAI Pacifica Radio 99.5 FM Brooklyn, New York. Reprinted with permission of WBAI Pacifica Radio 99.5 FM and General Manager Berthold Reimers

GUESS WHO'S COMING TO DINNER Copyright© 1967, renewed 1995 Columbia Pictures Industries, Inc. All Rights Reserved. Courtesy of Columbia Pictures.

Mandela, Nelson, excerpt used as epigraph from Long Walk to Freedom by Nelson Mandela © 1985 Copyright by Little Brown Book Group Limited. Reproduced with permission of the Licensor through PLSclear.

Copyright Peggy McIntosh, 1989: "White Privilege: Unpacking the Invisible Knapsack" (1989) In Peace and Freedom, July-August 1989, Phila., PA. Women's International League for Peace and Freedom

Peele, J. (2017). *Get Out*. Universal Pictures. Copyright Universal Film Exchanges LLC.

Rankine, Claudia, excerpt from *Citizen: An American Lyric*. Copyright © 2014 by Claudia Rankine. Reprinted with the permission of The Permissions Company, LLC on behalf of Graywolf Press, graywolfpress.org

Zinoman, J. (2017) "Jordan Peele on a Truly Terrifying Monster: Racism", *New York Times*. Reprinted with permission of Geoff Foster, Director of Special Projects, Monkey Paw Productions.

The following chapters are reprinted from a special section, "Psychoanalytic Conversations on Race," conceived of and edited by Michael Slevin and Beverly Stoute, published in *The American Psychoanalyst*, a membership magazine of the American Psychoanalytic Association. They are here republished with permission:

Hart, A. (2017). From multicultural competence to radical openness: A psychoanalytic engagement of otherness. *The American Psychoanalyst* 5(1):12, 13, 26, 27.

Jones, A.L. (2016). Relational dynamics of loss, grief, and fear in everyday lives of African American women. *The American Psychoanalyst* 50(3):2, 26–28.

Moskowitz, M. (2016). How I came to understand white privilege. *The American Psychoanalyst* 50(4):7, 22

Reichbart, R. (2016). On racism and being white: The journey to Henry's restaurant. *The American Psychoanalyst* 50(4):8, 23, 24.

Spielberg, W. (2016). Am I the only Black kid who comes here? *The American Psychoanalyst* 50(4):6, 21.

Stoute, B. (2017). Race and racism in psychoanalytic thought: The ghosts in our nursery. *The American Psychoanalyst* 51(1):10, 11, 16, 17–18, 28–29.

Vaughans, K. (2016). The shadow of slavery's legacy: Intergenerational trauma among African Americans. *American Psychoanalyst* 50(3):6, 26–29.

Appreciation for Funding

Funding that helped defray costs of editing the manuscripts was provided by the American Psychoanalytic Foundation through the American Psychoanalytic Association.

Introduction

The trauma of racism landed on the doorstep of America's consciousness on May 25, 2020, with the murder of George Floyd during a global pandemic. Black Lives Matter protests swelled; reverberations were felt worldwide. Anger and deep empathy for Floyd, his family, and Black and brown communities galvanized Americans across age, gender, class, and racial lines. The lens used to blur the painful reality that one group of people with white skin devalues another group with black skin had cracked. We asked ourselves, what could we do to help illuminate the complexity of the human experience of psychological and systemic racism? Could we contribute to the healing that needs to take place? The answer to our moment of trauma, we decided, was to write, to edit, to complete the collection of essays we had been working on for several years.

The authors of the chapters that follow have all borne witness, through activism, research, and writing, to the glaring societal disparities directly attendant to race. Although the horrors of racism have been present in our country for more than 400 years, laid down over time in intricate circuits of American sociology, culture, and politics, many white people were shocked. They recognized that individually and collectively they were responsible for, or at least acquiescent to, the unequal distribution of resources by race. Their privilege leveraged unjust access to employment, education, wealth, opportunity, and power. The trauma privilege inflicts on people of color was suddenly in the buzz of a national conversation. African Americans had known it all along, for they live the traumas and indignities every day. Many whites, though—even those long committed to racial equality—found that the emotion coursing through the public space connected them to the daily lives of people of color. New understandings surged from the margins to the center: that inequalities of race were embedded in contemporary structures created by whites; that racism and racial inequality—however painfully internalized by many Black Americans seeking to navigate intolerable and immovable realities—were a white problem.

Two realities—the murder of Black men by police and unequal distribution of illness and death by COVID-19—overtook our work on *The Trauma of Racism: Lessons from the Therapeutic Encounter*. Beverly Stoute redirected her attention to write her groundbreaking theoretical paper "Black Rage: The Psychic Adaptation to the Trauma of Oppression." Exploring her own response to the twin realities of death launched a journey to clarify how Black people productively manage their deep rage, experienced as though fresh by each generation. That rage, driven by the legacy of the Middle Passage, slavery, and Jim Crow, is a legacy that penetrates American society still. Stoute experienced, recognized, and then gave analytical expression to her own Black Rage. As a psychological adaptation of Black culture, she writes, it protects against the shocks and insults, old and new, of racism, while making it possible for people to endure and resist.

Stoute's essay is the linchpin holding together the book's Part One: Historical Perspectives and Part Two: Living with the Trauma of Racism. Our collection's Part Three: Learning and Relearning Race then pivots to Part Four: Being Aware of White Privilege. Engaging in a conversation about the complex reality of race from the platform of privilege evokes powerful feelings. With integrity and care, our authors describe variously anxiety, guilt, fear, regret, nostalgia, pleasure, grief, entitlement, and sorrow. As writers, they look inward, to confront themselves, and outward, to confront the racism embedded in our society. Seeking to understand and heal, they convey hope for a future that is more just. But their essays blaze a path across difficult terrain. Acknowledging the landscape, we conclude our book with a hard look at the present in Part Five: Interpreting Racism in Jordan Peele's *Get Out*. In the two essays there, Grant Shreve and Dionne Powell reflect on a film that, as it develops, peels layers off a racism that demolishes Black identities even as it appropriates Black culture and Black bodies for its own pleasure and advancement. Paradoxically, the film, as Grant Shreve writes, was greeted at its opening in Baltimore by an interracial audience among whom "a communal bond was forged" by Peele's stark truth.

The reality of trauma hovers over the essays in this collection. Sometimes explicit, often not, it informs the human narratives throughout. What is the narrative of racism from the perspective of trauma? It is the searing impact of the lash and the lasting scars left behind; it is the separation of child from mother, husband from wife; it is the corrosive action of a culture that in countless ways devalues Black lives; it is the systemic throttling of opportunities for education, housing, and employment as promised equality is dangled out of reach. The transgenerational transmission of these assaults on the psyches of African American citizens has left a deep and distinct mark on Black subjectivity. But the trauma of racism has affected us all. White people have responded variously to the suffering in their midst. Many, now shaken into awareness of their roles, witting or unwitting, in this national tragedy, have awakened to their lost humanity. They see the opportunities they, too, would derive from a more just society.

Our subtitle is "Lessons from the Therapeutic Encounter." Those lessons were learned in the consulting room, the schoolroom, the hospital emergency room, in media and film, and, as Mark Solms narrates, through reconciling the traumas lived on his South African wine farm. Our encounter is seen through the psychoanalytic lens, but this is a psychoanalysis free of the excesses of jargon, and an instrument for the recognition and elaboration of the experience of another. Psychoanalysis is a disciplined study of individual subjectivity as affected by stages of development, family dynamics, community, biology, culture, and history. As clinicians, we have employed it to explore and even heal the psychic assaults of racism. The investment our authors have made in their essays is palpable. Many speak autobiographically in tones immediate and intimate. Many are psychoanalysts sharing knowledge gained and deepened through the therapeutic encounter.

That knowledge offers insight into the way racism has been embedded in individual, family, and community histories. Individuals and the society within which they live are formed in the crucible of human relationships. While some relationships are created from realistic and empathic bonds, others are born of distortions, misinformation, misunderstanding, projections, and fear. The institutions, policies, and laws; the emotional structures, values, and behaviors; and the norms and governing symbols that structure our culture are orchestrated by human hearts and minds. While group processes and the larger societal structures—the province of sociologists, political scientists, novelists, architects, and philosophers—cannot be explained as direct manifestations of intrapsychic processes, they do coexist and interact with individual psyches in complex ways. Whether studying the underpinnings of authority in race relations, seeking to redress wrongs inflicted by the economic institution of slavery, or attempting to rehabilitate a community grounded in a history of systemic racism, the psychological knowledge, techniques, openness, and emotional integrity essential to psychoanalysis can deepen the work.

Each generation of psychoanalysts bears its own stamp. They shape their institutions and theories in the midst of a moment in time. That fact is in the ethos of our age, made manifest by psychoanalysts as they work to understand how culture and history are integral to the unconscious and to human relations. Through this work and much more, psychoanalysis recuperates from past theories on race riddled with the prejudices prominent in the society from which it emerged. The civil rights movement, the Black Power movement, and postcolonial studies have all influenced the field and its members. This book lives in the ferment of the George Floyd moment. We look through the resolving lens of today's psychoanalysis at the systemically and intrapsychically embedded traumas that have made American racism all but intractable. Doing so, we fervently believe, can help individuals and society break from their history and heal.

Part I

Historical Perspectives

Chapter 1

Racism and Health Equity
A Challenge for the Therapeutic Dyad

Beverly J. Stoute

A patient's race and zip code influence health care delivery more than any other variables. Mental health care disparities faced by members of racial—ethnic minority groups, Medlock et al.[1] contend, include "inequities in access, symptom severity, diagnosis, and treatment," as well as in treatment outcome. Removing the socioeconomic barriers to access does not level the health care playing field. Data on the significant effects of racial bias in mental health care delivery are overwhelming, too wide-ranging and copious to enumerate. In her riveting analysis, *Fatal Invention: How Science, Politics, and Big Business Re-Create Race in the Twenty-First Century*, legal scholar Dorothy Roberts writes, "Race is not a biological category that naturally produces health disparities because of genetic differences ... [but] a political category that has staggering biological consequences because of the impact of social inequality on people's health."[2]

The effects of racism permeate all levels of our health care system, regardless of the arena of medicine or psychiatry being practiced.[3] Racism manifests in many forms, from individual discriminatory acts to structural barriers, to beliefs based on unconscious ideas. We in the helping professions wish we were exempt. As mental health clinicians, we aspire to offer our patients, through treatment, an opportunity to achieve fuller and healthier lives—as Freud said, at work and play—but our own unconscious scripts guide us too.

Unconscious racism in the form of derogatory unconscious race fantasies about Blackness restrict our view when we least expect it.[4] Are Black patients with psychiatric illness really more dangerous than white counterparts and more likely to need involuntary commitment?[5] Is a psychotic Black male patient more likely to have schizophrenia

DOI: 10.4324/9781003280002-3

than bipolar disorder?[6] Why are the therapists' response rates to patients' calls for treatment slower if the callers are perceived to be Black?[7] Why are Black patients who experience anxiety disorder or depression less likely to receive care that adheres to established guidelines?[8] Why are young Black males perceived as older, more mature, and more dangerous than white, age-matched counterparts?[9] Unconscious racism—what we now call implicit bias—affects the practice of psychotherapy on many levels.[10] Racial bias influences whom we see in our offices or clinics and with whom we are comfortable in the consulting room. Bias affects how we diagnose and who makes it to our office to receive a diagnosis. It influences whether we recommend medication, which medications we prescribe, and in what doses. It affects our research protocols, including who and what is the priority of scientific study. It affects whom we deem appropriate for psychotherapy and who we think has the ego resources to benefit. It influences how we see race manifest in the transference or in the supervisory relationship—or whether we are blind to it as an entry point for treatment. In all of these cases, racialized thinking can be explored and understood psychologically and can be a subject of inquiry.

Even if we manage to initiate therapy, the literature teaches us that trust is a fundamental obstacle affecting interracial treatments.[11] It can be gained through effort from both sides of the dyad. Still, we are haunted by the ghosts from the Tuskegee experiments and the Sims gynecological procedures, two examples of unethical medical practices cited in Harriet Washington's startling book *Medical Apartheid: The Dark History of Medical Experimentation on Black Americans From Colonial Times to the Present*,[12] a work that barely scratches the surface in the long history of racist medical practices. This history is painstakingly detailed further in Byrd and Clayton's encyclopedic compilation *An American Health Dilemma: Race, Medicine, and Health Care in the United States (1900–2000)*.[13] Centuries of racist medical practice dating back to slavery dwell in the collective unconscious among people of color, perpetuating the cultural paranoia that obstructs care and trust.

The stress of racial discrimination exacts a biological toll on Black and brown bodies, thereby adversely affecting overall health, argues Yale historian Carolyn Roberts.[14] Experiencing discrimination is associated with stress and self-reports of ill health.[15] Accordingly, if patients from minoritized groups are matched with providers who do not acknowledge the realities of discrimination nor the challenges of living in a racialized society, the quality of care suffers.[16] Studies document higher patient dropout rates for interracial therapy dyads.[17] Clinician education about these important factors cultural sensitivity, and understanding of "racial or ethnic identity, cultural values, cultural mistrust, [and] therapist cultural competence and worldview…may moderate the [potentially limiting] impact of racial differences."[18]

In the practice of psychotherapy, understanding how the psychodynamics of race, racism, and discrimination are encoded in the derogatory unconscious fantasies held about Black people in our culture can open a multiplicity of rich entry points for interpreting transference and countertransference.

The fragmenting toll that discrimination can take, whether manifested as physical symptoms, depression, or anger, can be one reason a patient might seek medical care, including psychotherapy. A patient whose experience of racial trauma causes fractures in the sense of self, for example, may find racial trauma superimposed on or fundamental to a sense of brokenness, badness, or inferiority. In these cases, connection and identification in the transference with a therapist of color, if artfully explored, can be fruitful and healing to the patient. Exploration and analysis of racialized transference dynamics can also uncover damaging effects when racial trauma coincides with key developmental nodal points in childhood or adolescence.

Reports of racial violence in the media disproportionately affect patients of color, triggering anxiety and reviving trauma for which psychotherapy can be an important supportive intervention. In 2018, *The Lancet* published a study by David Williams's group at Harvard, examining mental health reports of African Americans and data on shootings of unarmed Black men in the United States.[19] Data correlation revealed that every time an unarmed Black American was shot, the mental health of African Americans in that state was adversely affected for 3 months while that of white Americans was largely unaffected. Could these findings guide research on what an appropriate community intervention might look like? Consider that over 2,000 Black Lives Matter demonstrations shook the country in the summer of 2020, in response to what, in effect, was a lynching of George Floyd by Minneapolis police and to the deaths of 300 African Americans per year that have been attributed to police shootings. The people involved in the demonstrations crossed race, class, gender, and national boundaries, and in my office almost every patient I saw contemplated the question, "Do Black lives matter?" Race, as a transference variable, can be a powerful entry point to explore deeper conflicts around vulnerability and early trauma that transcend the specific racial composition of the therapeutic dyad.

In my experience as an educator, well-trained and well-meaning therapists are often mystified about how to talk about race and how to recognize the way racism infiltrates psychotherapy. Historically, this subject has not been covered in clinical training programs or supervisions. It has not been addressed in clinicians' personal therapies or analyses. As a result, it is easy for therapists and patients alike to become unknowing victims of an enactment. In our private offices, it is also easy to settle into our privilege of blindness to the effects of disenfranchisement.

For white psychotherapists who are not comfortable exploring issues of race, this is treacherous territory. Anxiety inhibits their ability to deepen the treatment and threatens the working therapeutic alliance. Therefore, greater clinician training and self-study are needed. For white patients questioning parental or family attitudes around race, psychotherapy can provide a space to maneuver the conflict-laden terrain so as to retain the parental and familial love but excise and renounce a family member's racist attitudes. Race can also permeate the transference as a connector to other conflicts. For example, for a white patient whose life narrative reveals a privileged social position coupled with parental emotional neglect, the fantasy of the Black female therapist as caregiver or maternal object or as a displacement from a beloved nanny might activate in the transference the pain around narcissistic failures in the patient's family of origin. These are but a few examples of the ways race can permeate the treatment landscape; the possibilities are endless because all of us are affected in multitudinous ways by living in a racist society.

White therapists are often intrigued and surprised to find that they have not recognized the racial dynamics in same-race (white therapist, white patient) therapies; training and supervision never afforded them the tools to make better sense of these issues in treatment. Latent references to race often hide important entries to deep conflicts, as well. Even if the transference is not directly interpreted, therapists can develop an understanding of the ways race affects the therapeutic relationship and treatment compliance. Young trainees want educational programs to address these issues because their patient population is increasingly diverse and multicultural and because racism, in our culture, is all around us. And, yes, some "racist thinking" can be amenable to psychotherapeutic treatment. It is always illuminating after teaching on this topic to receive calls from therapists who now are beginning to hear and see issues of race emerge in treatment.

Racism robs our nation of rising to a greater humanity at all levels. We need racial equity and racial justice in the streets, in the courtrooms, in the classrooms, and yes, in our health care system. But change, as psychoanalytic theory teaches us, comes from within before it comes from without. Psychotherapy and psychoanalysis offer an opportunity for that personal change on both sides of the therapeutic dyad.

Notes

1 Medlock, M., Weissman, A., Wong, S.S., et al. (2017). Racism as a unique social determinant of mental health: Development of a didactic curriculum for psychiatry residents. *MedEdPORTAL*; 13:10618.
2 Roberts, D. (2011). *The Fatal Invention: How Science, Politics, and Big Business Re-Create Race in the Twenty-First Century.* New York: The New Press.
3 Dunbar, E. (2004). Reconsidering the clinical utility of bias as a mental health problem: Intervention strategies for psychotherapy practice. *Psychotherapy: Theory, Research, Practice, Training*; 41:97–111.
4 Kovel, J. (1970). *White Racism: A Psychohistory.* New York: Columbia University Press.
5 Snowden, L.R. (2003). Bias in mental health assessment and intervention: Theory and evidence. *American Journal of Public Health*; 93:239–243.
6 Akinhanmi, M.O., Biernacka, J.M., Strakowski, S.M., et al. (2018). Racial disparities in bipolar disorder treatment and research: A call to action. *Bipolar Disorders*; 20:506–514.
7 Wisniewski, J.M. and Walker, B. (2020). Association of simulated patient race/ethnicity with scheduling of primary care appointments. *JAMA Network Open*; 3:e1920010.

8 Young, A.S., Klap, R., Sherbourne, C.D., et al. (2001). The quality of care for depressive and anxiety disorders in the United States. *Archives of General Psychiatry*; 58:55–61.
9 Stoute, B. (2019). Racial socialization and thwarted mentalization: Psychoanalytic reflections from the lived experience of James Baldwin's America. *American Imago*; 76:335–357.
10 Wintersteen, M.B., Mensinger, J.L. and Diamond, G.S. (2005). Do gender and racial differences between patient and therapist affect therapeutic alliance and treatment retention in adolescents? *Professional Psychology: Research and Practice*; 36: 400–408. Also see note 1.
11 Griffith, M.S. (1977). The influences of race on the psychotherapeutic relationship. *Psychiatry*; 40:27–40.
12 Washington, H. (2006). *Medical Apartheid: The Dark History of Medical Experimentation on Black Americans From Colonial Times to the Present.* New York: Doubleday.
13 Byrd, W.M. and Clayton, L.A. (2002). *An American Health Dilemma: Race, Medicine, and Health Care in the United States (1900–2000)*, vol. 2. New York: Routledge.
14 Roberts, C. (2019). Braiding our pain. University Forum on Racism in America IV: Biological race: Has the old become new again? *Annual Meeting of the American Psychoanalytic Association*, New York.
15 Ren, X.S., Skinner, K., Lee, A., et al. (1999). Social support, social selection and self-assessed health status: Results from the Veterans Health Study in the United States. *Social Science & Medicine*; 48:1721–1734.
16 Jones, J. (2003). Constructing race and deconstructing racism. In *Handbook of Racial and Ethnic Minority Psychology,*. edited by Bernal, G., Trimble, J.E., Burlew, A.K., et al. Thousand Oaks, CA: Sage.
17 Sue, S., Fujino, D.C., Hu, L.T., et al. (1991). Community mental health services for ethnic minority groups: A test of the cultural responsiveness hypothesis. *Journal of Consulting Clinical Psychology*; 59:533–540.
18 Chang, D.F. and Berk, A. (2009). Making cross-racial therapy work: A phenomenological study of clients' experiences of cross-racial therapy. *Journal of Counseling Psychology*; 56:521–536.
19 Bor, J., Venkataramani, A.S., Williams, D.R., et al. (2018). Police killings and their spillover effects on the mental health of black Americans: A population-based, quasi-experimental study. *Lancet*; 392:302–310.

Chapter 2

Race and Racism in Psychoanalytic Thought
The Ghosts in Our Nursery, 2nd Edition

Beverly J. Stoute

Race, a biological fiction, is a social, cultural, and political construct. The tenor of this reality in the United States is sober and often quietly horrific, interwoven throughout private and public discourse. Race, as the daily news cycle, film, and song remind us, is stark and differentiating. It has been so since the early years of the colonies. *Brown v. Board of Education of Topeka, Kansas*, decided by the Supreme Court in 1954, did not alter that reality, nor did the tandem Civil Rights Act of 1964 and Voting Rights Act of 1965. Affirmative action policies, designed to right a long history of denied opportunity, could not dynamite the bedrock of racism. Not even the election of the first African American president could shake it. In twenty-first-century America, racism is alive and well. Complex economic, social, political, cultural, and psychological forces interact to make it a seemingly intractable challenge in the American conversation. Race is a challenge for all of us, and yet, as a profession dedicated to integrity and change, where has psychoanalysis been in this conversation?

In this chapter, I review the literature of psychoanalysis and related mental health disciplines for their writings on race, beginning with Freud and continuing to the present. Psychoanalytic literature has historically been fraught with ignorance about race and limited by racism, both overt and subtle. Yet, on a positive note, psychoanalytic thought is growing ever deeper and richer, as it has been influenced by work on race and racism in other fields of the humanities. Yes, psychoanalysis is finally catching up.

During my own analytic training, issues of racial difference permeated my patients' transference with threads, at times, in the parallel process of the supervision. One supervisor noticed, yet there was only one paper in the literature she could quote. When my training analyst asked me as our work began if our difference in race was influencing the relationship, I snapped back, "You ask the question as if I have a choice." I noted that at least she did ask, and she quietly tolerated my defensiveness; after all, I was the only African American at my institute.

My analysis began before Dorothy Holmes (1992) or Kimberlyn Leary (1997) published their seminal papers on race and transference. The published interview of Ralph Greenson, in 1982 (Greenson et al. 1982), with Ellis Toney, one of the first African American analysts, revealed that he and other early African American analysts were less fortunate than I. Greenson, a self-described "white liberal," paved the way for the Los Angeles Institute and Society for Psychoanalytic Studies to admit Toney, its first African American candidate (who graduated in 1948). Yet, he later confessed that during his analysis of Toney, he had become aware of his own unconscious racism. That bias distorted the work and made it more difficult. For example, Toney requested a change in the time of his analytic session because, being the only African American on the street in Greenson's white neighborhood at the appointed hour, the police would sometimes stop him (Greenson 1982; Abney 2006; Hamer, 2002). Greenson's response: an Oedipal interpretation of Toney's "paranoia." with no awareness of what we now call racial profiling. Their realities were disconnected, damaging the relationship and limiting the analysis. At that time, it was also not yet clear to the psychoanalytic world that establishing trust, a fundamental challenge in interracial analyses, is crucial to a working therapeutic alliance (Griffin, 1977). It is ironic that Greenson is known for his classic 2008 paper formulating the concept of the therapeutic alliance.

As a mature analyst, I came to understand with greater clarity the traumatic effects of racism in my life, and the family and defensive factors that shielded me. The fantasy that analytic understanding could be a radical tool of individual and social change had made me hopeful and helped me endure the micro- and not-so-micro-aggressions along the way. Naively, I did not expect to question whether my chosen field was prepared for the task I expected of it. But a review of the literature makes clear that latent racist attitudes had long impeded the development of psychoanalytic theory on racial difference and the underpinnings of racist thinking. That the field was not diverse—most analysts were white, living and working and white neighborhoods—some postulate, also kept many psychoanalysts from being curious about the manifestations of race in their clinical work (Powell and Hart, 2016).

Starting with the Founding Fathers

Where should we begin this conversation about race and racism? A developmental perspective leads us to start even before conception. Do we start with the architects of democracy who wrote, "We hold these truths to be self-evident that all men are created equal, that they are endowed by their Creator with certain unalienable Rights…" while also creating the Three-Fifths Compromise, which wrote into the United States Constitution that for the purposes of representation and taxation in the House of Representatives each slave would be counted as having only three-fifths the value of a white person. Many of the architects of our democracy owned slaves and considered Africans subhuman. Yet, the economic foundation of our democracy, expressed in our political system, was built by Africans, countless unacknowledged millions of whom died in the Middle Passage before ever reaching our shores. We must start, therefore, by stating that America was and is a racialized society. The language, "We the People," of the Declaration of Independence—taught to schoolchildren for over two centuries as representative of our democratic identity—was at best aspirational, hiding the darker reality of a country brutally split in two, as Isabel Wilkerson makes crystal clear in her 2019 book, *Caste: The Origins of our Discontent*. From birth, the structure of American culture and society socializes people into a world in which whites, subtly and blatantly, are the dominant, more highly valued caste. African Americans are subordinate.

Although America is said to be a great melting pot, successive waves of immigrants worked to assimilate to the dominant white caste. This included taking on the socially sanctioned mantle of power and privilege over African Americans, both slave and, free. The African American "other" became a container for disavowed hatred, envy, and prohibited sexual fantasies long before Kleinian theory (1946) gave it the language of "splitting," "projection," and "projective identification," before "otherness" as a theoretical construct existed. It was a reality before Freud wrote in *Civilization and Its Discontents* (1930), "It is always possible to bring together a considerable number of people in love so long as there are other people left over to receive the manifestations of their aggressiveness."

Freud, as did many Jews in Vienna, endured anti-Semitism throughout his medical training and professional career. In Smiley Blanton's *Diary of My Analysis with Sigmund Freud* (1971), Freud is reported to have said, "My background as a Jew helped me to stand being criticized, being isolated, working alone." Sander Gilman's (1993) well-known scholarly work in this area documents that Jews were thought of as "the Negroes of Vienna," psychoanalysis was a "black thing," and Freud was labeled a "Black Jew" (Altman, 2006b). Freud referred to anti-Semitism in *The Interpretation of Dreams* (1900) and to racial self-hatred in *Jokes and Their Relation to the Unconscious* (1905). It may be difficult for us in the postcolonial modern era to understand his reluctance to localize psychoanalysis culturally (Altman 2000; Altman 2004). In *Inhibitions, Symptoms and Anxiety* (1926), when Freud discussed childhood neuroses, he pointed out that "from our observations of town children belonging to the white races and living according to fairly high cultural standards, the neuroses of childhood are in the nature of regular episodes in a child's development," making it clear he had some awareness of the cultural and socioeconomic status of his patient population, though he chose not to emphasize those factors in his clinical work or theory.

In his 1936 paper "A Disturbance of Memory on the Acropolis," Freud identified the "limitations and poverty of our conditions of life in my youth" as contributors to his dissociative neurotic symptoms at the Acropolis, indicative of his success neurosis, which Holmes (2006) eloquently reinterprets with reference to Freud's social class and the anti-Semitism he endured. Freud's emphasis on oedipal conflict as a wholly adequate explanation for his success neurosis may have further contributed to the early focus on oedipal theory over deeper considerations of race and class in the field as a whole. Many believe also that Freud dissected out reference to race and culture from his universal theory of the human mind to avoid psychoanalysis being labeled as a Jewish science (Gilman, 1993; Altman, 2006a,b).

Although the classic psychoanalytic view posits a universal theory of the human mind, social and cultural influences did infiltrate the thinking of early American psychoanalysts, but did so in ways that were detrimental to the thinking and practice of a number of mental health disciplines. At the turn of the twentieth century, the scant analytic literature on the subject reveals that many American psychoanalysts adopted the prevailing theories of race inferiority. In 1914, a lead article, "Dementia Praecox in the Colored Race," in the *Psychoanalytic Review*, the first psychoanalytic journal published in the United States, A.M. Evarts asserts that the "colored man" is prone to dementia praecox and that "bondage in reality was a wonderful aid to the colored man." In the same journal, John Lind, in his article "The Dream as a Simple Wish-fulfillment in the Negro," (Lind, 1914) explains that the "Negroes' development is lower than the white race and…similar to those of the savage," that "their psychological activities are analogous with those of the child" and "their psychology is of a primitive type." In a subsequent paper, Lind (1917) cites an 1847 source to support the claim that "Negro children are sharp, intelligent, and full of vivacity, but on approaching the adult period a gradual change sets in.…The intellect seems to become clouded…, gives place to a sort of lethargy, briskness yields to indolence" and, he concludes, "after puberty sexual matters take the first place in the Negro's life and thoughts."

Formulating Prejudice into Theory

Early theories of prejudice followed Freud, who discussed individual and group antagonism at the level of group dynamics and group hatred. In *Group Psychology and the Analysis of the Ego* (1921), *Totem and Taboo* (1913), and *Moses and Monotheism* (1939), he discusses the role that the metaphorical killing of the primal father by the sons plays in fostering group cohesion and the binding of aggression within the group. This formulation provided the basis later for related psychodynamic speculation on the lynching of Black men by white men in the South (Resnikoff, 1933). In *The Taboo of Virginity* (1918), Freud describes the "hostility against intruders," which he termed "the narcissism of minor difference" and referenced further in *Civilization and Its Discontents* (1930). Early psychoanalytic theory was slow, however, to develop Freud's group formulations into a comprehensive theory which would include the processing of racial difference, a developmental formulation of racism and clinical c practice. Integrating into Freudian theory ideas about the influence of culture and race on the psyche has taken decades. Sparked by historical social and political forces—and the diversification of the field—the work is ongoing.

Though the conceptions of Negroes in the literature by some analysts were derogatory, the work of others did seek to question and reformulate them, but it was work against the rip-tide of unconscious cultural fantasies in which Blackness represents the bad, evil, or ugly in mind, spirit or action. That, combined with the negative attitudes toward the Negro present in the fantasies, dreams, and everyday life of white patients, and the limited experience with Negro patients and Negro people, made the work developing theory slow. Early authors describing individual cases of "the Negro" or of "a Negro" (Graven, 1930), wrote with a tone that subtly indicated the Negro people did not have a part in an otherwise universal human experience. Negroes were othered by a latent yet palpable racist tone. Psychoanalytically informed work by sociologist John Dollard, and later by psychoanalysts Abram Kardiner and Lionel Ovesey, were welcomed into the literature since the authors had actually interviewed Negro informants. Lillian Smith's autobiography made its way into analytic circles for similar reasons.

Dollard, who had had technical psychoanalytic training, studied a Mississippi town he called "Southerntown." The meticulous description in his 1937 work, *Caste and Class in a Southern Town,* made clear that the racialized caste structure maintained a hierarchical social and economic division between Negroes and whites that allowed whites, especially white men, to maintain a superior social, economic, political, and sexual advantage. It remains an important contribution. Dollard et al. advanced the "frustration aggression hypothesis" along with the "scapegoat hypothesis" by which the individual frustrated in achieving a goal reacts aggressively toward a scapegoated minority group that he or she holds responsible wrongly for blocking access to the coveted goal—often one of economic advantage (Dollard et al., 1939; Brierley, 1944). In the case of Southerntown, a white working class subgroup of similarly frustrated men and women, metes out toward Negroes the competitive aggression and envy it feels toward members of the upper class who have blocked them.

Lillian Smith's (1949) autobiography, *Killers of the Dream*, reviewed in *Psychoanalytic Quarterly* (Barrett, 1951), provided an eye-opening account of the splitting, projection, and crystallized fantasy inherent in the racism of pre-1960s Southern culture in America. She outlined segregation, white supremacy, and how she was taught that "masturbation is wrong, and segregation is right." She explained: "The lesson on segregation was only a logical extension of the lesson on sex and white superiority and God...that...Negroes and everything dark, dangerous, evil must be pushed to the rim of one's life...." There is no better outline in the literature of the oedipal drama played out in Southern culture. Her portrayal of the Southern white man defensively splitting and projecting aggressive and erotic conflicts while disavowing guilt lays bare the historical bedrock of American racism that is part of our collective cultural unconscious.

In *The Mark of Oppression,* Kardiner and Ovesey (1951) argue that the "Negroes' wretched internal life" is evidence of the "Negro personality," one indelibly scarred by racism. The authors considered it an insightful study of the traumatic effects of prejudice based as it was on their interviews of 12 and the psychotherapy of 13 Negro subjects. However, it was criticized by African Americans as a derogatory and oversimplified caricature; its generalizations about the Negro family were later challenged. Literature conceptualizing the intergenerational transmission of trauma and the effects of racism on family structure and resilience came much later.

In the aftermath of World War II and the Holocaust, many theories of prejudice focused on anti-Semitism. Gregory Zilboorg (1947), Gordon Allport (1954), and Brian Bird (1957) all wrestled to understand prejudice psychologically. They used anti-Semitism and group psychology as a theoretical base to argue that all forms of prejudice have common psychological roots, likening "the fear of the Jew to the fear of the father and trac[ing] anti-Semitism back to an unresolved Oedipus complex" (Loeblowitz-Lennard, 1947). Interestingly, Bird's (1957) formulation of prejudice involved the case history of a 19-year-old Jewish woman whose "attack of racial prejudice," her erotic hatred of Negro men was fruitfully analyzed as an oedipal displacement. Bird extrapolated his argument, as many did, to group antagonisms where, "by projecting its own unconscious forbidden impulses onto another race, the active group allows conscious expression of those impulses but escapes responsibility from them." In his seminal work, *The Authoritarian Personality*, Theodor Adorno and Else Frenkel-Brunswik (1950) similarly extrapolate from their research on the roots of prejudiced ideologies to postulate that a rigid and severe parenting style sets the stage for the development of extremist authoritarian thinking.

Richard Sterba's widely quoted 1947 paper on the Detroit race riots of 1943, "Some Psychological Factors in Negro Race Hatred and in Anti-Negro Riots," emphasizes the psychoanalytic framework for oedipal conflict and sibling rivalry. Drawing from the clinical material extracted from the analyses of 42 patients, Sterba revealed that the Negro in some dreams represented a "substitute object" for the newcomer younger sibling, while at other times "being threatened by a Negro [man was] ...understood as the expression and repetition of the dreamer's infantile fears of his father." Negroes served as displacement objects for aggressive and oedipal conflicts. The mob chasing the "Negro in race riots symbolized the hunting down of the cruel powerful father by the sons as did the lynching of black men similarly symbolize the killing of the primal father by the sons" (Resnikoff, 1933; Sterba, 1947).

The frequently cited case report by Terry Rodgers (1960) of an "anti Negro racist" chronicled the brief analysis of a racist whose family history, obsessional behavior, and defensive splitting mirrored the classic oedipal formulation in which the patient, a middle-class attorney who had the prototypic "Negro nurse" growing up, revealed his fantasy (from the analysis of a dream) that the Negro man was the displaced figure of his castrating father. As the patient's unconscious incestuous wishes were revealed in the course of the analysis, his murderous fantasies toward Blacks intensified, and he fled the analysis to join a [white supremacy-oriented] hate group, later sending the analyst pamphlets on race superiority. This is one of the few case reports in the literature in which conscious racist views could be traced back to oedipal conflict. Lillian Smith's autobiography, taken with Sterba's (1947) discussion of the Detroit race riots, Bird's case (1957), and Rodgers's case report, provided compelling clinical support for the attractiveness of oedipal theory as a theoretical framework for racism—a formulation summarized with great clarity by Joel Kovel in *White Racism: A Psychohistory* almost 20 years later.

A wave of literature in the 1950s and 1960s on the "Negro experience" emerged, and post-colonialism as a theoretical framework blossomed. The attention given Gunnar Myrdal's (1944) famous book, *An American Dilemma,* which emphasized the Negro experience, marked this change in the field of sociology. Theorizing about prejudice evolved to include literature on anti-Black racism, the Black experience, the challenge of American multiculturalism, the intergenerational transmission of trauma, and later, Frantz Fanon's works, *Black Skin, White Masks* in 1952 and *The Wretched of the Earth* in 1961. They marked intersecting nodal points for both psychoanalysis and sociology. Emboldened historically by the independence of India and African nations in the 1960s and the work of the United Nations, Fanon, in his work, drew attention to the social and theoretical importance of understanding colonialism and the colonized mind. In her 1996 encyclopedic review, *The Anatomy of Prejudices,* Elisabeth Young-Bruehl provides an unparalleled integration of history and theory in this connection.

The civil rights movement catalyzed a social and political shift, so conversations about racism in the fields of sociology, social psychology, and the humanities outdistanced the analytic literature. African American physicians were drawn disproportionately into community work (Fuller, 1999) and continued to publish in psychiatric journals articles about racism in psychiatric training and racism as a social defense (Comer, 1969; Pinderhughes, 1973; Bradshaw, 1978; Poussaint, 1980), but few pursued psychoanalytic training (Spurlock, 1999).

In his 1966 paper, James Hamilton explained the housing discrimination policies and practices against Negroes in Ann Arbor, Michigan, as representative of the latent "anal components of white hostility towards Negroes," whereby the "Negro represents feces of which money is a displacement or sublimation," which he justified by reaching back to quote Sandor Ferenczi's *The Ontogenesis of the Interest in Money* (1953) and Lawrence Kubie's (1937) "The Fantasy of Dirt," as a theoretical base; this was the theoretical foundation of the so-called anal theory of racism.

Personally, I was not sure that this racist "theory" influenced analytic thought until several older colleagues confirmed it, with one reporting that a supervisor had told him that "the Negro in dreams means feces, you know." Joel Kovel in 2000 similarly reported,

I had presented a patient's dream in which black people had figured as characters. "Oh, don't you know about that?" the supervisor had pronounced airily. "She means her shit. That's what black people always mean in the unconscious. It's the color, you know."

Although credited with the exposition of this "theory" in his book *White Racism: A Psychohistory*, Kovel (1970) confessed to struggling with this formulation, stating, "The idea was grossly reductive, subjectivistic, and, most of all, deeply offensive." He called this theory the "*thing*ification" of the Black man and "the radical loss of humanity," equating the Black man with feces. Kovel revisited this offensive formulation in his 2000 retrospective analysis of his own work, stating,

> The history of slavery reduced blacks to the level of chattel, and in this way perhaps in racism, a whole category of human beings was being regarded and treated as excrement ... Could it be that the special association of blacks with feces in the racist unconscious is grounded in the historical reality of their enslavement—that they had in fact been considered property..., held as degraded things?

Even if conceding a great deal with this explanation, it is difficult to understand the clinical utility of these crude, reductionistic (albeit racist) interpretations, but many analysts did not question this "theory." Psychoanalytic writers in the 1940s, 1950s, and well into the 1960s, however, conceptualized racism from this framework.

Kovel's book brought our psychoanalytic understanding into sharper focus by artfully summarizing the psychoanalytic literature from the 1930s to the 1960s, including the three major lines of psychoanalytic thinking to explain racism: the Oedipal framework "enlarged to a cultural apparatus," the anal theory of racism, and the race fantasies in American culture that defined African Americans as the repositories of aggression and hatred. His insightful delineation of the "types" of racists (bigots who act out and liberals whose racism is unconscious) and the unconscious collective race fantasies operative in American culture is still a useful conceptualization and punctuated the emphasis on Oedipal theory that dominated analytic theory. The powerful implications of conceptualizing and focusing on culturally perpetuated race fantasies embedded in the "cultural apparatus," formulated with chilling clarity by Fanon a decade earlier, was not appreciated or developed in analytic thinking until much later, after the integration of the postcolonial discourse and critical race theory.

Persistence of Racism in Theory and Training

In 1962, Nathaniel Siegel (1962) surveyed a sample of 100 psychoanalyst members of the American Psychoanalytic Association on the demographic characteristics of their patient population, endeavoring to characterize the population of patients undergoing psychoanalytic treatment. Of the 52 respondents who carried an aggregate total of 476 patients in their practices, not one psychoanalyst reported having a single Black patient. Siegel posed the questions: "Where do Negroes who require private psychoanalytic therapy receive their treatment? How does the matter of race influence a psychoanalysis? How many, and under what circumstances of training, are Negro professionals being trained in the practice of psychoanalysis?" (p. 156). These were profound questions at the time, but it is notable that the paucity of African American psychoanalysts in the membership of the American Psychoanalytic Association did not spark further curiosity in the mainstream of the field. These questions were not studied in depth until the post–civil rights era, when people of color slowly entered psychoanalytic training in greater numbers. With an unparalleled level of intimate detail and sophisticated analysis derived from what she call a "historiographic methodology," sifting through archives, letters, and organizational reports of the work of the early players involved Elizabeth Danto[1] (2014) tells the story of the community mental health movement evolving concurrently as a catalyzing force in this narrative of racial integration with Richard Wright and the Lafargue clinic in Harlem, the pioneering activist work of Viola Bernard (1953, 1972, 1998) and of African American psychoanalysts including Margaret Morgan Lawrence (1998), Hugh Butts (1963, 1971)[2] and others in breaking down the structural barriers that had limited access to the field for people of color as patients and as clinicians.

The first documented African American graduates of American Psychoanalytic Association-affiliated institutes were Margaret Lawrence in 1954 and Ellis Toney in 1958. By 1999, only 26 African American psychoanalysts were members of the American Psychoanalytic Association (Fuller et al., 1999) constituting 0.007% of the membership. Data from non–American Psychoanalytic Association institutes is not easy to compile. Veronica Abney (1998) located 57 African American psychoanalysts[3] for her dissertation study on the history of African American psychoanalysts, including graduates of American Psychoanalytic (ApsaA) Institutes and non-APsaA institutes. The groundbreaking work of African American pioneer psychoanalysts such as June Christmas (1964, 1967, 1974), Jeanne Spurlock (1985, 1991, 1994), Canino and Spurlock (1994) and Ruth Fuller (1980, 1988, 1993), all of whom published on related issues, has not been given due attention. Their work dovetailed with the activist interventions of white analysts such as Viola Bernard (1953, 1972), who had supported the application of Margaret Lawrence for training at the Columbia Psychoanalytic Center. Bernard's (1952), Butts (1969) and Judith Schachter and Hugh Butts's (1968) widely quoted papers on interracial analyses ushered in this new era of psychoanalytic inquiry into the transference-countertransference manifestations of racial difference in the analytic dyad (Curry, 1964; Fisher, 1971; Goldberg et al., 1974; Myers 1984) and racial difference in psychoanalytic supervision (Bradshaw, 1977, 1982), adding to the discussions already underway in the psychiatric literature (Calnek, 1970; Flowers, 1972; Kranz, 1973; Cohen 1974; Jones, 1974; Mayo, 1974; Carter, 1979; Brantley 1983). Harrison and Butts (1970) studied the difficulty of white psychiatrists in exploring racial issues, and British psychoanalysts later questioned if the lack of supervisory sophistication and the absence of training development on issues of race were contributing factors to the problematically low numbers of people of color in the field (Morgan, 2002, 2007, 2008).

As people of color and of different cultural backgrounds sought treatment in greater numbers in the 1970s and entered analytic training, African American psychiatrists questioned if racism was embedded in psychoanalytic theory (Thomas and Sillen, 1972). As these limitations in psychoanalytic thinking were critiqued, some white analysts persistently objected. Although known for her work on race awareness in children, Marjorie MacDonald, in her 1974 paper "Little Black Sambo," for example, recommended that "the black reader's rejection… should be interpreted," since there "appears to be no obvious evidence of racism, and the story of Mumbo and Jumbo, and their little son Black Sambo should be seen as a charming children's story of Oedipal conflict and childhood sexuality."

Richard Gardner (1975), in his reference to Phyllis Harrison-Ross (1973) and Barbara Wyden's *The Black Child–A Parents' Guide,* objected to the expressions of the "black is beautiful movement," calling them "the substitution of one racism for another," rather than recognizing the valuable contribution to positive self-esteem and ego ideal, which serve a protective defensive function in countering the traumatic effects of racism and discrimination. After reviewing many of these early papers, Farhad Dalal (2000) criticized many psychoanalysts for ignoring how the real, detrimental effects of racism limited their clinical understanding of patients and, further, the reformulation of psychoanalytic theory. In her 1975 classic paper "Ghosts in the Nursery," Selma Fraiberg seemed chillingly relevant as she helped us understand that when past trauma is endured but not metabolized for one generation, what is not spoken is embedded in the unconscious and enacted in disturbing ways in those generations that follow (Fraiberg et al. 1975). Did the unexamined racism of how people of color were viewed and othered, even by analysts, silently stifle our development as a field and theoretical discipline?

Many African Americans entering the field encountered prejudice (Jones et al. 1970). The contention that minority groups were not "analyzable" had grown out of Clarence Obendorf's (1954) caution against interracial analysis since the divergent cultural difference, he argued, made it untenable. Altman, in 1995, challenged this classical attitude that analytic treatments could not be used with minority groups and, in 2006, pointed out "the blind spot in the field of psychoanalysis to racism in the U.S." due to "its troubled history of exclusion and in-group domination." The prejudices expressed earlier by Richard Reichbart's colleague (in Chapter 16), who doubted that African Americans had the abstract thinking capacity conducive to psychoanalytic training, is equaled only by Veronica Abney's (2011) recounting of how a colleague informed her that, when he began his analysis, he was told that since he was African American, he did not have an unconscious. In Salman Akhtar's (2012) *The African American Experience*, Dionne Powell (2012) similarly confirmed that "early psychoanalytic writers were circumspect as to whether African-Americans, due to their history of trauma, and white analysts' unexamined fears, prejudices, and behaviors, could effectively be brought into treatment."

Schools of social work in the 1990s integrated social and cultural factors into clinical psychodynamic work, while mainstream psychoanalytic institutes lagged in realizing the need for diversity teaching in training programs and the need to integrate the influence of class, ethnicity, and race (Pinderhughes, 1989; Foster and Moskowitz, 1996; Altman, 2005, 2006). Our theoretical understanding of race and transference deepened with the publication of Dorothy Holmes's (1992) paper "Race and Transference in Psychoanalysis and Psychotherapy," and later, Kimberlyn Leary's (1997) "Race in the Psychoanalytic Space," both representing new psychoanalytic perspectives on working with race as a container in the transference with greater nuance. Holmes demonstrated that transference can be racialized (1992), that race and class provide unique "points of engagement" to further analytic understanding (1999), and that integrating the psychodynamic conceptualization of othering deepens our clinical understanding along these lines (2015).

The British psychoanalyst Farhad Dalal, in 2002, integrated and expanded on how understanding the dynamic processes of othering and racialization facilitates a deeper psychodynamic conceptualization of racist thinking, although both concepts had evolved into discourse on racism in the sociological literature (Dalal 2002, 2006; Miles and Brown, 1989; Clarke, 2003). In short, Dalal (2002) postulates that "more useful than the notion of racism is that of racialization—the process of manufacturing and utilizing the notion of race in any capacity," an idea mirrored in the sociological literature by Miles (1989), who

> prefers to use the term 'racialization' where social relations between people have been structured by the signification of… [race such that]…race is a social construct at the center of the racialization process, and this becomes racism (ideologically) when there is a negative valuation.

These scholars challenge us to question our use of the terms "race" and "racism" and suggest we refine our thinking and conceptualization as our conversations on race evolve.

Unlike early psychoanalytic formulations steeped mainly in Oedipal theory, modern conceptualizations revealed more nuanced interpretations of racial dynamics as an entry point in clinical work and integrated this new lexicon using the terms "racialization" (Miles and Brown, 1989; Dalal, 2001; 2002) and "othering," along with multi-layered concepts, including intersectionality (Crenshaw, 1991), whiteness (Gump, 2000; Suchet, 2004, 2007; Altman, 2006a; DiAngelo, 2012; Hamer, 2012), white privilege (Baldwin, 1993), racial melancholia (Eng and Han, 2000; Cheng, 2001), hate, hating and mapping racism (Moss, 2001, 2003, 2006), being hated (White, 2002), race as an adaptive challenge (Leary, 2012), intergenerational trauma (Apprey 1996; 2003, 2014; Bass 2003; Vaughans, 2014, 2016), distinguishing racism from neuroticism in African Americans (Thompson, 1987), anti-Semitism as contrasted with anti-Black racism (Apprey, 1996), relational perspectives (Altman, 1996; Jones, 2016), the construct of dignity in a racist society (Holmes, 2015, Stoute 2019), and the formulation of the "racist state of mind" (Keval, 2016). I cannot do justice in the space provided here to the recent rich extensions of theory in this regard, but I have tried to position for the reader how the evolution of psychodynamic formulating on otherness, and the culturally imposed traumas of racism was thwarted by the latent racism in the early history of our field The formulation of racism from the trauma perspective represents a generational and interdisciplinary advance towards clinically useful theorizing from the early years psychoanalytically oriented discourse.

At the outset of researching the literature to write this review, I had hoped I would find that psychoanalytic theory had explained the psychological forces underlying racist thinking, had developed a theoretical framework, had explained its developmental underpinnings, its evolution, and intractability, and could serve as a foundation for social intervention and change. My sad conclusion is that racism, subtle and overt, has impeded the development of psychoanalysis as a theory and as a field of practice, forestalling our further understanding of race, racialization, and racism.

Alas, the psychoanalytic world has not been immune to the racism deeply embedded in our culture and experience. Although the literature grows, more work is needed. Recent calls for attention to diversity in training and education in the American Psychoanalytic Association speak to our awareness of our neglect of these challenges. Institute curricula, training analyses, and supervisions are beginning to address issues of race and racism in clinical work and develop and require psychoanalytically informed coursework on race, diversity, otherness while also developing integrative perspectives on intersecting oppressions and social justice. Other medical and mental health professionals and professional organizations are following suit and revamping educational curricula and training programs. Continuing education and study groups for educators[4] to improve supervisory teaching on this topic are also necessary, especially if we are to equip ourselves for Dorothy Holmes's "fierce urgency of now"[5] and Anton Hart's "radical openness."[6]

Psychoanalysis Focuses on Itself: Occurrences since the First Edition of this Paper

In 2018, Celia Brickman published *Race in Psychoanalysis: Aboriginal Populations in the Mind*, a revised edition of her 2003 work. In a powerful, nuanced analysis from a postcolonial perspective of Freud's foundational texts, she shows convincingly that Freud's conceptual framework was indeed grounded in late-nineteenth-century racist anthropology. This meticulous excavation of these foundational texts reveals that race was coded as "the primitive" based on colonialist notions. By tracing "a covert racial subtext within psychoanalysis through an examination of the sociocultural, metapsychological and clinical dimensions of Freud's thought," (p. 6), Brickman furthers the exposition of and critical engagement with the legacy of racism in psychoanalytic theory and practice.

In a 2016 paper that quickly became classic, "Culturally Imposed Trauma: The Sleeping Dog Has Awakened. Will Psychoanalysis Take Heed?" Holmes pivots from an argument made by Emily Kuriloff in her 2014 book *Contemporary Psychoanalysis and the Legacy of the Third Reich: History, Memory, Tradition* to focus with laser intensity on United States racism toward its African American population. Kuriloff's insightful, psychoanalytically primed historical analysis revealed that early psychoanalyst émigrés from Vienna and Nazi Germany who fled Nazism to America "made no mention of their ordeals." Through meticulous research, Kuriloff argues that their inattention and silence on the traumatic events of the Third Reich and Holocaust are a "psychological response to trauma" that influenced the theory and practice of psychoanalysis in the United States. She proposes that the émigrés' experiences in Europe caused them to discount traumas inflicted socially and culturally on the psyche. Holmes questions whether turning a blind eye to Nazi atrocities created a dissociative template that thwarted development of the psychoanalytic profession. Holmes points out that:

> The psychologically damaging effects of slavery and its sequels on Blacks and Whites (post-Reconstruction decimation of rights, Jim Crow and its ugly truths including lynchings, and current-day mass incarceration of Black men) are not typically recognized by psychoanalysts as needing conceptualization and clinical attention. [Neither are] [o]ther cultural traumas ….

Not only can a dissociative template obstruct "knowing" as Holmes advances, but, Keval (2016; Chapter 8) theorizes further, inhabiting a "racist state of mind," can inhibit and pervert curiosity about the difference of others and this plays out in the transference relationship regardless of the racial particularities of the therapeutic dyad.

As a consequence, the conceptualizations of racism as a "culturally imposed trauma" with transgenerational and post-traumatic and developmental consequences have commanded due attention, especially in the post-George Floyd moment, including a necessary self-examination in the fields of all mental health disciplines.

During this period, a little-known paper, "Freud and his 'Negro': Psychoanalysis as Ally and Enemy of African Americans," by Claudia Tate (Tate, 1996), has commanded renewed attention. It analyzes and discusses the historical significance of a racist joke Freud was fond of telling. In it, he referred to one of his American patients as "my Negro." The joke had been circulating in the culture and represented in a cartoon published in Germany in 1876 (Jones 1953, 151). Freud's well-known biographer, Ernst Jones, documented that Freud rejuvenated the joke, which was then told throughout his inner circle. Reporting that Freud identified with the lion sitting on a perch, Jones reports the caption read, "Twelve o'clock and no negro" (p. 105). In her research, this writer through the German publisher (*Fliegende Blätter*) located a picture of the cartoon with its original caption. "For Christ's sake, it's almost 12:00 now—and no Negro yet!" which is the more accurate translation of the original German (Figure 2.1).

Figure 2.1 Stoßseufzer aus Afrika.

Stoßseufzer aus Afrika (Deep sight from Africa). Original cartoon caption: "Hergott noch einmal, jetzt ist's schon bald zwölf Uhr - und noch kein Neger!" (Translation: "For Christ's sake, it's almost 12:00 now - and no Negro yet!"). The image was published in Fliegende Blätter, 65.1876 (Nr. 1635, p. 164). Credit for locating this archived cartoon is given to Bettina Müller M.A., Kunsthistorikerin Universitäts-Bibliothek Heidelberg, Germany. The original cartoonist, Adolf Oberländer, died 70 years ago. The original date published in Jones' original volume was probably a typo as the archivist verified the publication year of 1876 not 1886 as Jones cites. Reprinted with permission from Universitäts-Bibliothek Heidelberg, https://digi.ub.uni-heidelberg.de/diglit/fb65/0167.

The multiple possible reasons Freud might have had for telling the joke suggested by Powell (2019) are speculative, but we could perhaps view Freud's views on race to be a reflection of his unresolved conflicts around identity (Stoute 2021).

This author's recent reformulation of psychoanalytic theory on racial trauma (Stoute, 2021, Chapter 10) considers Freud's unconscious racism to have reflected the unmetabolized racial trauma of a Jew who had suffered from the anti-semitism strongly present in Central Europe at that time—an interpretation supported by other scholars (Gilman, 1993; Starr, 2013; Gaztembide, 2019). The prevailing German cultural view held that Jews were a "diseased and deficient race," part of a devalued "Black race" (Gilman, 1993; Starr, 2013).

Over the years, as we wrote and edited the chapters of this book, the psychosocial examination of how and why psychoanalysts have ignored the importance of racial oppression and cultural trauma, of social and cultural context altogether, has become a topic of mainstream discourse. We have witnessed an explosion of scholarship within psychoanalysis proper on issues of race, racism, diversity, and otherness. As we witnessed psychoanalytic theory break free of its theoretical and social isolation, more thinkers began to posit, as demonstrated in some of the chapters contained in this volume, that social, cultural, and historical backdrops influence theory and practice, as well as psychic development (Stoute 2023). Further, we have come to accept that culture and intrapsychic phenomena are interrelated and co-created in the course of development such that cultural systems can be conceptualized as constitutive elements of the mind (Dajani 2020; Stoute 2022), that transgenerationally transmitted traumatic legacies of otherness intersect and manifest cross-culturally (Grand and Salberg 2017), and that the concept of a social unconscious has operational utility in expanding the psychoanalytic discourse in theory and in practice (Layton 2020). Since the 2017 publication of the first edition of this review, we have witnessed, as we stand in the wake, the tone and content of psychoanalytic discourse in upheaval, widening, evolving.

Conclusion

Whether one's cultural history points to slavery, caste, racial violence, ethnic cleansing, genocide, or Holocaust, there is a narrative of oppression trans-generationally transmitted in every culture. The ramifications and lived experience of racialized othering, of, destructive projection, hatred, violence, and transgenerational trauma are devastating in the modern world, domestically and abroad, and make urgent the call for analytic voices in our communities world-wide. My hope is that this limited review has offered sufficient scaffolding for analytically oriented scholars, teachers, supervisors, and practitioners to build the conceptualizations and practices to make race and racism, as operative manifestations of otherness, a focus for disciplined interest and exploration. President Barack Obama once said, "Change will not come if we wait for some other person or some other time. We are the ones we've been waiting for. We are the change that we seek." Can we rise to that challenge? If we do, then and only then can we demonstrate the radical potential that psychoanalytic thinking can offer as a tool of understanding and change in our world.

Notes

1 Dr. Elizabeth Danto provides an extraordinary level of historical detail in her analysis of the role each player contributed. Intrigued, I contacted her to clarify her sources; she replied, "I never met any of these players. But I do apply a historiographic methodology inspired many years ago by my mentor Peter Gay. My writing draws exclusively on primary sources like letters, diaries, oral histories and internal organizational reports. This kind of deep research yields an authenticity rarely found in secondary sources but requires a lot of time in archives." (Personal communication, October 2021).
2 At the Columbia University Center for Psychoanalytic Training and Research, Dr. Margaret Morgan was the first African American to graduate in 1954 followed by Dr. Hugh Butts later in 1962. Dr. Viola Bernard and Dr. Hugh Butts both later served as Training and Supervising Analysts at the Columbia University Center for Psychoanalytic Training and Research.
3 Abney (2006) listed 57 African American psychoanalysts in her study: Veronica Abney, Ph.D.; Joan Adams, M.S.W.; Bruce Ballard, M.D.; Earl Biassey, M.D.; Irma Blands, M.D.; Frances Bonner, M.D.; Veronica Abney, Ph.D.; Joan Adams, M.S.W.; Bruce Ballard, M.D Earl Biassey, M.D.; Irma Blands, M.D.; Frances Bonner, M.D.; Martin Booth, M.D.; Houston Brummit, M.D.; Hugh Butts, M.D.; June Christmas, M.D.; James Curtis, M.D.; Charles Deleon, M.D.; Constance Dunlap, M.D.; Henry Edwards, M.D.; Ruth Fuller, M.D.; Arthur Gray, Ph.D; Milton Hollar, M.D.; Dorothy Holmes, Ph.D.; Lee Jenkins, Ph.D.; Pamela Jennings, Ph.D.; William Johnson; Arnold Jones; Curtis Kendrick, M.D.; Edward Kirby, M.D.; Margaret Lawrence, M.D.; Orlando Lightfoot, M.D.; Henry McCurtis, M.D.; George Mallory, M.D.; Michelle Morgan, M.D.; Carlotta Miles, M.D.; Regina Mitchell, M.D.; Evan Moore, M.D.; Milford Parker, M.D.; Mercedes Peters; Jacqueline Robinson, M.D.; Robert Ross, M.D.; Naomi Rucker, Ph.D.; Mark Smaller, Ph.D.; Charles Smith; Rutherford Stevens; Cheryl Thompson, Ph.D.; Elizabeth Trussel; B. Lois Wadas; Sandra Walker, M.D.; Fred Weaver, III; Cleone White, Ph.D.; Quentin Wilkes, M.D.; Patricia Anagwelem, M.S.W.; Robert Hill, Ph.D.; Annie Lee Jones, Ph.D.; Arthur Burris, M.D.; Enrico Jones, Ph.D.; Charles Pinderhughes Sr., M.D.; Jeanne Spurlock, M.D.; Claudia Tate; Ellis Toney, M.D.; Bobbye Trout. Those not located at the

time of Abney's study were: Janice Bennet, Ph.D.; Anton Hart, Ph.D., Ph.D., Paula Kliger, Ph.D.; Kimberlyn Leary, Ph.D.; Marilyn Martin, M.D.; Dolores Morris, Ph.D.; Craig Polite, Ph.D.; Dionne Powell, M.D.; Dr. Argyle Stoute; Beverly J. Stoute, M.D.; Cheryl Thompson, Ph.D.; Kirkland Vaughans, Kathy Pogue White, Ph.D.; Samuel Wyche, D.O.
4 This changed in the three years following the first publication of this article. The American Psychoanalytic Association (ApsaA) and its member centers responded with new initiatives to call for diversity in training and curricula. As part of this shift, and following the murder of George Floyd in May 2020 during the COVID-19 and worldwide demonstrations for racial justice, the Holmes Commission on Racial Equality was created in the fall of 2020 to investigate systemic racism and its underlying determinants embedded within APsaA, and to offer remedies. With this tumult in the aftermath of George Floyd's murder, teaching institutions and professional organizations across the country responded similarly.
5 Holmes, D. (2017).
6 Hart, A. (2017).

Bibliography

Abney, V. (2006). African American Psychoanalysts in the United States: Their Stories and Presence in the Field; 2006, Copyright Registration Number TXu 1-771-916; August 11, 2011.

Abney, V. (2011). An Excerpt of African American Psychoanalysts: Their History & Presence in the United States, doctoral dissertation. http://icpla.edu/wp-content/uploads/2013/09/Abney-V-African-American-Psychoanalysts-in-the-United-States-Their-History-and-Presence.pdf.

Adorno, T. and Frenkel-Brunswik, E. (1950). *The Authoritarian Personality*. New York: Harper & Row.

Akhtar, S., ed. (2012). *The African American Experience: Psychoanalytic Perspectives*. New York: Rowman and Littlefield.

Allport, G. (1954). *The Nature of Prejudice*. Boston: Perseus Books.

Altman, N. (1995). *The Analyst in the Inner City*. London: The Analytic Press, pp. 74–118.

Altman, N. (1996). Chapter 10. The accommodations of diversity in psychoanalysis. In R. Foster, M. Moskowitz, and R. Javier (Eds.), *Reaching Across Boundaries of Culture and Class: Widening the Scope of Psychotherapy* (pp. 195–209). New York: Rowman & Littlefield Publishers.

Altman, N. (2000). Black and white thinking: A psychoanalyst reconsiders race. *Psychoanalytic Dialogues*, 10, 589–605.

Altman, N. (2004). History repeats itself in transference–countertransference. *Psychoanalytic Dialogues*, 14, 807–815.

Altman, N. (2006a). Whiteness. *Psychoanalytic Quarterly*, LXXV, 45–72.

Altman, N. (2006b). How psychoanalysis became white in the United States and how that might change. *Psychoanalytic Perspectives, 3*, 65–72.

Apprey, M. (1996). Broken lines, public memory, absent memory: Jewish and African Americans coming to terms with racism. *Mind and Human Interaction, 7*(3), 139–149.

Apprey, M. (2003). Repairing history: Reworking transgenerational trauma. In D. Moss (Ed.), *Hating in the First-Person Plural: Psychoanalytic Essays on Racism, Homophobia, Misogyny, and Terror*. New York: Other Press.

Apprey, M. (2006). Difference and the awakening of wounds in intercultural psychoanalysis. *Psychoanalytic Quarterly, 75*, 73–93.

Apprey, M. (2014). A pluperfect errand: A turbulent return to beginnings in the transgenerational transmission of destructive aggression. *Free Associations, 15*, 16–29.

Baldwin, J. (1993). *The Fire Next Time*. New York: Vintage International.

Barrett, W.G. (1951). Book Review of Smith, Killer of the Dream. New York: W.W. Norton & Co., Inc. 1949 *Psychoanalytic Quarterly*. 20: 129–130.

Bass, A. (2003). Historical and unconscious trauma: Racism and psychoanalysis. In D. Moss (Ed.), *Hating in the First-Person Plural*. New York: Other Press.

Bernard, V.W. (1953). Psychoanalysis and minority groups. *Journal of the American Psychoanalytic Association, 1*, 256–267.

Bernard, V.W. (1972). Interracial prejudice in the midst of change. *American Journal of Psychiatry, 128*(8), 92–98.

Bernard, V.W. and K. Kelly (1998). Some applications of psychiatry and psychoanalysis to social issues. *Psychoanalytic Review, 85*, 139–170.

Bird, B. (1957). A consideration of the etiology of prejudice. *Journal of the American Psychoanalytic Association, 5*, 490–513.

Blanton, S. (1971). *Diary of My Analysis with Freud*. New York: Hawthorn.

Bradshaw, W. (1978). Training psychiatrists for working with Blacks in basic residency programs. *American Journal of Psychiatry, 135*, 1520–1524.

Bradshaw, W. (1982). Chapter 10. Supervision in black and white. In B. Bass, G. Wyatt, and G. Powell (Eds.), *The Afro-American Family; Assessment, Treatment, and Research Issues* (pp. 183–201). New York: Grune & Stratton.

Brantley, T. (1983). Racism and its impact on psychotherapy. *American Journal of Psychiatry, 140*, 1605–1608.

Brickman, C. (2018). *Race in psychoanalysis. Aboriginal Populations in the Mind*. London: Routledge.

Brierley, M. (1944). *Frustration and aggression, book review. International Journal of Psychoanalysis, 25*, 94–95.

Butts, H.F. (1963). Color perception and self-esteem. *Contemporary Psychoanalysis, 1*, 147–152.

Butts, H.F. (1969). White racism: Its origins, institutions and the implications for professional practice in mental health. *International Journal of Psychiatry, 8*(6), 914–928.

Butts, H.F. (1971). Psychoanalysis, the Black community and mental health, *Contemporary Psychoanalysis*, 7, 147–152.
Calnek, M. (1970). Racial factors in the countertransference: The Black therapist and the Black client. *American Journal of Orthopsychiatry*, 42, 865–871.
Canino, I.A. and Spurlock, J. (1994). *Culturally Diverse Children and Adolescents: Assessment, Diagnosis and Treatment*. New York: Guilford.
Carter, J.H. (1979). Frequent mistakes made with Black patients in psychotherapy. *Journal of the National Medical Association*, 71, 1007–1009.
Cheng, A. (2001). *The Melancholy of Race: Psychoanalysis, Assimilation and Hidden Grief*. New York: Oxford University Press.
Christmas, J.J. (1967). Sociopathic treatment of disadvantaged psychotic adults. *American Journal of Orthopsychiatry*, 37, 93–100.
Christmas, J.J. (1974). Sociopathic rehabilitation in a Black urban ghetto: Conflicts, issues and directions. *American Journal of Orthopsychiatry*, 39, 651–661.
Clarke, S. (2003). *Social Theory, Psychoanalysis and Racism*. New York: Palgrave MacMillan.
Cohen, A.I. (1974). Treating the Black patient: Transference questions. *American Journal of Psychotherapy*, 28, 137–143.
Comer, J.P. (1969). White racism: Its root, form, and function, *American Journal of Psychiatry*, 128, 802–806.
Crenshaw, K. (1991). Mapping the margins: Intersectionality, identity politics, and violence against women of color. *Stanford Law Review*, 43, 1241–1299.
Curry, A. (1964). Myth, transference and the black psychotherapist. *Psychoanalytic. Review*, 51, 7–14.
Dajani, K. (2020). Cultural determinants in Winnicott's developmental theories. *International Journal of Applied Psychoanalytic Studies*, 17, 6–21.
Dalal, F. (2001). Insides and outsides: A review of psychoanalytic renderings of difference, racism and prejudice. *Psychoanalytic Studies*, 3(1), 43–66.
Dalal, F. (2002). *Race, Colour and the Processes of Racialization*. London: Routledge.
Dalal, F. (2006). Racism: Processes of detachment, dehumanization, and hatred. *Psychoanalytic Quarterly*, 75, 131–161.
Danto, E.A. (2014). Race unchronicled. A discourse of psychoanalysis in mid–20th century United States. *Revista Culturas Psi/Psy Cultures, Buenos Aires*, 2, 51–72.
DiAngelo, R. (2012). *What Does It Mean to Be White?*. New York: Peter Land Publishing.
Dollard, J. (1937). *Caste and Class in a Southern Town*. New Haven: Yale University Press.
Dollard, J., Miller, N.E., Doob, L.W., Mowrer, O.H., and Sears, R.R. (1939). *Frustration and Aggression*. New Haven: Yale University Press.

Eng, D. and Han, S. (2000). A dialogue in racial melancholia. *Psychoanalytic Dialogues, 34*, 667–709.

Evarts, A.B. (1914). Dementia precox in the colored race. *Psychoanalytic Review, 1*, 388–403.

Fanon, F. (1952). *Black Skin White Masks.* New York: Grove Press. Originally published as *Peau Noire Masques Blancs.* Paris: Editions de Seuil.

Fanon, F. (1961). *Wretched of the Earth.* New York: Grove Press. Originally published as *Les Damnes de la Terre.* Paris: Maspero.

Ferenczi, S. (1953). On the ontogenesis of interest in money. *Selected Papers.* New York: Basic Books.

Fisher, N. (1971). An interracial analysis: Transference and countertransference significance. *Journal of the American Psychoanalytic Association, 19*, 736–745.

Flowers, L.K. (1972). Psychotherapy: Black and white. *Journal of the National Medical Association, 64*, 19–22.

Foster, R.M.P., Moskowitz, M., and Javier, R.A. (1996). *Reaching Across Boundaries of Culture and Class.* New York: Rowman & Littlefield Publishers.

Fraiberg, S., Adelson, E., and Shapiro, V. (1975). Ghosts in the nursery: A psychoanalytic approach to the problem of impaired infant-mother relationships. *Journal of the American Academy of Child Psychiatry, 14*, 387–421.

Freud, S. (1900). The interpretation of dreams. In *The Standard Edition of the Complete Psychological Works of Sigmund Freud.* London: Hogarth, S.E. 4:136, 139, 196–197, 212.

Freud, S. (1905). Jokes and their relation to the unconscious. In *The Standard Edition of the Complete Psychological Works of Sigmund Freud.* London: Hogarth, S.E. 8:237–245.

Freud, S. (1913). Totem and taboo. In *The Standard Edition of the Complete Psychological Works of Sigmund Freud.* London: Hogarth, S.E. 13:1–162.

Freud, S. (1918). The taboo of virginity. In *The Standard Edition of the Complete Psychological Works of Sigmund Freud.* London: Hogarth, S.E. 11:191–207.

Freud, S. (1921). Group psychology and the analysis of the ego. In *The Standard Edition of the Complete Psychological Works of Sigmund Freud.* London: Hogarth, S.E. 18.

Freud, S. (1926). Inhibitions, symptoms and anxiety. In *The Standard Edition of the Complete Psychological Works of Sigmund Freud.* London: Hogarth, S.E. 20:147–148.

Freud, S. (1930). Civilization and its discontents. In *The Standard Edition of the Complete Psychological Works of Sigmund Freud.* London: Hogarth, S.E. 21:114.

Freud, S. (1936). A disturbance of memory on the Acropolis. In *The Standard Edition of the Complete Psychological Works of Sigmund Freud.* London: Hogarth, S.E. 22:239–248.

Freud, S. (1939). Moses and monotheism. In *The Standard Edition of the Complete Psychological Works of Sigmund Freud*. London: Hogarth, S.E. 23:1–138.

Fuller, R.L. (1980). Working mothers. In J. Spurlock and C.B. Robinowitz (Eds.), *Women's Progress: Promises and Problems* (pp. 91–108). New York: Plenum.

Fuller, R.L. (1988). Lovers of AIDS victims: A minority group experience. *Death Studies*, *12*, 1–7.

Fuller, R.L. (1993). Health care must be culturally relevant [column]. *Denver Medical Journal*, p. 5.

Fuller, R.L., Spurlock, J., Butts, H.F., and Edwards, H. (1999). Chapter 11. Black psychoanalysts. In Jeanne Spurlock (Ed.), *Black Psychiatrists and American Psychiatry* (pp. 163–186). Washington, DC: American Psychiatric Association.

Gardner, R.A. (1975). The kids all call me Schwartzer. *Contemporary Psychoanalysis*, *11*, 125–134.

Gaztembide, D.J. (2019). *A People's History of Psychoanalysis: From Freud to Liberation Psychology*. London: The Rowman & Littlefield Publishing Group, Inc.

Gilman, S. (1993). *Freud, Race and Gender*. New Jersey: Princeton University Press.

Goldberg, E.L. Myers, W.A. Zeifman, I. (1974). Some observations on three interracial analyses. *International Journal of Psychoanalysis*, *55*, 495–500.

Grand, S. and Salberg, J., eds. (2017). *Trans-generational Trauma and the Other: History Matters*, London: Routledge.

Graven, P.S. (1930). Case study of a Negro. *Psychoanalytic Review*, *17*, 274–279.

Greenson, R.E. (2008). The working alliance and the transference neurosis. *Psychoanalytic Quarterly*, *77*, 77–102.

Greenson, R.E., Toney, E., Lim, P., and Romero, A. (1982). Chapter 11. Transference and countertransference in interracial psychotherapy. In B. Bass, G. Wyatt, and G. Powell (Eds.), *The Afro-American Family: Assessment, Treatment, and Research Issues* (pp. 183–201). New York: Grune & Stratton.

Griffin, M.S. (1977). The influences of race on the psychotherapeutic relationship. *Psychiatry*, *40*, 27–40.

Gump, J. (2000). A white therapist, an African American patient–shame in the therapeutic dyad: Commentary on paper by Neil Altman. *Psychoanalytic Dialogue*, *10*(4), 619–632.

Hamer, F. (2002). Guardians at the gate: Race, resistance, and psychic reality. *Journal of the American Psychoanalytic Association*, *50*, 1219–1237.

Hamer, F. (2012). Anti Black racism and the concept of whiteness. In S. Akhtar (Ed.), *The African American Experience: Psychoanalytic Perspectives*. Lanham, MD: Jason Aronson.

Hamilton, J.W. (1966). Some dynamics of anti-Negro prejudice. *Psychoanalytic Review*, *53A*, 5–15.

Harrison, P.A. and Butts, H.F. (1970). White psychiatrists' racism in referral practices to Black psychiatrists. *Journal of the National Medical Association*, *62*(4), 278–282.

Harrison-Ross, P. (1973). *The Black Child: A Parent's Guide*. New York: Peter H. Wyden Inc.

Hart, A. (2017). From multicultural competence to radical openness: A psychoanalytic engagement of otherness. *The American Psychoanalyst*, *51*(1), 12, 13, 26, 27.

Holmes, D. (1992). Race and transference in psychotherapy and psychoanalysis. *International Journal of Psychoanalysis*, *73*, 1–11.

Holmes, D. (2006). The wrecking effects of race and class. *Psychoanalytic Quarterly*, *75*, 215–235.

Holmes, D. (2015). "I knew my mind could take me anywhere": Psychoanalytic reflections on the dignity of African Americans living in a racist society. In S. Levine (Ed.), *Dignity Matters: Psychoanalytic and Psychological Perspectives*. London: Karnac.

Holmes, D. (2016). Culturally imposed trauma: The sleeping dog has awakened. Will psychoanalysis take heed? *Psychoanalytic Dialogues*, *26*(6), 641–654.

Holmes, D. (2017), The fierce urgency of now: An appeal to organized psychoanalysis to take a strong stand on race, *The American Psychoanalyst*, *51*(1), 1, 8–9.

Jones, A.L. (2016). Relational dynamics of loss, grief and fear in everyday lives of African American women. *The American Psychoanalyst*, *50*(3), 2, 26–8.

Jones, B.E., Lightfoot, O.C., Palmer, D., et al. (1970). Problems of Black psychiatric residents in white training institutes. *American Journal of Psychiatry*, *127*, 798–803.

Jones, E. (1974). Social class and psychotherapy: A critical review of research. *Psychiatry*, *37*, 307–320.

Kardiner, A. and Ovesey, L. (1951). *The Mark of Oppression*. New York: World Publishing.

Keval, N. (2016). *Racist States of Mind: Understanding the Perversion of Curiosity and Concern*. London: Karnac.

Klein, M. (1946). Notes on some schizoid mechanisms. *International Journal of Psychoanalysis* 27:99–110.

Kovel, J. (1970). *White Racism: A Psychohistory*. New York: Columbia University Press.

Kovel, J. (2000). Reflections on white racism. *Psychoanalytic Dialogues*, *10*, 579–587.

Kranz, P.L. (1973). Toward achieving more meaningful encounters with minority group clients. *Hospital & Community Psychiatry*, *24*, 343–344.

Kubie, L.S. (1937). The fantasy of dirt. *Psychoanalytic Quarterly*, *6*, 388–425.

Kuriloff, E. (2014). *Contemporary Psychoanalysis and the Legacy of the Third Reich: History, Memory, Tradition.* London: Routledge.
Lawrence-Lightfoot, S. (1988). Balm in Gilead: Journey of a Healer.
Layton, L. (2020). *Towards a Social Psychoanalysis.* New York: Routledge.
Leary, K. (1997). Race in the psychoanalytic space. *Gender and Psychoanalysis, 2,* 157–172.
Lind, J.E. (1914). The dream as a simple wish-fulfillment in the Negro. *Psychoanalytic Review, 1,* 295–300.
Lind, J.E. (1917). Phylogenetic elements in the psychoses of the Negro. *Psychoanalytic Review, 4,* 303–332.
Loeblowitz-Lennard, H. (1947). The Jew as symbol. *Psychoanalytic Quarterly, 16,* 33–38.
MacDonald, M. (1974). Little Black Sambo. *Psychoanalytic Study of the Child, 29,* 511–528.
Mayo, J.A. (1974). The significance of sociocultural variables in the psychiatric treatment of Black outpatients. *Comprehensive Psychiatry, 15,* 471–482.
Miles, R. and Brown, M. (1989). *Racism,* second edition. New York: Routledge.
Morgan, H. (2002). Exploring racism. *Journal of Analytic Psychology, 47,* 567–581.
Morgan, H. (2007). The effects of "difference" of race and colour in supervision. In A. Petts and B. Shapley (Eds.), *On Supervision: Psychoanalytic and Jungian Perspectives* (pp. 187–203). London: Karnac.
Morgan, H. (2008). Issues of "race" in psychoanalytic psychotherapy: Whose problem is it anyway? *British Journal of Psychotherapy, 24,* 34–49.
Moss, D. (2001). On hating and in the first person plural: Thinking psychoanalytically about racism, homophobia and misogyny. *Journal of the American Psychoanalytic Association, 45,* 201–215.
Moss, D. (2006). Mapping racism. *Psychoanalytic Quarterly, 75,* 271–294.
Moss, D., ed. (2003). *Hating in the First Person Plural: Psychoanalytic Essays on Racism, Homophobia, Misogyny, and Terror.* New York: Other Press.
Myers, W.A. (1984). Therapeutic neutrality and racial issues in treatment. *American Journal of Psychiatry, 141,* 918–919.
Myrdal, G. (1944). *An American Dilemma: The Negro Problem in Modern Democracy.* New York: Harper & Row Publishers.
Obama, Barack (2008). February 5, 2008 Speech to Supporters. Recorded by the Federal News Service. www.nytimes.com/2008/02/05/us/politics/05text-obama.html (Last access February 2, 2022).
Obendorf, C.P. (1954). Selectivity and option for psychiatry. *American Journal of Psychiatry, 110,* 754–758.
Pinderhughes, C. (1973). Chapter 3. Racism and psychotherapy. In C.V. Willie, B.M. Kramer, and B.S. Brown (Eds.), *Racism and Mental Health* (pp. 61–121). Pittsburgh, Pennsylvania: University of Pittsburgh.

Pinderhughes, E. (1989). *Understanding Race, Ethnicity and Power: The Key to Efficacy in Clinical Practice*. New York: The Free Press.

Poussaint, A. (1980). Interracial relations and prejudice. In H.I. Kaplan, A.M. Freeman, and B.J. Saddock (Eds.), *Comprehensive Textbook of Psychiatry* (III, Vol. 3, pp. 3155–3161). Baltimore: Williams & Wilkins.

Powell, D. (2012). Psychoanalysis and African Americans: Past, present, and future. In S. Akhtar (Ed.), *The African American Experience: Psychoanalytic Perspectives*. New York: Rowman and Littlefield.

Powell, D. and Hart, A. (2016). *African Americans and Psychoanalysis, a Final Frontier: Collective Silence in the Therapeutic Conversation*. New York: The Association for Psychoanalytic Medicine.

Powell, D. (2019). Race, African Americans, and Psychoanalysis: Collective Silence in the Therapeutic Situation. *Journal of the American Psychoanalytic Association*. 66(6), 1021–1049.

Resnikoff, P. (1933). A psychoanalytic study of lynching. *Psychoanalytic Review*, 20, 421–427.

Rodgers, T. (1960). The evolution of an anti-Negro racist. *Psychoanalytic Study of Society*, 1(1), 237–247.

Schachter, J. and Butts, H. (1968). Transference and countertransference in interracial analyses. *Journal of the American Psychoanalytic Association*, 16, 792–808.

Siegel (1962). Characteristics of patients in psychoanalysis. *Journal of Nervous and Mental Disorders*, 35(4), 155–158.

Smith, L. (1949). *Killers of the Dream*. New York: W.W. Norton & Co.

Spurlock, J. (1985). Survival guilt and the Afro-American of achievement. *Journal of the National Medical Association*, 77, 29–32.

Spurlock, J. and Norris, D.M. (1991). The impact of culture and race on the development of African Americans. In A. Tasman and S.M. Goldfinger (Eds.), *American Psychiatric Press Review of Psychiatry* (pp. 594–607). Washington, DC: American Psychiatric Press.

Spurlock, J., ed. (1999). *Black Psychiatrists and American Psychiatry*. Washington DC: American Psychiatric Association.

Starr, K (2013). Chapter 12, Freud's anti-semitic surround, In K. Starr and L. Aron (Eds.), *A Psychotherapy for the People: Toward a Progressive Psychoanalysis*. London: Routledge.

Sterba, R. (1947). Some psychological factors in Negro race hatred and in anti-Negro riots. *Psychoanalysis and the Social Sciences I* (pp. 411–427). New York: International Universities Press.

Stoute, B.J. (2019). Racial socialization and thwarted mentalization: Psychoanalytic reflections from the lived experience of James Baldwin's America. *American Imago* 76:335–357.

Stoute, B.J. (2021). Black Rage: The psychic adaptation to the trauma of oppression. *Journal of the American Psychoanalytic Association*, 69 (2): 259–290.

Stoute, B.J. (2023). How Our Mind Becomes Racialized: Implications for the Therapeutic Encounter. In Holly Crisp, and Glen O. Gabbard, (Eds.), *Gabbard's Textbook of Psychotherapeutic Treatments* (Second Edition). Washington, DC: American Psychiatric Association, Publishing.

Suchet, M. (2004). A relational encounter with race. *Psychoanalytic Dialogues*, *14*, 423–438.

Suchet, M. (2007). Unraveling whiteness. *Psychoanalytic Dialogues*, *17*(6), 876–886.

Tate, C. (1996). Freud and his "Negro": Psychoanalysis as ally and enemy of African Americans. Jounal for the Psychoanalysis of Culture & Society, 1(1), Spring 1996, 53–62.

Thomas, A. and Sillen, S. (1972). *Racism and Psychiatry*. New Jersey: The Citadel Press.

Thompson, C. (1987). Racism or neuroticism: An entangled dilemma for the Black middle-class patient. *Journal of the American Academy of Psychoanalysis*, *15*, 395–405.

Thompson, C. (1995). Self-definition by opposition: A consequence of minority status. *Psychoanalytic Psychology*, *12*, 533–545.

Vaughans, K. (2014). Chapter 32. Disavowed fragments of the intergenerational trauma. In K. Vaughans and W. Spielberg (Eds.), *The Psychology of Black Boys and Adolescents*. Santa Barbara, California: Praeger.

Vaughans, K. (2016). The shadow of slavery's legacy: Intergenerational trauma among African Americans, *The American Psychoanalyst*, *51*(3), Fall 2016: 6, 26–29.

White, K.P. (2002). Surviving hate and being hated: Some personal thoughts about racism from a psychoanalytic perspective. *Contemporary Psychoanalysis*, *38*, 401–422.

Young-Bruehl, E. (1996). *The Anatomy of Prejudices*. Cambridge, MA: Harvard University Press.

Zilboorg, G. (1947). Psychopathology of social prejudice. *Psychoanalytic Quarterly*, *16*, 303–324.

Chapter 3

Race, African Americans, and Psychoanalysis
Collective Silence in the Therapeutic Situation

Dionne R. Powell

Both historically and currently, assaults on the Black body and mind have been ubiquitous in American society, posing a counterargument to America as a post-racial, color-blind society. Yet the collective silence of psychoanalysts on this societal reality limits our ability to explore, teach, and treat the effects, both interpersonal and intrapsychic, of race, racism, racialized trauma, and implicit bias and privilege. This silence, which challenges our relevance as a profession, must be explored in the context of America's racialized identity as an outgrowth of slavery and institutional racism. Racial identifications that maintain whiteness as a construct privileged over otherness are an obstacle to conducting analytic work. Examples of work with racial tensions and biases illustrate its therapeutic potential. The challenge for us as clinicians is to acknowledge and explore our racial bias, ignorance, blindspots, and privilege, along with identifications with the oppressed and the oppressor, as contributors to our silence.

    At the 2013 IPA Congress in Prague, psychoanalysts from around the world sat silently as moderators attempted to access their reactions to the theme of the congress: "Facing the Pain". Continuing from the 2007 Berlin Congress ("Trauma: New Developments in Psychoanalysis"), this was the first of a three-day large-group discussion for analysts, providing a forum to reflect and experience ourselves collectively returned for the first time since World War II to a region that was the birthplace of psychoanalysis. The silence was deafening. Its source was particularly unique to this region of Europe and the tragedies that had occurred there. Sitting with my colleagues, attempting to capture imaginatively the painful silence of the moment, I offered the following:

> I could only attempt to imagine what Prague means to most of you as you remember loved ones lost to Nazism, anti-Semitism, the Holocaust and Communism. Your experience reminds me of what is taking place in America right now, especially for a particular segment of the population: for a young teenage boy, Trayvon Martin, was visiting his father in Sanford, Florida. Walking back to his father's condo, talking to his girlfriend on his cell phone, anticipating the NBA All Star game; it starts to rain, and Trayvon pulls up his hoodie. He realizes he's no longer alone. Following Trayvon was George Zimmerman in his car, on the phone with the police: "These f-ing punks! These assholes, they always get away." George Zimmerman shot and killed Trayvon Martin and was acquitted of Trayvon's death, claiming self-defense. Trayvon was unarmed. If you were an African American parent, the next calls were to your sons, imploring them to be vigilant when walking down the street, to be mindful when it rains and you cover your head, and to caution that there's an extra price to pay in trying to be a normal kid when you're black!

After that the floodgates opened as analysts began to speak freely about their terror, joy, guilt, and loss, as though their ancestors were speaking through them. They were no longer "haunted" into silence. We were collectively facing the pain.

My observations in Prague came into focus as a foreign observer, an African American woman, of the unique trauma and atrocities that occurred in that part of the world, and yet I suggest that my outsider status provided the psychic space to contemplate and speak as the traumas of then (Eastern Europe) and now (the United States) intersected (Biale, Galchinsky, and Heschel 1998). Psychoanalysts have extensively explored the dynamics leading to the Holocaust, mass violence, genocide, and the seeds for within-nation conflicts that result in murderous violence, along with its psychological sequelae in a European context (Davidowicz 1975; Volkan 1988, 1997, 2001, 2003; Volkan, Ast, and Greer 2002; Kernberg 2003a,b; Casoni and

Brunet 2007; Kuriloff 2010).[1] Less explored is the psychic impact of American slavery on the minds of the nation's inhabitants. I wondered how, had my colleagues remained here, in Eastern Europe, where such massive trauma had occurred, their ability to work, to think, and to speak would have been affected. Or would silence have prevailed? This experience and others have led to my attempt here to understand our silence as American psychoanalysts when it comes to race, racism, and racialized trauma within the clinical situation.

We are confronted daily with the precariousness of the Black body: Black bodies that we encounter through social media and the news, milliseconds before and after their deaths.[2] Yet American psychoanalysts appear blind and mute to race, culture, implicit bias, racism, and white privilege as informing our therapeutic work. How attuned are we as clinicians, as fellow citizens, to the collective tragedy that is racism in America, especially as reflected in the clinical situation, but also within us? To imaginatively embody, and vicariously hold and contain, the trauma of another is the daily task of psychoanalysts. And yet racialized trauma, especially as it pertains to African Americans, is seldom discussed in the psychoanalytic literature, with a few notable exceptions (Fanon 1952; Kovel 1970; Fischer 1971; Wolfenstein 1981, 1991; Holmes 1992, 2006, 2016; Altman 1995, 2000, 2006; Young-Bruehl 1996; Leary 1997, 2012; Thompson 1998; Cushman 2000; Hamer 2002; White 2004; Bonovitz 2005, 2009; Layton 2006; Moss 2006; Davis 2007; Gump 2010, 2017; Akhtar 2012; Winograd 2014; Harris, Kalb, and Klebanoff 2016a,b; Stoute 2017).

It is still safe to assume that most people of color will not be treated by someone of their race, while white patients will. African Americans account for 12 percent of the 309 million citizens of the United States, but of the over three thousand members of the American Psychoanalytic Association, only seven in a thousand are black (US Census Bureau 2010).[3] If topics of race are engaged predominantly when the analyst belongs to a racial minority, then psychoanalysis will continually fail to speak to the experience of segments of the population that are most affected; it will also fail to explore the ongoing effects of racism on all Americans who seek treatment. Our silence will increasingly constrict the relevance of our profession for an increasingly diverse American population.

Within psychoanalysis, the absence of diversity, of otherness, in those we treat, train, and teach is notable. This absence has reached a level of acceptance such that in presentations of clinical work race for the most part is mentioned only when the patient is *not white*. How, as clinicians and academicians, can we understand the meaning of this absence or lack within our field—the psychoanalytic enterprise that values the dynamic unconscious, the multidetermined self, and the multidetermined other that forms our therapeutic edge? What role, if any, do we as mental health practitioners have in speaking to our patients, candidates, supervisees, and colleagues regarding race, racism, implicit bias, and white privilege as encountered in the arenas in which we function?

South Africa's Truth and Reconciliation Council succeeded in bringing a long-held trauma to the experiential level (Gobodo-Madikizela 2004, 2008). In the United States, similarly, race, implicit bias, racism, white privilege, and generational transmission of trauma require explication at an experiential level, in the here-and-now clinical encounter, in order to forge any comprehensive meaning or healing impact. This would require not only exploring the effects of institutional racism on our patients, but also a thorough consideration regarding our own racial biases, white privilege, guilt, and sense of superiority as they interface and interfere with our work (Balbus 2004). Christopher Bollas's plenary at the 2015 IPA Congress reminded the audience that despite the loftiness of the ideals espoused by America's Founding Fathers, the level of brutality present today is equivalent to what once drove millions to these shores, the fundamental difference being the race of those being persecuted. Bollas was not silent about the current tale of two Americas. With the death count rising, I believe we must face the pain of our collective silence regarding racism. It is an open wound that keeps on hurting, and a deep signifier of meaning. Breaking our silence as mental health professionals, analysts, and psychotherapists can let us bring meaning to our national trauma in a way that can benefit us, our patients, and perhaps America as a whole.

Historical Context

One does not need to look far through the annals of American history to discover evidence of mistreatment of America's Black population at the hands of whites (Skloot 2010). Instead of presenting a litany of atrocities visited upon the ancestors of today's African Americans, it should suffice to examine a particularly egregious phenomenon, as its purpose was to maintain a collective silence stratified along racial lines. Our silence as clinicians reflects the shared history of slavery, its aftermath, and the traumatogenic effects of racism for all Americans.

For a significant portion of America's history, lynching was a socially, if not legally, sanctioned reality whose purpose was to prevent the psychological emancipation of people of color. It was a form of terror and manipulation, with the intent to fortify impenetrable racial lines, that has its vestiges in modern society, contributing to the continued silence of our nation and our field. As evident in the August 7, 1930, lynching[4] of Thomas Shipp and Abram Smith in Marion, Indiana, witnessing of lynching was a communal American activity and inspired the poem "Strange Fruit" by Abel Meeropol, immortalized in song by Billie Holiday in 1939. The words of Colson Whitehead, in the National Book Award winning *The Underground Railroad*, capture this uniquely harrowing American form of terror:

> The corpses hung from trees as rotting ornaments. Some of them naked, others partially clothed, the trousers black where their bowels emptied when their necks snapped. Gross wounds and injuries marked the flesh of those closest to her.... One had been castrated, an ugly mouth gaping where his manhood had been. The other was a woman. Her belly curved.... Their bulging eyes seemed to rebuke her stares, but what were the attentions of one girl, disturbing their rest, compared to how the world had scourged them since the day they were brought into it? "They call this road the Freedom Trail now," ... "The bodies go all the way to town." "In what kind of hell had the train let her off?"
>
> (2016, pp. 152–153)

In 1909 alone, the year of the Freud-Jung lectures at Clark University, there were 69 documented lynchings of Black people in this country. Solomon Carter Fuller (1872–1953), America's first African American psychiatrist, was the lone person of color attending those lectures (see Figure 3.1, which had been arranged by G. Stanley Hall, the

Figure 3.1 Solomon carter fuller (top row, farthest to the right), Freud-Jung lectures, Clark University, Wooster, MA, 1909.

university's president. Fuller was Hall's personal physician and perhaps his analyst, and there is evidence that Fuller corresponded with Freud (Kaplan 2005, pp. 50–51; Akhtar 2011). The achievements of Fuller, W.E.B. Dubois, and other African Americans, when juxtaposed with the traumatic reality of lynching, encourage splitting, disavowal, and silence as the psychic sequelae of those unpunished crimes of terror. From 1882 to 1968, there were 3,486 documented lynchings of Blacks in the U.S., of whom 150 were women (four of them pregnant), occurring in forty-four of the fifty states, including New York, New Jersey, Michigan, Illinois, Pennsylvania, and Vermont. While there were instances of successful interventions against lynching, most white Americans would risk loss of property, job, or life were they to show any sign of opposition to these acts of domestic terror.

Although public lynchings no longer occur, the mass media provide a nearly daily menu of dead Black bodies for us to witness. The image of Michael Brown's lifeless body in Ferguson, Missouri, instantaneously broadcast throughout the world in 2014, is analogous to historical lynchings in terms of the fear and terror it generated[5]. We witness white supremacist groups that historically carried out public lynchings marching, emboldened and united with neo-Nazis, performing acts of domestic terrorism with impunity. Whether viewed or ignored, these incidents and images weigh on our consciences and contribute to a silencing antedating our becoming psychoanalysts; this silence requires acknowledgment that we might be mindful of its impact. As the history of lynching suggests, 250 years of chattel slavery and the Jim Crow America that followed have had lasting effects on Blacks and whites alike. Our silence as American psychoanalysts is persuasively predetermined by this racist system that predates our training and contributes to "racist states of mind" that have been internalized and require our recognition (Keval 2016).

Mindful of these effects, Donald Moss proposes in "Mapping Racism" (2006) that we are all afflicted by racial stereotypes, including how we locate others psychologically based on their race, class, and various differences. Results from the Implicit Association Tests confirm in part that the vast majority of us negatively and unconsciously characterize groups based on race, religion, gender, and/or sexual orientation (Greenwald and Banaji 1995; Greenwald, McGhee, and Schwartz 1998; Gladwell 2005).

The fields of clinical psychology and psychoanalysis are not free of culpability in contributing to America's fraught racial past in a way that leaves lingering ripples in present society. For instance, "drapetomania," flight-from-home madness, was a psychological term referring to an affliction of slaves who attempted to run away from their masters to gain their freedom (Thomas and Sillen 1972, p. 2). It was a commonly held belief that a slave must be ill to yearn for what every other person in America took for granted. To defend slavery, psychologists promoted pseudosciences claiming to demonstrate that the slave was an intellectually inferior, dependent subhuman requiring dominance and control (Gay 2016). Slavery was deemed preventative of the "dementia praecox, insanity and idiocy" that would result if the African were freed (Thomas and Sillen 1972, pp. 16–22). These lingering beliefs regarding the inferiority of African Americans are the unconscious legacy of slavery and continue to pervade modern society, including our clinical practices. African Americans were long considered "unanalyzable" due to white biases regarding their intelligence, reflective capacity, and psychological mindedness (pp. 67–82). These stereotypes, while decreasing, continue to require vigilance and active challenges.

The psychological assault on the mind and the challenges for African Americans who pursue analytic training are embodied by the experience of Margaret Morgan Lawrence, the first African American psychoanalyst to complete training in the United States. Her training was done at the Columbia University Center for Psychoanalytic Training and Research in the years 1946 through 1951. Lawrence's life has been lovingly told by her daughter, Sarah Lawrence-Lightfoot, in *Balm in Gilead: Journey of a Healer* (1988). Lawrence faced tremendous obstacles, including being a child of the deep South raised under the strictures of Jim Crow, encountering resistance toward her analytic training due to her race, and being treated as a foreigner in her own country. The opposition she faced at Columbia included Sándor Radó's questioning of Lawrence's preparedness for graduation. Despite the candidate's meeting all requirements and having the support of Viola Bernard and Benjamin Spock, Radó informed Lawrence that an additional consultation with Abram Kardiner, a member of the graduation committee, was required (Lawrence-Lightfoot 1988, pp. 178–184).[6] Although Lawrence refused to meet with Kardiner and the request was withdrawn, the impact of the additional requirement remained with Lawrence as a humiliating assault on herself (Margaret Morgan Lawrence, personal communication, 2010). While Lawrence's experience speaks to her time, I can attest, as a supervisor and mentor to several trainees of color, that racial microaggressions and pejorative racial bias continue to plague the candidate experience. Yet candidates today are more sensitively attuned and accepting of the multiply determined self as a gendered, racial, and cultural subject. Most important, they are ready to challenge these biases and prejudices actively within their training.

To address the silence in our field regarding race as reflecting American society more generally (Powell 2012), it is important to first establish the breadth and depth of the impact of America's sordid past on the present day by incorporating a sociological perspective. While I cannot give a thorough accounting of the sociological impact of racism, it is necessary to highlight a few concepts from sociology as a foundation for what will follow.

The sociologists Tricia Rose (2015), Lawrence Bobo (2001, 2004), and Eduardo Bonilla-Silva (2015) speak to the evolution of racism from overt manifestations such as slavery, Jim Crow, and lynching to more subtle contemporary manifestations, including implicit bias, color-blind racism, and laissez-faire racism. Bonilla-Silva (2015) argues that "racism creates race," in that the structuralizing institutions of colonialism and slavery promoted societal categorization based on one's closeness to a white ideal (p. 2). While the overtly racist legal systems that created today's racially stratified society have manifestly been dismantled, discrimination persists at every level of society, affecting access to health care, education, housing, and employment. The relevance of including and integrating social reality in analytic thinking is best captured by Wolfenstein (1991):

> I sometimes say to my patients that reality is the best defence against the experience of psychic pain. But if, e.g., a woman has been subjected to demeaning sexist behaviour, it is not analytic to deny that social reality. To put it another way: to bracket social reality is not to disavow it.
>
> (p. 546)

Generation after generation, oppression is externally experienced and internally reinforced by both the oppressed and the oppressor. This generational transmission of trauma has been foundational to the psychic structure of our country, where new arrivals face the implied questions of where do you stand, what are you willing to tolerate or ignore in order to belong, how white are you, and what are the compromises of your citizenship? Transformation from oppressed to oppressor is based on the ability to assimilate into the larger white society. Racial tribalism has thus become the signifier of our times, with whiteness its imprimatur.

In reference to Americans of African descent, DeGruy (2005) has coined the term "Post-Traumatic Slave Syndrome" for the multigenerational trauma and ongoing oppression that underlie their belief, justified or not, that the opportunities the rest of society enjoys are unavailable to them (p. 121). David Walker's *Appeal* (1830) captures this collective experience of slavery and its ongoing legacy almost two centuries ago: The "vile habits often acquired in a state of servitude are not easily thrown off" (p. xiv). Those "habits" are ingrained in the American psyche, to a large extent on an unconscious level. Thus, while America may continue to be experienced as the land of opportunity for immigrants who readily assimilate into white culture, for those who have not come from another country and whose ancestors were enslaved, the same opportunities are not perceived as available. And for too many that perception is true. This cultural binary of white and other, represented at one extreme by African Americans, becomes entrenched in the American psyche, at times with explosive and deadly consequences (witness the events of August 12–13, 2017, in Charlottesville, Virginia).

Finally, while we are reluctant to speak negatively of our founding father, Sigmund Freud, his racial hierarchy is available for our consideration. Freud did not discourage or prevent several early psychoanalysts from adopting his use of lower-order animals and the simplicity of children to analogize and describe people of African descent as primitive, simplistic, and not fully actualized adult human beings (Thomas and Sillen 1972, pp. 7–10; Rizzolo 2017). Specifically, there is the oft-referenced cartoon in *Fliegende Blatter* showing a lion yawning while muttering, "Twelve o'clock and no Negro," (cartoon reprinted in chapter 2) which Freud frequently took to stand for his noon hour patients (Jones 1953, p. 151). The phrase "my Negro" was later used jokingly by Freud in reference to an American patient (Jones 1957, p. 105). Several interpretations are readily available regarding Freud's frequent allusion to this cartoon; as an example of his paltry economic condition after his marriage to Martha Bernays; as an analogy for relying on his patients for his economic livelihood, like a lion awaiting its African/Negro prey; as a reflection of Freud's tenacious attempt to discover the primitive man, represented by the Negro; or as a displacement of Freud's strides toward legitimacy and acceptance in Viennese gentile society, needing to redirect his own otherness, his being Jewish, onto the Negro body and mind. Ironically, it would be America, for whom the Negro also represented foreignness, that would be entrusted with the preservation and survival of psychoanalysis decades later with the outbreak of war in Europe.

These are uncomfortable truths to bear. Ta-Nehisi Coates, in *Between the World and Me* (2015), states there is a "need to live in the discomfort—the chaos—that is race and to live in that truth" and not remain in what he calls "the dream" (a state of deception) (pp. 50–52). In our field the dream, a state of deception, manifests as our silence when confronted with race, racism, and otherness in the clinical situation (Dalal 2006).

Race and Psychoanalysis: Within and Without the Consulting Room

The following examples demonstrate how race arises as a concern to be worked through in the therapeutic conversation.

Years ago, Ms. A., a white professional in psychodynamic psychotherapy, was suddenly convinced that I was going to abruptly terminate her treatment. I initially believed we were in familiar conflictual territory surrounding her maternal transference of an aloof mother she thought preferred other activities over being with her daughter. We had spoken openly on many occasions regarding racial issues and tensions between us, including her steadfast feeling that I preferred my African American female patients, with whom she competed to secure my undivided attention. George Zimmerman's not guilty verdict led to an abrupt rise in Ms. A.'s anxiety. Noting the intensity of Ms. A.'s experience, I stepped away from a familiar dynamic between us and arranged an emergency meeting. Ms. A., shaking with fear, panic, and trepidation, described how an all-white female jury (including one light-skinned Puerto Rican) had acquitted Zimmerman of murdering Trayvon Martin.

MS. A.: I know you want to stop my treatment now.
ANALYST: What's led you to that conclusion?
MS. A.: An all-white female jury acquitted a murderer! I'm a white woman. This is horrible! How can you even look at me!
ANALYST: The intensity of your feelings, the shame and guilt, suggests there's more to what you're experiencing than the actual facts of George Zimmerman's acquittal.
MS. A.: Can't you see he's guilty and he's getting away with murder!
ANALYST: I can see that, but I also see your reaction as if you're personally affected, that *you* have acquitted a murderer.

She was now convinced I would expel her from treatment based on the jury's decision, as if she were one of the jurors. She feared that I had lost *my* capability of experiencing *her* uniquely, our years of intensive work evaporating, and that I identified her as belonging to the oppressive group that had freed a murderer.

Ms. A.'s projective identification was unabashedly evident. Manifestly, the connection between my patient's statements on the denial of justice in the Trayvon Martin case and her sudden fear that I would abandon her was readily ascribed to a disjuncture in the treatment along racial lines. But I was aware that her unconscious guilt and fear of punishment had earlier antecedents that would often attach themselves to racial events.

Later in the same session, Ms. A., slightly calmer, said, "It's my family, their history, my guilt again. It's difficult for me as a white woman. Based on my education, my wealth, and my privilege I should feel the verdict was justified. But I don't. I just feel guilty."

In this instance, her German ancestry, including both resisters and members of the Nazi Party, was a deeper contributing source. This was the unconscious connection of my patient's abrupt guilt and veiled fear of punishment for unspeakable crimes. What we were unaware of was the extent of her generational trauma. Interpreting and working through Ms. A.'s guilt and fear of punishment resulted in a de-escalation of her anxiety, along with renewed interest in social justice as reparative of crimes in both Germany and the United States.

Thus death, punishment, fear, silence, shame, and guilt emerge to be reexperienced through the prism of race. My patient's mother, reportedly, had silenced any curiosity about her history and her relatives' pasts, leaving my patient frightened that she would have to experience her current anxieties about us in isolation. When I moved from a position of apparent knowing, setting aside my established notions regarding her dynamics in terms of race, and instead operated from a position of curiosity that encouraged a mutual desire to understand, our work together, though challenging, deepened and progressed. My emphasis here is on the internal work required by the analyst/therapist to recognize and bring forward racial dynamics alluded to in treatment, dynamics that may reflect areas of psychic conflict, rather than dismiss reactions as reflecting a merely societal reality with no psychic meaning.

Mr. T., single and Jewish, entered psychoanalysis four times weekly on the couch, presenting inhibitions and anxieties that prevented his advancement in love and work. A key aspect of his background was his preference for the diverse urban environment of his early childhood, as against the religiously homogeneous upper-middle-class suburbs of his middle and high school years. He vividly recalled his father's unveiled dinner conversation about the "Black animals" he was "forced" to engage with at work. Although an erotic sadomasochistic paternal transference, presented in starkly racial terms, was prominent in the first years of analysis, this transference was defensive, serving to ward off affectionate and tender feelings toward me. Mr. T. was initially convinced he was receiving an inferior analysis because of my race. As his treatment deepened and drew closer to his identification with his father, his sadomasochistic masturbatory fantasies and aggressive behavior intensified. This included a prominent somatic symptom, occurring at peak moments of impotent rage and/or longing, that was understood as a displacement of his castration anxiety. Despite this intensity, or perhaps because of it, he would keep a tissue from my office in his pants pocket, which he would tenderly rub in moments of stress throughout the day. Mr. T. became convinced that I resembled his mother, or at least a fantasized maternal ideal that would be available and loving toward him. These expressions of a positive transference provided a psychic reprieve from the volatility of the analysis, suggesting a capacity for developing a reflective ego. What presented as an obstacle, his violent racial and sexualized attacks, was understood as defensive reaction to Mr. T.'s vulnerability, low self-esteem, and impotence whenever feelings of dependence and affection emerged.

Race, culture, and the effects of racism did not figure as topics in my formal analytic training. Thus, analytic silence was my default position in my work with Mr. T. In silence I would absorb and reflect on his racist and frequently sexualized attacks. My silence only escalated the tensions between us as I experienced within the transference his father's stranglehold on Mr. T. Recovering my ability to think, reflect, and be curious about these dynamics, first within myself and later with Mr. T., led to new levels of understanding.

Of equal importance was examining the superego inhibitions that led to my countertransferential disengagement, couched under the rubric of maintaining therapeutic neutrality. I would sanitize and attempt to mitigate Mr. T.'s stark language, thinly veiled eroticized dreams, and descriptions of his masturbatory fantasies, frequently of Black women, by, for instance, using less profane and charged language. Ultimately, my working through of my superego inhibitions allowed for more direct contact with Mr. T. This included exploring my own narratives regarding white men who loved, hated, and sexualized Black women in my familial past. During the peak of the transference neurosis, when he was virtually paralyzed by his somatic symptoms, I commented: "You are like a lion backed into a corner with a sharp thorn in your paw, and my job is to remove the thorn and not be annihilated."

MR. T: I'm in so much pain. I want to destroy you, fuck you, and love you. I feel so paralyzed and numb. I feel it in my body! This is so Freudian!

ANALYST: There's a lot of pain there that you don't know what to do with. How can we understand this pain, remove the thorn, and survive?

Exchanges like this were often followed by confirmatory dreams that increasingly allowed me to help him, but these were immediately followed by masochistic attacks imputing mercenary motives to me. These were understood as an internal saboteur that required Mr. T.'s absolute allegiance. My emerging understanding of the strength of this object relationship, in direct conflict with what he was experiencing within the new analytic relationship, became the focus of our work. The hate that was required for connection with his internal objects was in sharp contrast to his loving, vulnerable, and dependent feelings toward me.

The basic question that Mr. T. and I answered together was, "Is it okay to be different, one's authentic self, if that means separating from an internalized object that espouses and demands hatred in exchange for love?" As the positive transference deepened, Mr. T. became increasingly challenged by the depth of his paternal identifications, especially in his relations with ethnic others, most specifically his analyst. To work with Mr. T. effectively I had to confront my own negative identifications regarding whites, including my need to de-escalate the sexual hostilities and tension that Mr. T. used defensively. This allowed us to face what once seemed impossible to bear and to "play" with this highly charged regressive material with increasing depth and insight (Coen 2005).

Ralph Ellison's words from *Invisible Man* (1952) continue to capture the experience of being African American:

> I am the invisible man. ... I am a man of substance, of flesh and bone, fiber and liquids—and I might even be said to *possess a mind*. I am invisible, understand, simply because people refuse to see me.... When they approach they see only my surroundings, themselves, or figments of their imagination—indeed, everything and anything except me.
>
> (p. 3; emphasis added)

This sentiment is currently reflected in Claudia Rankine's musings (2014) on tennis great Serena Williams's difficulties with unfair line calls: "Again Serena's frustrations, her disappointments, exist within *a system you understand, not to try to understand* in any fair-minded way, because to do so is to understand the erasure of the self as systemic, as ordinary" (p. 208; emphasis added). As a psychoanalyst, as an African American, as a woman of a certain age, I view the struggle to see and be seen, understood, and witnessed as the core of the psychoanalytic and general therapeutic enterprise. As we function to help our patients become less opaque to themselves, we become more visible to ourselves as we appreciate the complexities of these mutual realizations. It is this fundamental capacity to be known by the other and to know one's self that is at the heart of our work.

As a first-year analytic candidate, I was reminded of the unique interior self-struggling for expression. Riding the subway uptown for my Freud class, I initially did not notice the large African American man sitting next to me and reading over my shoulder Freud's "Those Wrecked by Success" (1916). When his presence was acknowledged, he immediately reported that what he had read had happened to him. He had found it impossible to integrate the academic success he was having in high school with the realities of the street and his peers. He felt bad about leaving his neighborhood friends to actualize his potential in college. Eventually he involved himself with the wrong crowd and had only recently been released from jail, never having gone to college. He had no rational explanation for his behavior, except for feelings of guilt about leaving his friends and family behind and fears about what a future would mean in college and beyond, in a white environment less than accepting of his presence. His vulnerability, concealed beneath his size and bravado, was touchingly revealed. More importantly, this brief vignette illustrates a narrative that competes with black representation in the news media, "coverage" that typically lacks nuance and texture, focusing as it does almost exclusively on black criminality. This man not only wanted to tell his story, but also wanted to articulate and find meaning behind several conflicting narratives. Would he lose his community by pursuing his studies? Would he lose his credibility and identity by leaving his friends? His intelligence was an entrée to an expanded life, but how did guilt and shame over leaving family and friends impact his subsequent behavior and aspirational dreams? Dorothy Holmes's paper on success neurosis (2006) directly explores this dynamic, as African Americans have individual narratives heavily influenced by collective experiences as an oppressed group subject to discrimination. A focus on the narrative, of the interior, its existence, depth, and complexity, yields nodal points of confluence between psychoanalysis and clinical work with African Americans. Toni Morrison's *Beloved* (1987) eloquently renders the internal landscape of her protagonist and in doing so "rewrites the traditional slave narrative by *reconstructing* what those stories silenced: the *interior self* of the slave" (Glaude 2007, p. 41; emphasis added). The articulation of this interior world housed within the self, as a continuous dynamic dialogue with past and present, is similar to the basic foundation of psychodynamic theories and mitigates the oppressive forces that confront oppressed people.

To be invisible to the majority of Americans and yet so intimately aware of our cultural heritage is a juxtaposition inherent in being black in America. One might argue that my race as an African American would have to be part of my conversation with my patients. This fails to grasp that race is a readily available area of exploration for same-race pairings as much as for interracial dyads. How this is revealed is of course specific to the actual treatment pair. Ms. S., an African American woman in four-times-weekly analysis who presented with difficulties in romantic relationships, would constantly say to me with conviction, "You know what I mean?" Of course not, but yes I did "know" in the broadest context of being an African American woman in this country. But her words were a sort of shorthand that I *should* understand: she was ascribing to me knowledge about her as a fellow African American woman. Implicitly acquiescing to my patient's subtle pressure to resonate with her based on our being African American women would have bypassed exploring in depth the particulars of her narrative: sexual overstimulation at an early age, her mother's abandonment, and other offenses from loved ones in her past and current life that she projected into me as if we had experienced them together. I did not, of course, automatically know these aspects of her life, or the terror of being alone with these traumas. Within the treatment we confronted and discovered these things together, without the fantasy of knowing she wished to ascribe to me. My patient's fantasy was understood as her maternal transference involving simultaneous sexual overstimulation and neglect. This was my patient's apparent background of safety: that I would collude in re-creating this childhood trauma of seduction and avoidance, leaving Ms. S. to fend for herself (Sandler 1960). To presume a shared knowing within the analysis and forgo exploration would enact instead of explore the forbidden, the sexual, her desires, and, just as important, her neglect. This would be to possibly overexpose and overstimulate her, without containment or recognition of her terror. By not tacitly agreeing to a narrative superficially based on our shared race, and thereby foreclosing further exploration, depth and authenticity were maintained and the full gamut of her emotional landscape was open to be understood in all its complexities, including the maternal erotic.

In my work with African American patients, many implicitly assume that we share cultural norms regarding race, family dynamics, and perceptions of current events, as the preceding example emphasizes. These assumptions are often regarded as facts known between the two of us. Subtle but active attempts to pressure me into colluding or agreeing with a patient's leitmotif become part of the analytic dialogue. What I am describing is the tendency to regard cultural material as conflict-free, but it is not, or at least not always. Marianne Goldberger (1993) captures this phenomenon, referring to our "bright spots" when we fill in the spaces based on assumptions of our own (pp. 270–271). Early in my career as a psychoanalyst and psychotherapist, I would find myself getting far down this transference-countertransference road of bright spots, missing its subtlety before realizing what had occurred and having to rework material that had been understood quite superficially.

My final clinical example highlights the profound negative consequences of racial hatred, and the possibilities of bridging the racial divide through a dynamic therapeutic approach. As a third-year resident on my consultation-liaison psychiatry rotation, I was asked to consult on an elderly white man who had experienced a series of mild strokes that continued while he was in the hospital, despite exemplary medical care. His treating physicians were baffled. In reading the patient's chart and speaking to the referring medical team and other relevant medical staff before meeting the patient, I uncovered the following: the patient, Mr. J., was the descendent of a proud Confederate family renowned and vilified for their staunch views regarding "race" and "place." In the hospital, his symptoms, unbeknownst to his medical team, took a unique pattern: after the East Asian cardiologist consulted with Mr. J., his symptoms worsened, resulting in another small stroke. A similar fate occurred following his consultation with a Latino pulmonologist. The request for a psychiatric consultation followed the patient's request for a priest. It is easy to surmise Mr. J.'s response when a Chinese priest with clerical collar walked into his room to provide spiritual solace. None of this was obvious from his chart, but knowledge of his historical past and curiosity about why he continued to be symptomatic despite top-notch treatment led to exploration beyond the usual medical inquiries. Of note, Mr. J. did not exhibit these symptoms in his interactions with ancillary medical staff who were people of color: those who transported him to tests, brought him his meals, and drew his blood. They fit my patient's cultural norms, his racial map; they were "the help."

Armed with my data, I was ready to meet Mr. J., who had been informed that psychiatry had been consulted. At this point, he was looking for any form of relief. As I entered his room with my white coat, name tag, and brown skin, I quickly observed my patient become flushed, diaphoretic, and short of breath. Immediate action was necessary.

> Mr. J., I'm Dr. Powell, the psychiatrist called by your medical team to consult on your condition. I get it, if you could give me a minute to explain. You just want to be treated by white people, especially if they're going to be your doctors or your priest.

Mr. J. looked at me with bewilderment, relieved by the message if not the messenger. As he visibly relaxed, Mr. J. wondered aloud if he could be transferred to another country, perhaps in Northern Europe, his ancestral home; anywhere to escape and actualize the fantasy of a white utopia. As we explored the limits of that possibility in a world of increasing multiculturalism, we were able to agree that his racism was truly killing him.

We began a series of conversations about the importance of keeping the races separate, his acts of commission and omission when it came to his racial past in the South, and the regrets and consequences of a lifetime of hate. This hate was not confined to other races, but was also expressed toward his most intimate relations as they began to accept and even form close relationships with people that Mr. J. vilified as the enemy. He had become a very lonely and isolated man, hate his constant and sole companion, and a major cause of his physical symptoms. We worked together to find ways to honor his heritage and explored his deep identification with his family's past, in which hate was required to receive love, while moving away from his need to destroy others. It was painful, transformative work. Mr. J. looked forward to our talks and in a short time was discharged from the hospital with no further neurological events and an improved prognosis.

Examining Our Collective Silence: Race and Psychoanalysis

As analysts and mental health clinicians we remain silent in order not to foreclose or influence what may emerge, but are we also unconsciously conveying intentionality when we are silent about our patient's race or culture, or racial events that unfold in our multicultural milieu? While psychoanalysts are ambassadors of the talking cure, our working function is primarily spent listening, in silence. Silence provides a space to reflect, to synthesize, to construct, to feel, but also a place for defense, rationalization, and avoidance. As analysts, we accentuate the former and deny the latter. In this regard, silence isn't always golden, especially if it limits or forestalls active communication and curiosity. All too often our silence conceals our bias, prejudice, and racism under the rubric of staying with the patient's freely associative material.

Racism affects us all, particularly when we are least reflective on our privilege, distancing ourselves from those who are oppressed. In a rarely seen 1976 video interview, Ellis Toney and Ralph Greenson discuss the interracial training analysis the latter conducted during Toney's training at the Los Angeles Psychoanalytic Institute in the late 1940s and early 1950s (Greenson et al. 1982). In this interview, we witness Greenson breaking his silence as he acknowledges multiple incidences of ignorance. For example, Greenson accused Toney of being paranoid when Toney requested a different Friday appointment because he was routinely stopped by the police on his way to Greenson's Beverly Hills office. Despite Greenson's presumed liberalism, he is not shy in acknowledging his accent to naivete and his not being curious at the time to delve deeper into matters pertaining to Toney and the racial tensions between them. Greenson both speaks to and demonstrates his ignorance as he attempts to dominate Toney twenty-five years after the end of his analysis. In the interview they both speak to the institutional opposition to Toney's training, recounting incidents reminiscent of Margaret Morgan Lawrence's experience at Columbia (personal communication, 2010; Lawrence-Lightfoot 1988). Greenson and Toney also address features of their background that assisted the therapeutic relationship. They were able to establish a working relationship that stabilized the treatment, protecting it from racial assaults from within and without the consulting room. Transference remained the area of both resistance and deep therapeutic gains; despite the participants' being from very different worlds, they continued to seek out common ground. This is similar to my work with Mr. T.

Having doubts about one's liberalism is a salient feature of interracial analyses, and being able to be informed by our patients, seeing them as they want to be known, is essential in building the therapeutic relationship. This includes an expanding awareness of our own prejudices and racial blind and bright spots, and an ongoing desire to not foreclose but open up the therapeutic dialogue.

As in the larger society, we hide behind our professional veneer and turn a blind eye to race. There is a false sense of protection in white, heteronormative privilege (Galatzer-Levy and Galatzer-Levy 2012; Holmes 2016). To look at present reality for Black people, or Native American people or Latin American people is too frightening, too reminiscent of being singled out for one's religion or ethnicity, to be seen as the other. As we are all ethnic others to this land, the psychic reality of atrocities occurring in our homeland is difficult to believe (Keval 2016). And therefore we don't. Salman Akhtar and Emily Kuriloff propose that the majority of European analysts came to the United States not as immigrants but as exiles attempting to assimilate and not speak of their foreignness or their trauma (Akhtar 2006; Kuriloff 2010). As for immigrants of color, Eng and Han (2000) capture the racial melancholia that ensues:

> In the United States today, assimilation into mainstream culture for people of color still means adopting a set of dominant norms and ideals—whiteness, heterosexuality, middle-class family values—often foreclosed to them. The loss of these norms—the reiterated loss of whiteness as an ideal, for example—establishes one melancholic framework for delineating assimilation and racialization processes in the United States precisely as a series of failed and unresolved integrations.
>
> (p. 670)

Ruby Sales—civil rights activist, theologian, educator, and founder of the Spirit House Project—proposes that becoming "white" in America requires a form of ethnic cleansing that robs the soul and spirit (personal communication, 2018). Thus, attaining whiteness moves one further away from one's ancestral legacy, culture, and foundational roots. James Baldwin (1955, 1962) proposes that African Americans continue to serve as a mirror to what is sacrificed by *becoming* white: one's culture, soul, and spirit. Baldwin in this regard is privileging the Black experience as containing a rich cultural heritage of pride, identity, and familial connection that rejects assimilation and whiteness as the sole pathway to being an American. A possible counter to white assimilation, then, is to reembrace one's cultural heritage and thus reappropriate one's unique ethnicities and signifiers, which can mitigate whiteness as a construct supporting tribalism and other isms that fracture society. One can observe the beginning appreciation of our multicultural heritage in the expanding pursuit of DNA ancestry testing.

Racism does much of its damage psychologically, as my clinical examples have shown. An erasure of self, of family, of culture, and of historical signifiers occurs when we reduce ourselves to being merely black or white or other. We approach each other with our unique racial identity, both genetically and culturally imposed, along with dynamic identifications solidified over time. We map ourselves and others. We assume familiarity where there is none, and are vexed when someone falls outside our racial stereotypes. Embedded within what Keval (2016) refers to as the racist state of mind are envy and murderous rage toward what we lack, projected onto the other.

Now the silence within our profession is maintained at its peril, and challenges conceptualizations regarding empathy and the universal applicability of our field with all cultural, racial, and ethnic groups. It behooves psychoanalysts and other mental health clinicians to become curious and question issues of race, not only with people of color, but with all our patients. It is up to us, as therapists and analysts, to provide an atmosphere, a container, where communication is welcomed, with an eye to mutual understanding. An important part of addressing race entails accepting a certain humility, even a clumsiness, about addressing these issues straightforwardly with our patients. It also entails having a sense of doubt regarding our notions of the other, as well as an openness to relearning strongly held beliefs about one another and ourselves. Patients have described preferring an open and curious, if awkward, approach to discussing these issues, which overtly and covertly affect their lives, over considering issues of race, including trauma, microaggressions, and their own racially oppressive thoughts and behavior, as outside the boundaries of the therapeutic dyad.

Equally important, one cannot reconcile what is not recognized and acknowledged. As analysts we are witness, participant, and co-constructor. Exploring, accepting, and acknowledging our own racism, racial prejudice, and implicit bias allows us to approach our patients less defensively. None of this is attained overnight. It is a practice, not a cure.

Concluding Remarks

As analysts, we work with and through trauma. The history of America is a history of racial trauma that continues to this day, and affects us all. Our capacity to immerse ourselves in our patients' traumas is assisted by our ability to vicariously introspect and discover links with our own traumatic pasts (Kohut 1984; Leary 1997; Frankel

1998; Connolly 2011; Philips 2011; Peskin 2012), as my opening example illustrates.

As Kuriloff (2001) observes, these attempts to find common ground with our patients are not meant as "modeling or self-disclosure" but rather reflect "a less conscious quality of relatedness within the working dyad, changing what becomes possible for each participant to bear" (p. 680). Cultivating this ability allows us to approach our patients' traumas as they touch upon our own. Reflecting in silence, being openly curious about trauma revealed in subtle manifestations, and "speaking to" our patients' trauma and resilience can lead to profound understandings that are transformative.

It is important to add that while we bear witness to our patients' traumas, in this instance racial traumas, which tend to be chronic, we must simultaneously appreciate the resilience and adaptations that contribute to survival. This privileges the adaptive capabilities of the human spirit, mitigating revictimization.

Psychoanalysis and psychodynamic psychotherapy have the potential to heal deep-seated racial wounds, if we are capable of breaking our silence. Or, as stated over fifty years ago by Dr. Martin Luther King,

> Like life, racial understanding is not something that we find but something that we must create.... And so the ability of Negroes and Whites to work together, to understand each other, will not be found ready-made; it must be created by the fact of contact.
>
> (1967, p. 28)

We are no longer bound by silence. Silence regarding otherness, particularly regarding race and culture, threatens every facet of our field. It is not enough to wait until others bring up these topics to engage with them. We are charged to *make* contact. Doubt and exploration about our beliefs regarding race as engaged in treatment is essential. Curiosity and empathy, as clinicians and for our patients, is the only path toward understanding.

Notes

1 Rarely explicated are the psychological consequences of the uniquely American genocide of Native and African peoples forcefully enslaved in America. The United Nations defines genocide as any of the following

acts committed with intent to destroy, in whole or in part, a national, ethnical, racial or religious group, as such: killing members of the group; causing serious bodily or mental harm to members of the group; deliberately inflicting on the group conditions of life calculated to bring about its physical destruction in whole or in part.

As subjects of an intentional action to destroy a people in whole (Native Americans) or in part (for African slaves, destruction of enough of the self to internalize a subhuman existence dependent on white domination), both groups embody the psychological consequences of the dominant group's attempts at psychological destruction while simultaneously fostering pathological dependency.

2 The descriptors African American or Black should be taken to include individuals from the larger African diaspora: Caribbean, South American, African, and European. The ethnic, racial, and cultural diversity of New York City, where I practice, serves as a reminder of the uniqueness of the clinical situation, and the specificity of treatment pairs, which challenge any attempt to make global speculations, especially when addressing race and culture. Being mindful of our patients' race and culture, while aware of how this shapes the individual self, is critical.

3 Even though Black Americans seek therapy at lower rates than whites (around 38 percent less than the 40 percent of white Americans who do), there still are not enough Black analysts to keep up with demand. African Americans seek treatment less often than in society generally, due to (1) the history of racism in medicine, particularly within our field, and (2) socioeconomic conditions that suppress access to mental health care. If anything, African American reluctance to pursue mental health treatment and/or training is part of a pernicious cycle of silence that perpetuates unchallenged myths within the black community regarding the risks of pursuing medical treatment (e.g., the infamous Tuskegee Syphilis Experiment; Mississippi "appendectomies" and the forced sterilization of black women in both the North and the South [see Roberts 1997]). See also Skloot (2010) and Bahrampour (2013).

4 The well-known photograph, "Witnesses to the lynching of Thomas Shipp and Abram Smith, Marion, Indiana, August 7, 1930," inspired the poem 'Strange Fruit' by Abel Meeropol, immortalized in song by Billie Holiday in 1939." This photograph was published in the original article in the *Journal of the American Psychoanalytic Association* but the photograph was removed here due to a restriction in copyright laws so the permission to reprint in this volume could not be obtained.

5 The Figure of "Michael Brown: shot and killed by a police officer, Ferguson, MO, August 9, 2014" was published in the original article in the *Journal of the American Psychoanalytic Association* but removed due to a restriction in copyright laws and the permission to reprint here not be obtained.

6 Kardiner, with Lionel Ovesey, had recently finished *The Mark of Oppression*, a controversial psychoanalytically based exploration of Negro oppression and the resulting psychological damage from generations of enslavement, the development of within-race caste systems, and the ongoing necessity by whites to degrade the status of Blacks (Kardiner and Ovesey 1951). Lawrence refused to assist in the book's creation, having suspected the racist ideological overtones in the book that her presence at Columbia directly challenged. While the case studies present a two-dimensional minimization of multidetermined factors of development, there are in Kardiner and Ovesey's book prescient insights, including proper attribution of a "Negro personality" as being *not* genetically determined but, rather, built up during the multigenerational trauma of slavery and oppression (p. 50). Additionally, there are negative observations on whites, both Northern and Southern:

> The degradation of the Negro's status served to narcotize the white man's social conscience against the ethical issues involved in slavery. … Once you degrade someone in that way, the sense of guilt makes it imperative to degrade the object further to justify the entire procedure.
>
> (p. 379)

Unfortunately, as Thomas and Sillen (1972) note, the book is hampered by its own degradation of the Negro personality, characterizing Blacks as having low self-esteem, a sense of inferiority and a "wretched internal life."

References

Akhtar, S. (2006). Technical challenges faced by the immigrant psychoanalyst. *Psychoanalytic Quarterly*, 75, 21–43.
Akhtar, S. (2011). *Personal communication with Ivan Ward, director of education*, Freud Museum, London.
Akhtar, S., ed. (2012). *The African American Experience: Psychoanalytic Perspectives*. Lanham, MD: Aronson.
Altman, N. (1995). *The Analyst in the Inner City: Race, Class, and Culture through a Psychoanalytic Lens*. Hillsdale, NJ: Analytic Press.
Altman, N. (2000). Black and white thinking: A psychoanalyst reconsiders race. *Psychoanalytic Dialogues*, 10, 589–605.
Altman, N. (2006). Whiteness. *Psychoanalytic Quarterly*, 75, 45–72.
Bahrampour, T. (2013). Therapists say African Americans are increasingly seeking help for mental illness. The Washington Post, July 9, 2013.
Balbus, I. (2004). The psychodynamics of racial reparations. *Psychoanalysis, Culture, & Society*, 9, 159–185.
Baldwin, J. (1955). *Notes of a Native Son*. Boston: Beacon Press.

Baldwin, J. (1962). *The Fire Next Time*. New York: Vintage International, 1993.
Biale, D., Galchinsky, M., Heschel, S. (1998). *Insider/Outsider: American Jews and Multiculturalism*. Berkeley: University of California Press.
Bobo, L.D. (2001). Racial attitudes and relations at the close of the twentieth century. In Smelser, N., Wilson, W.J., Mitchell, F. (Eds.), *America Becoming: Racial Trends and Their Consequences*, (pp. 262–299). Washington, DC: National Academy Press.
Bobo, L.D. (2004). Inequalities that endure? Racial ideology, American politics, and the peculiar role of the social sciences. In Krysan, M., Lewis, A.E. (Eds.). *The Changing Terrain of Race and Ethnicity*, (pp. 13–42). New York: Russell Sage Foundation.
Bollas, C. (2015). Psychoanalysis in the age of bewilderment: On the return of the oppressed. *International Journal of Psychoanalysis*, *96*, 535–551.
Bonilla-Silva, E. (2015). The structure of racism in color-blind, "post-racial" America. *American Behavioral Scientist*, *59*, 1358–1376.
Bonovitz, C. (2005). Locating culture in the psychic field: Transference and countertransference as cultural products. *Contemporary Psychoanalysis*, *41*, 55–76.
Bonovitz, C. (2009). Mixed race and the negotiation of racialized selves: Developing the capacity for internal conflict. *Psychoanalytic Dialogues*, *19*, 426–441.
Casoni, D., Brunet, L. (2007). The psychodynamics that lead to violence: The case of "ordinary" people involved in mass violence. *Canadian Journal of Psychoanalysis*, *15*, 261–280.
Coates, T.-N. (2015). *Between the World and Me*. New York: Penguin Random House.
Coen, S.J. (2005). How to play with patients who would rather remain remote. *Journal of the American Psychoanalytic Association*, *53*, 811–834.
Connolly, A. (2011). Healing the wounds of our fathers: Intergenerational trauma, memory, symbolization and narrative. *Journal of Analytic Psychology*, *56*, 607–626.
Cushman, P. (2000). White guilt, political activity, and the analyst. *Psychoanalytic Dialogues*, *10*, 607–618.
Dalal, F. (2006). Racism: Processes of detachment, dehumanization, and hatred. *Psychoanalytic Quarterly*, *75*, 131–161.
Davidowicz, L.S. (1975). *The War against Jews, 1933–1945*. New York: Bantam Books.
Davis, S. (2007). Racism as trauma: Some reflections on psychotherapeutic work with clients from the African-Caribbean diaspora from an attachment-based perspective. *Attachment: New Directions in Psychotherapy and Relational Psychoanalysis Journal*, *1*, 179–199.
DeGruy, J. (2005). *Post Traumatic Slave Syndrome: America's Legacy of Enduring Injury and Healing*. Uptone Press.
Ellison, R. (1952). *Invisible Man*. New York: Random House.

Eng, D., Han, S. (2000). A dialogue on racial melancholia. *Psychoanalytic Dialogues*, *10*, 667–700.

Fanon, F. (1952). Black Skin, White Masks, translated by Philcox, R. New York: Grove Press, 2008.

Fischer, N. (1971). An interracial analysis: Transference and countertransference significance. *Journal of the American Psychological Association*, *19*, 736–745.

Frankel, J.B. (1998). Ferenczi's trauma theory. *American Journal of Psychoanalysis*, *58*, 41–61.

Freud, S. (1916). Some character-types met with in psycho-analytic work. In *The Standard Edition of the Complete Psychological Works of Sigmund Freud*, S.E. Vol. 14, 311–333.

Galatzer-Levy, B.A., Galatzer-Levy, R.M. (2012). Ordinary police interrogation in the United States: The destruction of meaning and persons: A psychoanalytic-ethical investigation. *American Imago*, *69*, 57–106.

Gay, V. (2016). *On the Pleasures of Owning Persons: The Hidden Face of American Slavery*. New York: International Psychoanalytic Books.

Gladwell, M. (2005). *Blink: The Power of Thinking without Thought*. New York: Little, Brown.

Glaude, Jr., E.S. (2007). *In a Shade of Blue: Pragmatism and the Politics of Black America*. Chicago: University of Chicago Press.

Gobodo-Madikizela, P. (2004). *A Human Being Died That Night: A South African Woman Confronts the Legacy of Apartheid*. New York: Mariner Books.

Gobodo-Madikizela, P. (2008). Trauma, forgiveness and the witnessing dance: Making public spaces intimate. *Journal of Analytical Psychology*, *53*, 169–188.

Goldberger, M. (1993). Bright spot, a variant of "blind spot." *Psychoanalytic Quarterly*, *62*, 270–273.

Greenson, R.E., Toney, L., Lim, P., Romero, A. (1982). Transference and countertransference in interracial psychotherapy. In Bass, B.A., Wyatt, G.E., Powell., G.J. (Eds.), *The Afro-American Family: Assessment, Treatment and Research Issues*, (pp. 183–201) New York: Grune & Stratton.

Greenwald, A.G., Banaji, M.R. (1995). Implicit social cognition: Attitudes, self-esteem, and stereotypes. *Psychological Review*, *102*, 4–27.

Greenwald, A.G., McGhee, D.E., Schwartz, J.L.K. (1998). Measuring individual differences in implicit cognition: The implicit association test. *Journal of Personality & Social Psychology*, *74*, 1464–1480.

Gump, J.P. (2010). Reality matters: The shadow of trauma on African American subjectivity. *Psychoanalytic Psychology*, *27*, 42–54.

Gump, J.P. (2017). The presence of the past: Transmission of slavery's traumas. In Harris, A., Kalb, M., (Ed.), *Demons in the Consulting Room: Echoes of Genocide, Slavery and Extreme Trauma in Psychoanalytic Practice*. New York: Routledge.

Hamer, F.M. (2002). Guards at the gate: Race, resistance, and psychic reality. *Journal of the American Psychoanalytic Association, 50*, 1219–1237.

Harris, A., Kalb, M., Klebanoff, S., eds. (2016a). *Demons in the Consulting Room: Echoes of Genocide, Slavery and Extreme Trauma in Psychoanalytic Practice*. New York: Routledge.

Harris, A., Kalb, M., Klebanoff, S., eds. (2016b). *Ghosts in the Consulting Room: Echoes of Trauma in Psychoanalysis*. New York: Routledge.

Holmes, D.E. (1992). Race and transference in psychoanalysis and psychotherapy. *International. Journal of Psychoanalysis, 73*, 1–11.

Holmes, D.E. (2006). The wrecking effects of race and social class on self and success. *Psychoanalytic Quarterly, 75*, 215–235.

Holmes, D.E. (2016). Come hither, American psychoanalysis: Our complex multicultural America needs what we have to offer. *Journal of the American Psychoanalytic Association, 64*, 569–586.

Jones, E. (1953). *The Life and Work of Sigmund Freud: Vol. 1. The Formative Years and the Great Discoveries, 1856–1900*. New York: Basic Books.

Jones, E. (1957). *The Life and Work of Sigmund Freud: Vol. 3. The Last Phase, 1919–1939*. New York: Basic Books.

Kaplan, M. (2005). *Solomon Carter Fuller: Where My Caravan Has Rested*. Lanham, MD: University Press of America.

Kardiner, A., Ovesey, L. (1951). *The Mark of Oppression: Explorations in the Personality of the American Negro*. New York: Meridian.

Kernberg, O.F. (2003a). Sanctioned social violence: A psychodynamic view—Part 1. *International Journal of Psychoanalysis, 84*, 683–698.

Kernberg, O.F. (2003b). Sanctioned social violence: A psychodynamic view—Part 2. *International Journal of Psychoanalysis, 84*, 953–968.

Keval, N. (2016). *Racist States of Mind: Understanding the Perversion of Curiosity and Concern*. London: Karnac Books.

King, M.L. (1967). *Where Do We Go From Here: Chaos or Community?* New York: Harper.

Kohut, H. (1984). *How Does Analysis Cure?* Chicago: University of Chicago Press.

Kovel, J. (1970). *White Racism: A Psychohistory*. New York: Columbia University Press.

Kuriloff, E.A. (2001). A two-culture psychology: The role of national and ethnic origin in the therapeutic dyad. *Contemporary Psychoanalysis, 37*, 673–681.

Kuriloff, E.A. (2010). The Holocaust and psychoanalytic theory and praxis. *Contemporary Psychoanalysis, 46*, 395–422.

Lawrence-Lightfoot, S. (1988). *Balm in Gilead: Journey of a Healer*. New York: Addison-Wesley.

Layton, L. (2006). Racial identities, racial enactments, and normative unconscious processes. *Psychoanalytic Quarterly, 75*, 237–269.

Leary, K. (1997). Race, self-disclosure, and "forbidden talk": Race and ethnicity in contemporary clinical practice. *Psychoanalytic Quarterly, 66*, 163–189.

Leary, K. (2012). Race as an adaptive challenge: Working with diversity in the clinical consulting room. *Psychoanalytic Psychology, 29*, 279–291.

Morrison, T. (1987). *Beloved*. New York: Knopf.

Moss, D. (2006). Mapping racism. *Psychoanalytic Quarterly, 75*, 271–294.

Peskin, H. (2012). "Man is a wolf to man": Disorders of dehumanization in psychoanalysis. *Psychoanalytic Dialogues, 22*, 190–205.

Philips, T. (2011). Race, place, and self in the experience of a bystander. *International Journal of Psychoanalytic Self Psychology, 6*, 405–426.

Powell, D. (2012). Psychoanalysis and African Americans: Past, present, and future. In Akhtar, S. (Ed.), *The African American Experience: Psychoanalytic Perspectives*, Lanham.

Rankine, C. (2014). *Citizen: An American Lyric*. Minneapolis: Graywolf Press.

Rizzolo, G.S. (2017). The specter of the primitive. *Journal of the American Psychoanalytic Association, 65*, 945–977.

Roberts, D. (1997). *Killing the Black Body: Race, Reproduction, and the Meaning of Liberty*. New York: Pantheon.

Rose, T. (2015). *How Structural Racism Works Project*. Brown University Center for the Study of Race and Ethnicity.

Sandler, J. (1960). The background of safety. *International Journal of Psychoanalysis, 41*, 352–356.

Skloot, R. (2010). *The Immortal Life of Henrietta Lacks*. New York: Crown Publishers.

Stoute, B.J. (2017). Race and racism in psychoanalytic thought: Ghosts in our nursery. *The American Psychoanalyst, 51*(1): 10,11,16,17–18, 28–29, March 2017.

Thomas, A., Sillen, S. (1972). *Racism and Psychiatry*. Secaucus, NJ: Citadel Press.

Thompson, C. (1998). Does insight serve a purpose? The value of psychoanalytic psychotherapy with diverse African American patients. In Jones, R.L. (Ed.), *African American Mental Health*, (pp. 455–503). Berkeley, CA: Cobb & Henry.

Volkan, V.D. (1988). *The Need to Have Enemies and Allies: From Clinical Practice to International Relationships*. Northvale, NJ: Aronson.

Volkan, V.D. (1997). *Bloodlines: From Ethnic Pride to Ethnic Terrorism*. New York: Farrar, Straus, & Giroux.

Volkan, V.D. (2001). September 11 and societal regression. *Mind & Human Interaction, 13*, 49–76.

Volkan, V.D. (2003). Traumatized societies. In Varvin, S., Volkan., V.D. (Eds.), *Violence or Dialogue? Psychoanalytic Insights on Terror and Terrorism*, London: Routledge.

Volkan, V.D., Ast, G., Greer, W. (2002). *The Third Reich in the Unconscious: Transgenerational Transmission and Its Consequences*. New York: Brunner-Routledge.

Walker, D. (1830). *Walker's Appeal, in four Articles; Together with a Preamble, to the coloured Citizens of the World, but in Particular, and Very Expressly, to Those of the United States of America*. Boston: David Walker.

White, C. (2004). Culture, influence and the "I-ness" of Me: Commentary on papers by Susan Bodnar, Gary B. Walls, and Steven Botticelli. *Psychoanalytic Dialogues, 14*, 653–691.

Whitehead, C. (2016). *The Underground Railroad*. New York: Doubleday.

Winograd, B. (2014). Black Psychoanalysts Speak. *PEP Video Grants, 1*, 1.

Wolfenstein, E.V. (1981). *The Victims of Democracy: Malcolm X and the Black Revolution*, Berkeley: University of California Press.

Wolfenstein, E.V. (1991). On the uses and abuses of psychoanalysis in cultural research. *Free Associations, 2*, 515–547.

Young-Bruehl, E. (1996). *The Anatomy of Prejudices*, Cambridge: Harvard University Press.

Part II

Living with the Trauma of Racism

Chapter 4

African American Boys
Adolescents under the Shadow of Slavery's Legacy

Kirkland C. Vaughans

Twenty years ago, I delivered my first talk on the topic of the intergenerational transmission of trauma among African Americans since slavery. Over the years, the body of theoretical and clinical literature on this topic has grown tremendously. Black novelists also have highlighted it, most notably Toni Morrison in *Beloved* (1987).

Although my focus on generational trauma in this chapter will be limited to Black boys, in no way do I suggest that only they, and not girls too, are the victims of the generational trauma of their families or society. It is necessary to understand that while racism of individual, cultural, and institutional types impacts Blacks in general, it also manifests in gender-specific ways.

From my clinical and research work, I have arrived at the theoretical position that the unresolved generational trauma among African Americans, and Black boys in particular, is a function of an unmourned, original, collective, historical trauma, as well as the episodic, persistent, terroristic, and oppressive social assault targeting the Black community at later periods in American history. In addition to their actual threat to life and limb, these later, contemporary experiences constitute an unconscious agitation or reawakening of unmetabolized earlier trauma, generating a sense of disease and a breeding ground for a number of dissociated responses toward off an impending sense of doom, loss, humiliation, failure, and a disconnect from society. Therefore, the redemption Blacks seek cannot be offered through individual psychotherapy or psychoanalysis alone, but must be obtained through a communal effort of liberating our colonized minds from cultural introjects.

It is the generative power of collective cultural consciousness, as witnessed during the civil rights movement of the 1960s and the Black Power movement of the 1970s, that holds significant therapeutic potential and has been reawakened in the current Black Lives Matter movement. Let me be very clear on this point: It is not that psychoanalysis and psychodynamic psychotherapy as therapeutic instruments would prove ineffective in pursuing such a goal; it is that the psychoanalytic community lacks the will, the commitment, and the interest to do so. Historically, it has failed to recognize its obligations to social justice, particularly where Blacks are concerned. Abram Kardiner and Lionel Ovesey's (1951) early and clumsy effort to explore the "Negro problem" is a classic testament to the crucial need for our community to explore ingrained racism and bigotry as a pedagogical and clinical prerequisite to engagement in the treatment of Blacks and other minorities. Should the psychoanalytic community dare such a transformation, it would result in the simultaneous psychic liberation of both Black boys and the psychoanalytic establishment.

First, I will contextualize how Black boys are socially portrayed or not portrayed in society. When national magazines highlight the plight of American boys on their covers, Black boys are conspicuously absent from the cover picture, as well as the cover story; further, their unique challenges are not addressed in many of the current bestselling books on the struggles of boys in general. The present plight of African American boys and adolescents in this country is quite disturbing, and often, the burden for improving their condition is perceived to rest with them, with little understanding of the role of the traumatic effects of racism.

Age Distortion

The title of this chapter is deliberate: It hits hard on the social and cultural disavowal of these boys' developmental stage of "boyhood." The media often portrays Black boys as being "at risk," as opposed to being "vulnerable." In my mind, the two terms connote very different affective responses. A vulnerable child needs guidance or help; an at-risk child at best has fallen prey to the luck of the draw and has failed to show personal responsibility. At-risk Black boys of 12 or

13 are called "men" by the news media; their white counterparts are called "youths." This misperception of Black boys is evident in the strong tendency in the juvenile justice system to try Black boys in the courts as adults, unlike boys who are white.

In general, Black male children are viewed as four to five years older than their actual age. This distortion of age, internalized, supports with ease the prized racism code of white people, especially police officers, who react with fear for their lives when in a confrontation with a Black male, distorting his potential dangerousness. The distortion of age is also a pretext for latent sexual anxieties that become manifest through the obsessional focus white police officers have with the bulge in the Black man's pants. This stereotypical threat is based on the historical descriptions of Black males used to rationalize their enslavement: They are described as immoral, highly aggressive, impulsive, and oversexed.

With the recent spate of "publicized" shootings of Black males by white police officers, as well as by private citizens, some Black males have come to consider themselves prized trophies in the quest for white nobility—an internalization of racist projections. During sessions, I observe the boys' desperation reflected often in their dazed facial expressions when I inquire, "Do you know what to do when stopped or challenged by a police officer?" Some jokingly reply, "Prepare to die," while others look like a stunned deer caught in the headlights.

Most often, it is the stereotypical, defensive, hypermasculinity of Black males that is commented on in the clinical or social literature. In my practice and research on Black boys, however, I have observed defensive tendencies away from machismo or *cool pose* posturing. A number have described feeling conflicted and tormented as athletic coaches pursue them to play sports for which, in fact, they had previously demonstrated a real gift. The social pressure comes not just from their schools, but also from family members and significant others within the Black community, all urging the boys to excel athletically as a means of authenticating themselves as Black young men. Many Black male youths then feel caught in a white–Black racial, class, and cultural crossfire, and as adolescents, they are conflicted in how to integrate these expectations as they struggle with identity formation and consolidation.

Disowning Racial Stereotypes

The term microaggression has received wide acceptance across professional domains. However, for Black boys, who are frequently exposed to these impingements, their situations constitute a condition more akin to cumulative trauma. The symptoms resulting from emotional assaults are an abiding sense of shame, depressive affect, a sense of futility, and a disavowal of the racial significance of these experiences.

Interviewing Black boys for a research project I was conducting, one question among many I put to them was, "How do other people describe you?" The most frequent responses included the following: honest, dependable, hardworking, reliable, studious, and trustworthy. It is not that I doubt the character of these boys contained such qualities; it is that the qualities they described were so directly counter to the racial stereotypes of Black males that they read like a Boy Scout creed. Implied is a powerful need to evacuate socially induced toxic introjects. In an attempt to distance themselves from painful racial characterizations, some run the risk of becoming socially isolated from their own racial peer group, which may perceive the boys as rejecting not racial stereotypes, but the peers themselves. In efforts to overcome imposed racial limitations, some students are at a complete loss to understand their particular circumstances.

This racialized drama, first appearing in the speeches of Malcolm X, constitutes a reenactment of the conflict between what was considered the "House Negro" versus the "Field Negro," a conflict dramatically depicted in the film *Django Unchained* by Quentin Tarantino. This splitting between the "good" slave and the "bad" slave is indicative of unresolved mourning of the Black community's historical trauma. Our shame and humiliation are embodied by or projected onto the House Negro; other compensatory efforts to evacuate this hideous humiliation are given to the Field Negro. In his unapologetic commentary, Malcolm X (1963) clearly articulates the shame and humiliation of Black people when he states, "You came here in chains, like a horse, or a cow, or a chicken." This collective dynamic is continued in our celebration of our African heritage—to the almost complete negation of that which our enslaved ancestors developed for us. A fashion movement in this direction might have featured the wearing of the cotton sack as frequently as we donned the dashiki. Such an action would diminish our shame by acknowledging our pain, lifting from the shoulders of Black boys this responsibility and restoring their rightful developmental stage of boyhood, of which they have been socially dispossessed.

The psychoanalytic community must begin to formulate, integrate, and make use of the development and trauma of Black boyhood in its theory and in its clinical practice. Until we do this, our attempts to bring more African American men into the field, our attempts to help the thousands of young men who suffer in our communities and jails, and our attempts to fulfill our social responsibility to help heal racism in American society will be doomed.

References

Kardiner, A. and Ovesey, L. (1951). *The Mark of Oppression*. New York: World Publishing.

Malcolm X (1963) Malcolm describes the difference between the "house Negro" and the "field Negro." In *Speech*. Michigan State University, East Lansing, Michigan. January 23, 1963

Morrison, Toni. (1987) *Beloved*. New York. Alfred Knopf, Inc.

Chapter 5

Loss, Grief, and Fear in Everyday Lives of African American Women

Annie Lee Jones

Over the years, I have learned that the photos of African American women on the walls of my office have become an integral part of who my patients perceive me to be. Some of the photos are of elderly former sharecroppers, others of poor women straightening their own or another's hair with hot combs; some are of nomadic women carrying vessels on their hips or heads.

My patients have told me that the photos have served as a kind of bridge to spaces in our work in which it is safe for them to wonder about me as their analyst. Additionally, patients have offered thoughts about what each photo represents to them based on their own backgrounds. It is through the *use* of me and my photos that we begin to formulate previously unarticulated psychodynamics and historical narratives.

Some have also said that during silent reveries in their sessions, they notice aspects of me reflected in the photos. Sometimes during the initial interviews, patients ask me direct questions about the photos and share their associations, along with their thoughts on why they selected me to begin treatment. The freedom to explore their perceptions of me in my office during the early stages of our work has proven to be very important to the treatment process. Some patients, making note of the fact that I practice in their neighborhood, wonder out loud if I live nearby. Others ask me about my own ethnic origin within the African American diaspora.

Shared encounters like these can quickly lead to transference and countertransference processes centered on mutually recognized experiences (Aron 1991, 1999). These shared encounters offer opportunities for exploration of the patient's introduction of recent life events that on the surface do not appear to be related to what has gone before, but can lead to the resurfacing of losses attached to their mourning process.

The patient's musings about the possibilities of their analyst's daily life can trigger some shared relational links to media-driven experiences of fear-inducing events that appear to be typical in the everyday lives of those who live and work in our community. Loss-grief, shame-embarrassment, and fear of repetition become shared in complex ways between patient and analyst as the patient tells the analyst who she is and where she came from. Many find the initial "taking of the developmental history" traumatic.

Impact of Lost Family History

It is not uncommon for the patient to starkly inform the analyst that she does not know anything about her grandparents, for example. Some patients struggle to describe feelings associated with paternal or maternal absences. War, migration, social upheavals, economic distress, and other forces have a tremendous impact on the personal histories of many of my patients. In most cases, they identify racial discrimination, caste and class-driven violence, and poverty as the cultural forces responsible for the major disruptions in their genealogy. It is common for them to announce that it grieves them deeply that they do not know their family history at the very point in their lives when they are poised to work in psychotherapy to get to know better the selves they are.

The psychoanalytic dyad of two African American women can offer possibilities for empathic recognition that facilitates treatment. The dyad and its mutually constructed dynamic can be informed by many factors not usually a component of psychoanalytic discourse around theory and training. The race-based and ethnically informed relational exchanges that shape the work are yet to be incorporated in contemporary psychoanalysis. Over the years, Megan Obourn and I, as well as others, have written about the way culturally informed racialized object relations work in everyday life (Thompson, 1995; Jones and Obourn, 2014).

Wolstein (1994) points to the relevance of these observations when he states that "clinical involvement with the larger social and cultural environment in which the therapist and patients live out their daily lives was considered novel" and that intrapsychic phenomena do not exist in a vacuum—they occur in the context of "extrapsychic phenomena."

I have written elsewhere (Jones and Obourn, 2005, 2008, 2014) about my understanding of how hatred and fear directed at the blackened object have historical, political, economic, cultural, and social implications for how our internal world is constructed. The legacy of chattel slavery is foundational and informs our group and individual psychodynamics. When current events reflecting injustice and inequality are brought into the session, our dyad's experiences of these events can be effectively utilized to provide both a space where such events can be metabolized and a space where the potential for replication of oppressive experiences can be reflected upon rather than acted out in self-destructive ways. In this conceptualization of our work, I can facilitate the patient's recognition that the larger social domain impacts the dyad's individual psychologies. In so doing, I affirm my patient's right to observe; such affirmation can soften resistances and open pathways towards illumination of internal conflicts requiring more in-depth exploration. As Hopper (2003) suggests, we live in a traumatogenic society that can be relationally explored.

When a patient in an intense, prolonged grief reaction gains a respect for the realities she has experienced, she can begin to consider altering her object relations to the lost loved one, as Freud suggested in 1917. In doing this, the patient begins to recognize pathways to understanding the aspects of her mourning process that stay linked to the loss and prolong the existence of the lost object's influence on much of her everyday life. Her loss lingers over narratives created in the dyad. When recognized by the dyad, she can use this new experience to explore shared and evolving awareness of affective links to past traumas. I have found Spence (1994) and Stern (1997) helpful in understanding narration and consensual validation.

As a person who began her training as a clinical psychologist and psychoanalyst in the Deep South during the heat of the Civil Rights Movement, it became important to me to create a treatment space where I could stabilize my own subjectivity as a psychoanalyst who is also an African American woman. I am fully aware of many of the forms of gendered racism that inform my everyday experiences. My patients often report that their outlook for the future is complicated by fears of loss and grief. As Claudia Rankine (2015) so profoundly put it, "The condition of black life is one of mourning... mourning lived in real time." Further, Rankine says (2015), "There really is no mode of empathy that can replicate the daily strain of knowing that as a black person you can be killed for simply being black."

Some recent immigrants who enter treatment describe a loss of hope when they realize they cannot avoid the plague of American racism based on skin color. Some have detailed the broad spectrums of skin color variances that were typical of households in their countries of origin. Even after including skin color associations in their treatment, they seem to dissociate their experiences in the United States from similar experiences they had back home. It is my impression that their encounters with prejudice in the United States based on skin color are uniquely traumatizing.

Fresh Acts of Violence

News of acts of violence against African Americans by the authorities or by other citizens are brought into the session with dysphoric affective links to the patients' own lived lives. Jones (2015) provides us with an example of this in her short piece, "The Lingering Memory of Dead Boys":

> Like many Americans, I have been glued to the television eager for details about the tragic murder of 17-year-old Trayvon Martin. I am not sure what I hoped to discover, as each new piece of evidence is more disturbing than the last. I listened to the recently released 911 tapes on my office computer and cried in public. I was up until after midnight scanning my Twitter feed for news and comfort, a 21st century vigil of sorts.... Learning about death and dying is part of growing up. If we are lucky, we come to understand that death is natural through the passing of a grandparent or some other elder. If we are lucky, we will be taught something about a life well lived. But for too many of us, we are made aware of our own mortality seeing our peers—the boys we want to go to the movies with, the boys who used to pull our hair—we learned that they could be killed for the crime [of] being themselves. Young. Black. And Male.

Along with many of my patients, I followed the unfolding details of the Zimmerman case after he killed Trayvon Martin. My patients reported that they found themselves crying out loud or weeping softly during each news update. During the immediate aftermath of the murder, some patients reported spending innumerable hours following Twitter feeds and other social media. While some dedicated large portions of their sessions to their experience of this material, others seemed to avoid detailing the daily news in their sessions and instead introduced dangerous encounters from their own childhoods. There were patients who also focused on their thoughts and feelings about their own mortality, which they related to the loss they imagined the mother of this child was enduring (Jones 2006).

Those patients who reported feeling that their days were saturated with news of this tragedy also seemed to be those who found pathways back to formerly unarticulated losses of their own. Some patients started to explore how they first encountered death and dying as children. These patients seemed to also return to the ways their unique mourning process had been eclipsed, interrupted, or stalled by current traumas in their own lives.

Patients also use the tragic death of Sandra Bland in police custody—referred to as "the Sandra Bland situation"—as shorthand for anticipatory fear that they relate to random encounters with law enforcement agents while traveling alone on the streets of their own neighborhoods. It may be that the co-creation of potential spaces in the treatment that allow for these types of associative explorations via the media offers the added benefit of reducing the personal negative impact of racial discrimination. This allows the patient room to reflect on and symbolize the pain of these experiences, rather than burying such pain or dissociating from it. She can then be freed up to turn back to what brought her to treatment.

Detailing the rash of media reports of violence and destruction of blackened bodies serves as a pathway to the individual's unresolved grief and mourning, processes that have sometimes been transmitted across generations in the patient's family. The legacies of repetitive losses are often encapsulated in individualized, developmentally charged expressions of the ways in which chattel slavery, caste systems, and generational losses could not be contained by the patient's family, or that the patient could not locate in prior relational spaces.

Sometimes, Black and dark skin associations mark each member of the dyad as participant, observer, and/or witness. The dyad can thus become/create a containing relational space.

It seems that as patients chronicled fears of racial animus that infused their daily lives, they became more able to identify personal aspects of their developmental history that may have inhibited the mourning of past losses.

Fear of Police

Fear of random violence at the hands of the police is shared by many of my patients. As a psychoanalyst, I have shared their terror as they recount experiences of contact with police and security guards. The patients' attempts to figure out ways to feel more secure in their homes and neighborhoods, and to develop strategies to avoid contact with the police when they travel outside their neighborhoods to work, can be fraught with difficulty. They often couple their descriptions of these efforts with how they struggle to explain to their children the reality of their lives lived in Black skin in America.

The ordinary, everyday lives of Black women in America can be plagued by the repetition of difficult-to-metabolize thoughts and feelings that can initially present as mild clinical states. Financially successful Black women living and working in urban areas describe how they cope with being seen through the mist of poverty. They describe how the experiences of the poor are mapped upon them when they move around their world. They report feeling socially and politically isolated from urban centers of power and opportunity.

When some women describe family members' experiences with the policing tactic of Stop/Search/Question/Frisk, what they seem to fear most is finding *themselves* in the presence of such phenomena and being caught off guard. They describe their fear of witnessing such police action, and they often indicate that they equate such experiences with other types of community-based violence.

I have found that unconscious, intergenerationally transmitted memories linked to trauma and loss are never dissociated; instead, they remain actively available in the reflective realm of the unconscious. A patient reported to me that whenever she was driving alone on her usual route to work, any news dispatches describing the shooting of a child, similar to the killing of the 12-year-old boy in Cleveland, induced her to become so overwhelmed with tears and breathlessness that she had to pull over immediately, blinded by her tears. Her description of the depth of her pain mirrored her description of discovering her mother dead in their family home when she was a child.

My work with patients often includes oral histories of ancestral enslavement and menial field work due to caste systems, as well as descriptions of heavy, often dangerous, underpaid factory work. Having finally made it to America, many people, paradoxically, begin to find the freedom to lament the limitations on their lives. They explore the effects of a prolonged, generalized sense of anxiety and remorse over the risk of sudden loss they had experienced. Their fears seem to link to fantasies of loss at the behest of unknown others.

The immediate transmission of threats and acts of violence against Black Americans via all forms of social media, television, and news outlets underscores the risk that these acts can seem normative.

It is common that the isolation stemming from institutionally sanctioned segregated housing and schooling in major cities in the United States reifies dissociative processes around current losses and also reactivates the trauma of those losses that have gone before (Jones 2009). This isolation and negation of the reality that African Americans experience foreclose the opportunity to experience a general sense of freedom to be oneself, including the opportunity to communicate the fear of past and present loss. In this connection, the relational experience for many of my patients of having an African American psychoanalyst serves as a validating relational affirmation that alleviates their isolation as they recall and metabolize these experiences. DuBois's (1953) formulation of the *double consciousness* that African Americans display, as contrasted with a more authentic self, is still useful for understanding the unique relational possibility of shared validation for my patients in this dyadic experience.

The racial and ethnic undertones of the 2015–2016 campaign cycle filtered into some of my treatments. These undertones amplified the fears I have been describing above, and there is no resolution in sight. Many of my patients are mourning the loss of their ability to imagine life free of the risks they face simply because of how they are perceived by others. At the time of writing this chapter, the Chicago

Police Department had just released a series of videos of the use of deadly force against its citizenry. I expect this news will surface in my practice, further complicating the relational dynamics of loss, grief, and fear in our psychoanalytic processes.

References

Aron, L. (1991). The patient's experience of the analyst's subjectivity. *Psychoanalytic Dialogues, 1,* 29–51

Aron, L. (1999). Clinical choices and the relational matrix. *Psychoanalytic Dialogues, 9,* 1–30.

DuBois, W.E.B. (1953). *Souls of Black Folk*. New York: Blue Heron.

Freud, S. (1917). Mourning and melancholia. In J. Strachey (Ed. & Trans.) *The Standard Edition of the Complete Psychological Works of Sigmund Freud*. London: Hogarth, S.E. *14*: 237–258.

Hopper, E. (2003). *The Social Unconscious: Selected Papers*. London: Jessica Kingsley Publishers.

Jones, A.L. (2009). "The Blackness in Me: Psychoanalysis 'Blind Spot. The Psychoanalytic *Activist*. Fall, issue #16

Jones, T. (2015). The Lingering Memory of Dead Boys. In Edited by Gray, K.A. & St. Clair, J., Wypijewski, J. (Eds.) *KILLING TRAYVONS: An Anthology of American Violence*. Petrolia, Calif.: Counter Punch Books. 49–50.

Jones, A. L. & Obourn, M. (2014). Object fear: The national dissociation of race and racism in the era of Obama. *Psychoanalysis Culture & Society, 19*(4), 392–412.

Jones, A.L. & Obourn, M. (2014). Blackness in Sigmund Freud and Andre Green's Construction of the Human Psyche. *Modern Language Association*, Philadelphia, Pa.

Jones, A.L. & Obourn, M. (2005). Audre Lorde, Andre Green, and the power of metaphor: An interdisciplinary approach to raced and gendered construction of identity. Minority Matters: Society, Theory, Literature: Proceedings of the 1st International Symposium on Minorities and Minor Literatures. January 2004, edited by Touaf, L & Boutkhil, S. Publications de la Faculte des Lettres No 92; Serie: Colloques et seminaries No 32, Oujda, Morocco.

Jones, A.L. & Obourn, M. (2008). A critical race analysis of intrapsychic space. *Invited Lecture at Mental Health Grand Rounds*. N. Y. Harbor Department of Veterans Affairs Health Care System, Brooklyn, N.Y.

Jones, A.L. (2006). Mothers, readers, race, and the analyst. *American Comparative Literature Association Conference*. Princeton University, Princeton, N.J.

Rankine, C. (2015). The Condition of Black Life is one of Mourning, downloaded: https://www.nytimes.com/2015/06/22/magazine/the-condition-of-black-life-is-one-of-mourning.html

Spence, D. P. (1994). *The Rhetorical Voice of Psychoanalysis*. Cambridge: Harvard University Press.

Stern, D.B. (1997). *Unformulated Experience: From Dissociation to Imagination in Psychoanalysis*. Hillsdale: The Analytic Press.

Thompson, C. (1995). Self-definition by opposition: A consequence of minority status. *Psychoanalytic Psychology*, *12*(4), 533–545.

Wolstein, B. (1994). The evolving newness of interpersonal psychoanalysis: from the vantage point of immediate experience. *Contemporary Psychoanalysis*, *30*, 473–498.

Chapter 6

Everyday Racism
Psychological Effects

Ivan Ward

Preamble

Let me start with an incident that happened to me during the first pandemic lockdown in London. I was out for a morning walk through the Regent's Park, wheeling my bicycle and doing a spot of birdwatching before cycling down the Broad Walk to my favorite bench to sit and read for ten minutes. An elderly couple walked past, and the man turned back and addressed me. "Excuse me, can you read English?"

"Er, yes."
"Well, why can't you read that it's *no cycling?*" he shouted.

My first response was confusion—cycling had always been allowed on the Broad Walk, so I wondered if the rules had changed because of the pandemic. "Are you sure there's no cycling on the Broad Walk?" I asked, trying to "engage." He said something that was angry and abrasive that I didn't quite catch and turned away. I checked and learned that the regulations had not been changed, but that's another story.

What was racist about this encounter? In the question, "Can you read English?" the racist assumption of otherness is inscribed in the question; it is the strategy by which another person is *being made alien*. The nonracist attack might have been "Can't you read?" Or even a shouted "Don't you know there's no cycling!" The racist part is a supplement to what could have been a simple act of aggression. This man's attack made me question my knowledge of the world—that something I thought I knew (in this case, the cycling regulations), I may not have known. My position—you might say my status—within a system of social rules and regulations, even within the rules of language which have symbolic power, was being questioned and undermined. The experience has stayed with me for some time; I've been mulling it over, trying to come to terms with what is, in truth, a trivial incident. I wish I'd been more on the ball and recognized sooner what was happening; bizarrely, I took his question at face value. Perhaps I should have said, "Well, I've got a first-class degree from Cambridge University, so I think I can be regarded as functionally literate, but why would you like to know, my good man? Stout yeoman." And then, I imagine, if he was being honest, he might reply (given, as I believe, that all he saw was the color of my skin), "Because I'm a small-minded f**king racist, and you've just broken a rule *I made up*, which gives me a chance to unleash my aggression and feel justified in doing so."

I sometimes like to distinguish between what I call the visceral and the ideological racist. The former is motivated by the pleasure/unpleasure principle, which comes from the id. He just feels uncomfortable around Black and brown people; to him, they seem a bit smelly and dirty, eat disgusting food, speak funny, harbor disease, and might be aggressive. The visceral response is mild disgust and wariness. The ideological racist's motivation seems to be a response to a perceived threat to the symbolic order. It comes from the superego and is elaborated into a delusional paranoid system. This man was clearly both. The aversion had a visceral quality, but the tone of moral superiority and self-righteousness pointed to an ideological derivation. You might guess which is more dangerous when I tell you Freud (1923) once described the superego as a "pure culture of the death instinct" (p. 53).

This stranger, who didn't know me, positioned himself as the authority over me and proceeded to humiliate me, as if it was the natural order of things. He became the arbiter of right and wrong, and I was to know my place. Incidentally, if you are a white person in a position of authority and you don't want to behave in a racist manner, there is an easy way to recognize whether there is this racist supplement within yourself. Do the "substitution test." Simply ask yourself, "Would I behave in the same way, say the same things, make the same decisions, if the person in front of me was white?" You might be a policeman stopping someone in the street, a shop manager dealing with a customer complaint, a foreman in a factory, a manager in an office, or a teacher dealing with an unruly pupil at school. If so and you want to go further, you could ask yourself this supplementary question:

> Why is it that I am quite so enraged, quite so unwilling to help, quite so *put out* by this person in front of me? Why is it that *in you*, as psychoanalyst Jacques Lacan (1978) might say, I see *more than you*. Why is it that I feel threatened in an obscure and indeterminate and "barely acknowledged way?"

Difference and Projection

It is often said that racism is connected to "difference"—either the inability to tolerate difference or the creation of artificial differences and systems of exploitation based on them. In fact, you might say that racial categories themselves have been created in order to provide an ideological justification for the domination, brutalization, and exploitation of other people. Within a structure of racism, the perception of difference is connected to valuations (good and bad, true and false, right and wrong, correct and incorrect) and power. One group is able to impose its valuations on the structure as a whole, and there is a basic categorization of the world in which both parties find themselves caught up, but to the significant detriment of one of them.

We ask, "What are the psychological effects of being regarded as different?" Being assigned an arbitrary marker of difference can reanimate infantile reactions to separation and individuation, envy, identification, and feelings of exclusion, or even "of not being regarded as better or as chosen." (Hamer, 2002) From a young age, you are aware that being different means being made less-than, and other-than, what you are different *from*.

The main psychoanalytic model for understanding racism involves the concepts of splitting and projection, which add a dynamic aspect to the idea of difference. Unwanted, disowned, and despised aspects of the (white) psyche—the dirty self, the rapacious self, the childish self, the "sinful" and humiliated self, and so on—are projected onto another group and become the basis for stereotyping, scapegoating, denial, and attacking that other group.

We might consider the main templates of the object of racism the idea that Black people and some other minorities are bestial, childish, monstrous, aggressive, rapacious, dirty, ugly, criminal, and so on.

This simple idea of racism tells us much about its psychological effects. The denigrated person knows that they are having to deal with somebody else's shit. That they are being dumped on. In describing the frightening experience of one of her phobic patients, psychoanalyst Hanna Segal (1954) talks of "fecal bullets" that seem to be attacking her patient from the outside. Being told that you *are* bestial, childish, monstrous, aggressive, rapacious, dirty, criminal, and hypersexual, as Black and brown people are told in subtle and not-so-subtle ways, is to be struck repeatedly by fecal bullets. Black people may be experienced as fecal objects themselves, as psychoanalyst Sharon Numa (Dugan and Numa 2020) states. If we think of racism as projection, then the experience of racism is the experience of these projections. Black and brown people are *subjected* to them, and therefore we can ask what it feels like to be indelibly marked by such negative characteristics. We can explore their nuances and specific content.

Being the Object of the Projection

First, there is the fact of the projection itself: You feel helpless because you cannot escape it. You feel claustrophobic, trapped in somebody else's fantasy. How do you respond? Do you internalize the fantasy and make it yours? Bring the racist assumptions into your inner world, creating what Fakhry Davids (2011) calls an "internal racist organization"—but in this case within the unconscious mind of the victims of racism, rather than the perpetrators? Think how difficult it is for children to not associate Blackness with all things "bad"—with ugly, mean, stupid, untrustworthy; with being forever judged and found wanting. With repeated exposure, it is understandable that the feeling of inadequacy is inescapably internalized into how Blackness is devalued. My daughter recently showed me a video of Kenneth and Mamie Clarke's doll test experiment, first developed in the 1940s and still used today. You can find it on YouTube. It is shocking to watch Black children consistently choose white dolls to hold everything "good" and Black dolls to be everything bad, ugly—unwanted. The projections and fantasies of the dominant group seep into your inner world and interfere with your relationships with peers, parents, children, and sexual partners. Not being recognized for who you are affects your sense of reality. Projections often operate on the basis of externally perceived or imagined differences involving sight, hearing, smell—so the victim of racism experiences a sharp split between his inner self and the outer self as others perceive it. You go through life trying to keep at bay a massive distortion of your sense of who you are. You feel continually used by other people (who are trying to make you be something for them—a kind of fetish—and to play the role that has been assigned to you). You are always trying to compensate for being regarded as a stupid child, or a dirty animal, or a threatening criminal—or even, as the James Brown song goes, a "sex machine." Eventually, it takes its toll.

Defending Against the Psychic Intrusions

What does the person of color do, psychologically, to cope with this unwelcome intrusion into one's psychic life? What are the defense mechanisms brought into operation to retain a sense of self-worth and a semblance of human dignity? Joseph and Anne-Marie Sandler (1986), two eminent British psychoanalysts, talk of "the gyroscopic function of unconscious fantasy." Something happens to destabilize your inner world, a little shock that knocks you off your perch, knocks you sideways, and the fantasy mechanism kicks in to reestablish equilibrium. There are also conscious daydreams that have the same function, just as I go over and over imagining what I might have said to the man in the park, taking up energy and time that I could otherwise use productively. I once gave my Cambridge University library card as photo ID when questioned by the police on Hampstead Heath. I'd been sitting on a bench looking out over one of the ponds in what I considered a particularly wistful manner when two policemen ambled over from an adjacent path 30 yards away. Clearly, a person of color sitting on a bench doing nothing is an object of suspicion that has to be investigated. The "gyroscopic" function can be seen in my response—as if I was saying to myself and them, "But I've got a Cambridge degree!," "But I've published books!"—while feeling as powerless in some measure, I wonder, as Freud's four sisters might felt as they were taken to concentration camps. I can imagine them pleading, "But our brother is Sigmund Freud!" And just to take some recent examples that have been in the news in the UK, think how ineffectual it has been to say, "But I'm a gold-medal-winning athlete," "But I'm a distinguished barrister," "But I'm a member of Parliament," if you are unaccountably stopped by the police and happen to be Black. And what about if you haven't got a gold medal, or a law degree, or 31,779 votes to support your threatened self-esteem? How then do you shore up the crumbling edifice of your inner world?

There are many other responses to this psychic intrusion. Sometimes you retreat into grandiose fantasies—so you call yourself "King" or "Prince" or "Duke," perhaps. I'm not thinking about well-known Black celebrities of the past or present, I'm thinking about friends from childhood. At other times you rage impotently against what you feel is the injustice of it all—"But I am not stupid, aggressive, rapacious, dirty, natural, sexual, or criminal. Or even exotic." You might try to release the tension and demand recognition through violence. Such might be an unmetabolized explosion mobilizing the Black Rage that Beverly Stoute describes in this volume. Or you withdraw into a narcissistic bubble, inhabiting a world of fashion and pop culture in which self-love is almost indistinguishable from self-loathing. Or you use sexuality to assert a feeling of power and self-esteem or to gain approval and love and to feel whole again. Or you become cut off from feelings for other people, as you imagine their feelings are cut off from you. Or you play the fool and use humor to deflect the disapproving gaze that you feel bearing down on you. Or you intellectualize and imagine you can think away the psychic assault as if a feeling of legitimacy or emancipation can be discovered in the pages of a book. Or you become excessively "good" and conscientious and polite—because who wants to be seen as yet another angry Black person?

The concept of projection provides enough material to keep going for years. We suffer projections and we react against them.

But there is another set of feelings having to do with being unloved or cut off from something nourishing and supportive. And there is the anxiety and depression generated by living in a world which does not understand you; even feelings of being forsaken and betrayed. Journalist Aditya Chakrabortty (2020) recalls being taunted as "rubber lips, n—r lips"[1] at a majority-white school in the 1980s, and he uses the word "helpless" twice in his short account, being most affected by the indifference of the teacher to whom he eventually went for help. What is it like to grow up in a society that values all that you don't have and denigrates your essential characteristics? Being the recipient of other people's projections is an abstraction that does not begin to convey the feelings of rejection and injustice that accompany being regarded as dirty or having rubber lips. In her magnificent sociological account of racism in the UK, Reni Eddo-Lodge (2017) looks at the emotional strain of being an anti-racism activist. "As a long-time depressive," she writes, "I know how much it can paralyze…." But perhaps, as I try to make clear in this chapter, it is the racist culture itself, not the activist, that holds these depressive affects.

Racial Stress

Freud says:

> Psychoanalysis warns us to abandon the unfruitful antithesis of external and internal factors, of fate and constitution, and has taught us regularly to discover the cause of an outbreak of neurosis in a definite mental situation, which can be brought into being in different ways.
>
> (Freud, 1913)

In other words, the inner world and the outer world are implicated and imbricated in our mental health. Which, of course, we knew already.

So let us assume that racism is a kind of mental stress and see if we can try to unpack what else that stress might consist of.

One type of stress may seem odd at first. It's "thinking of other people." Contemporary psychoanalysts often neglect Freud's insight that much of human behavior is designed to protect us from other people, rather than relate to them. When you think of other people all the time, you are like a less-dominant animal in a hierarchical social group, having to fear what the more-dominant might do. Being on your guard is stressful—spending ages trying to get that email just right because you can't be sure how it will be received or what arbitrary attack may be made due to a wrong word here or a missed nuance there. Being aware of the person walking toward you because *they* may feel uncomfortable and so you have to appear less threatening. Continually worrying about how you come across. People of color in a white-dominated culture grow up in a world with a question mark over how they will be received by other people, and this indeterminacy can seep into all areas of life.

Exclusions—the experience of being excluded from access to a social good because of your color—are yet another matter. Patricia Williams (1991) talks of the "blizzard of rage" that overwhelmed her when she was excluded from a shop in New York's SoHo neighborhood by a callow youth who mouthed "We're closed" as she pressed her brown face to the window and rang the bell to be admitted. She is a distinguished legal scholar and professor of law, but at that moment she wanted to smash the window, ransack the shop, and steal the sweaters she was hoping to buy for her mother.

Being ignored, not being recognized, facing indifference and rejection because of who you are—all these constitute stressful and everyday encounters for people of color, eroding self-confidence and undermining mental and physical health. There are now hundreds of studies of race-related stress showing the physiological and psychological effects of discrimination on individuals and communities.

The experience of being watched is at the opposite end of the spectrum. People with psychosis may have delusions of reference and imagine that they are being observed, but what happens when you *are* being observed, as people of color are in many parts of their lives—scrutinized, suspected, or even the object of benign curiosity? White people may not realize just how much of the UK is ... white. My eldest daughter and I used to walk around Chichester, near her grandparents' home, and not see another Black face from one year to the next. As soon as a person of color steps outside the enclave of their multicultural bubble, they become the objects of other people's intrusive gaze. A disturbing, destabilizing self-consciousness is the inevitable result. What Annie Lee Jones (2020), in a recent conference paper, calls "feeling dislocated" in the presence of the "white gaze."[2]

We can continue the list with ...

Domination, which may have reached its zenith in the antebellum South and under colonial rule, is still evident today in the number of Black and minority-ethnic men incarcerated in prisons, or in the greater likelihood that you will be Tasered while being arrested, or forcibly restrained in a mental hospital, if you are Black. A teenage aboriginal boy in Australia is more likely to go to prison than to university, and he's likely to die when he's ten years younger than his white compatriots.

The *emasculation* of (especially) Black men, which was grotesquely manifested by actual castrations in the past but which occurs symbolically today, through gratuitous humiliations of social life that engender a sense of powerlessness.

The *denial of dependency* needs of (especially) Black women, forever having to be "strong" and "independent" and "in control" and "formidable," as if prohibited from expressing even the simple need to be loved.

Expropriation, having something taken from you, as the legacy of historic expropriations still resonates, of things and freedoms and cultural resources. My eldest daughter was distraught one year when she saw that the Black Pride festival had, as far as she was concerned, been taken over by white people. She felt dispossessed of a cultural space. And perhaps most important, people of color in a white society have had taken from them a sense of entitlement, even a sense of agency.

Distortions of language and reality, attributing characteristics to you which you do not have, telling you that you are seeing things that are not there—the reason Reni Eddo-Lodge decided she no longer wanted to talk to white people about race.

The *uncertainty* generated by arbitrary rules and uses of power and the unfairness of a system rigged against you; the intense *frustration* of not being allowed to get what you want or need, and the more subtle but corrosive frustration of *not being heard*, and what may seem an odd characteristic to put on the side of stress: having to deal with *idealizations* projected from a dominant group or even the culture at large. Sometimes people of color may suffer in the same way that women who are "put on a pedestal" suffer: They know that their lofty position is not designed for their own benefit but to serve somebody else's psychic well-being or material interests.

There's just too much!

What we call mental stress (a term never used by Freud and one that effaces the specificity of subjective experience) could be related to the idea of mental pain or the psychoanalytic concept of anxiety. The idea that people of color may experience mental pain from being subjected to ordinary and systemic racism may be difficult for many white people to grasp. I know this is hard to accept, and I take little pleasure in pointing it out, but even if you are anti-racist and a "good person," you still might not get it.

We can derive three broad categories from the list above: (1) fears of being dominated by a more powerful figure and of the body being attacked and controlled by others. Kleinian psychoanalysts have used the term "persecutory anxiety," but it's not just in your head; (2) fears of being rejected and abandoned. Not quite the "depressive anxiety" of Klein (1957) but rather a hypervigilance to the signs of rejection in order to circumvent the more debilitating effects of depression; and finally, (3) fears of not being understood by, or being able to understand, the world. Some analysts have called this "confusional anxiety." Each of these cases incorporates the feeling that nobody cares or understands that the outside world does not function as a "container," in psychoanalyst Wilfred Bion's (1962) sense. There is not a container but a void into which you might fall and be lost, or a black hole into which you might fall and be crushed. Cultural identities, as modes of defense and attack, resistance and refuge, are generated in part as ways of coping in such a hostile environment. They enable the individual to achieve a measure of relief from the outside world, a modicum of happiness and creative self-expression, some sense of self-worth, and a modulation of anxiety. Cultural forms allow individuals to share the pain. In many minority communities, participation in the church and religion has served as the central pivot of the culture. The eminent American psychiatrist James Comer (1972), writing of his own upbringing, remembered the sermons in the Zion Baptist church that his family attended, which brought the audience to shouting and tears. "They were also designed to help a rejected and abused people feel good about themselves," he writes, "and enjoy a sense of purpose and worth."

He continues: "The intensity of the response reflected the sense of frustration and helplessness the people felt. The church was the place to discharge frustration and hostility so that one could face injustice and hardship the rest of the week."

Of course, not everybody bought into the cultural illusions equally. James Comer's mother was bothered by the "hereafter sermons", as she called them, and thought that instead of talking about golden streets and rewards in heaven, the preacher ought to be teaching the people about saving their money, buying homes, and taking care of their families. Many preachers did just that, and still do, but perhaps it was his mother's critical stance toward religious authority that nurtured Comer's interest in the self-reflective discipline of psychology.

The Assault on One's Sense of Reality

The basic valuations of a culture—what is good and bad, right and wrong, correct and incorrect, true and false, which I mentioned earlier—are tied up with our sense of reality. We are all split subjects, as Lacan insists, but the insufficiency to which human beings are subject is doubly marked by the stigma of racialization. Racism in a white-majority society entails that we live between two cultures, and it muddles things up in our heads.

On many occasions, the person of color feels like the victim in one of those old films where one person tries to drive another person mad by undermining their reality. Underlying the distortion is the loss of connection between the victim and his or her tormentor ("What's that strange sound?" "I didn't hear anything"). The same reality has two registers, or different realities may be insisted on as being the same. In a typical work situation, for instance, a minority worker may be regarded as "surly," while his or her white colleague is seen as "under stress"; one person will be seen as upset, the other as aggressive; two people may have different degrees of responsibility but may be regarded as the same. If the aggrieved person tries to address the situation and ask for accountability, he or she may be identified as a troublemaker or someone with a chip on their shoulder. It will come as no surprise to minority workers in academia that a recent UK report on education (Haque and Elliott, 2019) found that Black and ethnic-minority teachers were three times more likely to face disciplinary action than their white colleagues—and the same disparity exists in other workplaces.

The sense of being trapped in a distorted reality—a Kafkaesque world—means that many ethnic minorities feel assaulted by what can only be called a failure of logic. I was once charged a penalty fare on a train I had boarded at the last minute without having yet purchased a ticket. I was rushing to join the rest of my family to see my father-in-law, who had been involved in a car crash and had broken his neck in four places. I was puzzled that the ticket collector (who was selling tickets to other people on the train) not only assumed I was the sort of person who would make up such a story, but that as I stood in front of her with my wallet open to buy a ticket she perceived me to be trying to avoid paying my fare. I felt my brain shrinking trying to work out that logic, not wanting to go any further to consider what she was perceiving when I loomed into her field of vision and asked to pay my fare.

What she saw was a threatening, shifty Black man trying to get away with something. All my desperate attempts to humanize myself—to become somebody with a family and fathers-in-law and worries just like her—were met with implacable defiance. I told her my story. And she looked at me with pity and contempt. "You people," she said, "will say anything." And at that point my heart sank. Once the elementary gesture had been made to dehumanize the other, I knew there was no escape from being seen as the degenerate, drug-dealing freeloader of her imagination. In her eyes, then, I was no longer human. I had to beg to be regarded as such. To make a leap from my trivial encounter to one that has resonated around the world, perhaps when George Floyd was calling for his mother while being pinned down in Minneapolis, it was not only because that's what dying men do, but because he was desperately trying to communicate to his attackers that he was *somebody who had a mother*.

The Ongoing Sense of Depressive Anxiety and Threat

Depressive anxiety and the strategies to keep depression at bay are facts of life for people of color. There is fear that the self will be abandoned, bereft, and alone. All the casual little slights and insults that accumulate over the years, the intense feelings of rejection, of helplessness and hopelessness, become traumatic. But it's not just being demoralized by rejection and being knocked back continually by a system working against you, though that's bad enough. There are other reasons for depression that are less obvious.

In her extraordinary and harrowing book *Caste*, Isabel Wilkerson (2020) gives the example of a Black slave flogged to the brink of death for talking in an overly familiar way to his white owner. Would it be completely unwarranted to make a comparison between this incident and the microaggressions to which people of color are subjected today? Not with the shocking physical atrocities that were inflicted on the Black body, but with the concurrent mental scars of humiliation, powerlessness, and fear that were also the aims of slavery and are felt in everyday encounters that are intended to *put you in your place*. It's the pervasive sense of imminent threat that does the lasting damage. The fact that in the social landscape through which you try to navigate a path, you don't know where the next attack might come from. Kleinian psychoanalysts talk of "persecutory anxiety" to go alongside "depressive anxiety" and "confusional anxiety," and although I am not using these terms in their correct technical sense, they are resonant in evoking the fears of attack and abandonment and confusion that people of color feel in a significant part of their lives. All these forms of anxiety bleed into each other and comingle when experienced at the sharp end of everyday racism. When I was young, my father, a former prisoner of war, told me about the theory of "learned helplessness" that had just been invented. If you don't know when the shocks are going to happen, and you have no control, then you give up trying to escape. You allow yourself to be shocked over and over again, having lost hope and succumbed to a sense of learned helplessness. The theory was verified through brutal experiments with dogs, but its applicability to humans is obvious. The attacked individual is supposed to suck it up and move on.

Once again the feeling that it does *not make sense* exacerbates the trauma. A basic trust in the world is fundamentally disturbed. It also fuels the incandescent rage against the injustice of it all. It's just not fair. Confusional anxiety (Klein 1946) exists not only because of the arbitrary nature of the rules, the split between inner and outer self, and the destabilizing experience of living within two cultures, but because we live in a world in which racism is denied. Did anyone see the video of Neomi Bennett's arrest in London? She was a nurse waiting in her car when she was suddenly surrounded by police vehicles that blocked her in. The subsequent encounter was captured on the police body cam, later made public. The opening salvo of the arresting officer was a politely expressed, but telling, Freudian slip—"Your windows are too tainted—er, I mean tinted, sorry." Let's suppose that Bennett, an experienced nurse who had been decorated by the Queen, knew what was really tainted in the eyes of the law, and she decided to make a stand. To take the courageous step of questioning the authority of the police who stopped her for no adequate reason. It may have been a mini-Rosa Parks moment. All people of color, before and since, have had these moments in their lives, or at least felt them.

When interviewed later on the BBC, Bennett said, "I was confused. I couldn't understand what was going on. I didn't want to believe it was because I was Black," while the conscientious policeman could assert that he was simply "doing his job." We could say that confusional anxiety is characteristic of contemporary racism, what Joel Kovel (1970) has called meta-racism, which denies its existence at the very moment it implements its pathogenic effects.

If to be recognized by the outside world is a necessary life-affirming experience for a human being, racism entails an anti-life nonrecognition.

My last account addresses the impact of racism on the relations between parents and children, which I mentioned earlier in passing. This was an incident that happened when I was taking my youngest daughter to a classical music concert, trying to widen her musical education in an act of fatherly concern. As we were filing into the auditorium, with our numbered tickets for numbered seats, somebody suddenly pulled me back by the shoulder and, in what was clearly a racist attack, shouted "I'm English!" I was flooded with anger but controlled myself. My 12-year-old daughter was equally enraged and started to shout back at the man, and a few other people in the queue were also visibly shocked.

That was how I remembered the incident, anyway, and I used the story to think about the impact of the father's humiliation on his children. Freud (1900) had a similar experience, which he wrote about in *The Interpretation of Dreams*. His father told him of an anti-Semite who knocked his father's new fur hat into the gutter, telling him to get off the pavement, *you dirty Jew*. "And what did you do?" asked young Sigmund, wanting to hear his father say "Well, I gave the man a sound thrashing and sent him on his way." "I went into the gutter and picked up my hat" said his father, diminishing his status in the young Freud's eyes. More than a decade passed before Freud reassessed the difficulty and value of the father's restraint in his anonymously published paper "The Moses of Michelangelo."

The normal process by which the overidealization of parents is followed by denigration in later years ("You're full of crap!," as they say) is undermined when the parent is already denigrated in the social world and quite clearly "second class." Cultural values may be overidentified with in compensation, or strenuously rejected and denied. The perceived vulnerability of the parents becomes destabilizing. What happens when, in psychoanalytic terms, the father is already "castrated"? How does the child, and boys in particular, go through the indispensable process of symbolically killing the father and escaping from his influence? The fact that the father is seen to be a second-class citizen in a racist culture undermines this crucial moment; the child feels he has to sustain the father and protect him and is weighed down by this extra burden. Such was my daughter's experience on the evening of the concert.

When I spoke with my now-adult daughter about this incident, she remembered it differently, and I realized I had been engaged in a process of disavowal for over fifteen years. I had forgotten what might be thought of as the most significant aspect of the encounter. The man who accosted me, shocking myself and other people in the queue, did not just say "I'm English" as he pulled me back by the shoulder. He said, "No Black bastard is going to push in front of me. I'm *English!*"

It is sobering to think that racism can be denied even by those who suffer its effects. It can certainly be overlooked, misinterpreted, misremembered, and disavowed. For Black, Asian, and minority-ethnic communities and for the majority white population, we know it's there and we don't know at the same time.

Because who'd want to live in a world like that?

Notes

1 The N—r word references the pejorative word used to refer to people of African heritage. The traumatogenic effect of using the N—word is discussed in Chapter 11.
2 Franz Fanon (1952) spoke of the "white gaze," in *Black Skin White Masks,* Chapter 5, pp. 89–119.

References

Bion, W. (1962). *Learning from Experience*. New York: Basic Books. Jason Aronson Inc., p. 89.
Chakrabortty, A. (2020). There's a hidden epidemic of racism in UK schools—but it's finally coming to light. *The Guardian*, July 22.
Comer, J. (1972). *Beyond Black and White*. New York: Quadrangle Books.
Davids, M.F. (2011). *Internal Racism: A Psychoanalytic Approach to Race and Racism*. London: Palgrave.
Dugan, E. and Numa, S. (2020). Indelible racism: Roundtable discussion with Samir Gandesha, Maxine Dennis, Julian Lousada, and Fakhry Davids at the conference *Psychoanalysis and the Public Sphere: Social Fault Lines*. Organized by *Free Associations* journal and the Freud Museum.

Eddo-Lodge, R. (2017). *Why I'm No Longer Talking to White People About Race*. London: Bloomsbury Publishing.

Fanon, F. (1970). *Black Skin, White Masks* (Charles Lam Markmann, Trans.). Boulder: Paladin Press (original work published 1952).

Freud, S. (1900). The Interpretation of Dreams, In *The Standard Edition of the Complete Psychological Works of Sigmund Freud*, London: Hogarth, S.E. Vols. 4 & Vol. 5

Freud, S. (1913). *Totem and Taboo*. In *The Standard Edition of the Complete Psychological Works of Sigmund Freud*, London: Hogarth, S.E. 13:1–162.

Freud, S. (1914). The Moses of Michelangelo, In *The Standard Edition of the Complete Psychological Works of Sigmund Freud*, London: Hogarth, S.E., Vol. 13:21138

Freud, S. (1923). The Ego and the Id. In *The Standard Edition of the Complete Psychological Works of Sigmund Freud*. London: Hogarth, S.E., Vol. 19: 12–66.

Freud, S. (1950). Types of neurotic nosogenesis. In J. Riviere, A. Strachey and J. Strachey (Trans.) *Collected Papers* (pp. 113–121). London: Hogarth, Vol. 4, (original work published 1912).

Hamer, F.M. (2002). Guards at the gate: Race, resistance, and psychic reality. *Journal of the American Psychoanalytic Association* 50:1219–1237.

Haque, Z. and Elliott, S. (2019). Barriers report: The impact of racism on Black teachers. https://neu.org.uk/barriers-report-impact-racism-black-teachers.

Jones, A.L. (2020). White gaze, Black skin. Conference paper for *Race, Imperialism and the Contradictory Clinic*. www.youtube.com/watch?v=rpFml0cqDCM&feature=youtu.be.

Klein, M. (1946). Notes on some schizoid mechanisms. *International Journal of Psychoanalysis* 27:99–110.

Klein, M. (1957). *Envy and Gratitude*. London: Karnac Books.

Kovel, J. (1970). *White Racism: A Psychohistory*. New York: Columbia University Press.

Lacan, J. (1978). *The Four Fundamental Concepts of Psychoanalysis* (Alan Sheridan, Trans.). London: Hogarth (originally published 1973).

Sandler, J. and Sandler, A.-M. (1986). The gyroscopic function of unconscious phantasy. In D. Feinsilver (Ed.), *Towards a Comprehensive Model for Schizophrenic Disorders* (pp. 109–23). New York: Analytic Press.

Segal, H. (1954). A note on schizoid mechanisms underlying phobia formation. *International Journal of Psychoanalysis* 35:238–241.

Wilkerson, I. (2020). *Caste: The Origins of Our Discontents*. New York: Random House.

Williams, P. (1991). *The Alchemy of Race and Rights*. Cambridge: Harvard University Press.

Chapter 7

Thinking Clinically About Post-Traumatic Reactions to Racial Trauma

Anton Hart

In my experience, doing psychotherapy and psychoanalysis with people who are subjects of racism, incidents of discrimination can and regularly do result in emotional disturbances characteristic of post-traumatic stress reactions. The proportions of the discriminatory incidents need not be extraordinary, such as racial taunting by a mob or witnessing or being the target of bias-based violence, in order to have severe traumatic impact. This chapter provides a psychological conceptualization of how racial discrimination can lead to severe trauma and advocates the inclusion of racial discrimination—in our minds as analysts, if not on the pages of the DSM-5—as a regular contributor to the etiology of post-traumatic stress disorder and other resultant forms of emotional disturbance.

I would like to refer to the nonextraordinary event of racially biased treatment as "the discriminatory gesture" in order to emphasize its fluidity as an interpersonal event. This is in contrast to, for example, a "racial incident" or a "prejudiced act." Experiencing a discriminatory gesture is a unique source of trauma, particularly because it derives its destructive power from its occurrence in a wider contemporary context of pervasive racism and a historical context of slavery. If racism were not a fact of American (and international) life, imbuing virtually all cultural institutions and group and individual psychologies, then single acts of racial discrimination would cease to have meaning. It is because each discriminatory gesture evokes the existence of the contextual whole that the single event can seem slight on the surface yet the emotional toll can be great. Each discriminatory gesture carries with it the personally annihilating power embedded in the existence of the entire destruction-subjugation–oriented enterprise of racism.

If I am in a white group and hear a story in which one of the protagonists is described as "this big Black guy," then a whole system of fear and stigmatization is evoked for me, even if the story is being told by a "friend." If a store clerk addressing a person in the store with dark skin asks, "Can I help you?" when there are others without dark skin in the store who seem to be being left to their own devices, an entire social position and system of biased treatment is alluded to, and the feelings associated with it are, perhaps, evoked. Indeed, the language of the discriminatory gesture is always implicitly spoken with the grammar of the wider context of racism. It can be comprehended only if you already know the language. No single racially discriminatory event is an isolated incident; it is connected to the ubiquity of such events and to society's failure to sufficiently respond to or protect from them. The power of discriminatory words and deeds resides in the destructive forms of social organization they stand for. Accordingly, the psychological sequelae of the persistent trauma of living within a system of racial discrimination and oppression are potentially activated in every incident. Any single moment may yield the straw that breaks the camel's back.

I would like to present two case examples involving people whose skin is brown and whose experience of discrimination was a central—if unconscious—factor in their seeking psychotherapy. I will then elaborate on the themes I have encountered in my work with people who have been victims of prejudice. I will also present some thoughts on diagnosis and treatment in such cases and then will conclude with some thoughts about the obstacles faced by psychoanalysts and other mental health clinicians in recognizing and working with racial trauma.

Case Example I

K., an African American woman in her early 30s, entered weekly psychotherapy due to chronic depression, interpersonal isolation and loneliness, and difficulty with work and intimate relationships. She came to see me after seeking a referral for an African American psychotherapist from a minority-oriented local professional association. Her difficulties could only be understood, she reasoned, by someone who lived within the same racial experience. Although I am light-complexioned,

I qualified for K. because she had learned before meeting me that I was born of a Black father and a white mother; she assumed that I knew enough about being the subject of racial discrimination. A doctor, she practiced in a hospital and was a junior faculty member in the academic department of a medical school. She had relocated to take a teaching position, for which she had been heavily recruited for a unique expertise and, perhaps, for her minority status. Once in the department, though, she was given the least desirable courses to teach and was made responsible for serving on a disproportionate number of faculty committees, even for her status as a junior faculty member. Her minority status seemed to help legitimize those committees to which she was assigned by "diversifying" them.

There was no single incident that K. was able to identify as pivotally traumatic. Rather, there was an overall mounting feeling of being treated unfairly in her professional role as a result of "being Black." She saw herself as continually fighting an uphill battle to be recognized as competent and worthy of promotion. She believed that she was growing increasingly fatigued and depressed as a result of this professional frustration. Her sense of burden and frustration at work was contributing to an overall feeling of hopelessness in all areas of her life.

She was hesitant, however, particularly at first, to attribute her demoralized state to racial discrimination because, she believed, "No one is responsible for this mess but me." Indeed, this ideology of self-sufficiency and emphasis on personal competence had gotten her quite far throughout her education. Yet she suspected that there might be some link between what was happening in her work life—a part of her life that had had central importance for her since childhood—and her overall emotional outlook. And the straightforward and detailed account she gave of the events at work was strongly indicative of pervasive, insidious racial bias against her.

K. was isolated within her department, with virtually no mentors and a chairman who seemed unpredictably to be alternately supportive, neglectful, or punitive. The few other faculty members in the department who were also people of color, all senior to her, seemed competitive and unwelcoming. It was as if they had already been "broken" and were content to just go on surviving in the department, without the resources to lend any support to a person in the difficult position they had once been in.

Already tending toward an orientation of suspicion of other people for a variety of developmental reasons, K. became mistrustful of everyone in her department, feeling that she did not have a basis for evaluating their motives or their truthfulness. This sense of mistrust began to permeate some of her friendships and a romantic relationship she had formed with an African American man who worked as an administrator at the same hospital. She constantly tried to consider the "objective" information she could obtain about people, because she did not feel she could rely on her own interpersonal intuition or any other evaluative sense of them. And in the objective information she could obtain, she was usually able to find sufficient reasons to justify the view that people could not be trusted, that they had one or another hidden agenda, and that she had to "handle" them with extreme caution. This attitude came to pervade all of her work and personal relationships, including, during her most acute period of difficulty about one year into treatment, those relationships with her closest friends, and her relationship with me. In relation to friends, she had to rely on her ability to suppress her suspicions in order to prevent herself from cutting herself off from social contact and becoming completely isolated. This left her with a few ongoing friendships, but it created a state of affairs in which she felt routinely drained after spending time with friends by virtue of the fact that she felt compelled to be false and unreal while she was with them.

K. regularly reported events that sounded like subtle instances of bias at work, but she suffered from an increasing sense of doubt as to the validity of her perception that she was being treated unfairly. The experiences of neglect (or likely, sabotage) at the hands of her superiors at work, some of which seemed clearly due to racial bias based on our careful consideration of their details, led to increasing anxiety and depression. But she was not able to consciously connect her troubled state with the discriminatory nature of some of the traumatic triggers until much later, if at all. She would find it difficult to get out of bed and would binge-eat and fail to keep up with her regular routine of early-morning exercise classes. Alternately, she would become acutely anxious with attendant insomnia, shutting herself into her apartment for days at a time, fearful of the outside world. She would refrain from answering her phone or returning calls for extended periods. Her anxiety had no single or particular focus. Rather, it was characterized by an overarching sense of dread and hopelessness, a sense that she was completely alone, in emotional trouble, unable to come to her own aid, and unable to rely on anyone else.

In session with me, K. would fall into periodic bouts of suspicion of my motives. When this was most acute, she would skip sessions without calling, using the time away to protect herself from the danger that the therapeutic relationship had come to embody. She was also trying during these absences, I later learned, to protect me from the level of suspicion and hostility she was feeling towards me. She feared that I would become so alienated that I would be unable to go on working with her or alternatively, that I would become "justifiably angry" at her and lash out destructively in an attempt at retaliation.

Ordinarily quite articulate and organized in her thinking, when under stress K. had a tendency to become disorganized in her sentence construction and almost incoherent in her words, all the while presenting a facade of calmness and control. Her own mind seemed under attack. This was particularly the case when her feelings of dread were most acute. It was as if she had learned to go on acting as if things were OK, even when they seriously were not. She initially found it threatening, but later in our work experienced it as relieving, when I would try to articulate to her my sense that she was showing evidence that something was deeply disturbing her in the relative lack of clarity that her thoughts would take on.

She was, apparently, quite capable, but was not promoted as might have been expected. The extent to which her own interpersonal insecurity and tendency toward depression played a role cannot be known with absolute certainty. It is certain, however, that she was completely demoralized by the fact that she was persistently *used* at work and yet not promoted commensurate with the level of responsibility she was given. Severe anxious and depressive periods followed these multiple work disappointments and frustrations.

K. showed a fairly common combination of being both interpersonally suspicious and naive. Her life experience seemed to have taught her that she could not rely on her own capacity to discern whether or not she could trust another person. As a result, she would obsessively engage in an ongoing ruminative process of strategizing in relation to friends and lovers. The need to strategize came out of a sense of personal incompetence at "reading" other people. She always had to have a worst-case scenario, to be prepared for the danger she had a faulty capacity to detect. She would construe the data of her experiences with people not as emotionally informative but instead as requiring redundant, fine-grained, rational detective work. This led to a combination of her being extremely suspicious and rigid in her conduct on the one hand, and on the other, putting herself in situations in which the likelihood of disappointment, disillusionment, or betrayal by the other person was high.

The course of weekly psychotherapeutic work over a period of three years yielded moderate success in the sense that this woman became able to consistently verbalize her internalized troubling experiences—including those of various discriminatory gestures from the past and present—with increasing articulateness. The more K. was able to turn the disturbing experiences into expansively subtle and representative words conveyed to a receptive and interested other person—me, in the role of her psychotherapist—the more she seemed able to gradually gain mastery of the experiences. Articulation helped to detoxify them, transforming the incomprehensible and unspeakable into the painful and describable. Her capacity to utilize her considerable intelligence for such articulation increased as she was able to identify and describe more and more of what she went through. The emphasis in our work was not on *interpretation* of hidden meanings or motivations in what she said, but rather on the power of the process of putting into language the things that were bothering her, so that they could become available for internal and relational processing, for thought and dialogue. I believe that in order for this to take place she had to have, in me, a listener who was able to recognize the validity of her traumatic experience and who was willing to partake in making the experience increasingly vivid and detailed.

I sometimes felt the impulse to give K. strategic advice. But she did not need to be coached on how to handle her difficulties with being the target of discrimination. Indeed, she had had much strategic advice from friends and family members about how to handle the various obstacles that arose and their emotional impact. Regarding the latter, the fairly consistent message she had received was, "That's how it is. Do not let it get to you. Do not let racist ignorance stand in your way." Yet these were things she already knew. It was advice she was able to give to herself. The fact of the matter was that it already *had* gotten to her.

She lacked access to a way of emotionally handling the threats to her sense of her self and her existence as a human being that her experience of discrimination inflicted. It was only through the gradual speaking and considering of damaging experiences that she was able to identify their pervasive effects. Only then was she able to approach the task of developing a self-determined way of surmounting the trauma.

Our psychotherapeutic work was interrupted by K.'s taking a job in a different city, in a department that had a better reputation regarding its treatment of minority faculty. She was still quite prone to a suspicious orientation in relation to other people and suffered a major disappointment in a love relationship that had seemed promising but had devolved into a disillusioning withdrawal by her partner, a man who was struggling to maintain his own sense of self and self-esteem. (This man, I learned through my patient, had a story of his own regarding the damage inflicted by living with racism. He struggled to be perfect in his work life, rendering a superhuman effort to be reliable at all costs. In his personal life, in contrast, he relieved himself of the shackles of reliability while at the same time bolstering his fragile self-esteem by serially, deceitfully womanizing.) This disappointment clearly comprised another blow to her sense of trust in her own capacity for interpersonal discernment. Yet rather than become as deeply depressed as she had in the past, she was able to experience deep sadness and disappointment while at the same time examining the ways in which her defensive idealization in that relationship had contributed to her disavowing emotional perceptions that she actually had registered, if not formulated, along the way.

In our concluding session before her move, K. summarized the use for her of our work. She said that when she had started in therapy she had been suffering from things that had been so damaging for so long that she was unable to see them, much less describe them. It was only through my attention to the details of her experience, with the implicit message that her experience was valid, that she had developed her abilities to see and describe.

> I did most of the talking, but you were ready to listen to a kind of talking I don't usually do, or at least, hadn't done much of before. I still see myself as damaged, but at least I have a better sense of who I am.

Case Example II

J. was an African American professional who had graduated from a prestigious college and attended (but did not complete) law school. He came to treatment for reasons of difficulty completing writing assignments, social isolation, and a fear that he might be seriously emotionally disturbed without realizing it. I learned early on that J. had an extensive paranoid delusional system, the contents of which overlapped with some of the work he had completed dealing with issues of sexual harassment and discrimination. His persecutory anxieties and beliefs always ran close enough to actual forms of discrimination and persecution so as to be at least plausible, yet they were often vague in nature and tended to remain unsubstantiated. Paranoia had prevented him, up to the point when he scheduled a consultation with me, from seeking help. He was deeply fearful and suspicious of the psychotherapeutic process as one that sought to engender social conformity through an emphasis on the patient's own responsibility for his or her problems. What made him able to come and see me was that he knew a colleague of mine socially; this emboldened him to enter the treatment with the feeling of being more of my social equal than a "patient" who would be hierarchically "pathologized."

J. was born and raised in an extremely impoverished and dangerous neighborhood in which numerous friends and acquaintances had died from street violence or drug use. At the age of five, he was admitted into a Head Start program due, to the best of his knowledge, to his high intelligence as reflected on an IQ test. He was raised by his mother, who worked part-time as a housekeeper. He had no recollection of his father, who may have been present during brief periods of the first two years of his life but who either moved or died after that.

J. felt deeply ambivalent toward white people. On the one hand, he understood himself to have suffered the effects of racism all of his life, in both direct and indirect forms. He had thus arrived at a general sense that whites were his oppressors and his abusers. As far back as he could remember, his day-to-day life was imbued with discriminatory treatment. He also viewed his neighborhood and his family's poor circumstances as a product of economic injustice perpetrated by white people. On the other hand, he was indeed grateful to *some* white people and had close personal friends who were white.

There was an early teacher in his Head Start program who seemed to recognize his potential and take an interest in helping J. become more confident that he could be a smart student. There was a white professor in college, known for his high academic standards, who had become a sort of mentor to J. following several discussions during his office hours about independent reading that J. was doing on a topic within one of the professor's areas of specialization. Their friendship continued through periodic correspondence after J. graduated from college. There was also an idealized ex-girlfriend from college whom he "never fully got over." She was racially mixed, with one parent who was Black and the other white. During their relationship, J. had experienced her simply as "a light-skinned Black woman." Yet he did subsequently struggle with the awareness that when he was railing against white people he was also railing against an aspect of a woman whom he loved and idealized. This was a significant source of internal unease.

He was dissociatively divided between wanting to destroy his oppressors (or flee them, which took the form of an elaborate segregationist fantasy) or embrace them, trying to find a way to build on the close connections that he had with the few white people he considered friends in order to become "color-blind." Predictably, these issues were played out in J.'s relationship with me. He alternated between fearing and trusting me, feeling gratitude and disdain. My biracial background rendered me just sufficiently similar to and different from J. for him to feel initially safe enough with me. While I believe that these themes could have emerged in a therapy conducted by a therapist of a different racial background from mine, my racial background served as a point of entry for this very brittle, mistrustful man. What seemed most important in my work with J. was that he was able to come to experience me as a figure with whom he could enter into the psychotherapeutic process without feeling prohibitively threatened and with a belief that I could, at least at times, understand his experience.

J. suffered from delusions of omnipotence, including a belief that he was able to make clouds disappear by concentrating on them. He also believed that he could influence world events if he was able to meditate deeply enough and keep a desired political outcome clearly in his mind over a period of time. As a result of these beliefs, he spent a significant amount of time meditating, an activity which involved a combination of trying to clear his mind of "negativity" and trying to intentionally exert mental force on events in the world over which he wished to have impact. He regularly ruminated about world issues and was preoccupied with—and sometimes burdened by—what he viewed as his somber responsibility to help the world through his meditations and thought processes. I did not challenge his sense of omnipotence, and I empathized with his sense of burden. I was routinely interested in the details of his current world concerns and found them generally illuminating about aspects of world or national politics in their own right, even as they seemed grandiose.

As I got to know J. in the first year of our work, it became increasingly clear that he had a long history of harboring intense racial hatred and bitterness toward white people. This hatred took the form of multiple revenge fantasies that were constantly being pored over and revised. Many of these fantasies were hard to listen to for their abject destructiveness and rage, and they engendered a certain amount of dissociative distance on my part as I listened. His revenge fantasizing took up a good deal of his energy and time, compromising his productivity and rendering him somewhat remote and unspontaneous in his interpersonal style. He was prone to experiencing "rages" in which he would become afraid of his extremely violent and destructive fantasies and impulses. During these times, he would try to refrain from sleeping for fear of losing consciousness, and thus, self-control, which could result, he feared, in his committing some horrendous, destructive act.

J. tended to cope with the experience of fear by transforming it into anger and rage. Much of the psychotherapeutic process involved enabling him to notice his tendency to ward off anxiety with violent fantasies and his tendency to justify the fantasies with a hackneyed sense of persecution. There were extended periods of time during which J. would describe his beliefs and worries to me and I would listen to them attentively, refraining from challenging their contents yet seeking clarification when there was anything that struck me as vague. J.'s sense of comfort with my inquiring stance increased over time. Whereas at first he experienced my questions for clarification as my "playing dumb" or attempting to catch him in an inconsistency, he later came to experience me as "strangely curious about everything."

Over a period of several years of weekly psychotherapy, there was a combination of an increased openness to talking about his darkest, angriest fantasies and a softening of the contents of the fantasies as well. Economic disempowerment came to replace death as the vindicating vehicle. And as he became more able to tolerate anxiety and to experience himself as fearful, he came to view his ruminative fantasies as the products of traumatization, often linked to experiences of discrimination. In this way, he was able to locate a compromise between claiming personal responsibility and retaining righteous outrage at abuse. As it became possible for him to view himself as injured over the course of his life, he became an increasingly astute observer of both current and developmental experiences in which discrimination played a part. Yet his view of himself as a victim, in combination with his need to transform fear into anger, locked him into recurrent ruminations about retaliation; he couldn't move beyond the persistent, vindictive desire to right the injustices he had suffered.

Accordingly, the course of long-term psychotherapeutic treatment yielded only moderate improvement in J's overall emotional health. After six years of weekly psychotherapy, J. was able to function stably, but he never fully abandoned his delusional system and tendency toward retaliatory rumination. He was still prone to private retreats into suspicion and a sense of being persecuted. In the role of his weekly psychotherapist and then periodically scheduled consultant, I served as an intermediary between him and the outside, majority culture–dominated world; without that mediating link, we both thought it possible that he would lose further contact with reality, and his relationships with other people and his ability to function would suffer.

In working with J., I was perpetually uncertain about the extent to which it would have been advisable to bring a more direct consideration of his paranoid and persecutory anxieties—and their corresponding rage—into the therapeutic relationship itself. During the course of our work, I remained largely protected in the transference from direct expressions of hostility of the proportions that he clearly felt toward others. It seems likely that I unconsciously dreaded his direct expression of rage and also that I feared my own, likely retaliatory, rage as well. But consciously, I proceeded with the strong consideration that it was highly desirable to avoid a shattering destabilization of his connection with me that too much relational confrontation might occasion.

Discussion

What kind of trauma is possible when the context of racism is evoked in the discriminatory gesture? To begin with, in terms of symptoms, I have routinely encountered the following effects of being the subject of discrimination, many of which are evident in the two cases I have just described: depression, suicidality, anxiety, paranoia, phobic reactions, self-destructive or violent behavior, sleep or appetite disturbance, weight loss or weight gain, anhedonia, somatic problems (without a clear physiological cause), acute relational conflicts, chronic relational difficulties, memory and concentration disturbances, dissociation and related forms of discontinuity of experience, and substance abuse and dependency. Being the victim of racial discrimination is almost invariably destructive, sometimes to a high degree. Beyond symptoms, I have encountered the following psychological phenomena associated with both chronic and acute racially discriminatory trauma:

1 A conviction of arbitrariness of societal rules and absence of justice
2 An acute sense of helplessness and futility, one that extends to one's people and to potential allies or helpers
3 An inflated sense of the status, power, or pervasiveness of the discriminator
4 A destabilization of personal meaning and a disintegration of identity
5 A deterioration of self-esteem, sometimes including a feeling of being subhuman or nonexistent, or even depersonalization
6 Isolation in relation to the majority culture and the wider world; resignation to one's outsider status
7 A feeling that the original forms of oppression (e.g., slavery or segregation) essentially never ended, with attendant dreadful feelings of living in a world that would tolerate and even sanction hatred, destructiveness, and murder of oneself and one's group
8 A compromised sense of the acuity of one's perceptions; the feeling that one cannot reliably discern, interpret, or anticipate events
9 The regarding of suspicion and paranoia as legitimate stances that serve to compensate for one's insufficient ability to detect danger, with attendant hypervigilance and a pervasive mistrust of relationships

10 A tendency to hold prejudiced views toward those from different groups and those in one's own group alike

I find that each of these sequelae of racism may be linked to the connection between instances of discriminatory gesture and the broader social-historical context of slavery, genocide, devaluation, and injustice committed against people of color. The discriminatory gesture psychologically refers to a threat to the victim's existence, even if such a threat is not *overtly* present in the isolated incident.

I have observed in the course of doing psychotherapy and psychoanalysis with victims of prejudice the following process by which the experience of racial discrimination can become psychologically connected with mortal fear and trauma. First, the victim of racial discrimination's existence as a human being is negated through the discriminatory gesture. The victim is treated not on the basis of his or her particular individuality or humanity, but on the basis of being objectified as a member of a hated or devalued group. All at once, the victim is threatened with a connection to the fate of those who have come before (enslavement and death) and with the threat of not being recognized as a human being. Being treated as if you do not exist as an individual is an emotionally potent form of negation, because in asserting that you do not have a subjectivity, it is essentially an annihilatory communication. For better and for worse, we all are, as human beings, indelibly beholden to each other for affirmation and actualization of our sense of existing. We are relational beings. And because of this, the discriminatory gesture is persistently potent in its negating impact despite whatever attempts we may make to counter its validity. And so it can be more dreaded than restraint of freedom, unequal treatment, or, perhaps, threat to physical safety (since physical danger may be painful but may not be ultimately annihilatory).

Now, in experiencing annihilatory threat in the face of the discriminatory gesture, I have found that the victim often forms a defensive (and personally costly) compromise: He or she experiences the intense trauma of relational negation as physical danger in relation to the discriminator as a way of reaffirming a (threatened) personal sense of being, while registering (but not formulating) the interpersonal trauma at the same time. This proceeds by the emotional logic that if one is traumatized by extreme fear (i.e., of losing life or limb), at least one knows that one exists. The annihilatory negation of the discriminatory gesture is actually diminished by its concrete transformation into painful yet potentially survivable mortal fear.

I have consulted with multiple patients who have alluded to such a sense of being threatened with physical danger when, in retrospect, they were able to acknowledge the absence of such danger in the situation where they had, in the moment, experienced it vividly. Often the entry of conscious awareness of this disparity fuels a sense of shame and confusion. And there is a further price that is paid for such a hypothesized compromise transformation from annihilation of personal existence to physical threat. The greater the power of the discriminatory gesture to engender a sense of annihilation of the victim's existence, the greater the sense of physical threat that will be required to ensure some sense of psychological survival. And the greater the experience of concrete physical threat, the greater the potential for the kind of emotional trauma that may have lasting, fragmenting impact. In other words, the proportions of mortal fear are determined by the relative power of the discriminatory gesture's annihilatory message.

Another aspect of the trauma incurred by the victim of racism comes of the hatred and rage that discrimination engenders in its target, and this may be usefully understood as involving a process of projective identification. Powerful negative feelings in the victim of racial hatred may exceed the proportions of those same feelings that go into the discriminator's own racism. Through experiencing racism's negation, the victim enlarges the experience and feels like killing his or her victimizer. At the same time, having such induced rageful feelings is a disturbing experience, inherently threatening a sense of emotional integrity and cohesion. The victim becomes enraged, but the rage, as induced, is incongruous and out of sync with the victim's identity and ideals. Accordingly, part of the victim's rageful experience is then projected onto the victimizer, rendering the originator of the racial hatred a more potent and threatening figure, the representative of the victim's own induced rage experience. To reiterate: I am speaking of a twofold process of traumatization. The first part comes from the racist's projectively identified hatred, which induces an internal disorder in the victim-recipient, causing a rupture of the victim's own emotional experience and a sense of discord between the victim's feelings and his or her ideals. The second part comes from the victim's own projection (back) onto the victimizer. This has the effect of enlarging the threat, increasing the terror, and making it more likely that trauma will be the result.

Racism derives much of its toxicity from the intolerably corrosive, destructive feelings that the racist is attempting to evacuate by putting them onto and into the other, the object of racist hatred. Acts of racial hatred provide a channel for the racist's own hatred and rage to find interpersonal expression while simultaneously being disavowed. The bad, defective, dangerous other can be hated, so that the good, sound, safe other can be loved and the ideal self can survive. Love objects and ego ideals can thus be protected from the intolerable destructiveness originating from within.

It follows that the discriminatory gesture constitutes a powerful, interpersonally based security operation that has the power to induce a state that is simultaneously alien and destructive for the victim. This may provide some clues to the often-encountered incongruity between the demeanors of the indifferent racist and the enraged victim. The victim is, in effect, experiencing intolerable, extruded feelings for both parties, serving as a receptacle for those toxic feelings that are unbearable for each of them.

What a role for people of color to play: the hated, devalued, marginalized bearers of the unbearable. We sing the blues for a wide audience!

Why should it be that an individual suffers an acute trauma, perhaps resulting in a post-traumatic stress reaction, and does not readily recover? This is because post-traumatic stress reactions, as all symptoms, are not simply a product; they also serve a purpose in the psychological life of the individual. Clinically, post-traumatic stress reactions have both an acute survival function and a long-term memorializing function. Acutely, they serve to emotionally displace the full impact of experiences lest they be catastrophically overwhelming and destabilizing, threatening psychological annihilation. In an instantaneous compromise, the individual dissociatively saves some unprocessed experience for a later time, perhaps one characterized by greater ego strength and less immediate situational threat. In the long-term sense, post-traumatic stress reactions serve the mnemic purpose of commemorating experiences that are beyond words, those that defy the individual's ordinary process of memory encoding and yet have been registered nevertheless. In the dissociative process underlying post-traumatic stress reactions, overwhelmingly threatening experience is simultaneously jettisoned and preserved. The purpose is psychological survival in the wake of a horrendous experience. A brutal fact of being human is that no experience can simply be removed, even when it would seem better if the experience could be. Fractured by trauma, people absorb its impact and perhaps retain the possibility of returning to it later—at worst, in the form of flashback; at best, in the form of an opportunity for emotional processing and articulation.

What makes a traumatic event traumatic to the extent that it requires a pervasive dissociative defensive response is that the individual's psychological makeup did not prepare him or her for the event. A post-traumatic stress reaction preserves an overwhelming experience, yet does not help the individual think further about it; therefore the experience can be remembered in more integrated and psychologically benign ways. The process of articulation, inquiry, and understanding is not built in. At best, the delayed stress reaction can serve the purpose of returning the person to the traumatic experience such that a further attempt at mental and emotional processing may be made.

Conclusions

I think it is apparent in both of the case examples that I have been prepared to accept the legitimacy of the devastating impact of discriminatory experience. I believe that this preparedness is vital in the treatment of post-traumatic reactions to discrimination. My own life experience and what I have learned from the patients I have treated may have uniquely prepared me in this regard. But the capacity for being receptive to the reality of discriminatory trauma does not require one to have an identity as a therapist of color or even to have worked with many patients who come from minority backgrounds. And being a therapist of color does not guarantee that one will have sufficient receptivity and acceptance around such matters. I think it is clear that a therapist who is out of touch with the routinely destructive power of such experiences will have difficulty helping the patient who has been actually hurt and requires that this hurt be dialogically registered by the therapist. This forms a basis for proceeding with the arduous task of articulation and working-through. I think it is likely that the majority of therapists practicing today, as evidenced in part by the absence of acknowledgment in the DSM-5 of the primary role of racial discrimination in post-traumatic stress reactions, are not as prepared as they could be to help victims of racial discrimination with their post-traumatic emotional difficulties.

Mainstream society's dissociative lack of acknowledgment of the pervasiveness and destructiveness of racism mirrors victims' (and perpetrators') own dissociative defenses. The fact of the ubiquity of discriminatory gestures and their great toll is persistently disavowed. In this manner, the victim's own way of psychologically surviving persistent discriminatory treatment persists unquestioned by the discriminator, the victim, and society as a whole. This is analogous to a child molester, abused himself as a child, who then sexually abuses. His dissociative defense parallels his victim's, contributing to his difficulty in seeing the devastating impact of what he is doing. This represents a vicious cycle, one that is not the least helped by a societal refusal to acknowledge the terror taking place beneath the surface of conventional life.

The two case examples chosen for this paper involve highly intelligent and educated people who have been able to avail themselves of a high level of psychotherapeutic treatment, in part because they have walked in worlds in which getting such therapy is not anomalous. They have been able to be receptive to a form of processing and exploration to which the majority culture, both Black and white, has only limited access. But I have found in my work with people from varied educational and socioeconomic backgrounds that the utility of putting annihilating experiences into words and entering into dialogue around them has the same (universal) potential to restore health and heal trauma

If we can learn anything from the pendulum swings of psychological understanding of trauma, it is that both fantasy and reality are important.[1] Bad things can happen to people throughout their life spans, and these can be damaging. But all experience is mediated by its meaning for the person who is having it. The intrapsychic and interpersonal contexts of the traumatic event—that is, its individual and relational meanings—make all the difference as to the ultimate effect. This is why two separate people can go through the "same" ordeal and afterward come out very different. Their experience was not, in fact, the same, and this largely accounts for the differences in outcome. Some of us are more susceptible than others to the power of the other to affirm or deny our existence. And clearly, the terms on which affirmation is made are set by those who have the power to oppress.

The person who undergoes surgery will have an experience of a different order than the one who is slashed in an act of violence, even if in the latter case, the physical wound is less severe. The person who is forced into a sexual act has an entirely different experience than the one who willingly partakes, even if the level of physical trauma is equivalent. There are countless examples where the meaning of the event is largely responsible for determining the level of subsequent psychological injury. Clinical experience reveals that the greater the sense of self-agency, the less likely the event will result in post-traumatic stress, even when the proportions of the event are life-threatening. A boxer who suffers a concussion in the ring is less likely to suffer lasting emotional traumatization than a victim of a blunt-force head injury inflicted by an unknown attacker. But clearly, when there is a threat of annihilation there is a strong dimension of loss of control and helplessness, and the likelihood of post-traumatic damage goes up. The inherent loss of self-agency raises the likelihood of psychological injury as an aftereffect.

The discipline of psychoanalytically oriented psychotherapy has, to this point, largely failed to address the reality of racism's trauma. I would like to briefly touch on some of the reasons for this failure in the hope that a discipline-wide self-reflection would help psychotherapists and psychoanalysts to attend to this pressing matter.

First, the fact that the vast majority of our practitioners and our patients are white has direct bearing on the issues and concerns to which practitioners are exposed and that we personally and professionally engage.

Second, I believe that psychotherapists unconsciously (and sometimes even consciously) sense that by virtue of the combination of our own ethnicity, socioeconomic status, and professional identification, even as we intend to help those in need we still represent the discriminating oppressor, at least in part, for our racially victimized patients. I think significant shame and guilt are associated with sensing this. Such shame and guilt are likely to make themselves manifest in dissociative blind spots that interfere with the processing of these difficult yet potentially engageable and surmountable obstacles to the therapeutic processing of discrimination-based trauma.

Third, I think psychotherapists are aware (to varying degrees) of our own ongoing internalization and perpetuation of racism, an internalization that comes of being social beings who unconsciously absorb, participate in, and enact the values of the world in which we walk. As such, we experience a persistent concern that our own dissociated tendencies toward prejudice, objectification, and stereotyping will emerge in relation to patients who we are intending to help and protect. We fearfully engaging such patients on matters pertaining to their trauma, because we fear what their analysis will reveal about ourselves. The fourth obstacle for psychotherapists has to do with our proclivity toward dealing with trauma that has already happened. Even as we are prepared to work "in the here and now," and even while some of us may acknowledge the inevitability of retraumatization in the analytic relationship itself, the psychotherapeutic process tends to direct its attention to traumas that have some sense of safe (usually temporal) distance; the danger is usually not right in the office or out there on the street. If it feels that way to the patient, we are likely to attribute this to transference or paranoia or dissociation. But the experience of discrimination is precisely current, not just historical. Because of this, I think we lose some of the sense of safety and containment that temporal remoteness affords. It feels, countertransferentially, overwhelmingly difficult to face the patient's internalized trauma when lived experience yields perpetually renewed retraumatization.

I have attempted to demonstrate how the experience of a discriminatory gesture triggers a psychological sequence of events that often results in the victim's feeling threatened with both emotional and physical annihilation. This, in turn, forms a basis for understanding the frequency of clinically encountered instances of discrimination-based post-traumatic stress reactions. The point of questioning the DSM-5's omission of such a serious traumatizing phenomenon as racism from its list of causes of post-traumatic stress disorder is not to buy into the scientific reification of its diagnostic categories (including post-traumatic stress disorder). Rather, it is to point out the problem of the DSM-5's omission as a way of speaking to the clinical problem of attending to the psychologically unintegrated and dissociated experience of the discriminatory gesture and to the larger problem of societal denial and disavowal of responsibility for racism's persistently devastating effects.

Note

1 One could conclude, based on contemporary psychoanalysis's reestablishment of overt, objective trauma as the cause of many, if not most, emotional difficulties, that the subjective dimension of traumatic experience has receded in its importance to those seeking to understand post-traumatic stress and related disorders. Whereas the psychoanalytic tradition had at first based itself on the occurrence of actual abuse, then reversed itself with long-held emphasis on internal conflict and fantasy, there is now a consensus that abuse and trauma are indeed ubiquitous phenomena residing at the core of many forms of psychological damage. But it would be a mistake to appropriate this reaffirmation of the real for the purpose of a simplistic and concrete view that externally observable, objective trauma is all there is to it.

Bibliography

American Psychiatric Association (2013). *Diagnostic and Statistical Manual of Mental Disorders* (5th edn). Arlington, VA: American Psychiatric Publishing.

Chapter 8

From the Racially Provocative to the Evocative

Shaping the Destiny of the Racist Moment

Narendra Keval

When I came to Britain in the 1970s, racist graffiti etched across the walls and offensive chants on the street became the normal fabric of casual racism in our neighborhood. To a white person filled with hate, brown or black skin was felt to be a provocation, an insult, even an inflammatory presence to be extinguished if necessary. The racist has decided who you are in advance of knowing and discovering you as a person; otherwise, he risks his imagination, wandering from the familiarity of his knowledge to unknown vistas and imagined dangers of this intimacy, far away from his sense of self. The journey stirs up profound anxieties that have the potential for his undoing, and the more desperate this inner state, the more he is propelled toward hate. Perhaps it is not surprising that he should want to make this known through graffiti pasted on a solid brick wall and ritualized chants—which also protect him against inner collapse.

Retreating into a racist state of mind (Keval, 2016) offers a potential refuge from some of these urgent anxieties by trying to bolt down absolute certainty by shifting the focus from an inner threat to an outer one. What is felt to be internally unbearable is disavowed and grafted onto the ethnic characteristics of others. While it brings temporary relief to stabilize the self by establishing an immediate sense of location, meaning, and security, this is at the expense of distorting reality in ways that rob or silence the humanity of others, who can then be attacked with impunity.

While much has been written about the characteristics of defensive organizations, psychic refuges, or retreats (e.g., Rosenfeld, 1971; Steiner, 1993), very little has focused on how racist thinking and feeling can obstruct the potential for growth and development of the self through an attack on the capacity for curiosity about the ethnic *other*. Nor has there been sufficient focus on how to think about race in the clinical situation in a more nuanced way that considers the subtlety of movements between a patient's wish to engage and explore curiously and their wish to take refuge from perceived dangers, either in an openly provocative or more subtle way. Here, opportunities and challenges may open up for observing how various features of the analyst, such as their ethnicity and the peculiarities of their analytic setting, are made use of or misused to draw out their benign and malignant functions in the shades of feeling that are present in the patient's motivation from one moment to the next.

At one end of the spectrum, ethnic characteristics of others are allowed to be noticed with an inquisitive curiosity that expresses a wish to explore the self in relation to others. In contrast, temporary refuge can be sought in racist hate, where the atmosphere prevents thinking that would wander to unknown places in ways productive of spontaneity where meaning and creativity can merge with another. Of particular interest here is the extent to which these movements tell us something about the quality of the changing mental space inhabited by the patient. That is to say, they indicate whether productive links between thoughts are allowed to flow, which reflects a curiosity that expands as it accommodates, or contracts and collapses if anxiety becomes intolerable and has to be evacuated.

In this way, the racial dimension of thinking and feeling provides a pathway to navigate and attend to seminal moments, during which genuine curiosity flows or becomes obstructed or suppressed, triggering a retreat. The racial dimension also becomes a catalyst for exploring meaningful issues, bringing fresh life to past and present experiences and giving a particular shape and form to the therapeutic relationship (e.g., Schacter and Butts, 1968; Holmes, 1992; Leary, 1995). Our aim is to facilitate a move from the patient's provocative gestures, including those that are racially charged, toward a more evocative world of meaning to be discovered, a process that is not fixed and unidirectional but oscillates during the session. Some patients, however, have habitual tendencies to remain at the more extreme end of the spectrum where absolute certainty is sought in racist hatred. Inevitably, these psychic shifts between curiosity and hate are met with much feeling in the patient that requires tactful interpretation aimed at addressing their anxiety and predicament.

One patient's reaction to his increased awareness of feeling superior to and contempt toward less fortunate brown- or Black-skinned people (while ostensibly priding himself on being a charitable character) commented that while he found the recognition of his racism most unpalatable, it also brought him some relief. This was followed by his putting two fingers up at me from the couch, telling me he wanted to shout "f**k off" at me. He was enraged that I had the audacity to expose him in this way. It was clear how feelings of shame, narcissistic injury, and humiliation had a particularly excruciating quality for him as a white man whose sense of superiority was being threatened in the wake of an increased awareness of his ambivalence and vulnerability.

The case vignettes here focus specifically on the experience of working with white patients who habitually converted their infantile terrors and anxieties into racist hatred that got played out with me, an Asian analyst. I hope they also convey that patients who inhabit these toxic states of mind are caught up in a binary mental space that fiercely opposes any kind of curiosity that could signal triangulation. While the white patient–Black/Asian analyst dyad can present particular kinds of challenges, the intention here is to broaden our exploration of the role that *all* racial/ethnic preoccupations play in the clinical situation and the extent to which they are used and misused, regardless of the backgrounds of the patient and analyst.

Case Vignette: A Mind to Think Thoughts… Even Racist Ones

A white woman entered my consulting room for the first time looking both anxious and fascinated. She began speaking of what it was like coming to see me in a middle-class neighborhood which contrasted so sharply with what she described as a "scum" area, an impoverished housing development where she had spent most of her childhood. As a child, she had spent hours playing in an adjacent neighborhood whose families had had the opportunity to travel and discover foreign places. She told me this cheerfully as she looked around at objects and pictures from different parts of the world that may have felt unfamiliar to her. She said she wanted more out of life but was impeded by her mother's narrow-mindedness.

She thought the "scum" area was racist and associated this with her mother and sister, who could not stand the sight of Blacks, Asians, or foreigners in general. If she ever brought a Black man home she knew he would be kicked out of the house. She said she didn't consider herself racist because she had Asian and Black friends, and then rather sheepishly said she occasionally joined in the racist conversations that frequently took place in her home.

Her curious eyes explored the body of the consulting room, whose sophisticated objects contrasted sharply with her manner of talking, which devalued them and me with what felt like a scatter of hailstones. Her words were intended to hit, not convey meaning. While I found myself initially bemused by the ease with which she spoke—without embarrassment or shame or concern for how she would be experienced by this Asian man—I soon was rattled by this assault of words apparently intended to provoke a reaction. My countertransference was telling me that as much as her curious eye reached out to me—as I imagined it did with her Black and Asian friends—she also took refuge in the embrace of her racist family and could not stand the sight of my brown face. The moment she was in touch with the warmth of her curiosity, she would go cold, with words like the scatter of hailstones, intended to kick me out of her mind.

An opportunity had arisen in the immediacy of this moment to explore through her manner of relating to me her inner struggle as she sought to get more out of life. Her curiosity and the new possibilities she was able to imagine brought forth a fear of me followed by a racist phobic response. She could very conveniently locate this inner obstruction in her mother's narrow-mindedness that she needed to escape from in order to individuate into a woman in her own right. This struggle with her mother's narrow-mindedness, from which she needed to escape so as to individuate into her own person, was now present in a racialized transference.

Coming to my consulting room—on the other side of the fence, so to speak—was like being on the run from an internal object of "a racist mother"; it offered her refuge different from that of her family, but engulfed or curtailed her emotional freedom. When I asked what she thought about her own racist attitudes she became dismissive. Drawing a patient's attention to what is being disavowed often creates a counterreaction. However, naming it can bring some relief to the patient: Acknowledging that racist and racial thoughts and feelings can be difficult to think about helps with possible feelings of embarrassment, shame, or humiliation.

Acknowledging her own culpability as distinct from her mother's may have felt like a request to separate from her mother. Despite the desire born on childhood playgrounds, which, reawakened now, and had brought her to my consulting room, there lurked in the shadows the knowledge that if acted on in the analytic situation, this desire could only lead her far away from her mother and the apparent safety of her refuge in racist thinking. Not unlike her mother's threats to kick out any Black man who entered her home, she too tried to kick out, with her dismissiveness, what my comment had stirred up in her mind—but with only partial success.

In the following session, she was puzzled by how upset she had become, having thought it was just her mother and sister who were racist, whereas she thought of herself as being quite loyal to her Black and Asian friends. She had clearly mulled over our conversation and her ambivalent feelings, trying to reconcile her hateful and protective feelings toward the very person she had come to for help. A new possibility was emerging: she could acknowledge her own thoughts and feelings, even if they were racist and made her feel very uncomfortable. This struggle was then replaced with laughter and dismissal of what she was discovering about herself. She felt she was not being racist at all, but rather just joking—like her mother and sister, who thought it was a joke when they made cruel comments about others who were racially different.

This moment conveys something crucial in the experience of those on the receiving end of racism. If you take things to heart, you become the problem because of a "chip on your shoulder," but this is aimed at negating your experience when your emotional responses tell you otherwise—as my countertransference was telling me. It lodges an experience that belongs to the patient, namely that she had become upset and puzzled and then disavowed this by locating it in me. I suspect that, having recognized this upsetting fact, she once again retreated into her refuge of cruelty, establishing her loyalty to it by trying to belittle my experience to inflate her sense of superiority over me. This defensive maneuver to manage her racism also revealed how she habitually negated any discovery about herself, painful or otherwise. Another version of reality was to be substituted to convey what it felt like to be in her shoes, living in a family that threw words at each other like missiles, which fed seeds of doubt and, at their worst, became violent intrusions that questioned the validity of her experience. Here was a patient struggling to have some semblance of mind she could call her own.

Some patients who have been massively intruded upon psychically describe the experience as being akin to a psychic occupation, a thought or feeling belonging to others that has taken up residence in their mind and creates confusion as to who it is that is thinking the thoughts. This creates various clinical challenges as to how we might understand and speak to such a patient in a way that doesn't feel judgmental and shame-inducing (although the patient may well experience these feelings despite our best efforts). What is needed is an understanding about their predicament in navigating the ownership of unpalatable feelings.

At some point, I put to my patient that she had come to see me to discover her own point of view in relation to others such as her mother, sister, or me, without feeling she had to take sides. She replied thoughtfully that it was not just racism, it was anything different, like ideas, places, or people that her mother and sister hated because they were used to the same old ways of doing things, whereas she wanted to try things that were different.

I wondered with her whether her old accustomed ways stopped her from becoming more curious about herself, because if she were to abandon them she would have to separate from her mother. Thinking differently, she replied, made her feel afraid of herself. She remembered having had affectional feelings toward a knowledgeable teacher she looked up to which embarrassed her because her teacher belonged to an ethnic group my patient thought were "dirty scroungers on child benefits." She felt great shame for being two-faced.

I put to her that she found herself with feelings—such as embarrassment or shame—about needing help from me, a teacher she admired, feelings more complicated than the black-and-white thinking and feeling she preferred. She looked upset and said she often lacked the courage to speak out against the racism she encountered at home, such as her Spanish boyfriend's boasts that unlike the British, he came from a race that was pure and uncontaminated by foreigners. When her mother joined in the denigrating conversations, it became all the more difficult for her to challenge them. I suggested that I thought there were moments when she felt more able to speak her mind and other moments when she felt very alone and frightened to speak up, which made her want to run back into what was familiar: her racist thinking. She replied that it was too dangerous to speak out, as she had witnessed her relatives beat up her boyfriend for being racially different.

It is interesting how this woman's adolescent struggles to individuate are expressed through her preoccupations about geographical spaces and boundaries, some of which feel safer than others, with sharp demarcations of good/bad, racist/non-racist, and so on. These types of splitting were attempts to delineate an overwhelming internal confusion when she felt at particular risk of losing the contours of her precarious self. Perhaps her cold unfeeling words also conveyed her fear that she would be rejected, with a loss of warm, loving feelings, should she betray her loyalty to the racism intertwined with her mother. Her claim to be more tolerant and liberal than her mother and sister was some attempt (though one that failed) to punctuate a difference, to separate herself. Her choice of a foreign boyfriend was a further elaboration of a wish to separate and continue her journey into the adult world, one that made her feel both curious and terrified. Unfortunately, this separation was fraught with difficulties, as she found herself in a relationship with a man who also idealized racist beliefs.

Although the patient's struggles largely played out in terms of racial differences, embedded in these were all manner of other differences that were met with tyranny, as she reminded me. Challenging these racist sentiments brought profound anxieties in relation to potential threats of violence and being banished to a place where she felt utterly alone, without the internal resources to sustain her. This urged her to run back to what she perceived to be the safety of her refuge, one that claimed to offer her a modicum of certainty, even if it was delusional.

In this way, her adolescent journey became troublesome, a process made all the more difficult in the absence of a third object, such as a father, who could have helped her to triangulate and make a healthy transition, although it was unclear as to whether or not her father also held strong racist beliefs that would have created further complications on her developmental journey. While opportunities to explore her early life in more depth were limited, it is very likely that this racialized crisis around separation and individuation would have echoed earlier infantile crises that her adolescence had brought to the surface again (Blos, 1962).

However, the hopeful trend in her mental life connected her to memories of playing as a child that she associated with a particular geographical area, which brought her to my consulting room. In this sense, the ravages of her racist thinking did not manage to entirely colonize her capacity for play, curiosity, and embracing difference. Her struggle for emotional freedom from an engulfing mother found another opportunity of being worked at through the relationship with me, where our conspicuous racial differences brought fresh life to her internal predicament. One can see how these developmental struggles took on a more ominous tone when threats of thuggery and violence held her at ransom, shutting down any attempt made to achieve separation or acknowledge ordinary ambivalence.

Case Vignette: Thinking under Fire

An Italian man I saw for a consultation left quite an impression on me because of the rather dramatic nature in which our initial encounter unfolded. It seemed that his only means to communicate how frightening it was to be himself was to try to frighten.

He entered my consulting room, looking confident but suspicious as he placed his coat over mine on the door, sat down, stroked his chin, and looked at me patronizingly. I planned to see him briefly to discuss a treatment vacancy, but it was not long before he started his tirade. He said he was not going to be messed about, how experienced was I, and would his treatment end abruptly as it did with his previous therapist, as he was certainly not going to put up with that nonsense with me. I had a feeling from his demeanor and opening gambit that my being Asian had rattled him, as he managed to create an abrasive and volatile atmosphere within moments of meeting me. What unfolded next helped me make sense of this initial impression about his behavior.

When he insisted that there was only one version of events to comprehend (i.e., his), I wanted to kick him out of the room. Tuning into my violent countertransference response became an important source of understanding how he was provoking an enactment. First, my wish to kick him out, rather than engage and understand him, was a reaction he was accustomed to in his abrasive encounters with others. Although he was being aggressive in an effort to define a safe space for his treatment, by being provocative he courted rejection and yet another reason to be aggrieved.

I acknowledged his sense of urgency but needed him to tell me about his previous treatment and how it had ended so abruptly. I was under the impression that his cessation of treatment had been planned, but he was clearly disgruntled. He spoke without telling me anything about his experience of the therapy. His distress turned into omnipotent control and a demand to put things right. This prevented an exploration where he and I could think together; there was something about his experience with a previous therapist that appeared to have left him traumatized, with feelings of hurt, shame, and humiliation. Unable or unwilling to tolerate these feelings, he was determined to project them onto me, belittling me and questioning whether I would be robust enough to help him.

He became irritated, demanding that I stop pussyfooting around (exploration) and offer him treatment that would end only when *he* decided to leave. His mistrust and contempt were clear when he asserted that I should not try any of that therapy "lingo" with him, as he had heard it all before. This bullying stopped me in my tracks, unable to think for a moment. The litany was like a lawyer making a case for the prosecution. It felt as if he were demanding total control over whether I should even think my own thoughts! I could see that this form of abrasive engagement made him feel superior and triumphant. However, the inner place of desperation that was being converted into a demand for absolute control of me was difficult to reach.

When I was better able to gather my thoughts, I commented on his wish to test whether I could manage his abrasive behavior enough to help him. He replied, somewhat mockingly, that it was a shrewd observation. In his agitated state, although my attempts to empathize with his anxieties received fleeting recognitions, they made him feel even more vulnerable, increasing his anxieties and attempts to control me. With this man, naming his anxiety and frank terror of being with me could easily humiliate him and inflame his sense of injury, hence his desperate attempts to establish control. This escalated into a barrage of derogatory and racist comments about others and about my cultural background and by telling me the consulting room was smelly, before dismissing me as incompetent.

Two remarks were particularly telling. First, he demanded that only he should decide the ending date of any treatment that was offered. Second, he said he hated the silence in the room when I was thinking. I had a sense that these provocations expressed his terror that he might suddenly be left without anything to contain him, a catastrophic loss that would rupture his sense of continuity. This threw him into a paranoid state in which he demanded absolute control of others. His wish to stop me from thinking was intended perhaps to create an experience inside my mind in which I would be temporarily unhinged, unable to maintain continuity in my thinking. What would have been a disaster for the relationship was now playing out in my mind: my loss of control, risking even falling into an emotional abyss. It was a disaster I imagined he felt.

His use of racist thinking offered him temporary refuge that gave him a sense of feeling superior; it was a maneuver to help him avoid spiralling into a more severe breakdown. As these attempts failed him, he escalated his attempts to wound me. In this way, he could disavow his own feelings of the humiliation, of floundering in a mental and emotional mess. It is telling that by attacking my brown skin, which was unsettling him, he was displacing onto me his inner turmoil so that I experienced it.

Like the first patient mentioned, this man's provocation hid a desperation that was vital for me to reach. But it was difficult since he was determined to hurl everything at me to see if he and I could survive and continue to think. He attacked the very act of thinking. There is little space for curiosity to emerge for either patient and analyst in this state. I would argue that this was necessary for the patient as his psychic imperative was for the urgency of survival (unmetabolized terror) to be emotionally felt and understood. This patient saw that he could bruise me a little through the racist attacks that derailed my thinking, but not enough to stop my continuing to think with him to create an opening of a different type of space, even if momentary, to allow some exploration.

Despite all his bluster and noxious ways, this patient had taken the risk of coming to see me, knowing, at least from what he would have gleaned from my name, that we were racially/culturally different. Here was a hint, perhaps, that his more benign and hopeful feelings, however, faint, could emerge from the hateful and provocative inner world that he was trying to navigate. Despite the initial storm, the patient returned and stayed the course of his treatment with me, which continued to echo many aspects of that first meeting. However, as we both settled into being with each other, his volatility gradually took less of an upper hand. It took us both by surprise that he found himself able to speak with me from a place that felt less terrifying. Some moments emerged when he even seemed curious about my Asian background, trying to draw similarities and differences with his Italian background. As his need to take refuge lessened, a brief moment would open up for him to make use of me to explore his own emerging curiosity—that is, until a new threat was perceived on the horizon.

Conclusions

Preoccupations about difference in the form of ethnicity and race, including racism, are always present in subtle ways in the privacy of our daily thoughts, feelings, imagination, and dreams. Our clinical encounters are no exception, but they need close scrutiny to capture the nuances of what is being grappled with and communicated. I have suggested that regardless of the ethnicity of the therapeutic dyad, when racial preoccupations, whether explicit and provocative or more subtle, emerge in the clinical situation, they present us with particular challenges in how to listen to them as we tune into the emotional impact they have on us. I suggest a dimension of listening that tries to discern patients' use and misuse of the analyst as a pathway to understanding the wish to explore and engage with curiosity or to retreat into the refuge of racist thinking and feeling, respectively.

Exploring these movements with sensitivity and tact can allow us to understand the many layers of meanings they signify. Not unlike the racist graffiti on the wall I described at the beginning, some of our patients aim to provoke through the violence of words and even gestures in order to narrate their difficulties and predicaments. Both vignettes describe the storm created when racist moments arise in such a way as to bring out their feelings of racial superiority with particular intensity. When the atmosphere is volatile, there is a particular challenge of being receptive enough to be emotionally affected (but not masochistically submit) and continue thinking. This is not as straightforward as it sounds, given that some racist attacks are particularly cruel and designed to get under the skin to cause massive disruption to one's thinking and sense of self.

My patients' attempts to "kick out" the terrors and threats that pervaded their thinking—a wish that also appeared in my countertransference—was a regressive pull in words toward the concreteness of bodily action. The psychic action defended against disturbing feelings resulting from violence inflicted on their minds in the past and was indicative of early failures in the capacity to metabolize and transform infantile anxieties and terrors (Bion, 1962). We risk re-enacting the failures if we get drawn into being intolerant of intolerance in our patients. Or, just as the second patient placed his coat over mine or the first patient hurled her "scatter of hailstones" at me, we can unwittingly put an "analytic coat" over the patient through only an intellectual understanding (perhaps the therapy "lingo" referred to by the second patient) and fail to remain curious and emotionally present. Maintaining presence, on the other hand, can create small moments of thoughtfulness that, working incrementally, may turn the tide in the treatment. The patient can, with the force of an emotionally felt insight, find the strength to resist the turn to a racist solution for their difficulties. They can create an opening for their own curiosity to unfold, discovering moments of warmth, color, and common humanity. Put simply, our willingness to engage with the racially provocative to facilitate an evocative world of symbolic meaning has the potential for shaping the destiny of the moment.

References

Bion, W. (1962). A theory of thinking. *International Journal of Psychoanalysis* 43:306–310.

Blos, P. (1962). *On Adolescence*. New York: Free Press of Glencoe.

Holmes, D.E. (1992). Race and transference in psychoanalysis and psychotherapy. *International Journal of Psychoanalysis* 73:1–11.

Keval, N. (2016). *Racist States of Mind: Understanding the Perversion of Curiosity and Concern*. London: Karnac.

Leary, K. (1995). Interpreting in the dark. *Psychoanalytic Psychology* 2(1):127–140.

Rosenfeld, H. (1971). A clinical approach to the psychoanalytic theory of the life and death instincts: An investigation into the aggressive aspects of narcissism. *International Journal of Psychoanalysis* 52:169–178.

Schacter, J.S. and Butts, H.F. (1968). Transference and countertransference in interracial analysis. *American Psychoanalytic Association Journal* 16:792–808.

Steiner, J. (1993). *Psychic Retreats: Pathological Organizations in Psychotic, Neurotic and Borderline Patients*. London: Routledge.

Chapter 9

"And How Are the Children?"

Intergenerational Trauma and the Development of Black Children in America

Kirkland C. Vaughans

In her book, *Post Traumatic Slave Syndrome* (2005), Joy DeGruy Leary describes the traditional greeting of the Maasai, an African tribe. The greeting was *Kasserian ingera*, meaning "And how are the children?" and the traditional response was "All the children are well." Unfortunately, American descendants of Africans, who are living in a nation that has failed to recognize the trauma of the enslavement and oppression of African Americans, would not be able to respond, "The children are well." Furthermore, American society does not seem to want to know how Black children are, and psychoanalytic scholars and communities have not yet done enough to understand how Black children are or to support their psychological development. In this chapter, I ask the question, "And how are the Black children?" and begin to answer it by providing a historical framework that illuminates the current plight of Black children, which is a direct consequence of unresolved tensions from the institution of American slavery. I hope to show how crucial it is for psychoanalysts to inquire more regularly and consider more fully the ongoing and intergenerational trauma experienced by Black Americans and to imagine what role the psychoanalytic community might play in societal changes needed for the healthy development of Black children.[1]

As the historian Ira Berlin (2006) has observed, "Slavery is ground zero of race relations" (3). I will venture to demonstrate that despite considerable legal and social progress made by African Americans, slavery continues to cast its collusive shadow over the presence of Black and white Americans alike. W.E.B. Du Bois had prophesied that the "color line" was the problem for the twentieth century, but I fear that his prophecy must be extended by at least two centuries. Despite the time that has elapsed since the Civil War, many Americans find it difficult to examine slavery and abolition in our country with any sense of personal detachment: Its memory today remains fueled by animosity and conflict. Memorial statues dedicated to Confederate soldiers and battlefields physically and obviously symbolize and contain unresolved trauma, but the residues of slavery also live on through less-visible institutional policies and practices in our systems of juvenile justice, policing, education, and housing—institutions that often function in an unacknowledged segregated fashion and that perpetuate inequality and trauma (Logan 1997/1909). That significant and pertinent community and civic institutions serve as a repository for the historical ideology of white supremacy fosters the maintenance of a non-mentalization posture of American whites toward African American youth, as well as youth of Hispanic heritage. As the historian Patterson (1982) has demonstrated, these institutions have maintained and perpetuated perceptions of Black boys and girls that emanate from a historical period that challenged and denied their membership within the human family. Hence, racial injustice has become systemically institutionalized in ways that are often invisible and outside of people's conscious thought.[2] Furthermore, people who call attention to racial injustice and demand that we think about it as a nation often are accused of being divisive. I write and publish this chapter not to be divisive, but rather to attempt to articulate some of the causes of the existing racial divide. Like Eric Garner, I desperately hope to be heard, as I believe that, at present, American society has a lethal choke hold on many of its youth of color. That choke hold could start to be released if systemic racial injustice and its historical origins in slavery are made visible and if the effects of the intergenerational trauma of slavery are explicitly considered when caring for the psyches of Black children.

Intergenerational Trauma in Family and Nation

Generational trauma has not been consistently sanctioned by the APA or the DSM-5. In the 2017 two-volume *APA Handbook of Trauma Psychology*, for instance, the topic is indexed on one page, and it is not considered at all in the DSM-5. However, the topic is taken up by the *Psychodynamic Diagnostic Manual-2* (PDM-2), which emphasizes an epigenetic model for integrating the various models of generational trauma (Lingiardi and McWilliams 2017). It proposes the interplay between genes and environment as a major determinant of gene expression and not gene sequence. The epigenetic model suggests that we look at the "mode of inheritance" rather than inheritance itself. This conceptualization importantly involves the present social malaise as well as that of the past. Danieli (1998), the pioneering expert on generational trauma, observes:

> Multigenerational transmission of trauma is an integral part of human history. Transmitted in word, writing, body language, and even in silence, it is as old as humankind. It has been thought of, alluded to, written about, and examined in both oral and written histories in all societies, cultures, and religions.
>
> (2)

Danieli adds that, viewed from the vantage point of family systems, what impacts one generation can impact either a younger or older generation, although its expression may take on various forms. The trauma may be passed on as a family legacy. Although family values and means of coping with, defining, and adapting to trauma vary among cultures, Danieli views the family as the primary instrument for transmitting the traumatic legacy.

Even so, in an earlier study of Holocaust survivors (1984), Danieli concluded that society had a profoundly negative impact on survivors' post-traumatic adaptation, intrapsychic integration, and healing, as well as on their capacity to mourn their significant losses. Instead of being listened to, survivors were admonished to "let bygones be bygones." Survivors experienced similar punitive, judgmental reactions from mental health practitioners. This "indifference, avoidance, repression, and denial" was dubbed by Danieli the "conspiracy of silence" (p. 1).[3] Following atrocities such as genocide, denial often becomes an official instrument of the state and is greeted with cultural and historical collusion (Cohen 2001).

Ron Eyerman (2001) examines the identity formation of African Americans from a historical perspective based upon the trauma of slavery not as an institution as such, but upon the collective memory of slavery. Albeck (1994) similarly draws attention to the problematic propensity of psychology to focus on trauma as strictly an intrapsychic experience, without consideration of social, political, and historical factors. This neglect of the social aspects of trauma has resulted in a tendency to pathologize reactions to "abnormal events." In the introduction to their two-volume series on intergenerational trauma, Salberg and Grand (2017) explain:

> We now understand that psychic influence extends well beyond maternal dyads and Oedipal triangles. In the trans-generational model, the psyche is constituted by a much larger object world. This world is more multigenerational. It is also no longer exclusively hierarchical but is horizontal: inclusive of the communal cohort effect of massive trauma…. It expands our psychic world and our relational resources, as we also integrate the social/political/cultural markers of collective trauma.
>
> (3)

Slavery is generally recognized as the particular historical trauma for African Americans. Volkan (1997) describes such painful collective legacies as a "chosen" trauma, by which he means that a group's collective identification is developed through the memory of the injury that has been passed on for generations. The trauma is passed on through what Fromm (2012) refers to as "deposited representations," or what I have earlier termed "cultural introjects" (Vaughans 2015), a mechanism for the unconscious internalization of cultural phenomena in order to defend against the dread of knowing and, I would now add, against the mandate for repair.

This dread of knowing by individuals whose families have suffered trauma is exacerbated by the surrounding social denial and obfuscation of atrocities. As Warren (2016) points out, discussions of slavery are often greeted with intellectual exhaustion or impatience due to the dubious notion that we now live in a post-racial society and that such discussions of slavery have "exceeded the statute of limitations" (58). He contends, however, that despite the idea that slavery is in the past, the violence of slavery has never died but instead has been continuously "regenerated, reborn, and reincarnated" (59).

What, then, accounts for our nation's reluctance to have the adequate, needed conversation about this history of slavery and its ongoing effect on our country? If, as Salberg and Grand (2017) assert, "the psyche is constituted by a much larger object world," why is the effect of this larger world on the psyches of Black children not a more regular topic of psychoanalytic research? The analyst Volney Gay (2016) suggests that people tend to view their history through the psychological defenses of splitting and denial. However, he views idealization as the most "insidious" of all the defenses and notes that even "intelligence and learning" fail to diminish its power (p. 57). Unfortunately, these two anti-historical forces—the idea that discussions of slavery are no longer relevant and the idealization of America—thwart the very discussions of slavery and its aftermath needed to understand ongoing pressures on Black children. Instead, too many white Americans conflate history and heritage, buoyed up by Ronald Reagan's image of America as the shining light on the hill. Thus, America is an almost ahistorical creation in their minds. As a nation, we are held hostage to historical ignorance. Herman (1992) powerfully captures the essence of this phenomenon:

> The knowledge of horrible events periodically intrudes into public awareness but is rarely retained for long. Denial, repression, and dissociation operate on a social as well as an individual level. The study of psychological trauma has an "underground" history. Like traumatized people, we have been cut off from the knowledge of our past. Like traumatized people, we need to understand the past in order to reclaim the present and the future. Therefore, an understanding of psychological trauma begins with rediscovering history.
>
> (2)

It is with the intention of reclaiming the present and the future, particularly the future of Black children, that I turn to a brief account of slavery in America. In doing so, I attempt to disentangle the brutal reality of slavery from narratives that have evolved to obfuscate that reality. Even after having completed observance of 150 years since our nation concluded the epic historical crisis of the Civil War, few Americans know enough about American slavery, and since slavery and American history are inextricably linked, few Americans comprehend their history adequately. It is only by speaking the trauma of the centuries of slavery and the trauma of the various forms of oppression that followed slavery's abolition—it is only by understanding this past—that we can claim a more peaceful and equitable future.

Speaking the Horrors of American Slavery

In 1860, America had four million slaves, making it the largest slave-holding nation in the world, with enslaved Africans estimated at a value of three billion dollars. That tidy sum of money was almost three times more than the value of all of American manufacturing, seven times more than that of the holdings of all banks, and forty-eight times more than the expenditures of the entire federal government (Berlin 2006). In 1619, the first Africans arrived in involuntary servitude to Jamestown, Virginia, which has helped to augment the myth of slavery as a Southern phenomenon even though slavery was soon national in scope and practice. Massachusetts was the first state to legally regard slavery. Other Northern slave-holding states included Connecticut, Illinois, Maine, New Hampshire, New Jersey, New York, Pennsylvania, Rhode Island, and Vermont, which was the first colony to ban slavery (Hornsby 1997). In fact, prior to the Revolutionary War, New York City, with 20,000 slaves, had more slaves than any other populace north of Maryland. Another way of perceiving slavery's grasp upon the nation is the fact that twelve presidents of the United States owned slaves and that eight of them owned slaves while in office (Gay 2016).

Even with the present proliferation of scholarly research on American slavery, very little has focused on the lived experiences of children in bondage or of their experiences following emancipation during the period of the new Black codes to persecute and undermine Black Americans' newfound freedom. It is estimated that children constituted approximately one-fourth to one-third of those to cross the Middle Passage (King 2005). This crossing came to be known in Swahili as *Maafa*, meaning, "great loss, sorrow, or catastrophe." The experience of separation and loss would reverberate as a lifelong theme throughout their approximate 250 years of enslavement within the United States. Berlin (2010) documents this recurring trauma: "Few enslaved parents could expect to nurture their children to maturity, see their grandchildren grow up, or succor their own parents in their last years" (xxvi). The trauma of the separation of parents and children is vividly demonstrated in the narrative of Sojourner Truth (Truth 1998/1850) who, at the age of nine, finds her mother in tears shortly after her owner's death. She asks:

> "Mau-mau what makes you cry?" She would answer, "Oh my child, I am thinking of your brothers and sisters that have been sold away from me." And she would proceed to detail many circumstances respecting them. But Isabella long since concluded that it was the impending fate of her only remaining children, which her mother but too well understood, even then, that called up those memories from the past, and made them crucify her heart afresh.
>
> (6)

The dreadful fear of family breakup was known and exploited by white masters, whose phrase, "I'll put you in my pocket," was a warning of an impending sale if any question at hand was not resolved to the owner's satisfaction. Separation and loss were more feared than the pain of the lash. Thomas Jefferson, a large slave holder, readily endorsed this practice with the enslaved whose behavior he found intransigent (Berlin 2006). The fear of loss or being sold away was so pronounced that it was acknowledged in the wedding vows as, "Until death or distance, do you part." Paradoxically, the family of the enslaved child constituted a child's greatest source of protection as well as his or her greatest source of vulnerability. The ever-present threat of separation from family haunted children and parents, with unimaginably harmful effects on the possibility of the development of secure parent-child attachment.

A second common, if unspoken, conflict between a child's parents and master emerged from the master's patriarchal attitude toward all of his slaves, considering them as extensions of his own family and therefore his dutiful children. As the literal owner of enslaved children, the master's expectation was for the parents to educate them to be submissive and duty bound to him and him alone. Johnson (1996) asserts that the inherent principle in such a lesson is for the enslaved child "to experience their bodies twice at once, to move through the world as child and slave, person and property" (23). Slave holders employed a number of strategies to encourage enslaved children not to be frightened of them and, even more, to identify with them as benevolent mother and father figures. Schwartz (2000) documents how an enslaved girl, Hannah Scott, was taught to address her owners as "White Pa and White Ma" (93). In *Incidents in the Life of a Slave Girl*, Harriet Jacobs describes how perilous such a situation could be for the enslaved child when her brother is called by his mistress and his father at the same time:

> He hesitated between the two; being perplexed to know which had the strongest claim upon his obedience. He finally concluded to go to his mistress. When my father reproved him for it, he said, "You both called me, and I didn't know which I ought to go first." "You are my child," replied our father, "and when I call you, you should come immediately, if you have to pass through fire and water."
>
> (Yellin 1987)

A second painful memoir is offered by Caroline Hunter who, through teary eyes, told of her experience as an enslaved mother:

> During slavery it seemed like yo chillum b'long to everybody but you. Many a day my ole mamma has stood by and watched massa beat her chillum till they bled and she couldn't open her motf. Dey didn't only beat us, but they strap my mamma to a bench or a box an beat her wid a wooden paddle while she was naked.
>
> (Bardaglio 1992, 215)

By the age of eight or ten, enslaved children were expected to work a ten-to-twelve-hour shift in the field. Schwartz details how, in addition to this hard labor, enslaved children also were taught from a very early age to perform personal duties for the comfort or pleasure of the master, mistress, and overseer. Among these tasks were brushing away flies, fetching personal items, bringing a hot coal to light a pipe, cleaning and shining shoes, babysitting infants and small children, as well as emptying the chamber pot. Henry Bibbs recalled his childhood duties as a slave of "cleaning floors, polishing furniture, and pushing the rocking chair that the mistress sat in." He also complained that he combed her hair and scratched her hair because "She was too lazy to scratch her own head" (King 2005). Schwartz specifies that performing these tasks competently was insufficient: "Rather, each child had to perform the job in such a way as to emphasize the unequal relationship between servant and served" (92). Judith Herman's study of trauma (1992) illuminates the inter-/intrapsychic dynamics of the perpetrator with the goal of enslaving his victim. Herman explains how the perpetrator:

> relentlessly demands from his victim professions of respect, gratitude, or even love. His ultimate goal appears to be the creation of a willing victim. Hostages, political prisoners, battered women, and slaves have all remarked upon the captor's curious psychological dependence upon his victim.
>
> (77)

The effects and ongoing trauma of slavery are importantly rooted not only in brutal, forced labor but also in such coerced intimacy. Enslaved children were forced to feel a split obligation to master/mistress and father/mother, further eroding secure attachment between children and parents. Becoming the "children" of their masters and intimate caretakers of them fostered a complex psychological dependence of masters on slaves and slaves on masters.

Enslaved Girls and Women

As they approached puberty, female slaves were at great risk of sexual abuse from owners, overseers, and sometimes other enslaved men. In addition to their worries about sexual predators, enslaved girls were now at the prime age to be sold away from their families. Ahjum (2007) asserts that objectification of enslaved women as chattel—that is, as the personal property of the slave holder—made their "wombs little more than breeding sites" (91). Thomas Jefferson perpetuates the conceptualization of Black women as domesticated breeders when he observes, "A child raised every two years is of more profit than the crop of the best laboring man" (qtd. in King 1995). The profit for white slave holders who could impregnate slave women with impunity and secure the continuation of slavery through their wombs, however, was twisted into a judgment projected onto Black women as Mammy or a sexually licentious Jezebel (Morton 1996). Thus, enslaved Black girls and women not only suffered the trauma of sexual abuse and forced sexual slavery, but they also suffered the character assassination of the master's projections that justified that abuse.

The extreme consequences of slavery are made clear in the dramatic and tragic case of Celia, an enslaved girl. For years, Celia's sixty-year-old owner, Robert Newsom, raped her repeatedly, and Celia gave birth to two mulatto children. Pregnant with a third, she demanded an end to his sexual abuse, and when he refused to cease, she killed him. She was found guilty of murder since as his property he could do with her what he wanted to, and she was hanged. As of 1860, there were 405,761 mulattoes in the United States, comprising 12.55 percent of the African American population, the majority resulting from involuntary relationships.[4] This statistic speaks to how widespread sexual violence by white men against Black girls and women was. After Reconstruction, however, an extraordinary psychological defense of reversal occurs, in which white society promotes the fear of Black men pursuing white women. Once again, the violent and oppressive behavior of white masters is projected onto enslaved Black people. Although it is Black women who were victims of white masters' sexual violence, the narratives emerge that Black women are overly sexual or natural child bearers and that white women are especially vulnerable to Black male sexual violence. Such narratives not only erase the trauma of victims, but also blame them for the violence perpetrated against them. Such narratives also perpetuate oppression in ways that have become inherent in our cultural institutions.

Perpetuation of the Institutions of Slavery—Schools and Prisons

As Eyerman points out (2001), after Reconstruction and the rise of the Black codes to disenfranchise African Americans, Blacks quickly understood the amendments to the Constitution to be no more than a legal fiction and voiced their predicament in a blues sonnet about mass flight from the South:

> Boll Weevil in the cotton
> Cutworm in the corn
> Devil in the White man
> I'm good and gone.
> (154)

In the so-called "post-racial society," trauma is fueled by the systemic and endemic deployment of structural racism that impedes the psychic capacity for the resolution of the generational transmission of trauma among African Americans. I should note that other poor children of color, and especially those children with disabilities, also get snagged into this oppressive web of structural racism and prejudice. Structural racism is defined by the Aspen Institute as "a system in which public policies, institutional practices, cultural representations, and other norms work in various, often reinforcing ways to perpetuate racial group inequity" (Nguyen 2017, 2). By this definition, structural racism prescribes social relations through a hierarchical categorization of groups. The two principal institutions that I wish to focus on are education and "juvenile justice" (a misnomer) in combination with law enforcement. In addition, I will briefly touch on apartheid residential living. Even as unacknowledged racial trauma is embedded in such institutions, as Angela Davis (2003) observes, the social structures foster and perpetuate racism: "Racism has always found an easy route from its embeddedness in social structures to the psyches of collectives and individuals precisely because it mobilizes deep fears" (p. 66).It is thus particularly important for psychoanalysts to be aware of the impact of how social institutions affect the psyches of Black children and youths.

In my discussion of the educational and juvenile legal systems, I am borrowing the language of the educator Annamma (2018) and deliberately refusing to use the more familiar term "juvenile justice." Like Annamma, I do not believe that this system "remotely approximates justice." Moreover, I have come to conclude that the oppression of our youth through incarceration and the obscene failure of the educational system with children of color have co-inspired and co-created criminality in children of color. This amalgamation has come to be known as the school-to-prison pipeline. Schools in the inner cities have largely abdicated their responsibility for discipline and, through the use of national policies, have criminalized misbehavior, resulting in irresponsibly punitive measures toward students of color. The role of the legal system has been so vast and has profited so greatly from the imprisonment of our youth that it has come to be dubbed the prison–industrial complex.

In the United States, a free and compulsory education has long been considered the cornerstone of democracy. Thus, education is seen not only as an avenue for personal advancement or enrichment, but also as a necessary condition for the public good by developing an informed citizenry (Heitzeg 2016). However, it took the 1954 Supreme Court decision in *Brown v. Board of Education of Topeka*, for the empty promise of "separate but equal" to be acknowledged as inherently unjust. According to Jonathan Kozol (2005), by the 1980s, the high hopes that decision engendered had almost entirely waned, as evidenced in his visits to dilapidated inner-city schools across the nation. School segregation was so pronounced in New York City—it stood at a rate of 99.8 percent—that Kozol acknowledged being unable to distinguish between the legally enforced segregation of the South and the social and economic apartheid of New York City neighborhoods and those of other major U.S. cities. Although I do not wish to suggest that our educational system is solely responsible for the continued academic deficiencies of children of color, I do assert, as the researchers Thompson and Hickey (1994) conclude, that our schools "transmit inequality from one generation to the next" through their dual roles of "aiding and hindering" social mobility, the latter through limiting the learning opportunities of Black students.

Decades earlier, Kenneth Clark (1965) had warned that "When schools do not have confidence in their job, they gradually shift their concept of their function from teaching to custodial care and discipline" (133). Clark's words were indeed prescient, as seen in Henry Giroux's (2012) assessment of all American youth, especially those poor and of color, as "disposable." Giroux warns that compassion and moral and social responsibility toward youth have been replaced with punishment and fear and as a result serve as an instrument for the "savage inequalities" perpetuated within our school systems (Kozol,1991). With reference to the beleaguered African American students of Hurricane Katrina, Robinson and Brown (2007) point out:

> There is a curious pattern of unstated expectation by adults of children placed at risk and in vulnerable circumstances: That these children have at their disposal a package of strategies that they can access readily to rise above any adverse circumstance.
>
> (77)

This view of at-risk children maintains a functional popularity within the schools by administrators and support personnel, but it is in direct contrast to the research of developmental psychologists who characterize at-risk children as those with a limited range of potentially supportive resources within an oppressive environment. Michelle Fine (1993), in her critical analysis, argues that the construction of the idea of at-risk children distracts our attention as an "ideological diversion" from more fundamental issues, such as "an economy that is inhospitable to low-income adolescents, collapsing manufacturing sectors, housing stock, impoverished urban schools, and diplomas with very little exchange value across racial and class line" (106). For Fine, "the dropout" becomes the imaginary bogeyman that needs to be fixed and that obfuscates the real need to fix and transform our educational institutions. For Fine, the public obsession with fixing the dropout problem will be about as effective as changing the protocols in the obstetrician's delivery room in order to reduce the frequency of out-of-wedlock pregnancies. Unfortunately, however, most national educational policies—from President Bush's "Leave No Child Behind" to President Obama's "Race to the Top"—leave the sole responsibility for the child's education to his or her school, with no plan for improving the impoverished, segregated communities that are the very source of much of children's academic difficulties. Most efforts at educational improvement misguidedly focus on individuals, not the system. Furthermore, the fact that impoverished, segregated communities are rooted in our nation's history of slavery and systemic racial oppression continues to go unacknowledged.

Discussions of the school-to-prison pipeline have largely focused on the struggles of Black and Hispanic males, as opposed to girls and women of color. However, research by the Office of Juvenile Justice and Delinquency Prevention (2010) demonstrates that the incarceration rate of girls of color is increasing the fastest of all. A recent large-scale study conducted by the Georgetown Law Center on Poverty and

Inequality (Epstein et al. 2017) revealed that, compared to white girls, Black girls between five and fourteen years old were perceived as "in need of less nurturance, less protection, needed less support, needed to be comforted less, were more independent, know more about adult topics, know more about sex" (1). The researchers conclude that these attitudes constitute a kind of "adultification" of Black girls, which, by framing them as less innocent, in turn accounts for their disproportionately high rate of school discipline. Black girls are perceived as older than their biological age, a carryover from slavery to justify their work and sexual abuse. An example is offered when a fifteen-year-old Black girl was arrested, handcuffed, and taken to the police station for using a student MetroCard whose use is permitted only by those who are nineteen years and under. When her mother gave the police verbal confirmation of her age of fifteen, the police then demanded that the mother produce the girl's birth certificate, which the mother did. The girl was treated for damage to her wrists inflicted by the cuffs.

A second study by Georgetown's Juvenile Justice Initiative (Vafa et al. 2018) determined that there has been no evidence of an increase in girls' criminal or violent behavior, but that they are primarily detained, arrested, and incarcerated for status offenses. According to the findings, Black girls, who constitute 14 percent of the population, are 33 percent of detained and incarcerated girls; lesbian, gay, bisexual, and transgender (LGBT) youth are between 7 percent and 9 percent of the population but make up 20 percent of incarcerated youth. Boys in juvenile facilities identify as LGBT at the rate of 3.2 percent, whereas girls do so at 40 percent, and 85 percent of incarcerated LGBT youth are youth of color. Black girls who do not conform to the standards of white femininity (Winn 2011) are perceived as loud, hypersexualized, and even as helpers, but are rarely thought of as brilliant (Annamma 2018). According to Morris (2016), they are negatively labeled as being defiant, precocious, unladylike, disrespectful, and uncooperative. These stereotypes, in conjunction with get-tough policies such as "zero tolerance," lead school administrators to use much harsher disciplinary measures with Black girls than with white girls, even for documented identical offenses. When all of the stereotypes about Black females are compiled, they range from overly sexed to masculine, revealing quite confusion in white people's imaginations. Perhaps imagining Black girls as masculine and unladylike is a defense against imagining them as sexual.

Annamma further discusses the misconception that special education students are a protected school population. She points out that their suspension and expulsion rates are more than double those of general education students. While the national general education graduation rate is 83.2 percent, for white special education students it is 72 percent, for Hispanic special education students it is 58 percent, and for Black special education students, 55 percent. In addition, 58 percent of emotionally disabled Black youth drop out of school, and 73 percent of those students are incarcerated within three to five years. These critical determinants—Blackness, gender, class, and disability—affect Black girls in such a punitive manner as to cause them to be the fastest-growing group to be incarcerated. Indeed, a 1995 study conducted by Mauer and Kling demonstrated the rate of increase of 78 percent. How these factors intersect with such dismal opportunities and the encouragement of failure has caused the Black feminist Ann DuCille to quip, "One of the dangers of standing at an intersection ... is the likelihood of being run over" (qtd. in Annamma 2018, 144).

In the context of the over-disciplining of Black youth, it is important to note that the juvenile justice researcher Neil Bernstein (2014) reports that the number-one predictor of being imprisoned as an adult is not gang membership nor an absent father, but rather it is having been incarcerated as a youth. His research documents the racialization of the boundaries between youth and adulthood, whereby youth of color are significantly more likely to be sentenced as an adult. The dismal educational opportunities that challenge so many students of color are not viewed in any way as benign neglect by the educator Darling-Hammond (2007), who instead categorizes them as "aggressive neglect." The current hypercriminalization of Black and Hispanic youth, especially males, has resulted in an annulment of their constitutional rights as well as their right to be perceived as children and youth. Hillary Clinton's unfortunate 1996 remark about "the kinds of kids that are called superpredators,"[5] a name that strips these children of their status as children, has its historical precedent during slavery and in the post-antebellum period of American history.

Today, America has the largest prison population of any country in the world, reminiscent of its earlier dubious accomplishment of being the largest slave-holding nation in the world. The United States represents just less than 5 percent of the world's population; however, we incarcerate slightly more than 20 percent of it. The Sentencing Project, a social advocacy and research group (Mauer and King 2007), reports that since the 1970s there has been a 500 percent increase in the number of incarcerated persons, which means that 2.2 million people are currently incarcerated. They also report that Blacks constitute 900,000 of those incarcerated and that this increase in the prison population has had, at best, a "modest success" on public safety. They detail how, if the present rate of incarceration continues, then one of every three Black males born today will spend time in prison during the course of his life. Additional analysis of their data demonstrates that African Americans are imprisoned at nearly six times the rate of whites and that the rate for Hispanics is nearly double than that of whites. The prison–industrial complex is a source of a major economic boom for all involved, including those in the building trades, arms dealers, food industry, and real-estate investment, as well as being the source of thousands of jobs in local economies. Mumia Abul-Jamal once wondered that white Americans welcome and even compete for the building of new prisons in their communities even as they vehemently protest the development of homes or services for the underserved with the timeworn phase, "Not in my backyard." Incarceration brings jobs for whole communities where many people are out of work. In 1980, the total cost for incarceration was 6.9 billion dollars, and today it is approximately 80 billion (Stevenson 2014).

Such profiting by white Americans from the prison industry that disproportionately incarcerates Black Americans eerily echoes efforts to re-enslave emancipated African Americans. The Black codes, laws that pertained only to Black people, were hurriedly created to replace the slave laws that were no longer in effect after the Civil War. Other than skin color itself, these laws provided the primary distinction between Blacks and poor whites. Under these statutes, Blacks who refused employment offers by their former masters would be arrested, sentenced, and leased out to their former masters. The Black codes successfully resurrected white supremacy through massive terror, including thousands of public lynchings, the raping of Black girls and women, denial of the ballot box, and the return of enslavement through convict leasing. Statistics about "discipline" in institutions that are meant to educate our children and keep them safe reveal how, for far too many Black children, the institution of slavery has been reinvented in the institutions of schools and prisons. Schools that should promise to offer opportunities for change and growth instead perpetuate intergenerational inequality.

Conclusion

I have presented a long list of upsetting facts and ideas—historical and current. I have diagnosed a disturbing psychosociological condition. Do I have a treatment plan? I have only modest proposals that I offer as a "citizen psychoanalyst," a term coined by Prudence Gourguechon, former president of the American Psychoanalytic Association (Aron 2017). Gourguechon was advocating a social activism in order to help those in need, but also to develop and transform psychoanalysis beyond its present rigid borders. I, too, urge us to develop beyond our current borders.

My first proposal is that we reexamine our ranks and our institutional culture in relation to race and ethnicity. During this examination, I suggest that we include issues raised by the LGBT community, including our resistance to hearing them. My second proposal is that we take very seriously our capacity and our history as psychoanalysts and psychodynamically oriented clinicians to be catalysts for social change with regard to child policy. As Moskowitz (1996) points out, Spock, Brazelton, and Bowlby were all psychoanalytically trained, and all participated in the movements for women's liberation and for sexual minorities.[6]

The regressive pull of neoliberal policies is what makes our very loud silence on such social issues not only regrettable but also a license for those who would continue to inflict harm on children of color through the established conduit of the school-to-prison pipeline. In order to truly consider the developmental needs of the Black child, we must be willing to examine how they are educationally, programmatically, and legally tried and convicted not necessarily for an actual crime but by the policies that we put in place, like zero tolerance and broken windows. The researcher Nell Bernstein (2014) points out that even as crime is steadily declining, police arrest approximately two million children a year and that most are incarcerated for minor, non-violent offenses. Berlin (2010) researched and documented the forced interior migration of the enslaved population within the United States during the 1800s calling that the "Second Middle Passage" (p.100) which, like the first "Middle Passage," forever disrupted and broke apart homes, families, and communities. Presently, the massive numbers of Black men, women, and children who have become entrapped in the prison–industrial complex (Alexander 2010) which reeks ongoing collective racial trauma on the Black community, constitute what this author is terming the third, "Middle Passage." Franz Fanon (1967/1956) argued that "The habit of considering racism as a mental quirk, as a psychological flaw, must be abandoned" (p. 33). I would strongly suggest that in its stead we focus on programs designed to keep children and adolescents from an initial entry into the legal system: Even those who have had police contact can best be helped through a diversion program.

Of late, there have been a number of clinical articles focusing on cross-racial dialogue during treatment; however, I am unaware of any that discuss cross-racial dialogue among us clinicians. Yet, I am certain that any racially attuned analyst—white or Black—becomes aware of the subtleties and discriminating posturing that occur during psychoanalytic meetings and conferences, the origin of which, I believe, is a racial etiquette born during slavery. The Black historian Charles Johnson (1996), when interviewing Blacks about racial relationships, was told, "You got to treat them like a silk handkerchief on a barbed wire fence" (p.122). My third proposal is that we psychoanalysts and other mental health clinicians make every effort to break through such false etiquette and begin an open conversation about race in American institutions that will foster understanding of our national trauma and support the development of Black children.

Notes

1 As the historian Anne Mae Duane (2017) suggests, "The present. . . has the capacity to shift our perspective on the past, illuminating what we may well have overlooked, or even changing what we thought we knew in the first place" (2).

2 This lack of capacity for mentalization by whites toward Blacks was recently documented by Nicholas Kristof (2014) in a series of seven articles appearing in the *New York Times*, titled, "When Whites Just Don't Get It." Not "getting it"—or indifference—can be understood as a measure of social power rather than naivety or a lack of sophistication. According to Barton (2001), commenting on Ralph Ellison's novel *Invisible Man*: "The ability to render the world visible and invisible is a concrete form of power, and is a part of the social construction of race." The expression and hurtful consequences of this kind of white power also was addressed in a *New York Times* feature article in March 2019, "A Quiet Exodus: Why Black Worshipers are Leaving White Evangelical Churches."
3 Such a conspiracy of silence is not unique to survivors of the Holocaust: It too frequently becomes the official posture of the state after an atrocity, as when the Turkish government during WWI moved to exterminate or expel its Armenian population, resulting in approximately 1.5 million deaths (Kupelian et al. 1998). The Turkish government has consistently denied this genocidal catastrophe, for which no one has ever been officially punished.
4 Judith Herman (2017) reports that the United Nations considers gender-based violence the most universally practiced form of all human-rights violations.
5 Clinton is recorded in a C-SPAN video clip saying:

> But we also have to have an organized effort against gangs. Just as in a previous generation we had an organized effort against the mob. We need to take these people on. They are often connected to big drug cartels, they are not just gangs of kids anymore. They are often the kinds of kids that are called superpredators—no conscience, no empathy. We can talk about why they ended up that way, but first, we have to bring them to heel.

6 Moskowitz also cautions that the danger of taking credit for such positions means one also runs the risk of opening one's organization to having to take the "blame," as well.

References

Ahjum, S. (2007). The law of the white father. In *Women and Slavery*, eds. G. Campbell, S. Miers, and J. Miller. Athens: Ohio University Press, pp. 83–108.

Albeck, J. (1994). Intergenerational consequences of trauma: reframing traps in treatment theory – A second generation perspective. In *Handbook of Post-Traumatic Therapy*, eds. M.B. Williams and J. Sommer Jr. Westport: Greenwood Press.

Alexander, M. (2010). *The New Jim Crow*. New York: The Free Press, p. 24.

Annamma, S. (2018). *The Pedagogy of Pathologization: Disabled Girls of Color in the School-prison Nexus*. New York: Routledge.

Aron, L. (2017). Robert Jay Lifton: A witness and prophet who feels deeply and assaults our minds. In *Psychoanalysis, Trauma, and Community*, eds. J.L. Alpert and E.R. Goren. London: Routledge, pp. 231–237.

Bardaglio, P. (1992). The children of jubilee: African American childhood in wartime. In *Divided Houses: Gender and the Civil War*, eds. C. Clinton and N. Silber. New York: Oxford, pp. 213–229.

Barton, C., ed. (2001). *Sites of Memory*. New York: Princeton Architectural Press.

Berlin, I. (2006). Coming to terms with slavery. In *Slavery and Public History*, eds. J.O. Horton and L.E. Horton. New York: The New Press, pp. 1–18.

Berlin, I. (2010) *The Making of African America*. London: Viking.

Bernstein, N. (2014). *Burning Down the House*. New York: The New Press.

Clark, K. (1965). *Dark Ghetto*. New York: Harper & Row.

Cohen, S. (2001). *States of Denial: Knowing about Atrocities and Suffering*. Cambridge: Polity Press.

Danieli, Y. (1984). Psychotherapist's participation in the conspiracy of silence. *Psychoanalytic Psychology* 1:23–42.

Danieli, Y., ed. (1998). *International Handbook of Multigenerational Legacies of Trauma*. New York: Plenum.

Darling-Hammond, L. (2007). Countering aggressive neglect: Creating a transformative educational agenda in the wake of Katrina. In *The Children Hurricane Katrina Left Behind*, eds. S.P. Robinson and M.C. Brown II. New York: Peter Lang, pp xi–xx.

Davis, A. (1998). *The Angela Y. Davis Reader*. Malden: Blackwell Publishing.

Davis, A. (2003). *Are Prisons Obsolete?* New York: Seven Stories Press.

Duane, A.M. (2017). *Child Slavery before and after Emancipation: An Argument for Child-Centered Slavery Studies*. New York: Cambridge.

Epstein, R., Blake, J. and González, T. (2017). *Girlhood Interrupted: The Erasure of Black Girls' Childhood*. Washington, DC: Center on Poverty and Inequality, Georgetown Law.

Eyerman, R. (2001). *Cultural Trauma: Slavery and the Formation of African American Identity*. Cambridge, UK: Cambridge Press.

Fanon, F. (1967/1956). *Toward the African Revolution*, trans. H. Chevalier. New York: Grove Press.

Fine, M. (1993). Making controversy: Who's "at risk?" In *Children at Risk in America: History, Concepts, and Public Policy*, ed. R. Wollons. Albany: SUNY Press, pp. 91–110.

Fromm, M. (2012). *Lost in Transmission: Studies of Trauma Across Generations*. London: Karnac.

Gay, V. (2016). *On the Pleasures of Owning Persons: The Hidden Face of American Slavery*. New York: International Psychoanalytic Books.

Giroux, H. (2012). *Disposable Youth: Racialized Memories and the Culture of Cruelty*. New York: Routledge.
Heitzeg, N. (2016). *The School-to-Prison Pipeline*. Santa Barbara: Praeger Press.
Herman, J. (1992). *Trauma and Recovery*. New York: Basic Books.
Herman, J. (2017). Trauma and recovery: A legacy of political persecution and activism across three generations. In *Wounds of History: Repair and Resilience in the Trans-generational Transmission of Trauma*. eds. J. Salberg and S. Grand. London: Routledge.
Hornsby, A. (1997). *Chronology of African American History*. Detroit: Gale Press.
Johnson, C. (1996). Quoted in David M. Oshinsky's. *Worse Than Slavery: Parchman Farm and the Ordeal of Jim Crow Justice*. New York: Free Press.
King, W. (2005). *African American Childhoods*. New York: Palgrave.
Kozol, J. (1991). *Savage Inequalities*. New York: Crown Publishers.
Kozol, J. (2005). *The Shame of the Nation: Restoration of Apartheid Schooling in America*. New York: Crown Publishers.
Kristof, N. (2014). When whites just don't get it. *New York Times*, Sunday Opinion, August 30.
Kupelian, D., Kalayjian, A. and Kassabian, A. (1998). The Turkish genocide of the Armenians. In *International Handbook of Multigenerational Legacies of Trauma*, ed. Y. Danieli. New York: Plenum, pp 191–210.
Leary, D.J. (2005). *Post Traumatic Slave Syndrome*. Milwaukee: Uptone Press.
Lingiardi, V. and McWilliams, N., eds. (2017). *Psychodynamic Diagnostic Manual: Second Edition*. New York: Guilford.
Logan, R. (1997/1909). *The Betrayal of the Negro*. New York: De Capo Press.
Mauer, M. and Huling, T. (1995). *Young Black Americans and the Criminal Justice System: Five Years Later*. Washington, DC: The Sentencing Project.
Mauer, M. and King, R. (2007). *Uneven Justice: State Rates of Incarceration*. Washington, DC: The Sentencing Project.
Morris, M. (2016). *Pushout: The Criminalization of Black Girls in Schools*. New York: The New Press.
Morton, P., ed. (1996). *Discovering the Women in Slavery: Emancipating Perspectives on the American Past*. Athens: University of Georgia Press.
Moskowitz, M. (1996). The social conscience of psychoanalysis. In *Reaching Across Boundaries*, eds. R.M.P. Foster, M. Moskowitz, and R. Javier. Northvale, NJ: Aronson, pp 21–46.
Nguyen, K. (2017). *The Impact of Structural Racism on Mental Health: Dissertation Proposal*. Garden City, NY: Adelphi University.
Office of Juvenile Justice and Delinquency Prevention (2010). https://ojjdp.ojp.gov/library/publications/ojjdp-annual-report-2010 (Last accessed June 27, 2022).
Patterson, O. (1982). *Slavery and Social Death*. Cambridge: Harvard University Press.

Robinson, S. and Brown, C. (2007). *The Children of Hurricane Katrina Left Behind: Schooling Context, Professional Preparation, and Community Politics*. New York: Peter Lang Publishing.

Salberg, J. and Grand, S. (2017). *Wounds of History: Repair and Resilience in the Trans-generational Transmission of Trauma*. New York: Routledge.

Schwartz, M. (2000) *Born in Bondage: Growing Up Enslaved in the Antebellum South*. Cambridge: Harvard Univ. Press.

Stevenson, B. (2014). *Just Mercy: A Story of Justice and Redemption*. New York: Random House.

Stoute, B.J. (2018). Personal Communication.

Thompson, W. and Hickey, J. (1994). *Society in Focus: An Introduction to Sociology*. New York: Harper/Collins.

Truth, S. (1998/1850). *The Narrative of Sojourner Truth*. McLean, VA: IndyPublish.com.

Vafa, Y. et al. (2018). *Beyond the Walls: A Look at Girls in D.C.'s Juvenile Justice System*. Washington, DC: Georgetown Law Juvenile Justice Initiative.

Vaughans, K. (2015). To unchain haunting blood memories: Intergenerational trauma among African Americans. In *Fragments of Trauma and the Social Production of Suffering*, eds. M. O'Loughlin and M.C. Lanham. Lanham, MD: Rowman and Littlefield, pp. 226–241.

Volkan, V. (1997). *Blood Lines*. New York: Farrar, Straus and Giroux.

Warren, C. (2016). Black time: slavery, metaphysics, and logic of wellness. In *The Psychic Hold of Slavery: Legacies in American Expressive Culture*, eds. S.D. Colbert, R.J. Patterson, and A.L. Hussen. New Brunswick, NJ: Rutgers University Press, 55–68.

Winn, M. (2011). *Girl Time: Literacy, Justice, and the School to Prison Pipeline*. New York: Teachers College Press.

Yellin, J., ed. (1987). *Incidents in the Life of a Slave Girl, Written by Herself*. Cambridge: Harvard University Press.

Chapter 10

Black Rage
The Psychic Adaptation to the Trauma of Oppression

Beverly J. Stoute

> To be a Negro in this country and to be relatively conscious is to be in a state of rage, almost all of the time.[1]
> —James Baldwin

In his much-discussed and often disputed *Beyond the Pleasure Principle*, Freud (1920) posited the fundamental duality between Eros and Thanatos—the life and death instincts, our constructive and destructive forces—even before he fully elaborated the theory on aggression, and it is here that any psychoanalytic formulation related to racial hatred must begin. At the root of Freud's thinking is the ominous idea that there lurks something dark and destructive in all of us. The idea that racism can take expression in the most extreme forms of violence and inhumanity, in my mind, exemplifies the darkest realization of how racism can be recruited as an accomplice in humanity's potential destructiveness. Yet Freud formulated a theory of the "universal mind," detached from cultural and social context, which allowed him to disavow the pain of his own racial trauma, a precedent that made it difficult for psychoanalytic theory to subsequently recognize, formulate, and integrate the experiences of the oppressed. As a consequence, we have for a long time seen an extraordinary lack of reflection on how this silence on racial oppression has impeded the development of theory (Stoute 2017), limited the diversity of our professional organizations, and blinded many to the reality of racial violence in society generally.

Freud's Neglect of Race and Racism in Psychoanalytic Theory

Freud, as a Jew, had his own lived experience of racism. He knew poverty and discrimination; he knew devaluation, degradation, and despair at the hands of racial hatred, and, in his writings, he made many references to his Jewishness. That Freud endured anti-Semitism, especially during his medical training, is well documented. Sander Gilman's scholarly research (Gilman 1991, 1993) has documented that Jews were considered the "Negroes of Europe" and that "the male Jew and the male African" were seen as "equivalent dangers to the 'white races' in the anti-Semitic literature of the late nineteenth century," with Freud being referred to as a "black Jew" (1993, p. 19).

In evolving a universal theory, Freud had a dream, not unlike the African American dream, that he would be judged by the content of his character and understood by the content of his universal unconscious, regardless of color, creed, or race—in essence, that our shared humanity would trump difference. He did not theorize racial trauma as germane to psychoanalytic theory, and many have pointed to his quest to disidentify his theory with Jewishness even though he, as a Jew, was all too familiar with oppression. Understanding this aspect of Freud's history might allow us to reconceptualize his perspective as that of a racially traumatized Jew. Knowledge of the developmental aspects of racial trauma can help us understand why, despite this lived experience, he forged a universal theory that discounted social and cultural contexts.

Our connection to our group affiliation in racial and ethnic identity comes together in latency and early adolescence, and so racialized experiences at this nodal point in development, as in the following account, carry added valence (Stoute 2019). Moskowitz (1995), using Peter Gay (1988) as his source, recounts a story of a young Freud: When Freud was about ten or twelve

> his father told him about an incident in which the elder Freud was walking down the sidewalk, all decked out and wearing a new fur cap, when along came a Christian man who knocked the cap into the muck and shouted, "Jew, off the sidewalk!" Freud asked his father, "What did you do?" His father answered, "I stepped into the road and picked up my cap." The young Freud "was deeply disillusioned and developed fantasies of revenge. He identified

with the Semite Hannibal, who had sworn to conquer the mighty Romans. He also came to see himself as part of a suppressed minority that must always be in opposition to mainstream culture.
(pp. 550–551)

This fantasy of Hannibal—the humiliation and the identification with the minority—proved to be an important connector to an understanding of Freud's neglect of racial trauma and the subsequent effect on his theoretical writings. Extending psychoanalytic theory here to the more robust integration of racial trauma and psychic adaptation to trauma allows us to make sense of how the lived experience of racial trauma reawakened during the Covid-19 pandemic uncovered a dark reality for us all.

Our experience during the pandemic was a far cry from, but not totally disconnected from that of psychoanalysts in attendance at a meeting of the British Psychoanalytical Society during World War II. When air-raid sirens were heard during the meeting, D. W. Winnicott reportedly rose to say, "I should like to point out that there is an air-raid going on." Those present took little notice, and Winnicott sat down as the meeting continued (Phillips 1988, p. 61). During the 2020 pandemic, analysts could no longer ignore the external world, the social and cultural backdrop, as the threat of the virus and the threat of racism closed in on the analytic dyad, forcing a recognition anew of our shared cultural space (Winnicott 1967).

As I wrote this paper in June 2020, during the pandemic, the background noise was constant: It came from the demonstrations every day on the streets of the city where I live, and from demonstrations across the cities of our nation and the world. It prompted an essential question: How do we make sense of the disavowal of personal responsibility for the violence, cruelty, suffering, pain, and denial of promised freedom in understanding the narrative of the American psyche, the fact that our legacy of racism has prevented us from becoming a universal "we" even in a pandemic? It is not possible to present the theoretical formulation of Black Rage as the psychic force that galvanized a social movement without localizing my perspective as a psychoanalyst, because psychoanalytic exposition must involve a socially embedded narrative. If we formulate from the perspective of a socially embedded narrative, we come to the useful concept of a culturally embedded self that internalizes the influence of race, culture, ethnicity, gender, class, the social surround, and historical context. We have each brought our own psychic, cultural, racial, ethnic, gendered, and societal reality to this conversation on the pandemic, as we all grapple with the sense of ongoing threat in the social surround impacting our internal psychic reality.

As an African American, cisgender woman of mixed cultural descent, my American narrative, therefore, starts with the slave, is carried from slavery into freedom fighting, and includes migration and immigration; it is this cultural, intellectual, and religious history that centers me even as a psychoanalyst. The American narrative for me reaches back to that of the indigenous people, because they are the people with whom I share the first socially sanctioned position of the Other in this narrative. Akira Kurosawa's *Rashomon* attempts to get at the "truth" of an event while taking into account the perspective of each person who witnessed it. From my cultural context, the Black Panther Party cofounder Huey P. Newton takes up a similar idea in conversation with Erik Erikson: "People seem to think," he explains, "that because they live in the same geographical space and in the same period, they must be living the same reality, but there are several realities, and the official one is defined by power" (Erikson and Newton 1973, p. 30). Race in America defines psychosocial position, and that has never been more evident than during the pandemic. We went from the pandemic of the virus to a pandemic of anxiety to a pandemic of racism. We were forced to take notice together of the impact of social reality on our experience, our work, our theories; I will use psychoanalytic theory here to shed light on the unprecedented series of societal events that have unfolded. Integrating the story of a young Freud's racial trauma with a novel application of the concept of moral injury led me to a conceptualization of Black Rage as a defensive and mobilizing force at the heart of the 2020 uprisings across the globe.

Formulating How Black Rage Catalyzed a Mass Realization during the Pandemic

In March 2020, when the pandemic hit full force in the United States, I thought, as Freud might have, that the teams were human beings versus the virus, and in a pandemic, the virus knows no race. Patient and analyst faced the challenge together and simultaneously. We were all afraid. Like the crack in the Liberty Bell, though, the stark reality became clear as the data organized along the familiar racial fault line. The highest risk factor, the preexisting condition that affected my health status most, was being Black in America. This should not have been surprising, since accounts in the public health literature on epidemics in our nation's history—from the yellow fever epidemic of 1793 (Hogarth 2019a,b), to the smallpox epidemic of the 1860s (Downs 2012), to the Spanish flu pandemic of 1918 (Gamble 2010)—reveal similar racialized narratives: racism and segregation limited access to diagnosis and care and led to propagandized unsubstantiated prejudices about susceptibility to illness (Hogarth 2019a,b; Viboud and Lessler 2018). None of these epidemiological analyses predicted the challenges we faced as events unfolded for us.

Forcing us into a state of global anxiety and fear of annihilation, the pandemic had us trapped in our homes, quarantined for days, weeks, months on end. There was no shopping, diminished material indulgence, no bars, no in-person social gatherings; instead we were mesmerized by daily counts of the dead. Doctors were turned into frontline soldiers with inadequate protection. Some of the sick got care; others, often people of color, were turned away from hospitals to die at home. In Georgia, where 83 percent of Covid-19 cases were African Americans, Governor Brian Kemp, a white man, against all medical advice in April, shockingly lifted the state's shelter-in-place order to reopen businesses while infection rates continued to rise. And when Mayor Keisha Lance Bottoms of Atlanta, a Black woman, toed the public health line by maintaining the shelter-in-place, she received a disturbing text message that she then tweeted (see Figure 10.1).

Then the euphemism "essential worker" was coined. In the past, that term would have been a step up for slaves, but it stirs ambivalence now. What did we get? Rationalization, fanning of racial hatred, depraved indifference, blatant denial, a government that says there is no systemic racism. We, as citizens in a democratic nation, felt betrayed, as we all experienced some measure of devaluation by a government that acted immorally. The veil was lifted to reveal a deep violation of what is right for us all. If, before Covid-19 African Americans carried moral injury by proxy for generations as descendants of slaves, now

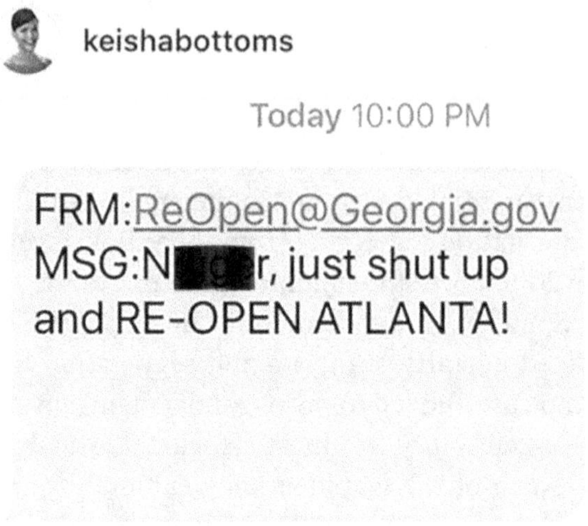

Figure 10.1 Racial epithet[2] received by Mayor Keisha Lance Bottoms.

it was moral injury front and center for all of us. We did not know it would be a perfect storm for an uprising, but maybe we secretly hoped, because how else could we discharge the rage of betrayal than by living out the American tradition— from the Boston Tea Party through the civil rights movement—of protesting injustice.

Against this social backdrop, on May 25, 2020, a murder—no, a lynching—shook our nation. George Floyd was an ordinary man, killed over a 20-dollar bill. The crime might have ended up in the police files, along with those of thousands of other ordinary, unarmed, murdered Black men. But Darnella Frazier, a 17-year-old high school student, in the face of four-armed Minneapolis police officers, stood her ground and videorecorded[3] the lynching with her cellphone. Her pictures exposed Officer Derek Chauvin's cavalier, almost casual expression—as if he were posing for a photo—as his knee compressed George Floyd's chest and neck for eight minutes, 45 seconds, while Floyd gasped "I can't breathe" sixteen times.[4] That video shook the world. Was it just the iPhone we needed to crack the disavowal of reality and personal responsibility for the endemic racial violence, and call attention to the fact that people of color live under constant threat every day? Amy Cooper's call to the police, for example, positioned Christian Cooper, an African American Harvard-educated birdwatcher walking peacefully through New York's Central Park on that same fated day in May, but one step away from becoming a twenty-first-century Emmett Till.

On June 7, 2020, CNN reported that demonstrations in Brazil, Argentina, Kenya, South Africa, France, Germany, and a host of other nations mirrored those in the U.S. A young Black man interviewed during a demonstration that day was asked by the reporter, "Being in the crowds, are you afraid of getting the virus?" He replied, "I can risk the virus if it means I fight for social justice." It is both profound and powerful that people willingly risked exposure during the pandemic of the virus to fight the pandemic of racism. The words of Claude McKay (1953) are uncannily apropos: in his poem "If We Must Die," written as a response to white mob attacks on African American communities during the infamous Red Summer of 1919,[5] he wrote, "If we must die, O let us nobly die/So that our precious blood may not be shed/In vain; then even the monsters we defy/Shall be constrained to honor us though dead!" (p. 36).

As the demonstrations waged day after day, we craved moral leadership. And so, it happened: In the absence of a moral leader to unite us, a symbol of injustice was created to mobilize the people. The hero of the moment became "we the people," who galvanized an uprising—the Black Lives Matter movement. George Floyd came to symbolize for the movement the moral injury that, for African Americans, stretched back generations, but now afflicted the nation. The parallel mirroring international demonstrations communicated to the world that the real pandemic was racism, and that Black Rage could be a shared, mobilizing human experience. Somehow, the daily demonstrations that month, almost two thousand nationwide, cracked the societal disavowal of personal responsibility for the violence, cruelty, suffering, pain, and denial of promised freedom in understanding the narrative of the American psyche; until then, the legacy of racism had prevented us from becoming a universal "we" even during a pandemic. The shocking effect of the Black Lives Matter demonstrations galvanizing the movement during a pandemic, however, made me ask, how did the murder of George Floyd catalyze a worldwide reaction that exposed a deeper questioning of the racial fractures in American society?

Moral Injury as Foundational

As I was pondering how to explain the basis for the moral injury—essential to understanding this series of events—without a lengthy exposition of American history, my unconscious took me to a book I had read at age sixteen that helped me integrate these ideas. Frederick Douglass's speech "The Meaning of July Fourth for the Negro" (1852) helped me organize a psychoanalytic framework to understand the connection of the social upheaval during the pandemic to the Black Lives Matter protests in response to the lynching of George Floyd.

Douglass escaped slavery in 1838 and lived as a free man in Massachusetts. In 1852, at the Ladies' Anti-Slavery Society in Rochester, New York, he spoke on the occasion of the Fourth of July. Here is what historians consider the most moving passage of his famous speech:

> What, to the American slave, is your 4th of July? I answer; a day that reveals to him, more than all other days in the year, the gross injustice and cruelty to which he is the constant victim. To him, your celebration is a sham; your boasted liberty, an unholy license; your national greatness, swelling vanity; your sounds of rejoicing are empty and heartless; your denunciations of tyrants, brass fronted impudence; your shouts of liberty and equality, (hollow) mockery; your prayers and hymns, your sermons and thanksgivings, with all your religious parade and solemnity, are, to him, mere bombast, fraud, deception, impiety, and hypocrisy— a thin veil to cover up crimes which would disgrace a nation of savages. There is not a nation on the earth guilty of practices more shocking and bloody than are the people of these United States, at this very hour
>
> (p. 192)

Douglass's speech helped me make the connection between enduring the sense of moral injury that dates back to slavery right up to myriad reports of contemporary racial violence in our country. In the American narrative, the two powerful stories of dehumanization and degradation are those of Native Americans and African Americans. Native Americans had their land stolen and suffered genocide.

Africans were kidnapped from their home continent and enslaved. The two groups are united in moral injury, a concept I will explain. It is at the core of our suffering as oppressed groups in America.

Jonathan Shay, a psychiatrist and classics scholar, coined the term *moral injury* while working with Vietnam vets. In his defining paper, Shay (2014) explains:

> Moral injury is present when there has been a betrayal of what is right either by a person in legitimate authority or by one's self in a high stakes situation. ... moral injury impairs the capacity for trust and elevates despair, suicidality, and interpersonal violence.
>
> (p. 182)

In *Achilles in Vietnam*, Shay (1994) finds the template for the concept in Homer's *Iliad*, in which Achilles is enraged when his commander betrays him. The moral injury of betrayal, Shay writes, "impairs a person's dignity by a violation of what's right" (p. 21). Shay describes Achilles's "indignant rage," signaling that this is rage at being treated unfairly, as the "word *dignity* [is] hidden in the word *indignant*" (p. 21). He distinguishes it from *berserk* rage, which refers to a "blood-crazed" state of fury (p. 77). Shay recognizes that the challenge is to exercise the rage of indignation while controlling the retaliatory murderous rage.

Mildred Antonelli (2017) further develops the moral injury concept to refer to "a core component of trauma that occurs when one's actions have profoundly violated one's code of ethics, when one has been a victim of such violation, or when one has been a passive witness of such violation" (p. 406). In essence, it is "inhumane behavior experienced as a betrayal of what is right" (p. 407). The concept of betrayal trauma in the literature on domestic violence also draws on the importance of this core element of the betrayal of trust (Platt, Barton, and Freyd 2009).

How do we understand the cause of the moral injury in this circumstance? My answer: Frederick Douglass indicts his fellow countrymen in an unparalleled, poignant address for betraying the Constitution's promise of liberty and protection for the descendants of slaves brought to this country from Africa. The betrayal occurs on many societal levels, whether it is the betrayal of their humanity by making their property or that of inflicting on them such violence that the contract of equal rights and equal protection under the law is broken. Those are betrayals reaching back generations for African Americans, and the national guilt has never been absolved.

This history of violence and injustice is recalled every time an unarmed Black man is killed. Approximately 300 Black Americans are killed by police annually. In 2018, *The Lancet* published a study by David Williams's group at Harvard (Bor et al. 2018). Mental health reports were correlated with data on shootings, revealing that every time an unarmed Black American is shot in the United States, the mental health of African Americans in the state where the shooting took place is adversely affected for three months, while that of white Americans usually remains largely unaffected.

If George Floyd's murder had occurred in isolation, the mourning might have been restricted to the African American community. But it occurred in the setting of a world crisis that magnified and extended the communal effect. The uprising carrying the indignant rage of moral injury—could we believe our eyes?—stretched across culture, race, gender, age, and national boundaries. As the uprising swelled with the Black Lives Matter movement at its core, it was carried along by the outcome of African Americans' moral injury: Our moral injury is a specific kind of rage—Black Rage. For African Americans, living in a racist society entails daily devaluation and degradation. Black Rage, conceptualized here as an adaptive mental construct, carries a unique transgenerational valence and, from a psychoanalytic standpoint, is a powerful and necessary defensive psychic force. Black Rage protects, preserving dignity and self-worth, thereby mitigating the impact of racial trauma. This point is essential in understanding racial trauma and its damaging effects at the individual and group level, as well as the protective value of nurturing and mobilizing Black Rage as an adaptive and dynamic defensive construct.

Having developed in the particular cultural context of African American history and oppression, Black Rage as a construct also contains the superego imperative of what is right and the collective unconscious store of transgenerational traumas and defensive directives that manifests in an enduring sense of moral injury. It can be said that there is a libidinal cathexis to the superego imperative when the sense of what is right is violated in moral injury. The rage is recruited intrapsychically to counter the attack from the racist's projection and the devaluation inflicted on the self. In this situation, the Black Rage construct does more than shield the self and the self's sense of worth. It protects the self from internalizing the devaluation of racism and, at the same time, reinforces a superego imperative that is experienced in a sense of moral injury. Shielding the self with the mobilized rage creates a metaphoric force field, as it were, protecting the vulnerable self with a counterphobic defense, as for the oppressed person there is an intrapsychic tradeoff: it is better to feel rage than fear or devaluation. If the person of color can modulate and control the activated rage affect, by mobilizing the Black Rage construct toward defensive aims when under racist attack, the individual is able to stave off retaliatory aggression, resist internalizing the incoming aggression and devaluation, and convert psychic turmoil into an adaptive response.

Would it surprise you to know that I, too, a Black psychoanalyst, have Black Rage?

It is well-encapsulated, stored in my mind; it protects my sense of self and fuels my drive to write, because Black Rage, as an adaptive construct, promotes defensive sublimations. The activated Black Rage construct serves a protective function as I work to modulate the reactive rage while living in a racist society that assaults my consciousness daily. Michelle Obama (2016) once said, "When they go low, we go high." Stacey Abrams fueled her rage at her manifestly unfair loss of the 2018 governor's race in Georgia into an historic grassroots campaign against voter suppression in the South. Without doubt, this campaign galvanized the 200 percent increase in voter turnout that turned Georgia from red to blue in the 2020 presidential election. Might one postulate that these are examples of controlled, functional Black Rage acting as a mobilizing force?

Another extraordinary contemporary example of Black Rage, which by definition promotes controlled and functional defensive operations, is depicted in Figure 10.2: a stretch of 16th Street in Washington, D.C., was renamed Black Lives Matter Plaza in response

Figure 10.2 Black lives matter plaza, Washington, D.C., 2020; photo by Jurveston, flickr.

to the many demonstrations for social justice. And if riots are "the language of the unheard," as Dr. Martin Luther King Jr. (1968) once remarked, then Mayor Muriel Bowser, in big bold yellow letters, silently screamed to the demonstrators "I hear you!" On the group level, as the rage was modulated and the call for justice given recognition, the Washington demonstrations became more peaceful. One might go so far as to say that the experience of recognition by Mayor Bowser had a therapeutic calming effect on the protesters. Harnessed on a global level, as we have all borne witness, Black Rage catalyzed a mass realization and galvanized a movement

In theorizing on the psychic resilience of oppressed people, it is necessary to point out that rage may not always be mobilized in an adaptive way. In the early days of the pandemic, as steam had been building in the pressure cooker of our society's unacknowledged racism, the sense of moral injury had become acute. At the time George Floyd was murdered, it was difficult to modulate the reactions of rage on an individual and group level. Here, the affect of rage in the rage reaction must be distinguished from Black Rage as an adaptive defensive construction. Unmodulated rage as an affect, if not mobilized adaptively, can be internalized or externalized to an excessive degree and should be distinguished from controlled, modulated Black Rage as a defensive adaptation. The sequelae of internalized rage, when it cannot be mobilized toward an adaptive end, can produce severe psychic consequences, including but not limited to mood symptoms and problematic effects on interpersonal functioning. If externalized, unmodulated and uncontrolled rage can be discharged and lead to violence, especially when the moral injury is not given recognition, as, for example, in the demonstrations of 2020 that led to destruction of property.[6]

That Freud's early work on conceptualizing trauma was foundational to psychoanalytic theory, and that psychoanalytic theory is conceptually crucial in understanding racial trauma, might seem ironic. His retreat from conceptualizing a theory of oppression and racial trauma demonstrates the extent to which internal conflict and trauma, even for a genius of his magnitude, had far-reaching implications inhibiting the development of psychoanalytic theory—and consequently, our field.

Conceptualizing Freud's Secret Black Rage

In "A Disturbance of Memory on the Acropolis," Freud (1936) identified the "limitations and poverty of our conditions of life in my youth" as contributors to his dissociative neurotic symptom at the Acropolis, which was indicative of his success neurosis (p. 247). Dorothy Holmes (2006) eloquently reinterprets this symptom with reference to the poverty and anti-Semitism Freud endured. His emphasis on oedipal conflict as a wholly adequate explanation for his success neurosis may have further contributed to the early focus on oedipal theory over deeper considerations of race and class in the field as a whole. That the young Freud fantasized about Hannibal is telling in this connection. Hannibal the Semite was actually an African general, a true conqueror feared by many, which fits quite nicely into the narrative.[7] For the boy whose father could show him no model to fight back against racist degradation and relieve him of humiliation, the secret identification with the Black general both encapsulated and expressed, I believe, Freud's Black Rage.

Freud stopped short of conceptualizing racial trauma as significant in theory, or race as a factor in the development of identity; however, I speculate that in fantasy Hannibal represented a powerful, wished-for African general father figure as a model who asserted Blackness, and that this fantasy served as an unconscious container of Freud's secret Black Rage. Freud's allusion to fathers in *Civilization and Its Discontents* (1930) lends credence to this focus on the importance of one's father as a role model and stabilizing force: "I cannot," he wrote, "think of any need in childhood as strong as that for a father's protection" (p. 72).

This unconscious reservoir of Black Rage contained in the fantasy of Hannibal, it is my contention, fueled Freud's ambitious climb to an intellectual Acropolis—an oedipal triumph that was a challenge for him to manage as he held at bay the humiliation and damaging assaults of anti-Semitism along the way. Imagining a psychic sphere in which there was no race with the vision of a universal mind idealized the dream of human equality and represented a defensive solace to endure the brutal anti-Semitism of which he was surely a constant victim. His internalized racism is still represented in his writings—in part, in his references to a primitive racial Other. There was no analyst to help heal his racial trauma, to help him mobilize his Black Rage further into an antiracist stance. In some ways, this crippled him intrapsychically from envisioning antiracism, even in theory.

Defining Black Rage as a Functional and Adaptive Mental Construct

The concept of Black Rage dates back to the seminal 1968 book *Black Rage* by William Grier and Price Cobbs (1968), both African American psychiatrists, who described the myriad ways Black people living in a racist society feel devalued. In *Black Rage*, published in the aftermath of the rioting that followed Dr. Martin Luther King Jr.'s assassination, amid the specific societal and cultural context of the civil rights struggle and the rise of the Black Power movement, Grier and Cobbs called for revised psychoanalysis of racism that located the afterlife of slavery in our psyche, not just our politics.

From their work with urban youth with substance-abuse disorders 40 years later, Hardy and Qureshi (2012) built on Grier and Cobbs's ideas to formulate the concept of rage as "the culmination of pervasive, chronic, and recurring experiences with devaluation and the dehumanization of loss without benefit of redress that is directly and poignantly linked to experiences with degradation, marginalization and devaluation" (p. 335). Rage can be dysfunctional if suppressed; internalized, it turns in on the self, especially in the face of ongoing trauma, leading to depression, self-destructive behavior, substance abuse, and even suicide. If externalized, dysfunctional rage can lead to violence. Black Rage is contextualized in African American culture, then, and defined as operative in the sustained response of oppressed people who endure repeated acts of injustice without opportunity for redress. Black Rage builds up as an accumulated adaptive reaction to experiences of racism and discrimination over generations and applies, specifically, to the reaction to ongoing oppression. In this context Grier and Cobbs, and Hardy and Qureshi, all seemed to recognize that Black Rage, if mobilized in a functional way, has a culturally specific adaptive potential that can be transformative.

Black Rage, formulated here as a mental construct, exists in a specific dynamic equilibrium as a compromise formation in the psyche that is a functional adaptation for oppressed people who suffer racial trauma and racial degradation, one that can be mobilized for the purpose of defense, adaptation, or even psychic growth. The connection to an enduring sense of moral injury makes clear its defensive protection of the dignity of the racial self[8] for oppressed people, for whom there is a libidinal cathexis to the superego imperative when the sense of what is right is violated in moral injury. Psychoanalytic theory is conceptually crucial in understanding racial trauma, and integrating the construct of Black Rage into our theoretical formulations extends our understanding of oppression and racial trauma with far-reaching implications for our theory and clinical work. Integrating the concept of Black Rage as an adaptational psychic construct into analytic theory validates and directs therapeutic attention to the traumatic experiences of the oppressed.

An Evolving Psychoanalytic Formulation of Functional Black Rage

The concept of otherness as a theoretical construct had not yet been formulated but was implied by Freud when he wrote, in *Civilization and Its Discontents*, "It is always possible to bring together a considerable number of people in love so long as there are other people left over to receive the manifestations of their aggressiveness" (1930, p. 114). Formulating the concept of Other on the basis of race came much later in psychoanalytic theory. In *Black Skin, White Masks*, Frantz Fanon (1952) wrote, "There is no longer any doubt that the true Other for the white man is and remains the Black man" (p. 206). Fanon wrote poignantly of the damaging consequences to the psyche of internalizing racism for the Black man who is the persistent object of devaluation, projected aggression, and racist degradation, substantiating the importance of psychic defense in mitigating the associated racial trauma. While expressions of racism can manifest in a multiplicity of ways, there is always a projected devaluation of the person of color which, Fanon maintained, is internalized by Black people as a sense of inferiority. Taken together, individual and group experiences become components of a social system that bombards people of color daily with evidence of systemic disregard and devaluation of a person or group's humanity in order that another group might assert its privilege and domination. A society structured by racism does this in many forms and in varying degrees, always creating a moral injury and individual racial trauma, as well as what I will term group *oppression trauma*. The oppressed know this, but the oppressors, who exist in a moral void, must be shown it.

To understand how race is recruited as a marker of difference in the American arsenal of Othering requires psychoanalytic formulation from the reference point of a socially embedded narrative. The American cultural ego ideal of greatness for whiteness thrives while projecting its destructiveness onto a racial Other; whiteness projects while Blackness endures. The construct of Black Rage psychically bolsters that endurance. As a construct in the mind, similar to the structural model, where mental agencies have psychic functions, Black Rage carries associated mental representations drawn from both the individual and the collective cultural unconscious and serves a crucial defensive and adaptive function. As such, these state and functional qualities influence how rage as an affect is experienced and expressed.

The construct of Black Rage as a mobilizing adaptive defense is a missing link in psychoanalytic theory conceptualizing the psychic functioning and resilience of oppressed people whose dignity is constantly assaulted. Black Rage as a construct functions as an adaptation to oppression trauma for those who endure the projected destructiveness in the position of a socially sanctioned Other living in a racist society. It proved difficult to construct this analytic scaffold. Rage, as a reaction, is not usually conceptualized as part of a defensive construct or adaptational response.

In a racist society, built on the paradigm of a white superiority/Black inferiority binary, socially sanctioned ego distortions, coupled with defective and regressive superego functioning, promote the disavowal of the persistent violence and aggression directed at the Black Other. A Eurocentric theoretical formulation devoid of social context that ignores racial trauma as a fundamental vicissitude in development, and the fact that derivatives of oppression can become intrapsychically embedded in traumatic ways, limits our understanding of otherness. To fully elaborate the adaptive function of the Black Rage construct, then, theory must factor in the contributing cultural effect of the white-supremacist social backdrop of American society, in which the individual is not "raceless" but is in fact a Black racialized Other. It is through white supremacy's racializing lens that Black people are othered and experienced as objects of constant threat. Indeed, the white-dominant, white-supremacist paradigm is projected onto the entire social frame, requiring ongoing psychic vigilance for the person or group of color.

Such vigilance requires that people of color modulate and control rage reactions on an ongoing basis. Mitigating and suppressing the reactive rage and converting the resultant psychic turmoil to an adaptive response requires the defensive operations of repression and sublimation.

Insistence on a moral imperative in the associated moral injury reinforces the individual's effort to resist retaliating, as they appeal to what is right is recruited from the unconscious transgenerational data bank of African Americans, which includes the cultural dictum to retain the capacity to love even when being hated. Even if this move is successful, it occurs at a psychic cost to the individual because the deflection of devaluation is never complete, and significant psychic energy is expended to quell the retaliatory rageful impulses stirred up. This transformation of initially helpless rage to a mobilizing defensive force is an aspect of what Dionne Powell (2020) has described as resisting "psychic enslavement" to achieve "psychic emancipation." Black Rage, and the social and cultural experience that is its context, can consequently be understood as a deeply held adaptation that enduringly impacts the individual's intrapsychic and interpersonal functioning.

A white-supremacist society, to formulate from a Kleinian perspective, operates on a paranoid-schizoid group level whereby racist projections invade the intersubjective space, and the Black racial Other is forced into the position of deflecting, defending against, metabolizing, or internalizing the toxic projections of the white-dominant society. Socially sanctioned projective attacking of the Black Other is raised from the individual level to the organizing frame of the culture. As the cultural norm, it becomes a ubiquitous contributor to the racial trauma invading the intersubjective field, both analytic and cultural. Early analytic theorists, having whitewashed the cultural field, had not identified this ongoing threat as coming from an external cultural source or realized that the analyst's unconscious racism might collude with the background culture in creating a racialized intersubjective field.

In understanding the significance of this defensive protection, Bion's concept of *linking capacity* (1956) is particularly helpful. Bion (1959) underscored that the main theme was not just an attack on the link but on the consequences of such an attack:

> on the one hand the ... disposition to excessive destructiveness, hatred, and envy ... [and] on the other the environment which, at its worst, denies ... the use of the mechanisms of splitting and projective identification, resulting in [what Bion terms] destructive attacks on the link.
>
> (p. 313)

So, to apply Bion's formulation, the Black racial Other is repeatedly forced into the position of psychic shock absorber struggling to withstand these attacks on linking, in order to preserve the capacity to think. The adaptive function of the Black Rage construct affords defensive protection in withstanding the damaging consequences of an attack.

For the Black Other in a racist society, then, the attack on linking is raised further to the level of the cultural frame, in which white supremacy, through its many sophisticated projective forms, dictates the norm and infiltrates individual intersubjectivities and intersubjective cultural spaces. It would seem logical, then, that in a racist society the oppressed are in a constant state of readiness to mobilize and modulate Black Rage as an adaptive defense, even when their affective state is manifestly calm. The social conditions of slavery and the subsequent period of Jim Crow lynching, out of which this adaptive strategy evolved, attest the great survival value of the strategy of holding indignant rage intrapsychically while appearing manifestly calm.

In a society operating on this paranoid-schizoid level, Black Rage would be a necessary construct for the healthy functioning of the Black Other. Attempting a psychoanalytic formulation of Black Rage raises the question of whether a theory of oppression must first be formulated in which the construct, as a functional adaptation, would be a normal developmental acquisition in preserving the integrity of the racialized self that must navigate a racist society. In theory, we would then be forced to posit that there exists a racialized self with a developmental trajectory integral to the formation of identity.

Black Rage Carries Transgenerational Mental Representations in Oppression Trauma

In the speculative work *Totem and Taboo*, Freud (1912–1913) theorized a type of cultural memory with associated mental representations that could be transmitted across generations; this laid the foundation for modern conceptualizations about the transgenerational transmission of trauma. Operating from his own cultural context, Vamik Volkan (Volkan, Ast, and Greer 2002) integrated his work with other psychoanalysts' work with Holocaust survivors (Freud and Burlingham 1942; Friedman 1949) and theorized a mode of transgenerational transmission in the setting of mass historical traumas. He formulated that

> transgenerationally transmitted self- and object-images ... belonging to the survivors of mass shared trauma often initiate specifically history-related *unconscious fantasies* in their descendants, whose task it becomes to deal with the shame, rage, helplessness, entitlement, and guilt that the previous generations have been unable to work through for themselves.
>
> (p. 17)

Volkan (2013)[9] wrote compellingly of "collective trauma," referring to specific mass historical events that have caused "a large group to face drastic losses, feel helpless and victimized by another group, and share a humiliating injury," the mental representations of which become intertwined with the group's core identity, and are thus labeled the group's *chosen trauma*. On a dynamic level, Volkan goes on to map out how

> large-group historical traumas are thus not simply comprised of static, shared conscious memories of the event. Rather, they are highly dynamic complexes of recollections, fantasies, affects, wishes, and defenses (i.e., mental representations) whose influences are transmitted from generation to generation…. It is this complex of mental representation that is passed to future generations who, as 'carriers' must cope with the unmastered psychological tasks.
>
> (Volkan, Ast, and Greer 2002, p. 25)

This concept of "mental representations" as part of the transgenerational transmission of group trauma can indeed be applied cross-culturally, and specifically to the African American experience. For African Americans, generations[10] of chattel slavery and its later derivatives, the Black Codes and Jim Crow segregation, promoted centuries-long socially sanctioned and culturally endemic traumatic mass violence. In addition, the related mental representations, oral traditions, and even social structures representative of slavery have become psychically imprinted, overlaid now by violent societal events that reactivate traumatic reactions. So, while mass traumatic events can become the focal point in a group's identification and history, as in Volkan's designation of the concept of chosen trauma, the more pervasive nature of ongoing racial violence in American history makes the more global term *oppression trauma* warranted as a descriptor of this culturally specific manifestation.

In a contemporary sociocultural analysis, Hardy (2019) similarly applies the term *oppression trauma*, to encompass "the interlocking of sociocultural oppression and trauma that is systemic, pervasive and protracted over time," and continues to postulate astutely that "race, class, ethnicity, gender, sexual locations and mental and physical ability ... are all social locations [that can be] connected to the experience of sociocultural oppression" (p. 135; see also Hardy 2013). The psychoanalytic formulation presented here integrates and makes particular to the African American experience the ideas of Volkan and Hardy. The traumas and systemic oppression endured by African Americans that began with slavery are represented mentally in the collective cultural unconscious, having been passed down transgenerationally, and are activated, amplified, and repeated by the ongoing violence of systemic racism. That is the definition proposed here of *oppression trauma*. From this perspective, the Black Rage construct as a mental agency operates as a focal vehicle carrying mental representations from the individual, transgenerational familial, and collective cultural unconscious and represents the convergence of psychic and sociocultural trauma embedded largely in the unconscious domain.

This oppression drama not only occurs on an individual level, but also connects on a transgenerational intersubjective level; African American parental role models and family oral traditions serve, in conscious and unconscious ways, to reinforce the cultural moral imperative of voicing the betrayal of the moral injury while also striving to retain the capacity to love while being hated.[11] As James Baldwin reminds us, African Americans generation to generation have demonstrated in word and deed to their sons and daughters, "Please try to remember that what they believe, as well as what they do and cause you to endure, does not testify to your inferiority but to their inhumanity" (1962, p. 8). Baldwin, in this letter to his nephew, demonstrated in *The Fire Next Time*, in so many ways, that for African Americans there is a transgenerational teaching of defensive strategies drawn from collective unconscious stores that foster group identification, cohesion, and survival. Black Rage, as formulated here, is an example. That victims of collective trauma pass down cultural teachings about threat, group preservation, and the sense of an "historical self" is a well-documented cross-cultural finding (Hirschberger 2018).

Surviving degradation, from slavery to Reconstruction and through Jim Crow to the civil rights movement, provided ample traumatic lived experience to perfect Black Rage as a transgenerational defensive and adaptational weapon that operationally suppresses and sublimates rage reactions to ongoing oppression. At the heart of

Baldwin's advice to his nephew, his namesake, is not only the directive to repress the rage but, further, to do it "with love": "We, with love, shall force our brothers to see themselves as they are and to cease fleeing from reality and begin to change"; he also reminded young James that "you come from sturdy stock … men who … in the teeth of the most terrifying odds, achieved an unassailable monumental dignity" (p. 10). It is this "with love" that is so powerful in Baldwin. He asks us to withstand hate, while maintaining our capacity to love, using

> the word 'love' here not merely in the personal sense but as a state of being, or a state of grace—not in the infantile American sense of being made happy but in the tough and universal sense of quest and daring and growth.
>
> (1962, p. 95)

I believe Baldwin recognized the need to protect (as Bion might interject, protect our linking capacity), to preserve the capacity for receptivity and mirroring inherent in the capacity to love while one endures devaluating attacks in being hated. The mantra *Love so as not to hate* is transmitted transgenerationally in African American families and in the symbolic function of the Black church as the mortar of psychic resiliency.

Creating a theoretical scaffolding for a theory of oppression trauma that encompasses racial trauma will facilitate our understanding of the individual familial and cultural mitigating factors that are protective. For African American individuals and families, especially those that are resilient, Black Rage is an internalized adaptive construct that is fortifying. If the defensive directives are cultivated, internalized, and passed down, Black Rage, as a mental agency with defensive functions, supports African American adolescents in acquiring the ability to metabolize their rage reactions to discrimination across development. An understanding of oppression trauma makes clear that developmental factors that enhance one's ability to tolerate frustration and promote what Bion (1963, 1970) termed the ability to "suffer experience" can be crucial to enduring racial trauma, especially when containing familial objects serve as role models.

This may speak to why historically Black colleges, for example, can provide protective growth-promoting environments for Black adolescents during this important developmental period, to expose them to role models who reflect and support the adaptive mobilization of Black Rage, foster group solidarity, and consolidate group racial identity. Acquiring and exercising Black Rage as a buffer relieves the developing racial self from absorbing the assault from persecution, demoralization, and the self-hatred that can result from internalizing devaluing experiences; it facilitates metabolization of these toxic experiences, thereby preserving the capacity for receptivity and connection, and affords protection of the dignity of the racial self.

Clinical Extensions of Black Rage as a Culturally Contextualized Adaptation

Enduring discriminatory experiences and the attendant racial trauma exact a biological toll on a physical and psychological level. If the rage activated in withstanding the discriminatory experiences of oppression trauma cannot be controlled and mobilized in a functional and adaptive way, retaliatory aggression cannot be contained. On an individual level, one is left defenseless, vulnerable to assaults on the self and at risk of internalizing one's degradation or devaluation, or acting out the stirred-up anger. Influenced by when in development racialized traumatic experiences occur, by the integrity of one's premorbid personality structure, and by accessible ego resources, a range of pathological manifestations result from withstanding racially traumatic attacks. Symptomatic manifestations include depression, substance abuse, and an array of other psychological and physical symptoms (Hart, Chapter 7; Roberts and Rollins, 2020; Stoute in press). A racist society presents ongoing threats, so the allostatic load of enduring these racially traumatic experiences provokes post-traumatic reactions (Hart, Chapter 7).

In working with patients in psychotherapy and analysis who have been victims of persistent racial trauma, Hart (2019, Chapter 7) reports, as does Hardy (Hardy and Laszloffy 1995; Hardy and Qureshi 2012), an array of symptoms that adult patients who have endured racially traumatic experience endorse upon presentation for treatment:

> depression, suicidality, anxiety, paranoia, phobic reactions, self-destructive or violent behavior, sleep or appetite disturbance, weight loss or weight gain, anhedonia, somatic problems (without

a clear physiological cause), acute relationship conflicts, chronic relational difficulties, memory and concentration disturbances, dissociation and related forms of discontinuity, and substance abuse and dependency.

(Hart 2019, p. 16)

For children and adolescents, the consequences similarly manifest in physical symptoms and mood symptoms but also as anxiety and behavioral problems (Brody et al. 2006). Defensive operations, as in the adaptive mobilization of the Black Rage construct on an individual level, foster resilience and mitigate the allostatic load of racial trauma. In the psychoanalytic theory of oppression proposed here could a developmental line be established, then, for the adaptive function of Black Rage in the defensive construct that promotes resilience in enduring the assault on dignity that oppression trauma poses for marginalized people of color?

Implications of Postulating Rage as an Emotional Drive with a Developmental Line

Panksepp's revolutionary theory of Affective Neuroscience (2005) debunks Freud's binary categorization of the instinctual drives, offering instead a nuanced, experimentally based formulation. Panksepp operates from the fundamental premise that "emotional feelings emerge from specific, evolutionarily dictated brain operating systems" (Davis and Montag 2019, p. 2). As demonstrated by experiments using electrical stimulation, pharmacological agents, and anatomical lesions of vertebrate brains, Panksepp identifies seven core primary process emotions that are shared universally by all human (and mammalian) brains; these core emotional systems, he theorizes, operate as "emotional action systems" that are localized anatomically to the limbic system of the human brain. Panksepp characterizes and documents seven primary-process emotional command systems: SEEKING/Expectancy, RAGE/Anger, FEAR/Anxiety, LUST/sexuality, CARE/Nurturing, PANIC/Sadness, and PLAY/Social Joy (Davis and Montag 2019, p. 3).[12] Based on Panksepp's taxonomy, Solms (2020) speaks to the formulation of RAGE, and each core primary emotion, as an emotional drive.

While the theory grounds these seven core emotional experiences in limbic response systems, childhood experience and cultural factors influence their expression throughout development. Although RAGE, for example, is a genetically based ancestral emotional drive shared by all mammals, Panksepp concedes that there is considerable variation in how and to what extent RAGE is expressed based on childhood experience, maternal–infant interaction, social learning, and cultural influence. Emotional learning and cultural socialization can also create unconscious associations that are trigger points for aggressiveness (Todorov and Bargh 2002). Further, in this new model, all the primary emotional systems, including RAGE, have developmental lines, and culture has an impact on development and expression.

Based on Panksepp's neurobiological formulation, I contend that Black Rage as a mental construct is one culturally specific developmental outcome for the expression of RAGE. Mental representations of oppression trauma, incorporated from the individual, transgenerational familial, and collective cultural unconscious, influence the progression and expression of RAGE. Black Rage, having evolved in the African American cultural context, has primed the defensive operations, on an individual and cultural level, that confer psychic protection and resilience in response to the assault on dignity of the dehumanizing experiences of oppression that began with slavery. Defensive operations that prioritize repressing and controlling overt expression of retaliatory aggression toward the aim of sublimation are given primacy and intergenerational solidity. In this way, social and cultural derivatives of oppression can enduringly embed trauma intrapsychically.

Conclusion and Moving Forward

It is too early to fully comprehend the forces that led to the Black Lives Matter uprisings of 2020 and the multiracial, multicultural global response, but I will offer a preliminary formulation. Perhaps the interweaving of the Covid-19 pandemic and worldwide uprisings sparked anew[12] our awareness of what I envision as a cross-cultural intersubjective space across the globe.

George Floyd became an icon of suffering for all African Americans, especially African American men. Remarkably, he has also become a *symbolic self* for people across the world who have suffered degradation and dehumanization, people who now identify with him—and, through him, with Black America. The image of the white policeman kneeling, with his hand in his pocket, on a Black man's neck, enacting the scene of "conqueror" and "conquered," evoked the deep sense of moral injury that I believe resides in all of us. Dare I hypothesize that these dynamics of devaluation and oppression reside in the collective cultural unconscious of all nations, and that the symbolic self of George Floyd allowed a reflective mentalization of suffering and recognition across nations? While not everyone who utters "Black Lives Matter" subscribes to the movement, many now see the reality that too often in our past Black lives did *not* matter, and our global community now identifies with the moral injury to which Black Rage corresponds. Without Black Rage as a mobilizing force to carry the moral injury of African Americans, the history of our nation demonstrates that racism would consume us—as individuals, as a nation, and maybe as a global community—and strip us of our moral integrity and humanity, one dead Black or brown body at a time.

The picture that shocked the world, and the iPhone video that amplified its dramatic effects, afforded a vast virtual witnessing and a recognition of racial violence by the global community. Citizens of the world came to recognize the operational moral imperative that Black lives must matter in order for all lives to matter. Black Rage as an adaptive and mobilizing force, and the moral injury it has carried for African Americans across generations, preserved an entry point for white America—and citizens across the globe—to experience symbolically and carry together our oppression traumas as shared, mobilizing human experiences.

Presented here, out of this specific historical and cultural experience, is a unique psychoanalytic formulation of Black Rage[13] as a functional and dynamic adaptive construct operating in the psyches of the oppressed, of its mobilization on a group level in uprisings, and of how, during the Covid-19 pandemic, it operated as an intersubjective connecting force across the globe.

Can we import the concept of Black Rage into the psychoanalytic lexicon? Psychoanalytic theory must allow a space for the protective function of RAGE as having a defensive adaptation. In theorizing about the psychic resilience of the oppressed, RAGE can be seen as a culturally primed emotional drive inherent in the Black Rage construct.

Importing the concept of Black Rage into the lexicon of analytic theory is crucial to constructing a scaffolding for theorizing on the psychology of oppression, the damaging effects of racial trauma, and the transgenerational transmission of trauma. We will never have more people of color in the field of psychoanalysis or other mental health fields, especially African American men, until we allow a psychic and theoretical space for the construct of Black Rage as a necessary adaptation to validate and allow for the traumatic experiences of the oppressed. No theory can become truly antiracist without integrating the functional utility of the Black Rage construct in its defensive protection of the racial self.

This opens a new chapter in our developing a psychoanalytic theory that recognizes the damaging effects of racial trauma and oppression as they impact individual subjectivity and the intersubjective cultural field. Further, this formulation elucidates the interface of the biopsychosocial dimensions of trauma on the border of the psyche and the internalization of culture. Not only do culture and the social surround impact the analytic dyad, but culture can be deeply and enduringly embedded in the psyche of the oppressor and oppressed alike.

We are a nation that boasts a Judeo-Christian tradition with a moral imperative at its core, but we will never realize *loving thy neighbor as thyself* or administer *liberty and justice for all* until we stop hating and projecting onto thy neighbor as the Other. In *Civilization and Its Discontents*, Freud (1930) wrote, "I may now add that civilization is a process in the service of Eros, whose purpose is to combine single human individuals, and after that families, then races, peoples and nations, into one great unity, the unity of mankind" (p. 122). Can this historical moment become a pivot point for more substantive conversation and action toward healing our culturally derived oppression traumas to recover and preserve our shared humanity? Black Rage is with us, in us and, as oppressed people have always known, can save us. Can we lean into and utilize the moral imperative carried in Black Rage as a radical catalyst for our shared psychoanalytic liberation?[14]

Notes

1 Full quote:

> To be a Negro in this country and to be relatively conscious is to be in a state of rage, almost all of the time—and in one's work. And part of the rage is this: It isn't only what is happening to you. But it's what's happening all around you and all of the time in the

face of the most extraordinary and criminal indifference, indifference of most white people in this country, and their ignorance. Now, since this is so, it's a great temptation to simplify the issues under the illusion that if you simplify them enough, people will recognize them. I think this illusion is very dangerous because, in fact, it isn't the way it works. A complex thing can't be made simple. You simply have to try to deal with it in all its complexity and hope to get that complexity across.

(James Baldwin, 1961 radio interview, WBAI New York)

2 On her Twitter account Mayor Bottoms revealed this racial epithet was texted to her phone number by an anonymous source. In her response she quoted the Rev. Martin Luther King Jr.: "Conscientious stupidity or sincere ignorance." The original tweet used the N—word. The "N—word" references the pejorative word used to refer to people of African heritage. It will not be reprinted in total here as it was in the original publication of this paper. The traumatogenic effect of using the N—word is discussed in chapter 11.

3 **Figure 2** of Derek Chauvin's knee on George Floyd's neck as Floyd gasped for air, a still image taken from a video by Darnella Frazier, which had been posted via Facebook via Agence France-Presse–Getty Image, was published under fair use laws in the original article in the *Journal of the American Psychoanalytic Association,* but permission to reprint in this volume could not be obtained by the publication date.

4 News reports at the time gave eight minutes, 45 seconds, as the time Floyd's neck was pinned by his assailant's knee. At the trial of ex-officer Derek Chauvin, however, it was revealed that Chauvin held his knee on Floyd's neck for nine minutes and 29 seconds, holding his knee in place even after his victim had stopped breathing and was dead. The prosecuting attorney, Jerry Blackwell, broke down this span of time into three intervals: "4 minutes and 45 seconds as Floyd cried out for help, 53 seconds as Floyd flailed due to seizures and 3 minutes and 51 seconds as Floyd was non-responsive" (CNN News, March 29, 2021).

5 On July 27, 1919, an African American teenager drowned in Lake Michigan after violating the unofficial segregation of Chicago's beaches and being stoned by a group of white youths. His death, and the police's refusal to arrest the white man whom eyewitnesses identified as causing it, sparked a week of rioting between gangs of Black and white Chicagoans, concentrated on the South Side neighborhood surrounding the stockyards. When the riots ended on August 3, 15 white and 23 Black people had been killed and more than 500 people injured; an additional 1,000 Black families had lost their homes when they were torched by [mainly white] rioters.

(History.com editors 2009, "The Red Summer of 1919")

Although the Black demonstrators were described in this *history.com* reference as "gangs," many other historical sources described them as demonstrators ("Red Summer of 1919: How Black WWI Vets Fought Back Against Racist Mobs" ©2019, A&E Television Networks, LLC, available at www.history.com/news/red-summer-1919-riots-chicago-dc-great-migration. All rights reserved. Used with permission).

6 The further extension of rage, and more complicated examples of how to modulate it in times of social upheaval, can be found in the mobilizing of rage toward revolution in colonialism, as discussed by Fanon, in the struggle for freedom by many African nations, later including South Africa, and in the civil rights movement in the United States. Fanon, in *The Wretched of the Earth* (1963), also pointed to the necessity of revolutionary counterviolence as the only way to overcome racialized trauma.

7 There is general agreement among historians that Hannibal was the son of Hamilcar Barca, the Barcas line being one of the most distinguished families in Carthage (Bradford 1981, p. 21). It is also often said that his family traced its origins back to Queen Elissa (Dido), the legendary founder of that great North African city. Little is known about his mother. There is historical debate as to whether being a native of a North African region implies Hannibal was a lighter-skinned African or a darker-skinned African (for a detailed historical review, see Chandler 1988). There are accounts of him as having a "dark-skinned face" (Donauer 1932, p. 244). Whether he was a Black (dark-skinned and indigenous) African or a light-skinned African, either would serve a role in the identification of African with Blackness. Freud was labeled a "black Jew," a curious racial/ethnic designation that had a connection to the social identity of Blackness as the symbolic oppressed minority. The line of historical debate, beyond my scope here, that speaks to the practice of intermarriage in North Africa at that time further complicates the issues.

8 See Holmes (2016b) and Stoute (2019), respectively, for discussions of how to define dignity and the importance of protecting the dignity of the self in racial trauma.

9 Volkan's lifelong work on conflict resolution, bringing ethnic groups together toward mutual understanding, peacemaking, and resolving interethnic conflict, has commanded accolades, awards, and international recognition including five Nobel peace prize nominations. Yet many LGBQT colleagues have expressed outrage at Volkan's reluctance to recant his writings, including a book edited with Charles Socarides (Socarides and Volkan 1992) about conversion treatments for homosexuality (1992), or renounce his past affiliation as vice president of NARTH (the National Association for Research and Therapy of Homosexuality), an organization that supports conversion therapy for minors. This, despite the fact that the American Psychoanalytic Association, as an organization, issued an apology to the LGBQT community in 2019 for discriminatory and exclusionary practices. At present, he is,

however, reconsidering these objections. Volkan's reluctance to recant seems ironic since it would be a logical extension of his theoretical position to extend his work to formulate that the discrimination endured by the LGBQT community is a culturally imposed mass trauma.

10 Wilkerson (2020) postulates that chattel slavery ran the course of 12 generations in America.

11 This cultural imperative was also reinforced during the civil rights movement through the model of Dr. Martin Luther King Jr. (1957), who took up the ideas of Mahatma Gandhi. Both espoused a moral philosophy of nonviolent resistance that, I would argue, was a derivative form of managing the rage of oppression toward a sublimated end while giving primacy to the sense of moral injury and assaulted dignity.

12 The capitalization is used to distinguish these emotional brain system labels as formulated in Panksepp's taxonomy from the use of the terms in ordinary language.

13 Winnicott (1967) speaks to this concept of cultural space in his classic paper "The Location of Cultural Experience." This idea was the conceptual forerunner of the concept of intersubjectivity, as Winnicott spoke to "the place where cultural experience is located in the potential space between the individual and the environment" (p. 370).

14 Erratum published *Journal of the American Psychoanalytic Association (2021), 69* (5): 1028.

In the article "Black rage: The psychic adaptation to the trauma of oppression" by Beverly J. Stoute (*Journal of the American Psychoanalytic Association,* Vol. 69, No. 2, pp. 259–290.

DOI: 10.1177/00030651211014207), an error appears in line 9 of the abstract (p. 259) and is repeated on p. 276, line 11. In both instances, the phrase "topographical model" should read "structural model." The correct language appears in this chapter.

References

Antonelli, M. (2017). Moral injury. *American Journal of Psychoanalysis* 77:406–416.

Baldwin, J. (1962). *The Fire Next Time.* New York: Vintage International, 1993.

Bion, W.R. (1956). Development of schizophrenic thought. *International Journal of Psychoanalysis* 37:344–346.

Bion, W.R. (1959). Attacks on linking. *International Journal of Psychoanalysis* 40:308–315.

Bion, W.R. (1963). *Elements of Psychoanalysis.* London: Heinemann.

Bion, W.R. (1970). *Attention and Interpretation.* London: Tavistock Publications.

Bor, J., Venkataramani, A.S., Williams, D.R. and Tsai, A.C. (2018). Police killings and their spillover effects on the mental health of black Americans: A population-based, quasi-experimental study. *The Lancet* 392:302–310.

Bradford, E. (1981). *Hannibal*. New York: Dorset Press.
Brody, G.H. Chen, Y.-F., Murray, V.M., Ge, X., Simons, R.L., Gibbons, F.X., Gerrard, M. and Cutrona, C.E. (2006). Perceived discrimination and the adjustment of African American youths: A five-year longitudinal analysis with contextual modification effects. *Child Development* 77:1170–1189.
Chandler, W.B. (1988). Hannibal: Nemesis of Rome. In *Great Black Leaders: Ancient and Modern*, ed. I. van Sertima. *Journal of African Civilizations* 9:282–321.
Davis, K.L. and Montag, C. (2019). Selected principles of Pankseppian affective neuroscience. *Frontiers in Neuroscience* 12, article 1025.
Donauer, F. (1932). *Swords against Carthage*. New York: Biblo & Tannen.
Douglass, F. (1852). The meaning of July Fourth for the negro: Speech at Rochester, New York, July 5, 1852, In *The Life and Writings of Frederick Douglass: Vol. 2. The Pre–Civil War Decade*, ed. P.S. Foner. New York: International Publishers, 1950, pp. 181–204.
Downs, J. (2012). *Sick from Freedom: African-American Illness and Suffering during the Civil War and Reconstruction*. New York: Oxford University Press.
Erikson, E.H. and Newton, H. (1973). *In Search of Common Ground: Conversations with Erik Erikson and Huey Newton*. New York: Norton.
Fanon, F. (1952). *Black Skin, White Masks*, transl. R. Philcox. New York: Grove Press, 2008.
Fanon, F. (1963). *The Wretched of the Earth*, transl. R. Philcox. New York: Grove Press, 2004.
Freud, S (1930). Civilization and its discontents. In *The Standard Edition of the Complete Psychological Works of Sigmund Freud*. S.E 21: 64–145.
Freud, S (1936). A disturbance of memory on the Acropolis. In *The Standard Edition of the Complete Psychological Works of Sigmund Freud*. S.E 22:239–248.
Freud, S. (1912–1913). Totem and taboo: Some points of agreement between the mental lives of savages and neurotics. In *The Standard Edition of the Complete Psychological Works of Sigmund Freud*. S.E 12:1–161.
Freud, S. (1920). Beyond the pleasure principle. In *The Standard Edition of the Complete Psychological Works of Sigmund Freud*. S.E 18:7–64.
Freud, A. and Burlingham, D.T. (1942). *War and Children*. New York: International Universities Press, 1944.
Friedman, P. (1949). Some aspects of concentration camp psychology. *American Journal of Psychiatry* 105:601–605.
Gamble, V.N. (2010). There wasn't a lot of comfort in those days: African Americans, public health, and the 1918 influenza epidemic. *Public Health Report* 125(Suppl. 3):114–122.
Gay, P. (1988). *Freud: A Life for Our Time*. New York: Norton.
Gilman, S. (1991). *The Jew's Body*. New York: Routledge.
Gilman, S. (1993). *Freud, Race, and Gender*. Princeton: Princeton University Press.
Grier, W. and Cobbs, P. (1968). *Black Rage*. New York: Basic Books.

Hardy, K.V. (2013). Healing the hidden wounds of racial trauma. *Reclaiming Children & Youth* 22:24–28.

Hardy, K.V. (2019). Toward a psychology of the oppressed: Understanding the invisible wounds of trauma. In *Re-visioning Family Therapy: Addressing Diversity in Clinical Practice*, ed. M. McGoldrick & K.V. Hardy. New York: Guilford Press, pp. 133–149.

Hardy, K.V., and Laszloffy, T.A. (1995). Therapy with African Americans and the phenomenon of rage. *Psychotherapy in Practice* 1(4):57–70.

Hardy, K.V. and Qureshi, M.D. (2012). Devaluation, loss, and rage: A postscript to urban African American youth with substance abuse. *Alcoholism Treatment Quarterly* 30:326–342.

Hart, A. (2019). The discriminatory gesture: A psychoanalytic consideration of posttraumatic reactions to incidents of racial discrimination. *Psychoanalytic Social Work* 26:5–24.

Hirschberger, G. (2018). Collective trauma and the social construction of meaning. *Frontiers in Psychology* 9, article 1441.

Hogarth, R. (2019a). A contemporary black perspective on the 1793 yellow fever epidemic in Philadelphia. *American Journal of Public Health* 109:1337–1338.

Hogarth, R. (2019b). The myth of innate racial differences between white and black people's bodies: Lessons from the yellow fever epidemic in Philadelphia, Pennsylvania. *American Journal of Public Health* 109:1339–1341.

Holmes, D.E. (2006). The wrecking effects of race and social class on self and success. *Psychoanalytic Quarterly* 75: 215–235.

Holmes, D.E. (2016b). "I knew that my mind could take me anywhere": Psychoanalytic reflections on the dignity of African Americans living in a racist society. In *Dignity Matters*, ed. S. Levine. London: Karnac Books, pp. 119–140.

King, M.L. Jr. (1957). Interview with Martin Agronsky: Nonviolence is the most powerful weapon. *Look Here* (NBC), October 27.

King, M.L. Jr. (1966). Interview with Mike Wallace. *Sixty Minutes* (CBS), September 27.

King, M.L. Jr. (1968). Remaining awake through a great revolution. Speech given at the National Cathedral, Washington, DC, March 31.

McKay, C. (1919). If we must die. In *Selected Poems of Claude McKay*. New York: Bookman Associates, 1953, p. 36.

Moskowitz, M. (1995). Ethnicity and the fantasy of ethnicity. *Psychoanalytic Psychology* 12:547–555.

Obama, M. (2016). Speech for the Democratic National Convention. July 25, 2016.

Panksepp, J. (2005). Affective consciousness: Core emotional feelings in animals and humans. *Consciousness & Cognition* 14:30–80.

Phillips, A. (1988). *Winnicott*. London: Fontana Press.

Platt, M., Barton, J. and Freyd, J.J. (2009). A betrayal trauma perspective on domestic violence. In *Violence against Women in Families and Relationships: Vol. 1. Victimization and the Community Response*, ed. E. Stark & E.S. Buzawa. Santa Barbara, CA: Praeger, pp. 185–207.

Powell, D.R. (2020). From the sunken place to the shitty place: The film *Get Out*, psychic emancipation and modern race relations from a psychoanalytic point of view. *Psychoanalytic Quarterly* 89:415–445.

Roberts, D. and Rollins, O. (2020). Why sociology matters to race and biosocial science. *Annual Review of Sociology* 46:195–214.

Shay, J. (1994). *Achilles in Vietnam: Combat Trauma and the Undoing of Character*. New York: Maxwell Macmillan International.

Shay, J. (2014). Moral injury. *Psychoanalytic Psychology* 31:182–191.

Socarides, C.F. and Volkan, V.D., eds. (1992). *The Homosexualities and the Therapeutic Process*. New York: International Universities Press.

Solms, M. (2020). Emotional drives and their place in human development. *Yellowbrick Journal of Emerging Adulthood* 7:4–10.

Stoute, B.J. (2017). Race and racism in psychoanalytic thought: The ghosts in our nursery. *The American Psychoanalyst* 51(1), March.

Stoute, B.J. (2019). Racial socialization and thwarted mentalization: Psychoanalytic reflections from the lived experience of James Baldwin's America. *American Imago* 76:335–357.

Stoute, B.J. (2022). How our mind becomes racialized: Implications for the therapeutic encounter. In *Textbook of Psychotherapeutic Treatments*, ed. G.O. Gabbard & H. Crisp. 2nd ed. Washington, DC: American Psychiatric Association Press.

Todorov, A. and Bargh, J.A. (2002). Automatic sources of aggression. *Aggression & Violent Behavior* 7:53–68.

Viboud, C. and Lessler, J. (2018). The 1918 influenza pandemic: Looking back, looking forward. *American Journal of Epidemiology* 187:2493–2497.

Volkan, V. (2013). Large-group psychology in its own right: Large-group identity and peace-making. *International Journal of Applied Psychoanalytic Studies* 10:210–246.

Volkan, V., Ast, G.A. and Greer, W.F. Jr. (2002). *The Third Reich in the Unconscious*. New York: Routledge.

Wilkerson, I. (2020). *Caste: The Origins of Our Discontents*. New York: Random House.

Winnicott, D.W. (1967). The location of cultural experience. *International Journal of Psychoanalysis* 48:368–372.

Chapter 11

Observations on the Use of the N-Word

Jyoti M. Rao

Introduction

At the first national psychoanalytic conference I attended, a senior white analyst spoke the n-word and a homophobic slur, both in their entirety.[1] To be clear, she did not direct these terms at anyone in particular, but rather used them in a sentence as if to speak about them. Since that time, I have noticed a remarkable occurrence so consistent that it rises to the level of a compulsion to repeat: in several analytic conferences I have attended that address race in any way a white person pronounces the n-word in its entirety. In one instance, it occurred at two different sessions during the same conference. As in the first incident, the many instances of its use I have witnessed since have never been plainly directed at another individual as personal invective. Often the person is quoting someone else, perhaps an overtly racist relative or patient; sometimes the epithet is dropped into a sentence as though it were an entirely ordinary word. I have heard people briefly hesitate, wondering aloud whether they should say the word, and then do so. Most people using the word may feel no conscious racial animus, and some are even committed to thoughtful reflection about racism and other forms of oppression. It is all the more curious, then, that an exceptionally charged word, laden with echoes of violent subjugation, seems to so regularly enter, almost unbidden, into the conversation of professionals trained to carefully track the nuances of language and affect. Who among us, after all, has not dedicated hours to poring over minute details in our process notes, attending to the most delicate shades of meaning, finely adjusting our phrasing, exercising restraint in the face of our countertransference, and attempting to attend to our most troubling associations to specific words?

DOI: 10.4324/9781003280002-14

What happens after the slur is uttered has been equally consistent, and equally notable. Some small part of the group, typically comprising the few people of color and others present who come from marginalized backgrounds, attempt to bring attention to what they have just experienced. Often they express palpable pain, clearly expressing the destabilizing effect of hearing a word strongly associated with white supremacy[2] spoken at a conference. Aside from occupying a marginalized social identity, those speaking are frequently earlier in their career; hold positions as graduate students, junior faculty, or analytic candidates; are less financially secure; and are speaking to people with greater institutional, organizational, and other forms of power. In response to hearing from these participants, the user of the word, and several other white people in the group, seem mobilized to counter what has been reported about the consequences of the epithet's use. They begin to explain that speaking the n-word is benign, even salutary, and advocate for why the word should be used freely by white people and psychoanalysts. In all the cases I have seen, the person using the word, as well as the people roused in support, have appeared unmoved, unreceptive, and unapologetic, even when it is repeatedly pointed out to them that their speech has caused harm. Again, this is especially striking among skilled practitioners who generally exhibit attuned sensitivity to others' feelings and a cultivated receptivity to others' subjectivity.

I will explore here some of the subtle processes underlying the pronouncement of the n-word and its aftermath in psychoanalytic spaces. Specifically, I consider unscripted moments in which the word emerges, rather than deliberate decisions made in the context of a formal presentation, as impromptu comments are especially dominated by unconscious process. I will emphasize structural factors on the scale of the group and society, working under the assumption that these factors ubiquitously and dynamically influence unconscious psychological registers. While individual experiences are idiosyncratic and hold meaningful variations, I address the power of social experiences, especially unresolved collective trauma, to fashion both psychic and social reality. Thus, I am not concerned here with the specific individuals who speak the word or their personal psychology. Nor am I interested in making a case for any sort of prohibition, or setting about the task of developing guidelines for speech in psychoanalytic settings—such endeavors would be entirely nonpsychoanalytic in their methods and aims. Rather, I wish to draw attention to a repetitive group phenomenon of which the utterance of a highly evocative racial slur comprises but a small part. In exploring the largely unconscious vicissitudes of these dynamics, my hope is to shed some light on their meanings and their links to broader social currents.

Unseen Harm

My personal choice to avoid speaking or writing slurs in any context, including this paper,[3] stems in part from my witnessing the intense degree of psychic harm suffered in my patients as a result of these words. The clinical literature, spanning decades, is full of examples of adult and child patients from a wide range of marginalized identities who have sustained psychic lacerations resulting from epithets directed toward them (Friedman and Downey 1999; Gardner 1975; Gehrie 1976; Halper 1970; Holmes 1992, 2016; Lousada 2006; Moss 2009; Stein 2004; Stoute 2019). Oppressed groups suffer from being used as "dehumanized targets of the majority's projections" (Akhtar 2014, p. 150). In addition to receiving projections, targets of prejudice are the recipients of more insidious projective identifications, which aim to alter the victim's internal mental processes by transferring venomous psychic contents from one person or group to another (Dajani 2017; Hart 2019). These intensely negative projections and projective identifications, when condensed into slurs, amount to weapons deployed against the psyches of those targeted in prejudicial attacks. Keval (2001) writes that such an attack may result in "puncturing and even shattering the individual's psychic skin and existing defensive organization," potentially shaking the psyche to its foundations (p. 34).[4] Slurs, like guns or whips or grenades, are designed to cause damage. Even when apparently brandished for another purpose, their original function is always nearby.

Many clinicians occupying marginalized identities report hearing these words directed toward them in the course of their clinical work and personal life, sometimes accompanied by physical violence or threats thereof (Butler 2019 Corbett 2001; Hamer 2006; Jones 2020; Leary 1997; Moss 2009; Tan 1993; White 2002). One consequence of the overrepresentation of dominant social groups in the psychoanalytic community is a marked underestimation of the degree to which our colleagues endure socially originated trauma. Relative protection from such forms of wounding is a significant privilege of social dominance. This protection is invisible to its possessor, as are all protections conferred by social privilege; one tends not to notice the absence of hostile attacks in one's life if such attacks have always been absent. Socially located trauma has potential to be revivified by the unexpected use of words typically aimed at individuals during expressions of atavistic hatred. Although analytic thinkers are generally savvy to even oblique expressions of hate, this fact may well be consciously overlooked by dominant group members in a form of nonrecognition that keeps certain experiences stubbornly unfamiliar. Thwarted mentalization aids this nonrecognition, facilitating a process of othering that is rationalized by the conscious mind, rendering it subjectively unremarkable (Stoute 2019).

Some may consider it a testament to our colleagues' resilience that traumatic socially inflicted injuries are so often managed privately by those who suffer them. However, these forms of nonrecognition have potential for grave material consequences. As Grace Kyungwon Hong (2015) asserts in her seminal contribution *Death beyond Disavowal*, the premature demise of many feminist scholars who are women of color is a direct consequence of the strain imposed by the structural and systemic forces under which they performed exhausting, exploitative intellectual and emotional labor. Intentionally paralleling remembrances of Black victims of homicide, Hong lists some of their names, poignantly stating,

> It is difficult to say and impossible to 'prove' that these women suffered early deaths because the battles around race, gender, and sexuality were being waged so directly through and on their bodies. ... Yet the names bear witness to [the] unknowable truth.
> (p. 147)

Like these scholars, marginalized psychoanalytic professionals perform labor under antagonistic conditions that are unshared and largely unwitnessed by their colleagues in dominant social placements.

Jones (2020) puts her long-standing lived experience of these battles in painful terms: "I am nearly 71 years old, but fear and terror have continued to be my constant companions when I move around ... in psychoanalytic spaces" (p. 80).[5] What are the consequences of living in unremitting terror among one's psychoanalytic colleagues over four decades, "speaking at [one's] peril, especially if heard" (p. 80)? Hong (2015) argues that a likely outcome is a systemically perpetrated collapse of the psyche-soma (Winnicott 1949). Some readers, based on a perspective shaped by their social location, may initially find the attestation of this degree of detriment excessive or unfathomable. Attentiveness to the accounts of our marginalized colleagues, students, supervisees, and patients in the field, especially with regard to the psychic and somatic sequelae of their more harrowing professional encounters, will confirm well-founded cause for concern.

The Violent World of the N-Word

It is certain that alongside any lack of awareness or bias that has its roots in differences in social position and lived experience, recognizable unconscious mechanisms are powerfully at work. Howard (2019), a professor of education and director of UCLA's Black Male Institute, advocates a zero-tolerance ban on the word's full pronouncement in schools, writing that the slur's history "is rooted in degradation, enslavement, dehumanization, hate, anti-Black racism, and a belief in [racial] inferiority.... countless African-Americans died hearing this racist slur as they took their last breath." The n-word first entered the institutional language of the United States Supreme Court in the context of the Reconstruction-era case *Blyew v. United States*, which in 1871 addressed a racial hate crime in which two white men "hacked to death several members of a black family," after making threats containing the slur; numerous legal cases followed in which the word's use was documented in instances of racial violence, arson, threats to life and employment, and other forms of extreme persecution (Kennedy 1999, p. 89). The children and adolescents who integrated Southern schools were relentlessly harassed with the word by white schoolmates and adults, often in the context of vicious physical attacks including being beaten, kicked, burned, and spat on (Asim 2007). For anyone acculturated to life in the United States, to claim a failure to know— or to seek an exemption from the fact—that the n-word is saturated in violently racialized and potentially traumatogenic meaning whenever used by a white person merits the highest degree of psychoanalytic skepticism. Yet these are precisely the assertions made repeatedly in discussions after the slur has been uttered in psychoanalytic circles.

Among white analysts who have spelled out the n-word in their academic publications, some have acknowledged that their doing so is fraught with weighty unconscious meaning and motivation. Altman (2006) uses the word, notably in a paper on the meaning of whiteness, in the context of representing the writing of both Black and white authors, including Baldwin and Faulkner. He astutely reflects on his dawning feeling of "getting away with murder" in using the word while attributing it to others, wondering that he "could use such a highly charged word without knowing that [he] was expressing something about [himself]" (p. 70). Similarly, Moss (2009), in his elegant discussion on use of the slur by a patient over the course of a treatment, explores his own developing understanding of "the brute fact" that writing the term in his paper meant that it constituted a part of his own personal language, allowing him to partake of the "pleasures and reassurances" offered by the "projective" and "essentialist" functions he attributes to the word (p. 837).

Both Altman and Moss initially imagined that they could write the invective out in full while remaining somehow separate from it, immune to its charge; both found this impossible. Both became distressingly aware that in writing the word in its entirety—even when discussing its use by a literary figure or patient—they were necessarily implicated in its use, and that this use was far from benign. Moss writes that regardless of his conscious intention, he could feel coursing through him the "pleasures, the powers, and the shame that adhere" to the n-word, concluding that despite the intention to use the word with civility, the "malign power" of slurs is inescapably persistent (p. 837). He asserts that the impact remains whether the epithet is spoken or unspoken; a similar stance is taken by Smith (2006), discussing Altman. I disagree with this latter claim. Speaking or writing slurs from a position of relative social power repeats well-worn and overdetermined lines of injury. Choosing not to do so disrupts the fault lines of splitting that undergird the normative unconscious process (Layton 2006) informing and upholding received social patterns. Such disruption can be potently reparative, a point to which I will return.

Perhaps the most developed psychoanalytic discussion about use of the n-word in one's professional capacity comes from Barrish (2002), a white professor of English who explores what he terms the "secret joys" of pronouncing the slur while ostensibly taking an antiracist position in teaching *Huckleberry Finn*. The description of his physical experience of leading his classes in "analytic discussions" of the n-word is rich with immediacy:

> To me these sessions always feel stressful and frustrating, sometimes unbearably so. But I also experience them as uniquely intense. They twist my viscera and sensitize the surface of my skin. I leave with churning feelings, mostly of guilt, confusion, and shame, as well as a sort of depressive helplessness. It is a dictum of Freudian thought, however, that where there is guilt there is also unconscious desire. What does it mean that I feel as if I've been caught red-handed in some shameful act every time I embark on a pedagogical attempt to discuss the word.... What secret desire might underlie the guilt? It goes beyond, I think, the excitement at breaking a taboo, at the repeating out loud of a forbidden word (which, of course, I know quite well before class that I will do)
>
> (p. 132)

Here we get closest to the bodily report of the conflict. Barrish finds himself feeling "caught red-handed," while Altman feels he is "getting away with murder." Both are aware that they are committing a transgressive, potentially harmful act that centers physicality, even as they proceed to commit it. Murder, bloodied hands, exposed viscera, and unpunished crimes are clear associations to chattel slavery and its horrors. These are made proximate by the demeaning term whose sole function was to be employed in the service of racist dehumanization.

Barrish's sensitized skin and twisted viscera are also plainly sexual, inviting us to consider the hidden dimensions of sexual violence and erotized aggression that are inextricably tied to the n-word. The "uniquely intense" "secret desire" and "excitement" to which he refers, as well as the "pleasures" and "powers" noted by Moss (2009, p. 837), reveal a link between use of the n-word by white people and the evocation of a sadistic sexuality tied to subjugation. Moss demonstrates some awareness of this possibility, stating early in his piece that "racist pejoratives ... gratify, sanction, and reward fantasies of codified, prepatterned sexualized violence" (p. 825). Gay (2016) notes that fantasies of sexual slavery are commonplace, and that erotica frequently features themes of omnipotent possession, conquest, control, and submission. These fantasies were pathologically concretized during slavery, resulting in untold violation: "American slave owners had no need for—and no use for—metaphors.... The realities of slavery, of owning other persons' bodies, included using those bodies for sexual pleasure" (Gay 2016, p. 41). Told from the point of view of those whose bodies were so used, one would speak not of pleasure but of unthinkable, relentless depredation.[6] In foregrounding the pleasurable uses of another's body afforded to white people in the context of slavery, it is facile to deemphasize the ravages of sexual terrorism inflicted on the bodies and psyches of people who were enslaved. Likewise, in writing about the exciting pleasures of their flirtation with racial slurs, white analysts and academics participate in a narrative in which they are not required to fully consider those violated by their words. They avoid awareness of their immediate adjacency to the most dire forms of racialized sexual violence in doing so. The nearness of such violence is unconsciously revealed in the inexorable honesty of associative testimony.

Nachträglichkeit

The dynamic meanings of the emergence of the n-word in psychoanalytic conferences are elucidated by two key concepts, *Nachträglichkeit* and the discriminatory gesture. The first of these, Freud's *Nachträglichkeit*, is translated with different emphases as "deferred action" and *après-coup*. Our tree-lined psychoanalytic neighborhood is experimenting with racial integration, only to find that swift, unconscious shifts occur in the ground beneath our feet. These silent earthquakes reveal weaknesses in our foundations, making small cracks more pronounced, and rendering seemingly hospitable spaces potentially annihilating. Present-day rumblings recall to us past tremors, with renewed exposure to the terrifying fissures they caused. This occurs when discussions about race summon the representation of white supremacy, which arrives, perpetually unmetabolized, in the form of the n-word blurted out by a white person.

In his early writings on hysteria, Freud observes the noteworthy occurrence of a memory arousing "an affect which it did not give rise to as an experience"; such a memory "only become[s] a trauma by deferred action" (Freud 1895, p. 356). Confusing, overstimulating events are especially prone to being unassimilable in their original experiencing, and therefore are subject to deferred revision (Laplanche and Pontalis 1967, p. 112). Such revision occurs in light of present experiences that shed new light on a memory such that it is experienced in a shockingly bewildering manner. *Nachträglichkeit* is central to a two-stage model of trauma, in which an event is "deposited in an individual, which is only activated later on" (Birksted-Breen 2003, p. 1501). It returns to us "what is left out of a story even when the whole story is told" (Ogden 2016, p. 160).

Freud's examples typifying *Nachträglichkeit* concern adult forms of sexuality encountered by a child, before the significance of these encounters may be registered. Rozmarin (2017) suggests parallels between potentially traumatogenic negotiations between childhood and adult sexuality and childhood and adult experiences in the social domain, indicating that early collective experiences "accrue social signification through repeated *Nachträglichkeit*" (p. 475). When adult experiences stir dormant memories of previously incomprehensible racialized aggression, these may be suddenly invested with overwhelming meanings and affect, generating trauma in the present.

Slavery involved repeated efforts to obliterate the subjectivity of the enslaved; an enslaved person's feelings were rendered entirely without meaning, inflicting "wounds on self and soma" transmitted intergenerationally (Gump 2000, p. 627). When a racial slur is spoken and defended, two levels of experience may be engaged. Most members of the targeted group are likely to recall memories of racial aggression and obliterated subjectivity, yet each will have their own specific, highly personal meanings made of those experiences via *Nachträglichkeit*, underscoring the importance of psychoanalytic working through (M. Levin, personal communication, July 15, 2020). Group-level identifications intersect with uniquely individual experiences; past intersects with present; internal life intersects with external events.

The Discriminatory Gesture

Repeated experiences of deferred action are at the heart of the concept of the discriminatory gesture put forth by Hart (2019). A discriminatory gesture, distinct from a racial hate crime or similar attack, is a seemingly everyday interpersonal occurrence that is destructive because it indexes present-day racism and the ongoing historical trauma of slavery. "Each discriminatory gesture," Hart writes, "carries the personally annihilating power embedded in the existence of the entire destruction-subjugation oriented enterprise of racism and white supremacy"; it is "always implicitly spoken with the grammar and vocabulary of the racist-supremacist cultural context within which it occurs" (p. 2). Seemingly mild references to racist oppression can contain the entire force of "foundational atrocities" (p. 12); slurs hold charge because of "the destructive forms of social organization and oppression" (p. 3) in which they originated and persist.

As a result, it is impossible for a white person to utter the n-word in any context without causing unconscious reverberations within the entire sociocultural matrix of white supremacy (historical and present-day) and slavery, replete with its violence and transgressions, its destructive sadism and dehumanization. In making use of people of color as repositories for unbearable anxieties and affects, discriminatory gestures pose "relentless attempts at enslavement," which engender ongoing retraumatization, and may precipitate post-traumatic reactions of great intensity (Hart 2019, p. 16). By contrast, the party generating the gesture is often apparently unfazed, stabilized by having projectively off-loaded extremely disturbing affect. Hart contends that a second traumatization occurs if the recipient of the discriminatory gesture attempts to project back into the originator, thereby "enlarging the threat, increasing the terror...making it more likely that lasting trauma will result" (p. 15).

I should note, as Hart does, that different people experience discriminatory gestures differently as a result of their personal histories and psychic structure. This may explain why some psychoanalytic professionals of color may not experience the use of the n-word by white colleagues to be especially noxious in any given instance. Indeed, some people of color have perceived an opportunity for psychoanalytic exploration in the emergence of the taboo term, a sentiment that has occasionally emerged in conference settings. McWhorter

(2019), an African American professor of linguistics, has proposed that some uses of the word by white people may be unobjectionable, and is critical of the idea that the slur's use in discussion is necessarily problematic. Nonetheless, a study conducted at an historically Black university showed that more than three-quarters of participants felt it was never acceptable for non-Blacks to use the n-word "with anyone in any situation," with 67 percent feeling it was never acceptable for anyone, Black or non-Black, to use the n-word, under any circumstances (King et al. 2018, p. 55); the possibility of serious psychological injury is always present. On a group level, such trauma is endemic but kept largely unconscious, and the unconscious climate favors recurrent minimization of its severity.

The Defensive Life of the Discriminatory Gesture

Holmes (2006) posits "a culture-wide defensive barrier to recognizing the implicit representation" of racism (p. 221). The sine qua non of the n-word is the implicit and explicit representation of the most brutal racism; slurs exist to conjure persecution. Awareness of this purpose must be defensively warded off to allow the n-word to be used in professional settings under any circumstances, especially ones in which the conscious intention is frequently an examination of race and racism. The unconscious awareness that the n-word evokes violence, bigotry, and subjugation in their most extreme degrees is strongly evinced in the alacrity of the defensive maneuvers that appear in the wake of its appearance in psychoanalytic gatherings.

The intensity of these defensive operations may amount to not registering the use of the word at all. After the first incident I witnessed, a few attendees believed they had not even heard the initial speaker say the two slurs she had uttered unmistakably, clearly, audibly, and rather forcefully. This is a striking example of the "perceptual defense" identified by Basch (1974, p. 92), which he conceptualizes as a failure in repression, or leaking out of highly charged content which must be secondarily erased, rather than evidence of successful repression. It is also a version of the dissociative "forgetfulness" exhibited by Southern apologists for slavery (Gay 2016, p. 57).

More commonly, those present will acknowledge that the word was spoken and heard, but then rapidly disclaim the meanings and significance attached to the epithet. This conforms to Freud's definition of disavowal, in which the conscious experience of the perception itself (i.e., hearing the slur spoken) remains intact, but the perception's "true meaning" is kept unconscious; "the percept's significance for the unconscious is not linked with conscious knowledge of perceived reality" (Basch 1974, p. 90). It is also similar to Steiner's concept (1985) of "turning a blind eye" (or plugged ear), an ambiguous relationship with internal and external reality in which we "seem to have access to reality but choose to ignore it because it proves convenient to do so" (p. 161). We cannot readily separate our reflexive responses from our more considered ones in relationship to highly charged speech, and both responses serve defensive functions (Moss 2019). In the case of the n-word, the enormous anxieties generated by acknowledging the legacy of slavery in our midst require enormous defenses, which may be deployed at the expense of reality orientation. These defensive processes also may facilitate the emergence of perverse forms of relatedness, as I will elaborate.

Using ancestral routes of projective processes, rights to which have been deeded intergenerationally, allows white people to achieve distance from feelings of ignorance, uncertainty, shame, guilt, inferiority, and badness.[7] Those who are socially empowered to employ discriminatory gestures are motivated to protect their use of them, as the gestures facilitate projections and projective identifications that are felt to be essential to psychological equilibrium within a racialized social-cultural system that has potential to traumatize in all directions. Additional motivation comes from unconscious awareness that access to particular defensive processes, including discriminatory gestures, are inequitably distributed. The option to make use of specific forms of defense is in fact an unconscious social privilege. This fact is not lost on those who receive the discriminatory gesture, though it likely known only unconsciously to the user of the defense.

Oppressive projective processes are not fully bidirectional; certain psychic contents move overwhelmingly from oppressor to oppressed. Hierarchies split culturally desirable attributes from undesirable ones, assigning the former to those with social dominance and the latter to those who are marginalized (Layton 2009). Repeated societal refusal to attempt any form of meaningful repair of societal trauma exacerbates these tendencies. Failures of the environment-mother, or culture-mother writ large, to reliably facilitate reparation "leads to a loss of the capacity for concern, and to its replacement by crude anxieties and by crude defenses, such as splitting, or disintegration" (Winnicott 1963, p. 78).

Disavowal

Primary among the defenses that recur in the wake of the use of the n-word is a disavowal which aims to omnipotently change the meaning of the slur, attempting to de-link the slur from its trauma-infused matrix; "surely, this time it didn't mean any of *that*." Unlike repression, which aims at managing affect, disavowal works on mitigating the troubles posed by ideas though "radical repudiation" of external reality (Hook 2005, p. 714). In the potent fantasy generated by such disavowal, the discriminatory gesture of the slur is imagined to lack destructive power because it has been psychically stripped of its actual, lived meanings, and uses. Moss (2009) writes of a depressive fantasy surrounding epithets, a search for a lost state of innocence in which the hatred held within the slurs is depotentiated, its harm located in the past rather than in the affect-filled present.[8] Hong (2015) makes a related observation, stating that contemporary educational institutions are "epistemological structure[s] of disavowal, a means of claiming that racial and gendered violence are a thing of the past" (pp. 10–11), while continuing pernicious forms of such violence.

Using the n-word in psychoanalytic meetings seems to hold within it an insistence on the comforting fantasy of a postracial world in which the slur has been rendered inert, or indeed, an even more compelling fiction in which slavery and anti-Black oppression never occurred and do not have an ongoing presence in our lives, despite ample daily evidence to the contrary. Access to these fantasies is restricted, however, and fantasies are not without their real-life consequences. Certain life circumstances and social locations allow some to readily enter, even in adulthood, fictional worlds in which racial and other oppressions are absent, while others must more fully confront nonnegotiable social realities from childhood. In this manner, the privileged person's comforting fantasy constitutes the marginalized person's discriminatory gesture, with destructive possibilities invigorated by the erasures inherent in repudiated reality. Every effort I may make to protect my defensive fantasy increases the traumatogenic potential of the gesture your psyche receives, filled with painful realities I cannot tolerate, but I insist you must tolerate for both of us. *Nachträglichkeit* links past and present experiences of erasure.

Identity Trouble, or "Who, Me?" and "Who Are We?"

Another repeating defense of the n-word spoken in its entirety in psychoanalytic settings is "My patients say that word all the time," or a corollary, "Should we forbid our patients to say these words?" These statements reflect an intense wish to be, in that moment, a patient-child in the presence of a receptive, accommodating analyst-caregiver rather than a professional among other professionals, held fully accountable for the consequences of their speech. In altering the scene from conference to consulting room, the speaker imagines him- or herself not as the containing analyst faced with metabolizing difficult experiences, but rather as the patient whose right to speak freely is being curtailed. This identification with a vulnerable, entitled party is consistent with white supremacist narratives that paradoxically allow white people to consider themselves endangered and innocently aggrieved while simultaneously asserting powerful superiority and narcissistic entitlement.

A related response is something along the lines of "I, too, would like to see certain words disappear, but I must tolerate their existence." This variation, typically made with reference to misogynistic insults, hints at the presence of chronic grievance. Grievance may be used to return to an omnipotently created ideal self, especially when reality has broken through and disrupted contact with such an object (Weintrobe 2004).[9] In this case, the ideal self quietly, gracefully, and patiently suffers insults and deprivations, and is ennobled in the process. Such an idealized self-disavows its own social power and narcissistic rage is damaged by the awareness of utilizing such power in racist enactments and must keep such awareness unconscious. This narrative, too, evokes long-standing white supremacist tropes that pit white cisgender women's interests against those of Black people, undermining the potential for solidarity against white supremacist patriarchy and its abuses.

Invocations of a psychoanalytic identity are another frequently heard defensive refrain—we are people who speak unflinchingly of difficult matters and therefore bravely speak slurs in their entirety at conferences. One analyst expressed this sentiment in her advocacy for the use of racial and homophobic slurs, writing, "I go deep and I go dark" (Maher 2018, p. 224). From this perspective, not using slurs, as in this chapter, is defensively euphemistic, and counter to psychoanalytic values of confronting painful realities. Some may contend that not saying slurs in their entirety is an evasion, a sign of unwillingness or anxiety about directly acknowledging the intense negativity held within these words. In my estimation, this critique is based on a misunderstanding of the function of the slur.

To slur or not to slur is not the question; contending with the full meanings of an epithet's use is. Psychoanalysis privileges the latent, the hidden, the obscured; the symptom is a provocation to discover, not the entirety of the communication. Speaking slurs may be considered a symptom that attempts to bind the anxieties generated by the return of the repressed. As a symptom, it is intensely protected in order to keep repressed, dissociated, and disavowed conflictual, trauma-filled material at bay. Those who slur must therefore consciously minimize the impact on others to themselves, justifying it as harmless speech, at least "just this once." Speaking epithets as if they are ordinary speech is hence more accurately understood as the evasion. The traumatic legacies of white supremacy are deep and painful indeed, and deserving of the most thorough psychoanalytic inquiry. They are instead enacted but left entirely unaddressed when slurs are pried from their meanings and impacts, a profound betrayal of psychoanalytic ethics.

Denial of Difference and Other Considerations

The notion that psychoanalysts, the vast majority of whom are white, should say racial slurs at conferences because it is psychoanalytic to do so also reveals a denial of racial and other social differences. Denial of difference is linked to the defense of disavowal, as such denial requires bending the reality that the self lacks qualities that the other possesses (Barrows 1995). Freud's definition of disavowal places central importance on defending against a perception's personal significance, its specific meaning to the individual (Basch 1983, p. 145). This extends to the personal meaning made of our perceptions of others' perception of us, the ways in which others read meaning into what we say based on their understanding of our social locations. However, much we may wish it otherwise, our unchosen social identities are constantly read by others—sometimes incorrectly, but read nonetheless—and have a role in shaping the meaning of our speech. Whiteness is rarely a salient identity to a white person; in fact it may be entirely overlooked as a part of one's self-concept (Altman 2006; Miller and Josephs 2009). Yet it may be the most salient identity to one's interlocutor. Acknowledging this to oneself as a white person may cause confusion and narcissistic injury.

Thus, one may attempt to defensively avoid the reality that it means something different for a white person, psychoanalyst or not, to speak a racial slur than it does for a person of color to do so. The former is a discriminatory gesture that evokes white supremacy. The latter is not, because racial trauma in the United States does not centrally feature Black people enslaving each other and perpetrating racial hate crimes against each other, but instead white people perpetrating ongoing racist harm against Black people. Similarly, a homophobic slur reclaimed for personal or in-group use by someone who is gay[10] means something entirely different from a heterosexual person's attempt to single-handedly diffuse the power of an epithet by speaking it, as the latter attempts an erasure of traumatic history even while invoking it. Centuries of social meaning cannot be undone through wishing. Psychoanalytic practitioners indulge in treacherous omnipotent delusions to the extent that we believe we may successfully separate ourselves from our social realities, including the conscious and unconscious meanings attached to our speech by our time, place, history, bodies, and social identities, both real and perceived. We may not.

It is possible that some choose not to say slurs as a reaction formation, adopting a guise of overweening sensitivity that obscures simmering, disowned racism underneath. However, it is likely more often the case that the ability to exercise thoughtful restraint with offensive terms is instead a developmental achievement, one that has been temporarily hindered, or not yet been accomplished, in those who use slurs in their entirety. In a case vignette involving a white patient who repeatedly hurls the n-word at his analyst Hamer (2006), the patient eventually ceases to say the epithet and instead begins to state that he feels "that way" (p. 201). This change occurs after skilled interpretive work on the part of the analyst, undertaken under the intensely charged and uniquely challenging conditions of sustained racial attack.[11] In evidence here is neither censorship nor evasion on the part of analyst or patient. Rather, we see a highly effective psychoanalytic treatment in which the patient exhibits developing concern for the other and an increased capacity for mentalization, resulting in the ability to better negotiate painful internal states without resorting to the violent projective processes indicated by the use of slurs. There is a corresponding shift from action, using the slur, toward thought and expression of affect, however vague: "I feel that way." Choosing not to use a slur also shows relatively intact reality orientation, a capacity to negotiate the intensely traumatic evidence of our human hatred for one another, as well as the realities of one's own social placement within those legacies. To choose not to use slurs, therefore, is akin to choosing not to wield a weapon; one has found other methods to manage anxieties.

Even among those who generally possess these capabilities in ample measure, all may be subject to impairment in the neighborhood of the discriminatory gesture. Such is the disorganizing force of racial trauma in the United States; "racism is ruthless in its violation of others" (Holmes 2016, p. 577). Epithets are perhaps best understood not as an opportunity to contend with the devastation incurred by human hatred, but rather as a miserable sound emitted by a canary in the coal mine, indicating toxic fumes released by subterranean antipathies rising to dangerous levels. When slurs are in evidence, whatever their conscious intention, it is a sign that our capacities for reconciliation with ourselves, each other, and our mutual implication in each other's suffering (Layton 2009) are under threat.

"Because I Want To"

The most thinly veiled defensive response, or secondary discriminatory gesture, arising in psychoanalytic spaces is the assertion of one's desire and right to speak as one wishes, expressing a defiant resistance to altering one's speech in any way. The reassertion of this right occurs in a range from quiet insistence to defiant outrage. Common related examples of this defense include balking at adopting a person's preferred gender pronoun or refusing to attempt to learn a name in a non-English language. The speaker voicing this point of view seems not to be saying, "I can say whatever I want," so much as "I can say the words that exert potentially dehumanizing power over you if I want to, and I want to." Gay (2016) believes that while sexual sadism certainly played a role in slavery, as noted earlier, comprehending the human capacity for the "nonsexual pleasures of ownership," including superiority, pride, status, wealth, display, and even a form of companionship, are most central to understanding the phenomenon of slavery in the Southern United States (p. 42). We may understand these pleasures as primarily narcissistic, extracted coercively from those who were enslaved.

Racamier's conception of narcissistic perversion (1992) is typified in the need to assert oneself at the expense of another and taking pleasure in doing so (Filippini 2005). Filippini (2005) suggests a distinction between sadomasochistic forms of relatedness and what she terms "relational perversions," the latter of which feature the absence of the potential for role-reversal and mutual pleasure in relatedness. In such an arrangement, as with a slave owner or a member of a dominant social group, only one party may enjoy the pleasure of exerting power over the other. Relational perversions centrally feature the infliction of psychological harm by one party upon another via narcissistically motivated dehumanization. Domination and coercion are means of extracting what mutual dependence would confer in other forms of relatedness (Gump 2010). Insisting on one's right to use slurs simply because one wishes to, especially when harmful consequences have been brought to one's awareness, seems to be an example of just such a psychologically abusive process, recapitulating the perverse processes that characterize white supremacy.

Those invoking this line of defense often engage in an unconscious reversal of social power, projecting a forceful tyrant onto the party made vulnerable by the discriminatory gesture of the slur. In doing so, they rewrite a bid for greater understanding, often made with the utmost trepidation, as a command from a powerful figure against whom one could be rendered helpless. They conjure a world of "thought police" and curtailed expression in which the powerful must suffer under the suppressive hegemony of fragile "snowflakes," casting those who seek self-reflection about charged language as "violently aggressive, controlling, and manipulative, with a victim mentality" (Maher 2018, p. 225). Absent is the idea that one may freely *choose* to be authentically caring in one's choice of language that one may desire to be sensitive to the others' feelings out of genuine, uncoerced regard. Depressive concern and the capacity for empathy are eviscerated in the neighborhood split asunder by patterns of subjugation; one is either controlled or the controller. Such primitive defenses damage "vital interpersonal connective tissue, replacing it with self-generated hostile or paranoid feelings, [with] serious consequences not only in relationship to others and the inner world, but in the capacity to test reality" (Aragno 2014, p. 271).

In its projectively identified form, this projected tyranny may result in apparent stridency on the part of marginalized people who feel they must repeatedly insist, sometimes frantically, that their personhood matters. It is often unclear to the observer that such a person is struggling against nothing less than a threat of annihilation (Hart 2019). Further projections lead to further intolerance, with both parties experiencing the other in undifferentiated fantasy as a violent, powerful, tyrannical oppressor. However, in reality, *only one party actually possesses the power to oppress with the full force of institutional, social, and epistemic power.* This is parallel to the relationally perverse arrangement delineated by Filippini (2005). In subjugation, persecutory fears are fully realized, leading to highly unstable, escalating fragmentation. The white speaker of the slur is filled with anxiety about loss of social esteem and entertains fantasies of being mercilessly shamed or "cancelled." The person of color addressing the harm done, who may already be in a post-traumatic state brought about by the discriminatory gesture, recalls past injuries and fears unconsciously motivated professional reprisal, sugar-coated aggression, and hate mail. Both are unsure whether their concerns are justified or paranoid, because it is unclear which psychic world is most dominant at any moment, internally and externally. Perhaps the new neighbors aren't as friendly as we thought.

The Gesture of the Open Hand

As noted above, oppressive projective mechanisms are asymmetrical, adhering to unequal distributions of social power and value. This is in part the reason why many forms of social reparation rest upon the willingness of those with social power to consciously resist conforming to expected, predetermined social scripts. When either oppressed or oppressor deviates from unconsciously prescribed roles and swims upstream against the projective current, generative potential results. The oppressed do this in various forms of protest and self-advocacy, as well as a willingness to engage in overtures toward repair. Oppressors do this by recognizing the ways in which they are pulled to inhabit oppressive internal stances and intentionally refusing to enact power in ways that are highly ego-syntonic, relinquishing the emotional spoils. Such a shift moves away from the potential of relational perversion (Filippini 2005) toward what Chétrit-Vatine (2014) terms "ethical asymmetry" (p. 33). This does not occur passively or unconsciously.

While a white person's saying the n-word will inevitably be experienced by many people of color as a discriminatory gesture, a white person who demonstrates sensitivity to the destructive potential of the word signals to the hearer that something new and different is taking place. Similarly, someone with membership in a dominant social group ceding time to a colleague from a marginalized social group is a powerful gesture precisely because it does not conform to expected behaviors that perpetuate normative marginalization. Listening closely and taking seriously the words and experiences of someone of less social privilege than oneself in a clinical hour, a classroom, or a meeting leaves lasting, consolidating impressions. A trans patient tells me with glee of having been greeted with everyday friendliness at a washroom sink; a friend with a visible disability reports with radiant pleasure an encounter in a supermarket in which he was treated as the capable person he is; a white student basks in warm pride when her instructor of color praises her skillful offer of repair after having made a racially insensitive comment to a classmate of color; the classmate is astonished because it is the first time she has ever received a sincere apology from a white person. Seemingly small moments such as these are intensely noticeable to the people receiving such gestures because they differ markedly from the norm.

I term such social overtures "gestures of the open hand," a reference to the *abhayahasta*, or "fearless hand" in South Asian iconography. The hand with open palm facing the viewer indicates beneficent concern for human welfare, a hand that is both fearlessly open and extending of reassurance that there is nothing to fear. In counterpoint to the discriminatory gesture, which derives its destructive power from the social terrors that have come before and rear their heads once again through *Nachträglichkeit*, gestures of the open hand derive profound restorative power by eliciting hope in a new and surprisingly benevolent future, reminding one of optimism instilled by past social nurturing. While discriminatory gestures trigger apparently disproportionately injurious reactions because of the ways in which they tap into traumatizing histories repeating themselves seemingly endlessly into the present and future, gestures of the open hand generate disproportionately reparative responses because they are unusual, unexpected, and generating of optimistic possibility, gifts from a new social object world that has not yet been realized. Discriminatory gestures index our deepest experiences of rejection and human hatred; gestures of the open hand index foundational, organizing experiences of acceptance and human love against all expectation. The act of fully witnessing the harm done by a discriminatory gesture may serve as a gesture of the open hand.

Gestures of the open hand may be considered a form of interpretation-in-action (Ogden 1994), symbolic actions that derive their meaning from the unconscious aspects of experiential context. Faimberg (2007) presents a broadened definition of *Nachträglichkeit* in which psychoanalytic interpretation may provide new, retroactive meaning to what may not be fully spoken as a result of trauma, suggesting that such meaning-making is key to psychic change and psychoanalytic efficacy (p. 1238). In this view, the meanings conferred retroactively through interpretation are not traumatizing, but rather have potential to integrate trauma; new meanings and capacities from the present are brought to bear on the past, rendering charged experiences in both past and present more assimilable. This facilitates a process by which "the patient acquires a history," and traumatic events may be placed firmly in the past as opposed to the ongoing present and feared future (Faimberg 2007, p. 1230). In the social sphere, this process becomes possible when clear signs are available indicating that what is occurring in the present differs from past socially traumatizing experiences.

As with interpretive action, discriminatory gestures and gestures of the open hand do not draw their life from the action itself, but rather from the entire universe of meaning held within the gesture. Psychoanalysis departs from other forms of social justice work in its understanding of this: the specific forms of action one takes are much less important than the conscious and unconscious meanings made of actions and inactions. By no means should I be read as making recommendations to cede time to colleagues, smile at strangers, and never voice a slur. Instead, I propose that gestures of the open hand are a spontaneous outgrowth of generative, constructive, creatively integrative processes that are well understood, theorized, and practiced within psychoanalysis. Cultivating environments in which such innate processes may begin or resume is the work of psychoanalysis, and it is increasingly crucial work. While the emergence of slurs and defenses thereof are a symptom of the collapse of such processes, the emergence of gestures of the open hand is a welcome sign of psychoanalytic well-being.

A Concluding Note on Epistemic Justice

In the preceding pages, I have reviewed the harms and unconscious significance of the n-word and discussed the possible meanings of the emergence of the slur in psychoanalytic conferences, as well as some of the many defensive processes that follow. I have identified both the utterance of the slur and the vocal defense of the word's use as discriminatory gestures, invoking the full force of centuries of subjugation in the present moment through intergenerational transmission of trauma, and generating traumatic experience through *Nachträglichkeit*. A third discriminatory gesture also takes place, that of epistemic injustice (relevant definition in Fricker 2007),[12] which occurs when the self-report of a marginalized colleague's subjective experience is not believed, delegitimated, or unrecognized. Psychoanalysis has within it the capacity to deliver epistemic justice, a recognition of disowned personal and collective subjective truth. Epistemic justice, in turn, may bring about the full promise of psychoanalytic modes of thinking, which have potential to usher in new ways of being (Rao 2020). To realize this promise, however, psychoanalysis as a discipline must address the epistemic injustices it has inflicted and continues to perpetrate.

Fricker's original concept of epistemic injustice includes two forms, "testimonial injustice" (2007), in which a hearer diminishes the credibility of a speaker because of the speaker's social location, and "hermeneutical injustice," which results in "having some significant area of one's social experience obscured from collective understanding" (p. 4–6, 155). In other words, we do not believe some people because of who they are, and we lack collective concepts to describe and make meaning of marginalized others' experiences. Both of these forms of injustice constitute discriminatory gestures that occur with regularity in psychoanalytic conferences, with potential to evoke the intense post-traumatic reactions outlined by Hart (2019).

Particularly because these injustices have to do with forms of thinking and knowing, concerns central to psychoanalytic identity, they issue deep cuts to those who suffer from epistemic marginalization in psychoanalytic communities, causing deleterious injury when elaborated through *Nachträglichkeit*. Jones (2020) piercingly communicates the cumulative impact of such jolting: "I cannot help but speak the wrong way in psychoanalytic spaces because I am a black woman in the United States" (p. 80). Psychoanalytically informed epistemic justice aims at remedying these injustices by paying particular attention to the ways in which we may ameliorate our unconscious participation in defensively prejudicial processes that marginalize others' ways of knowing, thinking, feeling, speaking, and being. Such offers of epistemic justice are true gestures of the open hand, ones that emerge out of generative conditions that allow seedlings of hope to take root in our neighborhood.

Notes

1 A discussion of this event was published some years later by the chairs of the roundtable session, including brief participant commentaries from the analyst and myself (Alcorn and Grand 2018a,b; Maher 2018; Rao 2018).
2 Throughout this paper, I use the phrase "white supremacy" as defined by the civil rights scholar Frances Lee Ansley (1989):

> a political, economic and cultural system in which whites overwhelmingly control power and material resources, *conscious and unconscious* ideas of white superiority and entitlement are widespread, and relations of white dominance and non-white subordination are daily reenacted across a broad array of institutions and social settings.
>
> (p. 1024; emphasis added)

3 I am aware that my using the phrase "n-word" is an imperfect and perhaps unsatisfying solution. A discussion of the strengths, weaknesses, and implications of various conscious stances when it comes to the use of slurs is beyond my scope here.
4 See Hart (2019) for a comprehensive list of psychological phenomena associated with chronic and acute racially discriminatory trauma.
5 Hong frames her inquiry around a question originally posed by Audre Lorde: "In what way do I contribute to the subjugation of any part of those... I call my people?" Jones's paper generously provides much to consider for those within psychoanalytic circles who wish to ask themselves this question. I encourage its careful study by anyone invested in the cultivation of the psychoanalytic community.
6 This is not intended as a critique of Gay. The avowed aim of his book is to imagine the "interior lives of [slave]owners," not enslaved people (p. xiv).
7 The degree to which such distance may be maintained is subject to a wide range of individual variation based on several factors, including personal experiences and organization, past introspection and dialogue about racial dynamics, and socially informed analytic work that cultivates increased tolerance of the charged feelings specifically engendered by racial difference. Some white people may more readily experience white guilt or shame, among other feelings, and will respond to the use of a racial slur in their professional environment accordingly. However, I have rarely heard these perspectives voiced during psychoanalytic conferences.
8 Although Moss writes of his awareness of the significance of having used the n-word in his paper, its malevolence and incivility intact, he does not address how he came to choose to use the entirety of the epithet in his paper's title. In doing so, I believe he is participating in the depressive fantasy he named.
9 See the cases of Amy Cooper and Lisa Alexander, widely reported in the news media, for examples of grievances generated for such a purpose.
10 See Asim (2007, pp. 200–202) for a comparative discussion of the reclamation of the words "gay" and "queer."
11 This is an example of the particularly taxing conditions under which clinicians with marginalized identities undertake forms of unacknowledged and unshared labor, often at great personal cost.
12 The concept of epistemic injustice was first formulated first by Fricker (2007),

References

Alcorn, M., Grand, S. (2018a). Coda: On pain and dialogue. Psychoanalysis, Culture, & Society 23:229–231.

Alcorn, M., Grand, S. (2018b). On process and traumatic repetition. Psychoanalysis, Culture, & Society 23:217–223.
Altman, N. (2006). Whiteness. Psychoanalytic Quarterly 75:45–72.
Ansley, F.L. (1989). Stirring the ashes: Race, class, and the future of civil rights scholarship. Cornell Law Review 74:993–1077.
Aragno, A. (2014). The roots of evil: A psychoanalytic inquiry. Psychoanalytic Review 101:249–288.
Asim, J. (2007). The N-Word: Who Can Say It, Who Shouldn't and Why. New York: Houghton Mifflin Harcourt.
Barrish, P. (2002). The secret joys of antiracist pedagogy: *Huckleberry Finn* in the classroom. American Imago 59:117–139.
Barrows, P. (1995). Oedipal issues at 4 and 44. Psychoanalytic Psychotherapy 9:85–96.
Basch, M.F. (1974). Interference with perceptual transformation in the service of defense. Annual of Psychoanalysis 2:87–97.
Basch, M.F. (1983). The perception of reality and the disavowal of meaning. Annual of Psychoanalysis 11:125–153.
Birksted-Breen, D. (2003). Time and the après-coup. International Journal of Psychoanalysis 84:1501–1515.
Butler, D.J. (2019). Setting (on) fire: Reply to discussions. Studies in Gender & Sexuality 20:171–176.
Chétrit-Vatine, V. (2014). The Ethical Foundation of the Analytic Situation. London: Karnac Books.
Corbett, K. (2001). Faggot = loser. Studies in Gender & Sexuality 2:3–28.
Dajani, K.G. (2017). Commentary on Yasser ad-Dab'bagh's "Islamophobia: Prejudice, the psychological skin of the self and large-group dynamics." International Journal of Applied Psychoanalytic Studies 14:192–196.
Faimberg, H. (2007). A plea for a broader concept of Nachträglichkeit. Psychoanalytic Quarterly 76:1221–1240.
Filippini, S. (2005). Perverse relationships: The perspective of the perpetrator. International Journal of Psychoanalysis 86:755–777.
Freud, S. (1895). Project for a scientific psychology. In The Standard Edition of the Complete Psychological Works of Sigmund Freud. S.E 1:295–397.
Fricker, M. (2010). Epistemic Injustice: Power and the Ethics of Knowing. New York: Oxford University Press.
Friedman, R.C., Downey, J.I. (1999). Internalized homophobia and gender-valued self-esteem in the psychoanalysis of gay patients. Psychoanalytic Review 86:325–347.
Gardner, R.A. (1975). The kids all call me Schwartzer. Contemporary Psychoanalysis 11:125–134.
Gay, V. (2016). On the Pleasures of Owning Persons: The Hidden Face of American Slavery. New York: International Psychoanalytic Books.
Gehrie, M.J. (1976). Aspects of the dynamics of prejudice. Annual of Psychoanalysis 4:423–443.

Gump, J.P. (2000). A white therapist, an African American patient—shame in the therapeutic dyad: Commentary on paper by Neil Altman. Psychoanalytic Dialogues 10:619–632.

Gump, J.P. (2010). Reality matters: The shadow of trauma on African American subjectivity. Psychoanalytic Psychology 27:42–54.

Halper, I.S. (1970). The counterpoint of racial and oedipal themes in the psychotherapy of a negro patient. Psychoanalytic Review 57:169–180.

Hamer, F.M. (2006). Racism as a transference state: Episodes of racial hostility in the psychoanalytic context. Psychoanalytic Quarterly 75:197–214.

Hart, A. (2019). The discriminatory gesture: A psychoanalytic consideration of posttraumatic reactions to incidents of racial discrimination. Psychoanalytic Social Work 26:5–24.

Holmes, D.E. (1992). Race and transference in psychoanalysis and psychotherapy. International Journal of Psychoanalysis 73:1–11.

Holmes, D.E. (2016). Come hither, American psychoanalysis: Our complex multicultural America needs what we have to offer. Journal of the American Psychoanalytic Association 64:569–586.

Hong, G.K. (2015). Death beyond Disavowal: The Impossible Politics of Difference. Minneapolis: University of Minnesota Press.

Hook, D. (2005). The racial stereotype, colonial discourse, fetishism, and racism. Psychoanalytic Review 92:701–734.

Howard, T.C. (2019). It's time to completely ban the n-word in schools. Education Week, Opinion Section, October 28.

Jones, A.L. (2020). A black woman as an American analyst: Some observations from one woman's life over four decades. Studies in Gender & Sexuality 21:77–84.

Kennedy, R.L. (1999). Who can say "nigger"? and other considerations. Journal of Blacks in Higher Education 26:86–96.

Keval, N. (2001). Understanding the trauma of racial violence in a black patient. British Journal of Psychotherapy 18:34–51.

King, W., Emanuel, R.C., Brown, X., Dingle, N., Lucas, V., Perkins, A., Turner, A., Whittington, D., Witherspoon, Q. (2018). Who has the "right" to use the n-word? A survey of attitudes about the acceptability of using the n-word and its derivatives. International Journal of Society, Culture & Language 6:47–58.

Laplanche, J., Pontalis, J.-B. (1967). The Language of Psycho-Analysis, transl. Nicholson-Smith, D. New York: Norton, 1973.

Layton, L. (2006). Racial identities, racial enactments, and normative unconscious processes. Psychoanalytic Quarterly 75:237–269.

Layton, L. (2009). Who's responsible? Our mutual implication in each other's suffering. Psychoanalytic Dialogues 19:105–120.

Leary, K. (1997). Race, self-disclosure, and "forbidden talk": Race and ethnicity in contemporary clinical practice. Psychoanalytic Quarterly 66:163–189.

Lousada, J. (2006). Glancing over the shoulder: Racism, fear of the stranger and the fascist state of mind. Psychoanalytic Psychotherapy 20:97–104.

Maher, A.L. (2018). Participant commentary from Alice Maher. Psychoanalysis, Culture, & Society 23:224–226.

McWhorter, J. (2019). The idea that white people can't use the n-word. The Atlantic, August 27.

Miller, A.E., Josephs, L. (2009). Whiteness as pathological narcissism. Contemporary Psychoanalysis 45:93–119.

Moss, D. (2009). On three strands of meaning associated with the word *nigger* used during the course of a psychoanalytic treatment. Psychoanalytic Quarterly 78:819–842.

Moss, D. (2019). Free speech, love speech, hate speech, and neutrality: In and out of the consulting room. Journal of the American Psychoanalytic Association 67:313–327.

Ogden, B.H. (2016). The good story: Exchanges on truth, fiction, and psychoanalytic psychotherapy. Rivista di psicoanalisi 62:149–167.

Ogden, T.H. (1994). The concept of interpretive action. Psychoanalytic Quarterly 63:219–245.

Rao, J.M. (2018). Participant commentary from Jyoti M. Rao. Psychoanalysis, Culture, & Society 23:227.

Rao, J.M. (2020). The promise of epistemic justice and the repair of psychoanalysis. Unpublished manuscript.

Rozmarin, E. (2017). Immigration, belonging, and the tension between center and margin in psychoanalysis. Psychoanalytic Dialogues 27:470–479.

Smith, H.F. (2006). Invisible racism. Psychoanalytic Quarterly 75:3–19.

Stein, H.F. (2004). Countertransference and organizational knowing: New frontiers and old truths. Free Associations 11:325–337.

Steiner, J. (1985). Turning a blind eye: The cover up for Oedipus. International Review of Psychoanalysis 12:161–172.

Stoute, B.J. (2019). Racial socialization and thwarted mentalization: Psychoanalytic reflections from the lived experience of James Baldwin's America. American Imago 76:335–357.

Tan, R. (1993). Racism and similarity: Paranoid-schizoid structures. British Journal of Psychotherapy 10:33–43.

White, K.P. (2002). Surviving hating and being hated: Some personal thoughts about racism from a psychoanalytic perspective. Contemporary Psychoanalysis 38:401–422.

Winnicott, D.W. (1949). Mind and its relation to psyche-soma. In Through Paediatrics to Psycho-Analysis: Collected Papers. New York: Basic Books, 1975, pp. 243–254.

Winnicott, D.W. (1963). The development of the capacity for concern. In The Maturational Processes and the Facilitating Environment: Studies in the Theory of Emotional Development. London: Hogarth Press, 1965, pp. 73–82.

Part III

Learning and Re-Learning Race

Chapter 12

Racial Socialization and Thwarted Mentalization

Psychoanalytic Reflections from the Lived Experience of James Baldwin's America

Beverly J. Stoute

> *No one is born hating another person because of the color of his skin or his background or his religion.*
> —Nelson Mandela (1985)

James Baldwin, with eloquence and depth, articulated the lived experience of being Black in America (Baldwin 1962b). He understood the defensive psychological forces operative in binding aggression and hate in racial attitudes at a time when psychoanalysts were dissecting race and culture out of our theory of the mind, and struggling to understand racist thinking. We had not yet conceptualized othering as a psychodynamic process, or the relative importance of dignity as a construct. The social sciences came to the conversation on race and racism before the fields of psychiatry and psychoanalysis, and even now, we have a long way to go in understanding racism on a psychological level and elucidating how our unconscious racial attitudes affect healthcare delivery and practice in the field of mental health.

Ta-Nehisi Coates' publication of the acclaimed Between the World and Me (2015), a letter to his son in homage to James Baldwin, reminds us of the necessity for dialogue made stark by the ongoing public outcry after the shooting of Trayvon Martin (shot on February 26, 2012; Blow 2012) and numerous unarmed Black men, including a mental health worker, by police officers (July 22, 2016 as reported in Grimm, 2016). These deaths haunt us as a society and return us to the conversation on race and racial socialization spearheaded by James Baldwin early in his career. Published initially in The Progressive in 1962 for the anniversary of the Emancipation Proclamation, James Baldwin's letter to his nephew entitled "My Dungeon Shook: Letter to My

Nephew on the One Hundredth Anniversary of the Emancipation" was reprinted as the first chapter in his acclaimed work, The Fire Next Time (Baldwin 1962a). The May 17th, 1963 issue of Time magazine with Baldwin's picture on the cover, published three months before the March on Washington, contained a review of The Fire Next Time. This jumped it to the top of the nonfiction bestseller list, winning Baldwin international acclaim. The reviewer wrote, "In the US today there is not another writer—black or white—who expresses with such poignancy and abrasiveness the dark realities of the racial ferment of the North and South" (Chaliapin, 1963, p. 26). Today in 2019 that can still be said. Baldwin's letter to his nephew in The Fire Next Time, though a literary source, still has contemporary relevance to the timely discussion of how our perception of racial difference and our unconscious race fantasies impact us daily, even as clinicians.

As a child and adolescent psychiatrist and psychoanalyst, I will speak to my understanding of James Baldwin, and position his letter to his nephew in a developmental context of what African American parents have communicated for generations in what I will call a story of the trans-generational transmission of trauma, and the trans-generational transmission of dignity and defense in the lived experience of racial socialization in America. Drawing on a developmental perspective, I will review certain orienting data on race awareness and racial socialization not taught in most training programs in psychiatry or psychoanalysis before addressing what we, as clinicians, can learn from a re-examination of Baldwin's work. I will demonstrate using clinical examples the invaluable importance of psychodynamic understanding in deconstructing how we process racial difference in treatment situations.

The awareness of and curiosity about racial difference begins early and occurs spontaneously in the course of development. Studies demonstrate that infants as young as three months of age have a preference for faces of their own race, while infants at six months can recognize racial difference (Katz, 1976, 1982; Bar-Haim et al., 2006). By the age of three, children develop a sense of "outsiders"—people who are different from them (Lasker 1929; Fishbein, 1992, 2002). Mary Ellen Goodman's classic research on Race Awareness in Children (1952) demonstrated that pre-school age children of three and four years were clearly aware of race—making the connection to appearance and color but not yet to the concept of race as a social construct.

Kenneth and Maime Clark's (1953) landmark work, which became the foundation of the data reviewed by the Supreme Court in the Brown vs. Board of Education of Topeka (1954), confirmed these early findings. When given a doll and asked, "Which is most like you?," at age three, 37% of children responded accurately in terms of race and by age seven, 87% of children responded accurately in terms of race. As Kenneth Clark put it,

> Learning about race and racial differences, learning one's own racial identity, learning which race is preferred and which is rejected—all these are assimilated by the child as part of the total pattern of ideas he acquires about himself.
>
> (p. 23)

Clark confirmed that children perceive and internalize the racialized symbols of our society—in his era segregated schools—and these social symbols demonstrably shape children's view of themselves in relation to others—be they Black or white (Clark, 1963).

As pre-school children evolve from what Piaget called pre-operational thinking to the stage of concrete operations (Ginsburg and Opper, 1979), the cognitive task of recognizing categories clearly lays the foundation for the capacity to identify the defining attributes of group membership—and later consolidating one's own racial identity in relation to others (Derman-Sparks et al., 1980; Derman-Sparks and Ramsey 2004). As their cognitive development advances, children rely less on appearance and more on the ability to categorize. By age seven, children can define group preferences and group affiliation, and come to appreciate that ethnic affiliation is constant (Piaget, 1951; Derman-Sparks et al., 1980; Derman-Sparks and Ramsey 2004; Lieberman et al., 2017). Therefore, how we become aware of difference, experience difference, respond to difference, and integrate those experiences into our view of ourselves and of others is a process that has conscious and unconscious developmental components, cognitive components, and social and cultural determinants. If you spend time around children, it is obvious that the awareness of racial difference and curiosity about racial difference occurs spontaneously

(Burnett 1997). Children are refreshingly open about this. Here are a few illustrative clinical vignettes.

Vignette 1

A three-year-old biracial Asian girl (one parent white European, one Chinese), referred for assessment of anxiety connected to her parents' divorce, is playing with dolls in my cabinet. She inspects them and assigns the Black dolls to me and the white dolls to her; she assigned the Black mommies and daughters to me, and the white ones to herself. As the treatment deepened, and her transference relationship with me evolved, she would shift and give me one white and one Black doll, asking can this be the mommy to that baby, or can this doll be the wife (white) to this husband (a Black male doll) shifting back and forth between same race and mixed-race pairs.

Vignette 2

Sally was a precocious bright five-year-old Jewish girl with oppositional and impulsive behavior, obsessive-compulsive rituals, and demanding rage at her mother who betrayed her with the birth of a baby brother who stole her prized position in the family. About a month into the treatment she posed the question: Are we alike? Are you like me? She asked this question repeatedly session after session. I told her I was very curious why it mattered so much if we were alike or not, and I wondered what she thought? She explained, "If we are alike, then you are like my family." After months of exploring this question, she entered the office one day and announced, I have figured it out! I welcomed her answer. We are alike. Both of our people were slaves, so you are like me and like my family, and I can trust you.

Vignette 3

Susie, a charming petite six-year-old little girl, was referred for psychiatric assessment of symptoms of poor focus, distractibility, and anxiety with the possible diagnosis of attention deficit hyperactivity disorder. On the initial visit, Susie picked up the toys and remarked to me, "My Mommy did not tell me you were brown. I thought you would be white like Dr. Smith." I asked, tell me more, I am interested in what you are thinking—about my being brown. "Oh. It's just a surprise. My nanny is brown, and you are brown like her."

As the next two vignettes show, the awareness of difference is constantly reworked over the course of development and affected by life experience.

Vignette 4

Sarik, a nine-year-old Hindu boy adopted from birth by white protestant parents, was presented with autistic spectrum traits, obsessive behaviors, daily outbursts, and fragilities in his reality testing. Although my working diagnosis had been Disruptive Mood Dysregulation Disorder, the diagnostic picture was complex and involved the assessment of fragilities in his reality testing. Sarik's mother had made me aware that his class was studying segregation in school the weeks before the following incident which she knew about because Sarik had come home in terror and said, "Back then, Mommy, we could not have gone to the same school!" In that moment of recognition their racial difference became a stark reality. On the day in question, in the second year of a three-time-a-week treatment, Sarik showed me the scratch on his right flank that he had been picking at; he asked why the skin from the healing scar was a different color from the rest of his skin? I explained that when you have brown skin and you have a scar when the scab comes off, the skin heals but the new skin looks lighter because it takes a while for the brown pigmentation to come back. I asked him why he picked the scab. He evaded answering the question. I explained to Sarik that I hoped he knew he could talk about his feelings of being brown; after all, he had pointed out before to me that I am brown too, so maybe I might understand. After much avoidance, finally at the end of the session, he told me, "I am trying to pick the brown away, and be white like my Mom and Dad—I want to be white like everyone else in my family."

Vignette 5

Ms. P, a 38-year-old Hindu woman, had achieved considerable professional success rising to the top of her field but was not married. One day, in the early stage of the treatment, she talked about her conflict between two men with whom she had dates: An educated mature Hindu man of distinguished heritage proposed as an arranged marriage, and an engaging white artist from a working class background, less financially situated, but with a warm engaging personality, to whom she was attracted. I interpreted that while there were many issues with this choice, she seemed to still be struggling with sameness and difference; she responded by talking about her sadness of how difficult it had been being the only family of color in a southern rural town. This opened the door to an avalanche of associations. A close white school friend distanced himself from her when they reached middle school when other kids teased him for playing with the "colored girl." She was shunned. As she put it, "People thought I was different." When she went to high school, no one asked her to date. Describing how she understood these experiences she explained, "I felt different, unattractive... inferior?" When I recommended analysis and referred to her core sense of self that was damaged, she replied, "It goes back to when I was a child." A school friend got the attractive blonde leading role in the school play, and she wanted to try out for the lead too, but "they [the other kids] said no"; "they called me a big [...] Black thing."

"Yeah, they call that a microaggression." I replied, "When you are a child the aggression is not so micro." She responded, "My early conception of myself was that I was this ugly damaged thing."

The coincidence of these experiences with puberty and her physical development merged these issues into a sexual inhibition that she related to her sense of herself as damaged and undesirable. The useful concept of a culturally embedded self integrates the influence of race, culture, and ethnicity as factors in the development of identity, and, further, elucidating the vicissitudes that coincide with the stages of psychosexual development can be fruitful especially when treating patients whose life experiences require that they metabolize these traumatic racialized experiences at key developmental nodal points.

In the pre-adolescent years, children develop a deeper understanding of what racism is and can talk about their racial attitudes as they encounter people from different backgrounds (Katz, 1976; Aboud, 1988; Aboud & Doyle, 1997).

By adolescence, social factors including peer influences shape and consolidate prejudiced thinking. Group affiliations are utilized as a source of identification (the we) or as an object of projection (the them). As adolescents pull away from infantile object ties peer groups become a pivot point to negotiate familial conflicts and consolidate their identity. Adolescents internalize their shared experience as their ethnic group identity is consolidated; they come to appreciate that their shared group experience differs from that of other groups (Young-Bruehl, 1996; Tatum, 2017).

From a related perspective, Vamik Volkan in his 2013 paper on Large Group Identity and Peace Making talks powerfully about the narcissistic investment in what he calls, "large group identity" in clan, nationality, ethnicity, religion, or political ideology that becomes consolidated also in adolescence, as one's group "identity" creates, what he terms, an individual's "inner working model" reference point from which to operationally measure sameness and difference.

As children grow, parents, teachers, media images, and the social setting of interactions with different groups all powerfully facilitate or thwart children's openness to interaction across racial and ethnic lines.

In his work entitled Shades of Black: Diversity in African-American Identity, William Cross Jr. (1991) draws from the early studies of Eugene and Ruth Horowitz (1936), and Kenneth and Maime Clark (1953) on identity development in Black children, and postulates that "self-concept follows the same two-factor model formulated by the Horowitzes (1936) in which self-concept is thought to consist of a general personal identity (PI) domain, and a racial or group identity (GI) domain." Cross later elaborates that, "racial, ethnic, and cultural identity overlap at the level of lived experience, and can be understood by utilizing what Cross terms a racial-ethnic-cultural (REC) identity model" (Cross, 1991 p. 156). According to this model, children—socialized from early childhood—are exposed to beliefs, values, and images that reinforce the dominance of the majority so-called White cultural superiority and to the stereotypes and distortions of Black and white. In the pre-pubertal period, which he termed the period of "pre-awareness," environmental cues about color are communicated to children who use them to internalize how blackness is viewed.

Cross's earlier 1983 study performed an in-depth comparison of the "everyday activities" of a cohort of young, urban, middle-, and lower-class Black and white mothers of pre-school children. Black mothers reared their children to be what Cross termed "biculturally competent" (i.e. aware and comfortable with people of different cultures and practices). In contrast, white mothers, though not overtly racist, gave little "indication [of understanding that] the child's everyday activities could be used as vehicles to increase awareness that the world consists of people who are different [culturally]" (p. 119), so white children relied on TV as the primary source of their images about people of color, and developed, what Cross termed, a "monoracial group orientation." As a result, white children developed social networks with a "white-oriented monoracial reference group orientation," while Black children developed social networks with a "biracial reference group orientation" or "bicultural competence." In fact, in a recent comparative study, British and American white children at ages 6–10 years demonstrated a consistent implicit group preference for white racial groups over Black racial groups with a frequency comparable to adults (Baron & Banaji, 2006; Raabe & Beelmann, 2011), whereas the "bicultural competence," developed by Black children gave them, in contrast, an adaptive advantage in their ability to function in racially heterogeneous environments (Cross & Cross, 2009).

Black adolescent males incorporate another crucial aspect of this socialization process at an earlier age than other children that is of paramount importance in the United States—that is "legal socialization." Legal socialization is defined as "the process by which individuals come to understand and appreciate the law, the institutions that create those laws, and the people who enforce those laws"; legal socialization occurs at a younger age for Black males, especially those who live in urban environments, and this is intensified in urban schools where there is a significant police presence (Henning, 2017).

In the literature on legal socialization, a telling study exploring police perceptions of childhood innocence revealed that police officers consistently overestimated the age of adolescent Black male suspects by five years and they underestimated the age of adolescent white male suspects by one year; further the older the officer thought the adolescent offender was the more culpable for the crime he perceived him to be (Henning, 2017). In another study that examined the perception of a child's innocence, it was revealed that children aged 0–9 years are perceived as equally innocent regardless of race

(Goff et al., 2014), but, as children mature, this changes: In general, Black children are seen as less innocent; Black children aged 10–13 are perceived as equivalent in innocence to non-black children aged 14–17, and Black children aged 14–17 are seen as equivalent in innocence to non-black children aged 18–21 (Goff et al., 2014). Studies in the cognitive sciences have now shown that even white subjects who espouse egalitarian beliefs can still demonstrate racial bias on implicit measures (Olson & Fazio, 2003; Nosek, Hawkins & Frazier, 2011), and, therefore, may not have conscious awareness of these racialized attitudes.

In their work entitled "The Psychology of Black Boys and Adolescents," Kirkland Vaughans, and Warren Spielberg (2014) chronicle the overwhelming data on the direct and indirect "hostile messages" in schools and in the media that Black boys face and analyze, from a psychoanalytic perspective, the defensive strategies Black adolescent boys employ to cope. They artfully integrate Fonagy and Target's work on mentalization (Fonagy 2003; Fonagy & Target, 2003; Fonagy, 2011).

In their classic paper on mentalization, Fonagy and Target (2003) postulated that the ability to mentalize involves a self-reflective and interpersonal experience that creates the capacity to observe and reflect on the mental state of the other. In doing so, we develop a foundational ability to imagine the lived experience of what others may be thinking, feeling, and experiencing. Spielberg points out that when adults and authority figures are "rejecting, hostile, or difficult to understand," the child is less open to the mind and influence of others. Recognizing the hostility of meaningful adults then would be too difficult, so the child wards off his awareness of the mind of that adult who could be a parent or teacher, and as an adaptive strategy closes his mind to these figures in his life; this impairs the development of the child's reflective capacity (Spielberg, 2014, p. 57).

Vaughans and Spielberg (2014) point to the inability of educators and police to mentalize Black boys, and the defensive utility of the so-called cool pose that Black boys adopt to protect themselves psychologically from these "toxic" messages. In writing about police violence against African American boys, Vaughans (2016) concludes that the resulting "social dilemma" alienates adolescent Black boys from society and robs them of the "social acceptance and support" that they, as adolescents, need to foster their development. The loss of a loveable self-image is instead replaced by what he calls "a denigrated self-image" that is popularized throughout the national media (Vaughans & Harris, 2016, p. 174). Physical violence is perpetuated then, Bateman and Fonagy (2006) further postulate, when we doubt the Other has a mind or when we see the Other as a member of an alien group so that the Other is seen as separate and disconnected from you. So, this vicious cycle of thwarted mentalization is rationalized, but can be understood in psychoanalytic terms.

Case Example: Preston

With the above background on racial socialization and the power of mentalization, I will now present the case of Preston, an adolescent boy I treated early in my career. Rest on, a seriously disturbed 13-year-old tenth-grade African American boy, was hospitalized with depressed mood and disruptive behavior at school after a suicide attempt. Without enumerating the many traumas in his life, I will emphasize that both of his parents had abandoned him. Preston's parents met in college, and his mother got pregnant by accident. She had a history of serious psychiatric illness and drug use, unstable relationships with men including one boyfriend who physically and sexually abused Preston; his father had been inconsistent throughout. Preston's mother, after getting involved with a new man, dropped him off with his paternal grandparents as a young boy; his grandparents, recognizing the striking family resemblance, accepted Preston without reservation. His grandparents and paternal aunt had been his consistent caretakers since, but even their consistency could not heal his sense of abandonment and loss.

In the early weeks of his hospital stay, Preston was difficult to manage. His daily aggressive outbursts, suicidal threats, and attempts necessitated placement in seclusion and four-point restraints. He made a noose out of his bed sheets, tried to break open the window to jump, and flew into rage at the least provocation. After several incidents requiring four-point restraints to control his aggression, he began to voice how he liked the restraints. This connected to his underlying conflict since they drew maximal attention and physical contact which he craved but could not directly acknowledge. The

Black male staff mental health workers were not afraid of Preston, and endured his aggression in these many outbursts although white staff members seemed quietly more cautious. We worked on elaborate behavioral contracts— he earned his way out of his room over a period of three weeks requiring intensive staff monitoring and medication adjustment.

In the differential diagnosis, a review of Preston's prior outpatient medications trials of Imipramine, Mellaril, and Prozac revealed that none had controlled the symptoms of depression, distractibility, impulsive outbursts, or volatile rejection sensitivity. At the time of this treatment Diagnostic and Statistical Manual of Mental Disorders IV (DSM IV) had not been released; the DSM-III diagnostic impression was that of attention deficit hyperactivity disorder, dysthymia, and oppositional defiant disorder; a careful review of his history made us entertain, but not substantiate a diagnosis of bipolar disorder. If one retrospectively makes use of DSM V, in addition to attention deficit hyperactivity disorder, combined type, and oppositional defiant disorder, a diagnostic reformulation might consider disruptive mood dysregulation disorder and concomitant post-traumatic stress disorder, with delayed expression from the physical and sexual abuse. Given the family history of depression, anxiety, and substance use, the recommendation of lithium was made, and in combination, a higher dose of immediate release methylphenidate dosed three times per day proved helpful. Although neuroleptics were considered, Preston refused to take them, insisting, "I am not psychotic." Finally, although the DSM did not allow the diagnosis of a personality disorder at such a young age, it was clear that borderline and narcissistic traits seemed a potential liability. His need for attention was insatiable. He exhibited the classic defenses of splitting, denial, and projection and his distortions of interactions with co-patients bordered on paranoid as he would often say, "no one believes me; no one cares; you're using me like a guinea pig." Although medication adjustment was helpful in decreasing the intensity of his mood lability, Preston was only intermittently motivated to control his anger, and this was addressed in the therapy that unfolded.

Achieving better control and connecting to me in the therapy was the preamble to organizing, articulating, and voicing his rage. I saw him for sessions daily, Monday through Friday, five sessions a week.

Now this was not a classical analysis, but this case speaks to the power of utilizing an analytic framework to understand trauma and apply a psychodynamic psychotherapeutic approach even in an inpatient setting.

I could discuss many aspects of this treatment. I could talk about the self-defeating sadomasochistic enactment with the physical restraints, and his unconscious struggle to make himself unlovable. After all, we know that traumatized children must re-enact elements of their trauma in an attempt to give expression to, work through, and master the trauma. I could talk about the psychodynamic perspective on how adolescents can use their peer group or, in this case the unit staff, in a process analogous to projective identification, to mobilize the staff to act out his conflicts and reject him. But, the relevant point I want to emphasize here is how the process of joint mentalization helped me to help the staff and, in family meetings, his family, rework their vision of Preston from that of a dangerous out of control Black youth to that of a needy traumatized boy afraid to trust and afraid of abandonment. You see Preston was one of the many Black boys hospitalized with a description of "dangerous" who was seen as more threatening than his white counterparts. From the outset, this image of him as dangerous interfered with the staff's ability to see him as depressed and traumatized, and empathize with his pain.

My meetings and discussions with the staff focused on helping them to process their frustration with how difficult Preston was to manage, and their fear of Preston's "dangerousness." I helped them talk about their racialized perceptions and asked them, just how "dangerous" was he really? I challenged the staff members to think about their disproportionate fear of this Black adolescent boy compared to white male adolescent patients. I explained to them how Preston's pain and trauma were undercurrents of his aggressive and self-destructive behavior, and how this enactment in the repeated cycles of provoking rejection was a repetition in service of mastering the trauma, abuse, and broken attachments that Preston had endured. We discussed these issues in staff meetings and the derivatives in community meetings because he had troubled peer relationships too.

Individual sessions with Preston were slightly atypical because we did not always meet in my office. You see, Preston could only talk to me after he had a snack. While on the unit, we would stop by the dining hall. When he was able to leave the unit to walk across the street to my office, he discovered the NY deli on the corner. He insisted I buy him a snack from the store, rationalizing that he needed better food than what was on the hospital unit and I, being a doctor, must have the money to afford it. This became a ritual. Eating, or being fed, seemed to settle him down before the session; it was the base he needed if we were to process the many levels of loss and trauma he had endured. In my mind, he was an angry, insatiably hungry boy who needed to process the painful abandonments by his parents, and to understand how he scared away peers and adults in his life with his anger.

As he became engaged, I began to interpret to him my sense that he feared that he was unlikeable—and maybe unlovable—because of his experiences being abandoned by his parents. To counteract and master those feelings, he wanted friends; but his rage and aggression scared people away. Preston acted as Winnicott presents in his 1949 paper "Hate and the Counter-Transference": "The child without parents is traumatized; to recover when he finds a new home, he must first," as Winnicott points out, "start to test out the environment he has found, and seek proof of his guardians' ability to hate [him] objectively," and then, "It seems that he can believe in being loved only after reaching being hated" (p. 72).

As Preston became more consciously aware of his conflicts about attachment, he began to acknowledge his sadness. Talking about his demanding attachment to me, and his wish that I be his mother, paved the way for him to discuss what it meant to him that I was not, leading to how it felt to have a mother with serious psychiatric illness and an uninvolved father. This helped him talk about his fear of trusting, his insatiable need for attention, and difficulty tolerating disappointment. As he put his rage and anger about having been abandoned into words in the therapy, he was able to control his behavior; this paved the way for him to elicit more positive responses from his grandmother, his aunt, and the staff members. They responded positively to his need for them to engage, and he was better able to connect and identify with them. In the transference, I had become the new mother from whom he demanded food and wanted love, and the hospital staff—his extended family. With us and through us, he processed his conflict about wanting and demanding to be taken care of, then pushing away those who responded; he did this by learning to give voice to his pain. Having a whole staff with whom to share and process his rageful reactions made the transference bearable. Preston decided to write his parents each a letter, an act he processed in therapy. His mother answered from an inpatient rehab center, explaining to him that she loved him but was unable to take care of him: This was helpful and affirming. His father never answered and we processed his sadness.

Toward the end of his hospital stay, he was a changed person; he became the darling of the community. He was an active voice in community meetings, able to discuss anger and conflict, and encourage peers to do so as well. To get attention, he engaged staff members in positive ways. Eventually, placement in a therapeutic residential school forced us to conclude our work. In the last days, Preston talked about missing us all, and in his final group therapy session on the unit, a peer asked what advice he would give to the other adolescent patients, he replied, "You can't fight the system; you have to work with it." When asked, "Can the system help you?" he answered, "If you want it to."

I learned many things from Preston at that early stage in my career: That regardless of the treatment context, psychoanalytic understanding can provide a mutative force; that adolescents use the analyst as transference figures and as real figures in their attachment to us, especially when trauma and abandonment have impaired their early development; that more than any interpretation we make to our patients, they know what we reflect back in our image of and compassion for them; for traumatized children, the absence of an adult attachment figure who bears, shares, and reflects back their pain and a sense of them as loveable can thwart their capacity for attachment and maybe even love; and, that our capacity as psychoanalysts to see our patients in their struggles to be more fully human and to continue thinking as we do, no matter where we find ourselves working, gives us the opportunity to offer a vehicle for change.

A key component of this treatment, I believe, was how I was able to mentalize Preston despite his many attempts to ward off connection. His so-called "dangerousness" did not deter me from attempting to develop a treatment relationship, nor did it forestall my using a psychoanalytic framework to make sense of his painful inner world, and hunger for attachment. I think he knew that—consciously and unconsciously—through my compassionate attitude towards him and my having given in to his demands to be fed. But there was the additional element—you see Preston is Black and so am I. In fact, he knew I was the only Black attending doctor on the inpatient psychiatric staff at that time, and that I was the inpatient Unit Chief. He was very proud of this. He internalized the image I had of him that was reflected in my attitude towards him in the treatment. He idealized me as the Black doctor-mother who was in charge, and through whom he was able to see a reflected capacity for power, strength, and compassion that he wanted to internalize for himself. He was bright, had skipped two grades in school, and toyed with the idea of whether he could one day be smart like me. He also became attached to certain Black staff members whom he leaned on as surrogate parental figures. In the shared reflective mentalization with an important adult, an adolescent, like Preston, can identify with and internalize aspects of ego functioning and a reflected self-image, and go on to develop an ego ideal through identification with that important adult who mentalizes him. This allows the adolescent to connect to and identify with other adults in his life and take in the mentalized image the adult(s) may have of him.

After being placed, Preston returned to visit the hospital staff from time to time in the first year after he left; then we never saw him again. One day, 20 years later I had confirmation of the success of my work with Preston. At the age of 33, Preston called me to tell me that he needed to track me down. He asked if I remembered him. He told me he needed me to know how much he appreciated that I had seen who he was then, and understood his pain; and he never forgot that. Now a man, at age 33, successful in managing his life, he wanted to tell me that he had kept the image of me and had hoped I remembered him. I told him that yes, I did remember him, still had the vase on the bookshelf in my office that he had given me as his goodbye gift, and that I was heartened to hear that he was doing well. Jokingly he said, "Oh and Dr. Stoute, I also had a crush on you back then, too."

Relevance to James Baldwin

Now, you may ask, how is this story of Preston related to James Baldwin? In Notes on a Native Son (1940), James Baldwin contemplated the dilemma faced by Black parents in America, that is "how to prepare the child for the day when the child would be despised and how to create in the child—by what means—a stronger antidote to this poison than one had for oneself" (p. 106). As he spoke to his nephew in The Fire Next Time, he reframed the challenge: How "to strengthen you [James] against a loveless world" (p. 7).

Baldwin, the eldest of nine, watched his father struggle against poverty and against racism; he watched the assault of racism on his father's dignity; he saw the internalized hate and reactive rage eat away at his soul. In his late adolescence, Baldwin fled to Paris and, from a distance, came to terms with his racial, and sexual identities and, through his writing, worked through his own pain, anguish, and conflict. In the letter to his nephew, his namesake, James Baldwin, decades before psychoanalysis could articulate it, explicated what is now called the trans-generational transmission of trauma; and, more specifically, the shared trauma that he knew first hand of the denigrated image mentalized in the American consciousness of Black men that young James would face. Though not a parent himself, as the eldest of nine, Baldwin was caretaker to his younger siblings including the brother to whom he was closest and who became his confidante, David—young James' father. Baldwin reminds us also, of what I call, the trans-generational transmission of defense that African American parents pass down to their sons and daughters in this cycle. While I emphasize sons here since Baldwin spoke to his nephew, the struggle of Black girls and Black women is no less arduous or important.

I reread this letter in the summer of 2016 when murder after murder was blast across the news of police violence against unarmed Black men in the wake of a racially polarizing presidential campaign. You see, that year my son got his driver's license and my husband and I had to tell him that his upper middle-class background could not eliminate the obstacles he would face as a Black man confronting racism in America. My kind-hearted, good natured, 6' 6" tall, scholar athlete son, for whom most of his life Barack Obama was President, naively said, "But Mom, if I am not doing anything wrong, I should be ok." We made him read Ta-Nehisi Coates' Between the World and Me. I explained to my son, then 16, the social context of who James Baldwin was and how Coates had leaned on Baldwin's cultural and literary example. When I was writing this paper, I told a colleague that I was not sure I felt developmentally ready to discuss this topic because the anxiety about letting my son go as he prepared to leave for college was too immediate and scary. As Charles Blow, a writer for the New York Times, put it in a CNN interview (2016) on the topic, we have to clip our sons' wings when we should be encouraging them to fly.

So Black parents, have "the talk," as people now refer to it, to help our sons' fashion, what I call, the psychic shield they will need to insulate their sense of self to ward off the racialized projections of hate. We warn our sons, guard your body, when you encounter the police: "Keep your hands where they can see them." "Ask the officer before you reach for your wallet. And then wait before you reach for it." "Do not wear black hoodies at night." "Do not run when you see the police."

Baldwin, however, does not describe in this letter the degree of terror he must have felt, nor does he describe the dehumanizing violence of racial assault he must have witnessed growing up in Harlem in the pre-civil rights era America. The pure unadulterated police brutality portrayed recently in the movie Detroit during the 1960s Detroit race riots is an example of the disturbing dehumanization that Baldwin feared for young James. It is not that racial brutality assaults who you are, it assaults that you are, your very existence. It seeks to strip you of your very humanity. Dorothy Holmes (2016), adapting the term from Leonard Shengold (1989), describes such practices of systemic racism as "soul murdering."

Inherent in Baldwin's thinking is the powerful conceptualization of dignity; no conversation on the trans-generational transmission of resilience in facing racism is complete without a discussion of dignity. Baldwin refers to the "unassailable monumental dignity," of African Americans passed down in families in this trans-generational tale of trauma, decades before psychoanalysts had conceptualized resilience and dignity in psychological terms as constructs operative in protecting the self in circumstances of discrimination and dehumanizing trauma.

According to his biographer, David Leeming (1994), Baldwin wrote another letter. In 1952, on returning from Paris to New York to visit his family when he was publishing his first book, his mother requested he write a letter to his younger brother, Wilmer, who had been mistreated by white officers in the army. According to Leeming:

> He [Baldwin] reminded his brother that racism is based on fear, that when the white racist confronts the black man, what he sees is not the individual man, but a "nightmare" of his own creation.

> Above all he [Baldwin] said, "you must take care not to step 'inside' his nightmare, his guilt and his fear, his hatred. To step inside the nightmare is to justify and to relinquish the soul's freedom and the control over one's life. To enter the nightmare is to become a 'nigger.'"
>
> (Leeming, p. 81)

In these letters, Baldwin admonishes both men to protect themselves: Do not step into the nightmare. Baldwin instructs them on how to forge a psychic shield to ward off internalizing the hate which he had seen destroy his father. Maintaining one's dignity, Baldwin knew, is essential to protecting one's self-worth when deflecting the projective assault of racist hatred. While Baldwin is more often quoted for speaking about love, I think this subtle point about dignity should be given due emphasis.

Psychoanalysts are just beginning to understand and conceptualize the importance of dignity—that irreducible aspect of one's self-worth—that protects the emerging ego ideal especially in situations of dehumanizing trauma. Dignity, however, is an elusive construct to define. Although Freud used the term twenty-three times in his Standard Edition (Levine, 2016), the first psychoanalytic attempt in the literature to define the term, written by Eli Marcovitz in 1966, existed in relative obscurity until Susan Levine (2016) reprinted it in her edited book entitled Dignity Matters. Marcovitz (1970/2016) pointed to dignity as "an intra-psychic and a social phenomenon" the formation of which begins in infancy and develops as the child experiences "the feeling of being nurtured, protected, and valued" (as cited in Levine, 2016, p. 64). Dorothy Holmes (2016), in her paper in Levine's volume entitled "I Knew That My Mind Could Take me Anywhere: Psychoanalytic Reflections on the Dignity of African Americans Living in a Racist Society," points out that "dignity—[is that] irreducible human worth that persists and motivates against all odds. Dignity is inseparable from what it means to be human" (p. 119). Holmes explains further,

> There is no psychoanalytic theory or definition of dignity per se [...] Dignity is a construct that embraces that larger sphere of influence whereas more usual psychoanalytic constructs such as

self and self-esteem limit their considerations [...] the psychoanalytic concept of self allows for the self to be fragmented [...]

dignity is a more robust construct than the self, because dignity cannot be fragmented. It is fundamental to human nature and is indivisible [...] Growing up Black in America is inherently perilous in terms of one's dignity since racism by design attempts to reduce one's worth.

(p. 120)

As Dr. Martin Luther King, Jr., once said, *One's dignity may be assaulted, vandalized, cruelly mocked, but it can never be taken away unless it is surrendered.*

If dignity bolsters the sense of self in withstanding the damaging effects of dehumanizing trauma, then a sense of dignity seems essential in preserving our capacity for human connection and maybe even love when the sense of self is assaulted.

Donna Hicks in her evocative 2016 paper entitled "A matter of dignity: building human relationships," points out that when children are not treated with dignity by caregivers, they do not develop a sense of worthiness. Further, Hicks postulates, children interpret being treated badly to mean they are bad, so, by implication, internalizing this sense of badness is destructive to their sense of self-worth and impacts later interpersonal functioning. All of this Baldwin understood from his lived experience in this trans-generational drama. As a psychiatrist and psychoanalyst, then, I ask how is dignity constructed developmentally especially in the face of dehumanizing trauma? Can understanding this construct developmentally add to our understanding of how some people emerge more intact than others when subject to horrific trauma, and help us clarify the differentiating individual, familial, and social factors that foster this human endurance? Can we integrate this construct into our theory of the formation of self-esteem and ego ideal? And can this understanding help us in our clinical work with patients?

As a mature psychoanalyst now, I have come to understand with greater clarity my personal tale of the trans-generational transmission of trauma and transmission of defense in my life. The psychic shield passed down in my family contained the centering belief that human beings have the capacity to change; and that capacity for change is best exemplified by the radical potential psychoanalytically oriented theory and practice offer to detoxify hate and heal trauma. So James Baldwin's letter to his nephew, I would argue, with clarity, simplicity, and eloquence, is a powerful psychoanalytic text that tells us the condensed story of the trans-generational transmission of trauma of African Americans, and the trans-generational transmission of defense.

Although I have used James Baldwin, a literary source, to venture into thinking about race and its impact on how we as clinicians view our patients, we can learn from his challenge to our society that we face together the ongoing trans-generational traumas of our country's racialized history. The Baldwinian directive to work to release us from the painful history of our collective trauma and "force our brothers to see themselves as they are and to cease fleeing from reality and begin to change," is, my dear colleagues, at heart a psychoanalytic directive. As clinicians, we too can exercise a social conscience in how we see our work with patients and we can expand our world-view and our view of ourselves. As educators and clinicians, are we ready, then, to make race and racism a subject of disciplined inquiry, study and focus in our theoretical formulations, in our research endeavors, in our teaching, our supervisions, our therapies, our analyses, our academic panels and conferences, our professional organizations, in our daily conversations wherever we may be? Can we widen the scope of psychoanalytic influence on understanding the related issues in our communities, and our world? Can we work together to challenge the social resistance to confronting racism head on by first examining our own attitudes about race as individuals and as a field? James Baldwin said, "I do believe we can become better than we are." That is the challenge before us my dear colleagues. Can we, as individuals and as a society, rise to that challenge? In a world where racial hatred and aggression dominate the world stage, what most scares me: What will happen if we don't?

References

Aboud, F. (1988). *Children and Prejudice*. Blackwell: Oxford.
Aboud, F.E. and Doyle, A.B. (1997). Does talk of race foster prejudice or tolerance in children? Canadian Journal of Behavioural Science, 29(3), 161–170
Baldwin, J. (1940). *Notes on a Native Son*. New York: Harper & Row.

Baldwin, J. (1962a). A letter to my nephew. *The Progressive*, December 1, 1962. https://progressive.org/magazine/letter-nephew/ (Last accessed July 2, 2022).

Baldwin, J. (1962b). *The Fire Next Time*. New York: Vintage International.

Bar-Haim, Y., Ziv, T., Lamy, D., and Hodes, R.M. (2006). Nature and nurture in own-race face processing. *Psychological Science* 17(2):159–163.

Baron, A.S. and Banaji, M.R. (2006). The development of implicit attitudes: Evidence of race evaluations from ages 6 and 10 and adulthood. *Psychological Science* 17:53–58.

Bateman, A. and Fonagy, P. (2006). *Mentalization-based Treatment for Borderline Personality Disorder*. Oxford, England: Oxford University Press.

Blow, C. (2012). The curious case of Trayvon Martin. *New York Times*, March 16.

Blow, C. (2016). You are being forced to clip your own child's wings. CNN News, July 7.

Brown vs. Board of Education of Topeka, 347 U.S. 493(1954). Landmark decision which declared that separate but equal segregation in schools is unconstitutional.

Burnette, E. (1997). Talking openly about race thwarts racism in children. *APA Monitor*, June 2.

Chaliapin, B. (1963). Nation: The root of the negro problem. *Time*, May 17.

Clark, K. (1953). Desegregation: An appraisal of the evidence. *Journal of Social Issues* 9(4):1–75.

Clark, K. (1963). *Prejudice and Your Child*. Boston: Beacon Press.

Coates, T. (2015). *Between the World and Me*. New York: Random House.

Cross, W., Jr. (1983). The ecology of human development for Black and White children: Implications for predicting racial preference patterns. *Critical Perspectives of Third World America* 1(1):177–189.

Cross, W., Jr. (1991). *Shades of Black: Diversity in African-American Identity*. Philadelphia: Temple University Press.

Cross, W.E. and Cross, B.A. (2009). Theory, research, and models. In *Handbook of Race, Racism, and the Developing Child*, S.M. Quintana and C. McKown, eds. New Jersey: John Wiley & Sons, pp. 154–181.

Derman-Sparks, L., Higa, C., and Sparks, B. (1980). *Children, Race and Racism: How Race Awareness Develops*. Retrieved from www.teachingforchange.org/wpcontent/ uploads/2012/08/ec_childrenraceracism_english.pdf.

Derman-Sparks, L. and Ramsey, P.G. (2004). *What if all the Kids are White? Anti-Bias Multicultural Education with Young Children and Families*. New York: Teachers College Press. Dissertation No. 104, Columbia University.

Fishbein, H.D. (1992). Factors important in the formation of preschoolers' friendship. *Journal of Genetic Psychology* 146:37–44.

Fishbein, H.D. (2002). *Peer Prejudice and Discrimination*. New Jersey: Lawrence Erlbaum Associates.

Fonagy, P. (2003). The development of psychopathology from infancy to adulthood: The mysterious unfolding of disturbance in time. *Infant Mental Health Journal* 24(3):212–239.

Fonagy, P. (2011). What is mentalization? The concept and its foundation in developmental research and social-cognitive neuroscience. In *Keeping Children in Mind: Mentalization-based Interventions with Children, Young People and their Families*, N. Midgley and I. Vrouva, eds. London: Routledge.

Fonagy, P. and Target, M. (2003). Chapter 12: Fonagy and Target's model of mentalization. In *Psychoanalytic Theories: Perspectives from Developmental Psychopathology*. New York: Brunner-Routledge, pp. 270–282.

Ginsburg, H. and Opper, S. (1979). *Piaget's Theory of Intellectual Development*. New Jersey: Prentice-Hall, Inc.

Goff, P., et al. (2014). The essence of innocence: Consequences of dehumanizing black children. *Journal of Personality and Social Psychology* 106:526–45.

Goodman, M. (1952). *Race Awareness in Children*. California: Addison-Wesley Press.

Grimm, F. (2016). North Miami dodges bullet after police shoot innocent health care worker. *Miami Herald*. July 22, 2016.

Henning, K. (2017). Boys to men: The role of policing in the socialization of Black boys. In *Policing the Black Man*, Davis, A., ed. New York: Pantheon Books, pp. 57–94.

Hicks, D. (2016). A matter of dignity: Building human relationships. In *Dignity Matters*, S. Levine, ed. London: Karnac Books.

Holmes, D. (2016). "I knew that my mind could take me anywhere": Psychoanalytic reflections on the dignity of African Americans living in a racist society. In *Dignity Matters*, S. Levine, ed. London: Karnac Books, pp. 119–140.

Horowitz, E.L. (1936). The development of attitude toward the Negro. *Archives of Psychology*

Katz, P. (1976). How the twig is bent. In *Towards the Elimination of Racism*, P. Katz, ed. New York: Pergamon Press, pp.13–14.

Katz, P. (1976). The acquisition of racial attitudes in children. In *Towards the Elimination of Racism*, P. Katz, ed. Pergamon Press: New York, pp. 125–150.

Katz, P. (1982). Development of children's racial awareness and intergroup attitudes. In *Current Topics in Early Childhood Education (Vol. IV)*, L.G. Katz, ed. New Jersey: Ablex Publishing Corporation.

Lasker, B. (1929). *Race Attitudes in Children*. New York: Henry Holt and Company.

Leeming, D. (1994). *James Baldwin: A Biography*. New York: Arcade Publishing.

Levine, S., ed. (2016). *Dignity Matters*. London: Karnac Books.

Lieberman, Z., Woodward, A.L., and Kinzler, K.D. (2017). The origins of social categorization. *Trends in Cognitive Sciences* 21(7):556–568.

Mandela, N. (1995). *The Long Walk to Freedom: The Autobiography of Nelson Mandela*. New York: Little Brown & Co.

Marcovitz, E. (1966/2018). Dignity. In *Dignity Matters*, S. Levine, ed. London: Karnac Books, pp. 61–72.

Marcovitz, E (1970). Dignity. *The bulletin of the Philadelphia Association for Psychoanalysis*, 20: 105–116. Reprinted In *Bemoaning the Lost Dream: Collected Papers of Eli Marcovitz M.D.*, M.S. Temeles, ed. Philadelphia Association for Psychoanalysis, 1982–1983.

Nosek, B.A., Hawkins, C.B., and Frazier, R.S. (2011). Implicit social cognition: From measures to mechanisms. *Trends in Cognitive Sciences* 15:152–159.

Olson, M.A., and Fazio, R.H. (2003). Relations between implicit measures of prejudice: What are we measuring? *Psychological Science* 14:636–639.

Piaget, J. (1951). The development of children of the idea of the homeland and of relations with other countries. *International Social Science Bulletin, III* 3:561–578.

Raabe, T. and Beelmann, A. (2011). Development of ethnic, racial, and national prejudice in childhood and adolescence. A multinational meta-analysis of age differences. *Child Development* 82:1715–1737.

Shengold, L. (1989). *Soul Murder*. New York: Random House.

Spielberg, W. (2014). Chapter 2: Trying Not to Know. In *The Psychology of Black Boys and Adolescents*, Vaughans, K. and W. Spielberg, eds. Santa Barbara, California: Praeger, pp. 45–73.

Tatum, B. (2017). *Why Are All the Black Kids Sitting Together in the Cafeteria?* New York: Basic Books.

Vaughans, K. and W. Spielberg, eds. (2014). *The Psychology of Black Boys and Adolescents*. Santa Barbara, California: Praeger.

Vaughans, K. (2016). African-American boys and adolescents under the shadow of slavery's legacy. *The American Psychoanalyst*, Fall 2016 50 (3): 6, 26–29.

Vaughans, K. and L. Harris. (2016). The police, Black and Hispanic boys: A dangerous inability to mentalize. *Journal of Infant, Child, and Adolescent Psychotherapy* 15(3):171–178.

Volkan, V. (2013). Large group psychology in its own right: Large group identity and peace making. *International Journal of Applied Psychoanalytic Studies* 10(3):210–246.

Winnicott, D. (1949). Hate in the counter-transference. *International Journal of Psychoanalysis* 30:69–74.

Young-Bruehl, E. (1996). *Adolescence and the Aims of Hatred in the Anatomy of Prejudices*. Cambridge, Massachusetts: Harvard University Press.

Chapter 13

From Multicultural Competence to Radical Openness

A Psychoanalytic Engagement of Otherness

Anton Hart

> "Multicultural competence–I wish that term would be banished from this earth. Competence? We're going to be *competent* in relating to the other?"

Of all my lines in the film, "Black Psychoanalysts Speak," the 2014 PEP video by Basia Winograd, this is the one that has garnered the most response. It seems to have resonated with people's misgivings about the emphasis in many approaches to multicultural "training." I read in this resonance a dissatisfaction with the aspiration of "becoming competent" at relating to human beings who are different from oneself, with studying the other in an acquisitive, non-participatory, and, in all likelihood, objectifying manner. Later in the film, I elaborate:

> I'm very critical of the multicultural competency movement because I don't think that reaching across cultural or racial boundaries is something to become competent at. I think it's something to become open to. There's something about the notion of competency which still keeps people who are different from you as other, like they're this commodity that we have to get better at dealing with.

I am surprised when psychoanalysts and other practitioners, sometimes those who are Black like me[1] or with some different otherness status, seem to embrace such a competency emphasis without sufficient criticism. Multicultural competency might be well intentioned in that it is attempting to help people increase their empathic availability while decreasing tendencies to distance or callously offend. Multicultural training tries to offer a rudimentary script so that necessary conversations across the divides of difference take place rather than the participants fleeing and avoiding those conversations. But this is not going sufficiently deep. This is why many people with whom I have spoken convey that they feel a sense of dread about having multicultural competency training required of them in their organization, and why many complain that the training they have received was concrete and, oftentimes, deadly boring. Such training inherently promotes a defended, prepared manner of addressing difference and otherness, with all of their attendant anxieties and defenses, and this represents a major lost opportunity for personal reflections and deeper engagement.

The heart of the matter is learning how to become increasingly undefended around matters of diversity and otherness such that you can be open: open to the other person who will be, in some significant ways, most certainly different from you. A psychoanalytic sensibility suggests to us that genuine openness can only emerge in the context of an unscripted dialog, one that involves making contact with and participating in an exchange that will, necessarily, threaten the dialogic participants' understandings, identities, and perceptions.

Because it is a talking cure, and because it prizes the continually refined formulations and understandings of its participants (in the context of a relationship between those participants), psychoanalysis holds the potential to open up and enrich dialogue across boundaries marked by racial, ethnic, and cultural difference in a way that is deeply personal. It encourages the participants to take the risk of losing understandings they have of themselves and of each other that constitute prejudices. In a sense, a new language must emerge in each dyad, one that is intended to grasp both the overlapping and the contrasting experiences of the two participants, while at the same time allowing for articulation of the emergent, combined experience of the two together. This experience will inherently challenge, threaten and revise the understandings that the co-participants bring individually to the conversation owing to their histories and their unique contexts, be they cultural, racial, sexual, socioeconomic, or otherwise.

Unformulated Dialog

Cross-cultural interlocutors must grapple with new ways of communicating, not just in the sense that they are encountering other whose background may be different and unfamiliar, but also in the sense that the deepest and richest forms of contact and conversation between people are emergent rather than fixed. In contrast, the multicultural competency approach emphasizes gaining a form of mastery or at least rudimentary ability in speaking the language of the other, on becoming aware of the other's customs, vocabulary, and syntax. A psychoanalytic sensibility holds that the participants in the analytic dialogue—nalyst and analysand, supervisor and supervisee, student and teacher, colleague and colleague—attempt to lose their own senses of mastery-based relating, to relinquish the feelings of cultural knowing and competence that they may have held prior to entering into each new conversation with each new other. Psychoanalytic engagement with issues of otherness involves repeatedly trying to not assume understanding and to be open to receiving understandings, insights and formulations—always temporary and limited in their scope. Such trying-not-to-assume-while-instead-trying-to-be-receptive involves the repeated, deliberate abandonment of presumptions, about both self and other while simultaneously maintaining a disposition of curiosity.

This is where what I have come to call *radical openness* comes into play. Radical openness involves a disciplined psychoanalytic stance of attempting to notice, question, and relinquish presumptions about oneself and the other. In order to do this in analysis, the psychoanalyst must be willing to be both curious about his or her own emergent experience and that of the analysand, and also be a responsive subject in relation to the analysand's curiosity. (And it is important to clarify here that by "responsive" I do not mean "self-disclosing." While some instances of intentional self-disclosure may serve the cause of fostering an analytic environment of reflectiveness, curiosity, and openness, some disclosures may have the opposite effect. The openness here refers to a receptivity to that which is unexpected in relation to oneself and in relation to the other.)

In talks I've given about diversity and otherness I have tried to acknowledge the good intentions inherent in people's attempts to get trained in how to be with people who are different from themselves. But I've wanted to urge people to go deeper. Competency in relation to the other might be seen as a starting point rather than an ultimate goal, like taking a crash course in a foreign language before you go to a new country in order to have some working phrases. I would propose that even without that course, you could still find a way to connect.

If you have enough courage, your experience could be more interesting than it would have been if you used your handy book of words and phrases to get what you want more efficiently. Throwing away the book, you would need to approach foreign strangers with a kind of interest, a turning towards their faces, listening to what they say and what you say, and how you both seem to be hearing each other. And you would have to be prepared to listen for the responses, including the negative ones, and to reflect on how you seem to be taking in—or keeping out—the responses you are getting. In that case, no matter what is said, whatever awkwardness comes out of your mouth, because of your own limited frame of reference or previously acquired fluency, you are going to be able to work toward reciprocal communication.

You might wind up, along the way, saying something that's not the "right" thing to say, something that may even offend. But if you approach the dialogue with a willingness to consider things that are out of your awareness (unconscious, unformulated), things that have not occurred to you before, then maybe the other can tell you about their problems with what you are asking and how you are asking it. But this useful information can only be conveyed to you if you convey, in your way of both speaking and listening, that you're interested in hearing about how you misunderstood, how you got things wrong, how you failed to understand, and how you were experienced as presuming rather than listening with an open mind. In this way, you can come to participate in a cross-cultural dialogue that will be stimulating and interesting rather than non-offensively safe, mannered, and probably boring (which in and of itself suggests a defensive turning away from the other).

The problem of racism and discrimination largely comes from a defensive process of disavowing one's unwanted parts, one's unwanted impulses and insecurities, locating them in the other person and then hating that other person in order to protect one's self. Rather than saying, "I hate these aspects of myself, or these are really difficult, frightening aspects of my own experience," it's easier for many people, perhaps most people, to experience those not as aspects of oneself, but aspects of the other, and then to hate the other. Othering, in this sense, would seem to be inherent in the human condition. It describes this process where people rid themselves of the things about themselves they can't tolerate, by projecting them onto others, or attributing them to others, and even by inducing them in others, and then hating or destroying them in those others. The psychoanalytic project aspires to help people be curious about and, perhaps, to recognize what they are doing in the process of othering, and to help them see they are using people for internal security in ways that have external, invariably destructive consequences.

When it comes to the problem of prejudice, psychoanalysis offers a more profound remedy than trying to teach people not to be prejudiced or to watch what they say. Because psychoanalysis is interested in understanding what would make one person hate another and is inherently interested in creating contained opportunities for dialogue. Psychoanalysis aspires to help people to become more aware of the ways ignorance is self-protective and that prejudice involves using people to manage dreaded internal experience.

Psychoanalytically, it is axiomatic that both ignorance and its self-perpetuating variants such as prejudice and paranoia reside in all people. When we work to analyze transferences we are working towards the dismantling of such defensively held ignorance. In this regard, transferences can be understood as prejudices acquired early in life, as ways of surviving the anxieties stemming from the problems of dependency and relatedness. Accordingly, the goal when addressing prejudice is to discover blindnesses and defensive biases, how they may have been established and perpetuate themselves, not erase them or cover them with more desirable or socially acceptable thoughts and manners of speaking.

Psychoanalysts look at otherness and how that otherness profoundly alters the interaction people have with each other. Whether conceived of in terms of identifications, introjects, or multiplicities of self, contemporary psychoanalysts understand the importance of context, looking at unconscious fantasy from the inside and considering the relational and broader social context from which fantasy may arise.

Critical theory, queer theory, hermeneutics, field theory, each of these has been incorporated by contemporary psychoanalytic thinkers and creates a richer and more complex analytic perspective for approaching racism, discrimination, and the many forms of othering. We cannot simply assert that racial discrimination involves the projection of unwanted, unconscious aspects of self onto the other. We now propose that racism represents a failure of curiosity, an intolerance of ambiguity, and complexity.

In contemporary psychoanalytic thought, in which the boundaries of self and other are understood as being constantly in flux and never fully clear or known, traditional categories of self and other are pushed to their limits. When you start considering things like the existence of more than two sexes, or multiple selves, or that the sense of continuity and cohesion that each person normally possesses might be an illusion that dissociatively obscures annihilatory dread, then you open the door to dissembling the constructs of race, culture, and other determinate categories and their validity. Psychoanalysts now are more likely to practice in a manner that acknowledges that what the analyst *doesn't* know is as important as what the psychoanalyst *does* know.

In relational and social constructivist thought, there is an emphasis on not knowing, and the psychoanalyst's capacity for, or tolerance of, not knowing. This becomes a crucial aspect of the psychoanalyst's role, one that has direct application to breaking down the categories that serve to perpetuate the defensive, discriminatory operations of othering: the ability to not know and to hold a position of not knowing for the analytic dyad, even when the analysand inevitably seeks to flee from the anxieties associated with such not knowing. The psychoanalytic endeavor aspires to avoid jumping to conclusions, even when they seem quite compelling and even when they would seem to resolve, or at least help to avoid, anxieties in the participants.

Finally, a psychoanalytic approach offers a unique tool for addressing the universal problem encountered when people try to talk with each other across the borders of interpersonal differences and race, culture, and discrimination, as they try to articulate their experience of both difference and commonality. That problem is the breakdown of speaking, of the ability and perhaps desire, to keep on working to create a sharable language for mutual recognition, understanding and transformation. The psychoanalytic process shows us it is those moments in which things break down, when speaking comes to a halt, that we experience some of the most difficult, yet most important, moments of all. As we become aware of our uneasiness, there is the opportunity to look at what goes wrong between us, how it happens, and what it tells us about our experience of difference. We look at what is going wrong when the analysand is trying to say whatever comes to mind, how it is happening, and how it could go otherwise. It is in this territory that we are likely to find the most basic anxieties human beings possess along with their associated, self-destructive and other-destructive defensive "solutions." It is also where, if we can stand to stay in the conversation (and encourage our dialogic others to do so as well), we may gradually be able to accept responsibility for the injuries we are sometimes causing and to relinquish—to lose— the self-protective blindnesses and biases we contain in favor of novel ways of seeing and being with different people.

In our attempts to encourage and to welcome people who are different from ourselves—who are *other* in one way or another—into our consulting rooms (and our institutes) we must, as psychoanalysts, ask more of ourselves than competence. We must mobilize the best of what psychoanalysis has to offer: a stance of openness to the unknown, the unfamiliar, even the frightening, in our patients and in ourselves.

Note

1 I am multiracial, with a Black father whose ancestors were African American, Native American, and Western European, and a white, Jewish mother whose ancestors were from Russia and Poland. I consider myself to be both Black and white, and, also, not simply either.

Reference

Winograd, B. (2014). "Black Psychoanalysts Speak," 2014 PEP Documentary (accessible through American Psychoanalytic Association Psychoanalytic Electronic Publishing database) https://www.youtube.com/watch?v=N8-VIi7tb44 (Last accessed July 2, 2022).

Chapter 14

On Psychoanalysis, Race, and Class in an Urban ER

Michael Slevin

> *At the core of the medical field are a number of dicta. One is, "Physician, heal thyself." At the core of psychoanalysis there are also a few dicta. One is, "Know thyself." Knowledge doesn't come all at once, however.*

When I was in my mid-20s, I suffered excruciating lower back pain following a running injury. My internist diagnosed a pulled muscle of little consequence. But when the pain continued, he referred me to a rheumatologist. In the course of the interview, the rheumatologist said to me that 50 percent of lower back pain is psychogenic. After a 20-minute consultation, he made the acute observation, "You have trouble finishing things." And in fact, the running injury had stirred up old fears and angers from an injury I had incurred in childhood. When I was six, a neighbor backed her car into me, fracturing my pelvis—and cutting me off from finishing a tower, fraught with personal meaning, that I was building in a pile of sand by the roadside. Desire, fear, and anger had coalesced with that traumatic scene, and, unthought and unresolved, had remained dangerous to feel into my adulthood. For years, when I felt compelled to stop a task before completion, I experienced intense anxiety as I was faced with feelings wrapped up in the memory of that trauma. A few days after the visit with the rheumatologist, the severe pain resolved. And as I worked in my own psychoanalysis, emotionally connecting those dots, the remaining lower back pain disappeared. It has never returned.

I work in the emergency room of an urban hospital, evaluating people in psychological crisis. Are they a danger to themselves or others? Are they suicidal? Homicidal? Are they safe? Should they be admitted to an inpatient psychiatric unit? This is a simple understanding of what I do; it is also a rigorous understanding of what I do. As I learned the ropes, I worked with restless anxiety. So much at stake for my patients, so much dread I might be mistaken. It took three years for the needed knowledge to distill, for me to be comfortable making these decisions.

Those three years were also years I sharpened my skills as a psychoanalytically oriented psychotherapist in private practice. Working psychodynamically over time allows emotions and defenses to repeat and evolve; a patient can reach, observe, and change fundamental patterns and metaphors of their life. In my private practice, a patient and I would create an intense, complex relationship over months or years. In the ER, on the other hand, every interaction is an intense, complex phenomenon with multiple moving parts. It happens fast. While the essential task is to protect life, within the stillness of an interview there is opportunity to connect, to understand, to heal.

Today, decades later, I remember the exact encounter with my rheumatologist: his office, his desk, his request as he said goodbye: "Could I keep your list of symptoms?" For I had written out a day's timeline of shifting somatic pains that were expressions of the intrapsychic conflict. His wish to use it for teaching was apparent. I was reluctant to let go, but equally, I saw I could contribute. I am struck still by his quick and ready understanding of my plight. Unhurried yet efficient, he had, using his knowledge of psychodynamic processes and principles, uncovered a moment of childhood developmental crisis living on in present time, a moment of the mind expressing itself through the body. And by making the unconscious conscious with new meaning, he helped heal me.

As I write this essay, I seek to connect that encounter to my present work in the ER and to explore how, broadened and deepened, it shapes a means to work with, help, and even, at times, heal the largely impoverished and working-class patients I see. For them, current practice, available resources, and the historical assumptions of psychoanalysis say "no." For my African American patients, historical events embedded in cultural memory and historical misapprehension of the psychological underpinnings and potential of African Americans add weight to that "no." Grappling now with my patients' needs requires that I work to understand the psychological effects on them of class and, notably in the healthcare system, of structural racism. Writing this essay requires that I tease out and confront my own experiences of race and class and the professional role I play in the social and economic system. Yet the journey seems promising.

Alliance and a Psychoanalytic Approach

A white, middle-aged man was admitted to our emergency room. He said he was suicidal and homicidal. He told the triage nurse and the attending physician he was hearing voices telling him to kill himself. I approached him and gently asked where he was living, whether he had friends, did he speak with his family? I asked him if he were safe now. He answered, "Yes." I asked if he would be safe if he went home. He looked up at me from where he was lying flat on the hallway stretcher, his blanket pulled up to his chin, and said quietly, "Yes." So I asked what had brought him to the hospital. He said, "I'm lonely."

How was it that the answers I got were so different from those he had given moments before? How was it that he could now tolerate his loneliness enough to return home? I believe it was because he felt heard. He felt heard because I had engaged him fully as a person, so he could trust himself and me with his emotions. He had come to the ER with a plan: to be admitted to an inpatient psychiatric unit. Most likely, the physician or nurse asked him questions from a mental checklist: Are you hearing voices? Do you want to hurt yourself? Have you ever been an inpatient before? Do you use alcohol? Cocaine? Heroin? How much? Last time? Questions he knew how to answer to get an inpatient admission. Questions that were a wall with no door to his actual experiences and true wishes: I want to be around caring people. It's cold outside. I can't stand the fighting at home.

Trust and connection are essential to my work in the ER. For a patient to lower the drawbridge and allow passage to-and-fro, they must feel that an inner world, often betrayed, violated, or in multiple other ways damaged, is safe. An intense African American girl in middle school said, in response to my soft voice, "I can't hear you." I laughed and said, "Well, we don't want that." She replied quickly, "But it makes me want to talk to you." A white student at a public school, terrified of her inner world, spoke for the first time, in fits and starts, with guilt and shame, of voices telling her to kill her lab partner.

She was relieved that a hospital stay would happen. Yet other times, distrust is palpable. A six-year-old African American boy sat on the white sheet of his hospital bed, feet dangling, and stared directly at me. His eyes, black, round, and frightened, shielded by street smarts beyond his years, dared me: "You want to find me out? I do not want to be here, and I will tell you nothing that might keep me here."

Few children and adolescents wish for an inpatient admission. Young children especially fear being separated from their families. Adolescents, even those who say they are lonely, resist separation from friends and social media. To both, being hospitalized speaks of punishment, and to adolescents concerned with acceptance by their friends, it reeks of stigma. Patients may, on feeling safe, tell me of suicidal impulses and plans but deny them as soon as they realize it means being admitted to a hospital psychiatric unit. Yet some adolescents, on speaking of previously unvoiced secrets and painful experiences and seeing that they are heard, find their agitation settle or their sorrow lift. Hope that their anger, suffering, or chaotic feelings might end, and ambivalence about suicide, lead them to an acceptance of an inpatient stay.

A parent or legal guardian must sign paperwork to admit a child or adolescent into a psychiatric unit. A vein of distrust, though, runs through the African American community, especially among those with fewer resources, who rely on the ER for medical care. White people thought Black people, being less than human, could not feel pain, physical or psychological. Further, and this is a view once prevalent in psychoanalysis, African Americans did not have the psychological strength or social and cultural resources to sustain challenging treatment. These currents colluded with a view in the African American community—perhaps a defensive reaction to being devalued—that mental health care is for white people, the "worried well." And there is risk: Mental health workers (along with the police) can commit you. They can take your children, your freedom. So psychological difficulties, denied and untreated, build until an ER admission becomes unavoidable. Feeling threatened by The System and devalued through cultural beliefs and by history, African American families with fewer resources often carry into the ER encounter a tension born of deep distrust of people who say, "We can help you."

In the interview that I hope will lead to help for my patient—Black or white, likely working class or poor, often homeless—I often must overcome their uncertainty, suspicion, or anxiety to form an alliance. My understanding of my patient's developmental age shapes that process. My youngest patient ever was five; my oldest, in her 90s. One evening, a white man in his 80s came to the ER. He had mild dementia and was living alone, simply, on a limited income. He had become tearful, depressed, unable to fix meals, and detached from the caring neighbor who had brought him to the ER. He could not tell her what troubled him except that he was old. With that starting point, I engaged him in a life history of memory and reminiscence. I learned about his son, who had died prematurely. I learned about his life working in the market stalls that no longer existed in the city. It soon became apparent that he had been traumatized by numerous losses—both of people and of a way of life—and that he had not yet been able to mourn. He hadn't developed the resilience in early life to absorb the buffeting of his later life. His loss of mind and function had been the tripwire to his withdrawal. As I listened with curiosity and empathy, he told his story with deepening emotion. As he spoke, he heard the echo of loss succeeding loss and began to mourn.

I had become a guide to his underworld of suffering. Personally and professionally I was engaged, but I also had to be detached. I had to use my own internal, unconscious universe of feeling, experience, wish, and imagination: being shaken by a lost love, an opportunity mourned, being of an age when one starts to look back as well as forward and acknowledge, with joy or pain, what has been and is no longer. Sitting there, an ache went through me. Yet my alliance with my patient also had to navigate differences—not only the circumstances, developmental and otherwise, of his life, but also those of age, class, and occupation. I had a quiet but deep-seated drive in that moment to know. By knowing myself, I could know him by our similarities; by knowing myself, I could recognize our differences. As I was able to be curious about and tolerate our differences, he had space for dignity in his separate and unique grieving. I was so intent on his world, I forgot about the neighbor sitting a few feet away. When the man and I emerged, she spoke: "I never knew this about him."

To unearth the metaphors and patterns of a particular life may take years of dedicated work with a therapist, but when a patient is in crisis the story is often there in the moment to be noted, respected, and cherished. A young, white freshman woman transitioning to college life came to our ER, suicidal, brought in by her brother. She told me, tentatively, of having gone that evening to a crowded student party where she knew only a few people. She told me of a boyfriend who had left her when he went to another state to go to school. She still longed for him and, when she happened to learn at the party that he had a new girlfriend, had become anxious and agitated. Blaming herself afresh—without cause, I thought—for the breakup, she felt lacerating guilt. All was futile, and she turned an unrecognized jealousy against herself. She had intended to kill herself. Fortunately, her brother had read between the lines of a text message and rushed to pick her up.

As I took a brief history, she spoke of a father who criticized her choices at each turn of the road; of a father who divorced her mother, with whom she then lived and identified; of how she could never be a good enough student or friend; that she would never be good enough for anyone. As I listened, guiding her recollections gently, she caught glimpses of the painful pattern of recurring guilt built on ambivalent love, hostility, and identification as successive developmental crises interacted with her world and, like struck tuning forks, resonated with each other. With churning emotions, from those of a toddler to those of an emerging adult, she surprised herself by saying, "I caused my parents' divorce." The suicidal impulses began to subside.

Sometimes, I would relax a little when a patient was white and middle class, or on or past a certain trajectory of four-year college and a professional career. I would experience a feeling of familiarity—and shame. Shame because despite my upbringing leavened with ideas of color-blind equality and my discomfort with the wealth of my neighborhood, I had succumbed to my privilege. Yet to see this young woman's suffering, I had to recognize and deflect this homogenizing myth of liberal, upper-middle-class whiteness, a myth I knew had once caused and defended against the pain of my own early inadequacies in school. Having done so, I could look into the way her world was fractured, her future uncertain. I could see myself, I could see her, and I could, with deeper imagination and fuller humanity, experience the aspirations of some of my adolescent, African American patients who wanted a college education but whose desires were impeded by family conflict and structural racism.

In my second year working in the ER, an African American girl in high school was admitted one evening with chest pain. The attending physician found no physical cause, yet the patient remained terrified she was dying. So, the attending referred her to Psychiatry for an evaluation. Reviewing the girl's chart, I noticed she had been an ER patient eight or 10 times over recent years: chest pain, abdominal pain, headache, and so forth. Sometimes the doctor prescribed medication, but the diagnoses were always inconclusive. The doctor would discharge her, but she would return two or six or 10 months later with a different complaint.

Reflecting on her checkered history with the ER, I remembered my own back pain. I wondered if there might be a relationship or trauma in my ER patient's life that could be causing a similar displacement of suffering. As I took a history, following her emotions, I inquired about trauma in her life. She said that some years earlier, a great-uncle who had helped raise her, and with whom she had spoken about intimate feelings and problems, had suddenly had a brain aneurysm burst. He died in front of her. Today's ER admission was occurring on an anniversary associated with this relative. It became clear to us both that the ER visits and her fear of dying repeated her terror, uncertainty, and confusion when her uncle died. As she realized this, her slumped body straightened. Facing her trauma and her loss, she could begin her slow journey absorbing into consciousness and accepting the trauma of her great-uncle's death and loss, with its full meaning. In the intimacy of the moment, with our intersecting histories, despite our difference in age by two generations and our differences of race and class, we connected deeply.

Racial Differences in the ER

One White Therapist's Response to Blackness

As I reflect on my experiences as a white clinician with patients who are primarily Black, I forage for memories and tags of my being white and others being Black in my youth. I was brought up in the white suburbs of Washington, DC, where houses and yards were large, and doors were left unlocked. There were sailing lessons and vacations at white beaches. Children were expected to go to college, and most did. I had the privilege of education, aspiration, and opportunity. Unconsciously, I had the privilege of power. To be Black was to be

Katie, a maid to whom my mother was close, or the picture framer at Brooks Photographers, where I took out the trash in the afternoon; it was the March on Washington, civil rights in the newspapers, and the neighborhoods along U Street and New Jersey Avenue that I thought of as poor and deprived as I looked, with a bit of anxiety, out my crosstown bus window on my way to an internship on Capitol Hill.

When I turned 20, I emphatically chose to leave behind the all-white suburb in which I was raised for the city, to live in housing on the ragged edge of the racial divide. Although I lived many of my adult years in urban communities that were diverse and often majority African American, I did not visit in my neighbors' kitchens or go to their churches. In many of those years, I kept to myself. I had little knowledge of the psychological forces driving me. I knew little of the psychological implications of the structural racism that divides white and Black in housing, education, employment, and health care. Yet that diversity of race and class drew me, enlivened me, made me feel true to myself.

To understand my patients in the ER, I needed to listen closely, drawing from my knowledge of myself and the rich, if fragmented, puzzle of my own years living in the diverse neighborhoods of downtown Washington, DC. At work in the ER of an urban community hospital, as I entered the room of a child or adolescent patient, meeting a parent or guardian, possibly with a sibling, grandmother, or social worker also present, I would be attentive but holding back, aware of my role and unsure of my audience. At times I wondered, "How do they hear *me*?"

While I was aware that many impoverished Black families lacked fathers in the household, I also knew that for some whites that fact had morphed into a belief that *all* urban Black men were unemployed, unfaithful, and irresponsible. The racism behind this belief made me uneasy, and I asked myself, "Did my white skin make my adolescent patients think *I* believed that?" How was I to be comfortable, how was I to make my patients comfortable, when what I often needed to ask was, "Tell me about your father."

A middle-school girl I worked with told me about her father with pain she could not numb. He had been shot in the head and killed when she was five, an age when little girls have very intense feelings for their fathers. Her mother remarried. A few years later, her stepfather was stabbed to death. When I saw her in the ER, she was severely depressed. I responded to her anguish deeply; a door had cracked open to a world barely touched by crime-blotter newspaper stories tinged with racial difference. That she had allowed me to know her sadness plunged a bucket into a deep well for me.

The depth of darkness into which I plunged was not one of gun violence, it was one of abandonment. At age two and a half, having fallen from a second story window, alone in early dawn, I was carefully watched throughout the day at home. Then, taken to the city hospital for a head x-ray and overnight observation, my father had left me to the care of nurses–abandoned me, as I could best then understand. Along with this young girl, backed into her pillows, who had twice had fathers ripped from her life, I had feelings of profound isolation and father abandonment.

As My Black Patients See Me

Race can unsettle us, throwing up roadblocks to listening and being heard. How I am heard by my patient can be very different from how I imagine myself speaking. When I do not recognize that I am crossing the divides of race, class, and power, there can be consequences. Early in my ER career, an African American patient who was homeless would come in frequently. She could afford housing—she had a disability income that she husbanded throughout the month—but she was particular. And entitled. She repeatedly rejected housing possibilities offered by a nonprofit organization because they did not meet her standards. So, she would come to the ER, say she was suicidal, get a meal and a night's sleep in a warm bed—and in the morning, deny she was suicidal and leave. Frustrated at the waste of healthcare dollars, one evening I said to her, as she lay on a stretcher, "Ms. X, this is not a hotel." She spun around, lifted herself on her elbow, and shouted, "You fucking white overseer!" Her furious, racially loaded insult, in response to what I thought was a mild scold, set me back on my heels. I was stung, angry, unsure how to respond. Her reminder of the trauma of slavery, condensed into a symbol of her pain and flung as a weapon, hit home.

We came to an understanding after that: She would not tell me she was suicidal, and I would say to her, "Would you like a meal before you leave?" It was an accommodation that gave us a balance of power.

Each of us had come to a deeper respect for the other. Yet when she showed up in the ER, I used at times a defense of bemused outrage with my colleagues. It hid what I now know was the deep pain and personal memory that drove my side of the accommodation.

My mother's Texas roots were as much a part of my identity as the assimilated New York Jewish household my father had been brought up in. But there were stories my mother told, stories with a whitewashed subtext of race. At the outbreak of the Civil War, four brothers—I am a direct descendant of one—had gone to Sam Houston and asked, "Should we fight?" He reputedly said, "I do not support this war, but I support my State." The brothers signed up and fought in the West for the Confederacy. It is a story of privilege and power, a dark and brutal reality I had avoided confronting for years: Members of my family had fought to defend chattel slavery. Not only that, but an ancestor on the other side of my mother's family owned nine Black human beings. Since memory is represented in and used by the present, I wonder how I might have understood my patient, what depths of hurt in her I might have been able to reach, had I then felt not only the anguish I now feel, but also the culpability I had tolerated well into adulthood by being blind to the reality of my mother's story.

It is with open eyes that I continue to navigate the distinctly different religious histories my parents brought to their marriage. In the ER, I wondered about the implications for my patients. The Christian church is a nurturing presence that for over two centuries has helped sustain the Black community through its suffering. The rituals and manner of worship are infused with African traditions, including ideas and practices of the healing arts. How, then, am I, a white man who practices a rather odd form of treatment, with personal and methodological roots in Western Europe, perceived by my patients? How am I, a man whose lineage is half Jewish (some say it is apparent in my features), perceived, given the troubled historical relationship, filtered through distortion, falsehood, stereotype, and myth, of Jewish shopkeepers and Jewish numbers runners in Black communities? I have spent many years working for therapeutic institutions with Jewish affiliations serving an African American community, and yet only a handful of times has a patient spoken to me of these tricky currents. Once, while I was working for a clinic, an African American patient let slip, with a raw edge in her tone, that her friends didn't trust that "Jew hospital" in their community. I was shocked; I wanted to know more. She clammed up, and even though I would work with the woman for many more years, she never again allowed me entry to that corner of her world.

In my private practice, I am a psychotherapist; in the hospital, my title is psychiatric evaluator. But by license, I am a clinical social worker. In the African American, urban community surrounding my ER, I belong to the social service system; I am known as a worker. Once I became more familiar with the community, for a while I would appropriate the word worker to myself, imagining myself into belonging to the community of my patients. But I pulled up short and never said it out loud, for the sword has a double edge. The worker is a vital member of the impoverished community served by an urban ER, but one held in ambivalent regard, often derogated with an assignment of lesser value than that to which I assigned myself. The worker represents The System. And I am white. What were the outlines of trust and distrust that defined my work?

Patients with mental illness often resist treatment. Any of their many defenses may lead them to turn away help, to deny the reality of their illness. Those with severe and persistent mental illness—bipolar, schizoaffective, or schizophrenic disorders—may have cognitive limitations contributing to their psychological resistances. But in fact, African Americans with a mood disorder are more likely than whites to be misdiagnosed with the more severe schizophrenia, and research shows that, if psychotic, they are, on average, prescribed higher doses of antipsychotic medications. Further, African Americans have an especially difficult legacy to deal with: Throughout slavery and on to incidents as recent as the 1980s, their community has been used, because of its impoverished, dependent status, as a laboratory for medical research. The Tuskegee syphilis study, James Marion Sims's gynecological research, the lead paint studies by Johns Hopkins University researchers are but examples. The poor and the Black were considered expendable. That legacy combines with a continuous reality of substandard care to produce a high level of distrust of the healthcare establishment.

Although most of my interactions with patients and their families were polite and respectful, sometimes I could taste the distrust. A tense African American man admitted to the ER for a psychiatric consultation looked at me with suspicion. He had requested a medication refill. Until now, he had received his medication from a clinic across town. Propped on his elbows on his bed in the half-dark he had requested, he told me that the white clinic doctor, believing the medication had not been working, had changed his doses and added a new pill. My patient had become mistrustful of all of his prescriptions and quit taking his medicine entirely, saying to me, "I don't know what's in that pill." I wondered if he felt, as other patients occasionally had said when I spoke with them: "Don't experiment on me." Soon after he quit taking his medicine, the voices he heard in his head, which had been quieted, returned with a roar. Disturbed by the voices and mistrusting the clinic he felt had not taken his suspicions and concerns seriously, he now wanted to return to a medication he had taken years before. Now the only doctor he trusted was himself.

Encounters with the System

A societal system of structural racism and devaluation on the basis of class looms over many of my patients. It affects their expectations coming to the ER, how they see me, the options I have to offer them, and how they receive those options. Housing, education, and employment segregation are all part of the world most of my ER patients live in, as is the structural racism of the healthcare system.

Having learned through my own analysis that cultural and societal forms and historical events affect my internal world, I attended to how these realities, especially of race and class, affected my patients. Several years before George Floyd was murdered, the ER medical team asked Psychiatry to evaluate an African American man in his late 40s. The man had once sold drugs but had left the street world behind. Brothers from that time were out to get him, he said. He had caught them on his home security camera hiding drugs in his car. He was afraid to drive his car or to look for the drugs for fear it was a setup for an arrest for possession. He said he had driven to a police precinct to tell his story and have the police look for the drugs. But he feared that if they did find drugs, they would arrest him, so after sitting in the parking lot in the dark for an hour, he drove away. As I sifted out what was paranoia and what was reality in the man's story, I presented the case to a visiting psychiatrist from Asia. Curious, he interviewed the patient. But coming from a country where adherence to authority was embedded in community culture and less fraught with a history of slavery, current oppression, and ambivalence toward the police, the psychiatrist disbelieved any element of the patient's narrative that stitched together paranoia, anxiety, and realistic fear. He curtly dismissed that a traffic stop could put my patient at risk. Unaware of the complexities of street life, he denied possible police duplicity. He missed the legitimate anxiety threaded through my patient's story and found him more profoundly disturbed than I ultimately decided was truly the case.

The Shadow of Child Protective Services

Black boys and girls are all too often perceived as older, more responsible, more sexually mature, and more threatening than justified given their age. One door frequently leading to crisis treatment for African American children on the lower rungs of the socioeconomic ladder, especially boys, is disruptive behavior at home or at school. Once that door has opened, things can escalate quickly. In school, disruptive behavior can start with a taunt, throwing objects, overturning a desk, leaving the classroom, or leaving the building, all resulting in multiple, even daily, calls to a distressed parent or guardian, suspensions, an individualized education plan, and visits to an overtaxed school-based social worker. Educational policies, therapeutic approaches, a paucity of resources, and a lack of time will often lead well-meaning and caring therapists and administrators to respond with efforts to manage the external behavior rather than address the underlying, unconscious emotional conflict. The fact that unconscious racial bias results in administrative actions escapes attention. The data overwhelmingly show that even with minor infractions, Black children are dealt with more harshly, more often suspended, more often referred to the juvenile justice system, less often diagnosed with learning disabilities, and less often seen as smart. As a result, nothing fundamental changes, and the suffering continues; as the student seeks again to master the anxiety, the disruptive behavior returns. Then, often with ideas—or plans—of suicide in play, there might be a call to the police, an emergency petition (EP) requiring a psychological evaluation, and an ambulance or squad car ride to the ER.

Having a disruptive child evaluated in an ER under an EP can evoke anxiety, distrust, and resistance. Real-world distrust of the police, who can execute the EP, and of a health-care system that can commit a child to a hospital or recommend an investigation that might remove them from the home, can increase the anxiety of a patient and their parent. Child Protective Services (CPS) is a dark shadow, a force to be reckoned with in an impoverished community. African American children and adolescents are more likely to enter the system of investigations and interventions, including foster care and juvenile detention, than any other racial group—and to stay in the system longer. Once in the system, with attachments in disarray, distrust rampant, and behavioral problems inadequately addressed, the child or adolescent may be transferred from one foster home to another to yet another.

One evening, a boy in his early teens was brought to the ER. His foster mother, feeling threatened and frightened by his outbursts, had called the police, who had brought him in under an EP. I determined that he was not a danger to himself and did not require hospitalization. But his foster mother refused to take him back. The foster care agency responsible for him took him to their office overnight while they searched for the next placement—as he absorbed yet another traumatic rejection.

Another patient brought to the ER by the police was an African American girl in her mid-teens, perhaps on her way to foster care and feisty, angry, and sullen. The girl would leave her house in the middle of the night and skip school the next day. Then, one day, she left the neighborhood and disappeared into the city. She was reported missing. A few days later, the police found her on a street corner with a teddy bear and ten dollars, speaking gibberish. Now, in the ER, she was speaking intelligibly, but she was desperate to go back to the city before her grandmother arrived. I feared for her safety. I wondered if she were being groomed for trafficking. I wondered if either her home or The System had the resources to help her.

I *am* The System in the ER. I can recommend that a patient be kept against their will or the will of their family for up to 72 hours for a psychiatric evaluation. That evaluation might result in a recommendation for a psychiatric hospitalization the patient and family don't want. Although it is rare with children, more common with suicidal adults, I can recommend that a physician commit the patient to the hospital against their will for up to a week until a review by an administrative law judge. I can make a report to CPS, most likely resulting in an investigation. It is not surprising, then, that I am sometimes challenged angrily by a distraught or righteous parent. To different degrees, patients and their families distrust The System. And so they distrust me.

The outcomes of my actions as a mandated reporter can be significant. The law requires that if a child or adolescent I treat has been abused, mistreated, or severely neglected, I must report it to CPS within hours. On occasion, the circumstances are clear-cut. One distraught aunt brought in her nephew, who was under her care. He was emotionally unstable, skipping school, getting into shouting matches, and breaking things at home. She was frightened of what might happen were he to act out defiantly in the community. She didn't recognize that his extreme behavior was an effort to master an internal turmoil, and so her attempts at discipline didn't work. The behaviors were worse after the child had been left alone with her boyfriend. With his "spare the rod and spoil the child" mentality, he had beaten the boy to end the acting out. In a combustible mix in which the medical system was mistrusted and mental health treatment was considered a sign of weakness and unmanliness, he was again threatening the child.

Although he had no legal standing, he was pressuring the aunt by phone to return home with the boy. Despite her alarm at her boyfriend's disciplinary methods and her strong desire to seek help, she was torn. An abrupt departure against medical advice was possible. The boy was having thoughts of self-harm. I recommended to the attending physician that she quickly fill out and sign an EP requiring that the boy have a psychiatric evaluation. She did so. With the decision taken from her, the aunt settled and the boyfriend retreated. As the situation stabilized, the aunt was able to accept what became a recommendation that her nephew be admitted to an inpatient psychiatric unit. I did not need to make the extreme request I was considering, that CPS take emergency guardianship to protect my patient's life. I did request that CPS investigate the boyfriend's role in my patient's life.

Other times, the circumstances are murkier. What might be perceived as neglect on the part of the parent or caretaker, such as not providing guardianship papers, not returning phone calls from doctors and other ER workers, or being unavailable to sign a child into an inpatient unit, may be due to external factors rather than intentional neglect: The parent may have a job with little leeway or might have to meet the demands of other children without an available relative or neighbor or friend to help. Sometimes, what looks like neglect is simply the disorganization caused by exhaustion or a wrong phone number. The child, it turns out, has not been abandoned. Yes, I have seen the rare parent, pushed to her limits by a destructive, unruly child in a system where she has inadequate resources, throw up her hands and say, "Let foster care take him" or simply not show up until contacted by CPS. I recall one angry mother shouting at her child, "I am finished with you." But she responded to my nonjudgmental attention to her emotion, her distress, and her almost unworkable circumstances and found a reservoir of love and commitment for her child that allowed her to once again engage The System for the child's benefit. I did not call CPS.

Sometimes, the ER reveals the consecrated dedication of members of the African American community to their children. One woman, whose family difficulties were telegraphed by the fact that she had kinship guardianship, alternated between being choked up and effusive that I had spent the extra hour needed to line up and explain to her the option of a day hospital admission for the child in her care. Another strong woman from the African American community was guardian for quite a few children not her own. She had resigned her job as a midlevel agency worker to care for otherwise unsupervised, ungoverned, and unloved foster children, while working The System for housing, food stamps, government stipends, Medicaid, Big Brothers Big Sisters mentors. And yet, she was about to lose two of her rambunctious and previously traumatized charges because she had violated government regulations, including one mandating public housing occupancy limits, that ignored the realities of her community. I took time to listen, to acknowledge, to not judge, while seeking to untangle The System's strictures. I knew the odds she was up against, and I thought: "I could not give up my career to do what she is doing." She decided, slowly, to open up the tightly held purse of her story to me, a white, male worker. Her investment allowed me to recognize her plight, and her to take a deep breath, exhale, pull herself together, and believe, at least for a minute, that by working what we both knew was a broken system, she might actually succeed in her mission to provide a future for the children in her care.

I stand quite in awe of some patients who, with grit and flexibility, have navigated through a childhood and adolescence of exploding munitions and broken lives. In a brief ER interview, I am sometimes unable to divine the unconscious springs of the strength and resilience I observe.

An agitated white girl on the edge of adulthood, with suicidal impulses but no plan, walked into the ER alone one day. She was frightened and didn't feel safe—from an abusive and controlling older boyfriend, or from herself. She had grown up in the inner city in dilapidated housing, raised by a mother who had prostituted herself in the apartment to pay for her severe drug habit. As a preteen and teen, she had been raped by men connected to her mother. She was often hungry. She had missed weeks of school and been in foster care. Taking from The System what she could, managing despite a system that for years had failed her, she had found the inner strength to finish high school and was learning a skilled trade. She had a toddler of her own and was raising her half-brother, struggling to see that they got fed, got off to preschool or school, had toys and playmates, did homework. Now she had found a refuge from her abusive boyfriend with a relative who lived in a safe and distant suburb.

As she and I talked, I leaned carefully in the direction of her brighter future; she oscillated anxiously between opportunity and perceived stability, risk and familiarity. Nurtured by my gently supportive interview, her agitation lessened, her thoughts became more organized. Then her phone rang. She didn't answer; then she did. It was her boyfriend. Her old patterns, which had made her resilient and had protected an inner core against her many traumas, seemed to kick in. Her shoulders slumped and tightened. Her damaging, familiar world called. Her inner struggle was visceral, visible. She determined to return, to make it work. As she walked out, I felt admiration for all she had accomplished, against the odds. And deep sorrow for all she was giving up.

Seeking Recovery from Substances

Many of my patients self-medicate, using alcohol and marijuana to excess. It's also common for patients to test positive for cocaine or heroin. More than a few men and women in their 40s and 50s come into the ER saying bleakly, "I'm tired of this life"—tired of the cycle of using, coming down, seeking, and using again. Yet given the opportunity of a substance rehabilitation program, many turn it down, leaving for the streets and another high. The physical and psychological dependence are too much to overcome with the 28-day programs they have tried in the past. Such programs begin the healing process, but due to the structures of insurance coverage, the substance abuse—the symptom—becomes the focus of attention, not the particular experiences and underlying suffering the substance use is covering up. Probing beneath the surface of addiction, one often discovers a pain driven by deep-seated trauma: rape, abuse, loss, neglect, crushed aspirations, a broken heart, racism. As clear as the link may be between addiction and trauma, I have too few effective resources to offer a patient wanting to get clean.

Conclusion

Psychoanalysis in the United States has traditionally been a practice of long-term, individual therapy conducted within the safe and comfortable surroundings of a consulting room. Increasingly, attention is being directed to applications in the community at large. In either setting, the work demands much of us. Applying the analytic framework challenges us to continually sample and make sense of our inner world—our biases, memories, fantasies, and personal traumas—and then employ what we can learn from them for the benefit of someone in pain. The circumstance of being a white clinician in an urban ER is at once one of the most challenging applications of psychoanalytic ideas and techniques and an exemplar of the fundamental relationship.

My patients, Black and white, compel me to ask, "Who am I to them? Who are they to me?" I have come to realize that racial myths and realities affect both me and them and are central to our relationship and our work. Recognizing that I have benefitted from opportunities provided by structural racism, and that this has psychological implications for my patients as it does for me, has enabled me to better understand, negotiate, and build upon the intricate dynamics of interactions in the ER. Reflecting on my defensive reaction to the pain of being called a "fucking white overseer" uncovered my anguish stemming from a distant family legacy of which I was only dimly conscious. I believe that this insight has been essential to my ability to effectively hear and help my patients.

Crossing the racial divide demanded that I look at how both history and systemic but generally unspoken racism have shaped us and continue to shape us through thousands of daily interactions. In the ER, even as I do my best to understand, empathize with, and act for the good of my patients, I'm forced to maintain the unpleasant awareness that, for many of them, I am The System, which holds power and controls access to resources. Haunted as we are by the traumas of our history and our society, an authentic human connection across the racial divide is a hard-won victory. My psychoanalytic sensibility and curiosity have allowed a fuller use of myself; in the difficult work of developing them, I have learned that the more I face painful realities with my patients, the greater my empathy and effectiveness in meeting their needs.

Part IV

Being Aware of White Privilege

Chapter 15

How I Came to Understand White Privilege

Michael Moskowitz

"When I call your name, come to the front of the class and form a circle," my first-grade teacher, Mrs. Wright, announced. We were going to learn to read.

I waited anxiously, barely able to sit. I was not called and continued drawing warships in battle. Then the first group returned to their seats and a second group was called. I was not in it. I ran to Mrs. Wright and begged, "I want to learn to read."

"You'll be in the next group," she said.

It soon became clear that the next group was the "gifted" group. I didn't know how this group was chosen. I don't remember any tests, though there may have been one. I do remember that in the third group the girls seemed snootier, and no one wore torn or dirty clothes as some did in the other groups. This is my first memory of privilege, benefiting from an unearned advantage by belonging to a group. Not only was I chosen, I had felt entitled to ask. Not everyone had. It was not exactly white privilege. Everyone in the school was white, and everyone in the town was white. In a way, I was less than white. Of the approximately 300 students and 20 or so teachers and staff at the elementary school, I was the only Jew—and I was seldom allowed to forget it.

It was rare to walk the five minutes to school or back home without being taunted: "Dirty Jew," "Christ killer," "Kike." The words were often accompanied by punches and sometimes by beatings. It was the same on the playground. Yet, somehow, I knew I'd get through it, that this childhood would be escaped, and I would emerge relatively powerful and privileged. Perhaps it was because at some level, even at age six, I knew that my parents, aunts, uncles, and cousins had suffered much worse anti-Semitism and had gone on to achieve enough success to garner respect. Perhaps it was because watching television with my parents or relatives always involved calling out, "You know he/she is a Jew." Milton Berle, Phil Silvers, Melvyn Douglas, Lauren Bacall, Shelly Winters, the Marx Brothers, Elizabeth Taylor, Peter Lorre, Paul Newman, Sammy Davis Jr, Benny Goodman, Jascha Heifetz, Justice Brandeis, Einstein, and Dr. Grawi.

Dr. Grawi was our neighbor in a grand house on a hill I passed every day on the way to school. He had fled Germany in the '30s and was now a modestly prosperous GP who drove to the city for opera and theater. My parents independently and repeatedly said about him, "They could take away everything, but they couldn't take away his education," which I took to mean, if you do well in school you can always find some place to live well, even if it means fleeing thousands of miles to an alien culture to be safe.

I never doubted I would escape the oppressive, often violent place of my childhood. Though the town was only a two-hour drive from New York City, in the '50s it was more an impoverished Appalachian town than an exurb. It still is. In 1828, it become a canal town—rechristened Port Jervis—just before the decline of the canals, then a railroad town before the decline of the railroad. It was a factory town until the flight of the factories. And when the highways came, they passed Port Jervis by.

Because my father was a plumber and owned a small plumbing supply store, we lived in the poorest part of town, and we were poor. But because we were Jewish, most neighbors thought we were rich, which bestowed another kind of privilege. Most of my classmates' parents worked in the factories or were laborers. Many were descendants of French Huguenot and Dutch settlers and were now poor whites. Others were children and grandchildren of Irish and Italian immigrants. Very few expressed any interest in leaving the area, whatever their talents. Diane, my first crush, the smartest student in school—I knew because I looked through the principal's files when I was in detention—got pregnant and left school when she was 14. Some of the Christian kids planned to go to college. Most of those were the children of the professional class, the doctors and lawyers. Of those who left, many returned, some to join their father's practice, others to start their own.

My parents made light of local anti-Semitism. It was nothing like they had suffered in the old country. My father did not come to my defense or teach me how to fight back. "Ignore what they say. It's just words. They're ignorant. They're jealous. This is a country of laws" were some of the things he said. As new citizens, my parents knew their rights and their privileges. They taught their children not to trust authority. It could be challenged, not flamboyantly but by the law. "You can always call your lawyer" was an essential part of the talk. I'll say more about the talk later.

Conspiracy of Silence

The first important Black person in my life was Malcolm X. I'm not sure how it happened. Maybe because of his "chickens coming home to roost" comment after the Kennedy assassination, saying what no one else dared speak. Maybe it was something my sister at college said. Maybe it was by way of Muhammad Ali. I know I heard Malcolm's Oxford Union debates in 1964. I was in awe of how he spoke out against his racist oppressors and by the intellectual precision of his rage, like Moses to the Pharaoh. I wished he were my father. Then in 1965, my first year of high school, he was killed, and I wondered again, as when Kennedy was killed, did heroes have to die?

After leaving home, through college and graduate school, I met, but did not get to know, a few Black students. This was in the revolutionary '60s and early '70s, and they were most often radical, like me. I assumed that like Malcolm X, they felt that they had the right to speak truth to power and that they could rely on the law to defend them, as could I. It was not until my second internship and first job at the West Haven VA in Connecticut, working closely with Black nurse's aides and Black and brown Vietnam veterans, that I learned how careful and fearful Black and brown people often are. Low-key at work, the aides never questioned a doctor's or nurse's decision, even when they knew better. It was different outside of work, when some talked to me about their anger and discontent. I did not quite get that what I was seeing was institutional racism and white privilege, covered by a conspiracy of silence. At first I attributed it to class and education. Then I saw it in a way I could not deny.

Everyone who was working at the new Vietnam Vet Center, an off-site program of the West Haven VA, was attending a training conference in a white suburb of St. Louis. After dinner, Dan Campbell and I went for a walk. Dan was a Black Vietnam vet with a master's in counseling who worked with me planning the Vet Center. After we walked and talked for a while, he said to me, "I couldn't walk here alone." I asked why, and Dan explained. It's a screen memory, I'm sure, an après-coup, coalescing what I saw and what I did not want to see because it implicated me among the privileged. Dan did not grow up with his teachers assuming he was smart, with his white neighbors assuming he was rich. Dan, a sweet and mild man, was assumed to be dangerous and was the object of their fear and rage. Maybe I was not the whitest white, but I was white enough to pass, white enough to feel free to walk where I wanted and say what I wanted, and white enough to know if things got rough, I could pick up and leave.

I needed to do something. Around 1984, I started postdoc psychoanalytic training at NYU. I asked for a meeting with the director of the program, Bernie Kalinkowitz. I expressed my concern about the relative absence of Black psychoanalysts. He agreed and introduced me to Kirkland Vaughans, a Black first-year student, who had expressed similar concerns. We then became co-chairs of the first psychoanalytic diversity committee. As we were getting to know each other, he told me about the racism he had borne in the course of his education to become a psychologist and psychoanalyst. When I said, "You should talk about it. You should tell people," he'd smile and nod. Over the years, I heard similar stories from other Black psychoanalytic colleagues, who often added something like, "I'm used to it. What good would it do?" Then, in the light of Barack Obama's presidency, I suggested forming a new group, Black Psychoanalysts Speak, and no one I asked to participate said no.

While reading Ta-Nehisi Coates's *Between the World and Me*, a talk to his son about being a Black man in America and about its dangers, I realized I had received a talk of sorts from my parents, as well. Like Coates's, it took place over time. The content was different, though like Coates's it did include, "Don't trust police just because they're police." But it did imply you could rely on the law. Also, "Know your lawyer. Bribery is sometimes necessary. Keep your passport current. Have some cash, gold, and jewelry in the safe. Get an education you can take with you. It can happen here."

White privilege has shades. Did your mother or father ever give you the talk, the talk about the dangers of a world in which more people have been killed by their own governments than at the hands of the enemy during war? If neither did, then they are either in denial, or they are very white. You are very white if you think it can't happen here, because it happened here and continues to happen right now. It happened to the Native people, to those in slavery, to Japanese Americans. It is happening now to those who have spent years in Guantanamo without trial, to the many thousands who are imprisoned without reason, to the millions too poor to buy decent food or get medical care, to the refugees we turn away. I've told my children. Have you?

Chapter 16

On Racism and Being White
The Journey to Henry's Restaurant

Richard Reichbart

> *My schooling gave me no training in seeing myself ... as a participant in a damaged culture.*
> —Peggy McIntosh, "White Privilege: Unpacking the Invisible Knapsack"

I am sitting at Henry's restaurant on the Upper West Side of Manhattan with the group of psychoanalysts from "Black Psychoanalysts Speak," the Psychoanalytic Electronic Publishing (PEP-Web) video for which I wrote the grant, and which followed upon two conferences of the same name (the psychoanalytic conferences were unique because the audiences were predominantly people of color). I am white, as is Michael Moskowitz, who envisioned those conferences, and Alexandra Woods, but everyone else there—Kirkland Vaughans, Annie Lee Jones, Craig Polite, Kathy White, Janice Bennett, Anton Hart—is Black. There are a number of other Black analysts who are not present (Cleonie White, Dolores Morris, Dorothy Holmes, Cheryl Thompson), and subsequently there will be two added to our group (Dionne Powell, Beverley Stoute). I am relatively quiet. In fact, after our dinner, Annie Lee emails me and asks: "Why so quiet?"

I sidestep by saying I have been preoccupied by being president of my institute, the Institute for Psychoanalytic Training and Research (IPTAR), but in fact her question gives me pause. Here is my extended answer.

I need to listen. I *have* to listen. Yes, I have a history of being involved, of committing myself to the importance of culture and doing so passionately, of advocating for justice—actually, of unknowingly, for years, metaphorically searching for the Black maid who left our family precipitously when I was four years old (a dynamic that I understood as a result of my first psychoanalysis). I was arrested in the Free Speech Movement at Berkeley in 1964 in protest against the University of California's forbidding solicitation by the Congress of Racial Equality (CORE) on campus; I worked for Martin Luther King's Southern Christian Leadership Conference as a civil rights worker in Georgia and Alabama in the summer of 1965; after Yale Law School, I lived and worked on the Navajo reservation in Arizona and New Mexico as an Office of Economic Opportunity legal services attorney for Dinebeiina Nahilnabe Agaditahe (attorneys who work for the economic revitalization of the Navajo people); and subsequently, I represented Native Americans who sat in at the Bureau of Indian Affairs (BIA) office in Littleton, Colorado, and were accused of trespass. I successfully defended them before an all-white jury by introducing cultural testimony that touched on Native American practices—from the invocation of tribal elders to the preparation of berry soup—and showed they had no intent to trespass, that they were not "wild Indians" but families who had brought food and ceremony to the BIA, which had accepted them as guests before their sudden and unexpected arrest.

The fabric of cultures, the texture, the theories of causality that are embedded within them, fascinated me. Thus, I wrote about the nature of Navajo thought as revealed in its healing practices. And as a civil rights worker, I learned the wonders and beliefs of Black culture, the back-and-forth of congregants and preacher at church, the power of gospel music. I applied my knowledge to one of my first clinical psychoanalytic papers, to show that the folk belief system of the Southern mother of a Black 12-year-old boy was central to understanding the way in which her child's emotional problems were formed and expressed. It should not be surprising that my early psychoanalytic heroes include George Devereux, Geza Roheim, and Weston La Barre or that I believe psychoanalysis itself should struggle with the same racial issues as have many great American authors, each in his own way: Ellison, Melville, Faulkner, Twain, Wright.

In a visceral way, I can remember living with Vivian Prater and her family in Fort Valley, Georgia; the safety of being on the unpaved-red-Georgia-clay Black side of town; dinners of collard greens, fried chicken, and grits; learning about the importance of church and song.

But the fact is, in all of these situations, my skin offered me a magic protection. I might not be safe on the white side of Fort Valley—it was indeed dangerous back then—but my skin was my passport and permitted me always to leave for home, for a place where I was safe.

So yes, I know about the concept of "white privilege" introduced in the work of Peggy McIntosh (which every psychoanalyst should read), defining racism not as invisible acts of meanness but as an invisible system that confers dominance, and the 50 very simple but poignant examples McIntosh gives of the "daily effects of white privilege," such as "If a traffic cop pulls me over, I can be sure I have not been singled out because of my race" and "I can choose bandages in flesh color and have them more or less match my skin" and "I can arrange to protect my children most of the time from people who do not like them."

Microaggressions

In the video "Black Psychoanalysts Speak," Kathy White poignantly asks whether any white person could conceive the effect of or even tolerate the daily microaggressions (Janice Bennett has referred to them as microassaults) to which Blacks in this culture are subject without terrible rage—without, in effect, "losing it." I would like to suggest that embedded in a culture that favors whites, there is something analogous to the microaggressions that Blacks encounter that takes place for white people who are aware of the racist structure of our society. I do not mean the obvious discriminations, nor the awareness of different ways in which one is privileged as white that McIntosh reports, but the daily things that happen to each white person that can invoke the commonality of one's white body at a price.

They could be labeled "microchallenges to one's integrity." White people do not talk about how we constantly come across these things. Yet every white person knows them. Let me give some examples: I am having a root canal by a skilled Asian dentist in my suburban, largely white town. The dentist expresses fondness for other members of my family he has treated, and I make some remark, just as he is about to drill down, about diversity in the suburbs. It is clear in his reply, however, that he thinks of diversity differently than I do and places Blacks in a different category, and because I am white, he assumes my agreement. Mouth open, vulnerable, I tell myself this is definitely *not* the time, but afterward I am still silent. I think, What is the point? But at what expense do I think that?

Or again: We have dinner with a couple, a friend to whom I have turned at difficult moments in my life and whose career has brought him into intimate contact with Blacks in the music world, and his wife. To my complete surprise, he tells me, despite the fact that he knows I have worked on "Black Psychoanalysts Speak," that Blacks do not have the abstract reasoning power to be psychoanalysts. Stunned, I disagree with him, but this does not reflect fully how I really feel. What I am thinking is that it will be difficult for me to enjoy a social occasion with him again. I probably have lost a dear friend, although he does not realize it. My heart is aching. Should I thrash it out with him? I do not, I let it go. But at what expense?

Close to Home

Let me bring this even closer, to white psychoanalysts at my institute, wonderful analysts from whom I have learned, who in their comments to me sometimes create the same internal sinking feeling I experienced with my friend. Their bias is not as obvious sometimes, but still, from my perspective, they too often exhibit a lack of understanding of the pernicious nature of our white privilege. They say such things as "Very few members of our institute have Blacks in their practice. How many have applied to our institute? Our focus should be on helping members with their practices and keeping a psychoanalytic stance." They say these things to me as if I should agree as their white president, even when they know something of my personal story and that I am trying to change the demographics and culture of my institute. And, of course, they are saying, as subtly implied in this construction, that if one is active in trying to change the culture of our various psychoanalytic institutes, one is not a good analyst; that psychoanalysis is directed toward changing oneself as opposed to society, as if the two are incompatible and the revolutionary core of Freudian thought, as shown so ably by Elizabeth Danto in *Freud's Free Clinics*, never existed. Are our institutes to remain unaware of the cultural ocean in which we all swim, and are we not to say that our white skins lead to our constantly being confronted with these microchallenges to our integrity? On another occasion I will expand this to show how these microchallenges play out in the analyses of our white patients.

Annie Lee Jones, in a prose poem, tells the story of watching white policemen manhandle a Black adolescent at a bus stop and being paralyzed, not able to do anything, distraught, but for one moment making eye contact with one of the policemen. In that moment, that "crack in time," they shared their humanity, seemed even to understand, and then it was over. As a white man, I feel in these microchallenges that I—in the white body that has been my protection and that I have in common with the aggressor—am in danger of being like the perpetrator and in danger of being paralyzed as well. All I can think is: If Annie Lee were there, if any of the Black psychoanalysts at Henry's restaurant were there, would I prove worthy of their gaze? Or would I use the magic talisman of my white skin and compromise my integrity?

So I *have* to listen to the Black Psychoanalysts Speak analysts at Henry's restaurant to hear the personal stories they tell: How you protect your Black son who wants to drive your red sports car for the first time and *will* be stopped by the police; how the white analyst, knowing nothing about Black hair, has no idea why a Black woman is reluctant for years to put her large Afro on the analytic pillow, and attributes her reasons to be characterological. I need to hear that give-and-take that occurs at Henry's restaurant, that kidding, that humor and sadness, that insight into the dark heart of our culture, and that daily shared bravery and determination among these Black analysts, from whom (strangely) I learn about myself.

Chapter 17

"Am I the Only Black Kid That Comes Here?"

Warren Spielberg

"Am I the only Black kid that comes here?" asked David, an 11-year-old African American boy who had been referred to me because of behavior problems.

The question caught me off guard and made me anxious. I reverted to the usual, "I am glad to answer your question, but perhaps you can tell me why you are asking?" He answered with silence.

A few minutes later, he said, "I like your chair. Can I sit there?" I thought about it. I liked my chair, too. But I was trying to build a relationship with a child who did not trust me.

"OK, you can sit there for a while. But eventually I will like it back." I got up, and he settled into my big, comfortable leather chair. I sat on the smaller chair that was reserved for the children who came to see me.

"Why do you think your mother brought you here?" Again he did not reply. I waited a minute, long in therapeutic time. Eventually, my annoyance gave way. "Did you hear what I said?"

"Yeah, I heard you. You know why I'm here. Now stop bothering me." He moved the chair over to examine my toys.

He had a point. I did know. He had been suspended from his public school for "defiant behavior" and was now enrolled in a parochial school. Like so many boys of color, David was not thriving in school.

For our book *The Psychology of Black Boys and Adolescents*, Kirkland Vaughans and I interviewed over 50 boys and young men about their school lives. Most felt uncomfortable with their teachers. Many reported being singled out for discipline and being asked to sit in the back of the class. However, most were unable to voice their feelings about these experiences. If they did allude to them, it was with much uncertainty and hesitation. Most of the time, they "tried not to know" they were the objects of fear or dislike, because this would be unbearably painful to acknowledge. Although they were unable to discuss their feelings and fears about school, they readily enacted them. Many used defiance or withdrawal to protect themselves from their fear of rejection. Sadly, many blamed themselves. By third grade, school participation and achievement among Black boys begin to decline, a process that will continue through high school.

I believe the "mentalization" capacity of boys and adolescent males of color becomes compromised in school. Peter Fonagy (1997) has discussed the relationship between the hostility of authority figures and the inability of children to develop self-awareness and advanced cognition. This is an adaptive strategy on the part of a child subjected to deprivation or rejection, as to recognize the hostile thoughts of a meaningful adult would be too frightening and painful. However, as Black boys close their minds to important adults like teachers, they also become afraid to think about themselves. They become unable to use what is in their own minds to create and achieve.

The current cultural climate of most schools undermines the developing capacity of the Black boy to see himself as cherished in the minds of teachers. In my view, the "achievement gap" reflects a "relational gap" between boys of color and their teachers. Many more white teachers than Black teachers describe boys of color as larger physically, less innocent, and more delinquent. Even when they do well in school, they are often accused of cheating, as their success runs counter to implicit stereotypes. Their positive qualities and selves are "invisible" to others, as A.J. Franklin has noted. They are not seen when they are gifted, intelligent, helpful, and decent. This trauma of nonrecognition leads to a lifelong feeling of jeopardy if they try to be seen.

Jared, a tall, handsome young man we met in Montclair, remarked, "I stay in the middle. I won't do badly in school, but I don't want to stand out either," echoing a common sentiment we encountered. To stand out or to do too well will lead to some kind of targeting. Black teachers and boys also experience ruptures based on clashes in culture and class. Boys and young men of color are suspended and expelled at six times the rate of their white counterparts. Once suspended, Black boys see their graduation rates declining by 30 percent. This sets many of these young men up for a life in the streets and involvement with the criminal justice system.

David could be defiant and uncooperative, but underneath he was frightened of being thought to be stupid and fearful of being punished. And now he was required to be in therapy. In treatment, he seemed to be treating me as one more demeaning authority figure. But now he was in the driver's seat (my chair had wheels), and I was the one in an inferior and more vulnerable position. David held my chair hostage for a few months. Often I was "forced" to sit in a smaller chair. I would request my chair back. But he would not relent. Sometimes I would make a mock run for the chair before he could get into it. But he was much faster and more motivated.

Meanwhile, I would speak to him of my frustration, longing, and helplessness about losing my chair. I wondered aloud, "What have I done to deserve being ripped off in this manner?" Once, after a few months, he said, "You don't deserve it."

"Why?" I asked. No answer. He went back to building a large Lego structure.
At the end of the session, I commented, "You are very creative, but many people in your life have never noticed." He nodded.
The next session he observed, "You're being nice to me because you want your chair back."
I replied, "I can understand why you think that, but I really do admire you. But yes, it's true I would like my chair back."
"You don't deserve it," he replied, "because you have not been honest with me."
"How so?" I asked.
"Every time we play checkers, you pick the white pieces. Not the black."

David's comments took me aback. Although he was soft in his tone and attitude, he put me on the spot. Despite my anxiety, I tried to be reflective. Had I really chosen the white pieces because of my own racial preference? Further, what did my choice mean to him, and why did he focus on it? My thoughts broadened. I remembered a piece of history. There was a time in many Southern states when Blacks and whites were not allowed to play checkers together. David's mother came from South Carolina. A deeply religious and somewhat distant woman, she was typically deferential, but she could be angry and mistrustful with David and with me. Perhaps he was also expressing *her* mistrust and doubt about my dedication to her son. Perhaps both wondered if I could love him as much as he needed, despite my being white.

I also began to think of my own racial history, of my fights with boys of color who had bullied me when I was growing up in a very polarized city. Although I was fortunate to have very close friends from other ethnic and racial backgrounds, I had also experienced the violence that lies in the transitional space between Blacks and whites. Was this contributing to our impasse? These reflections penetrated my consciousness, and I began to see our conflict in the context of a larger struggle.

But after six months, David had directly addressed what he felt and feared to be my racist attitudes. I took his directness and courage as a positive sign that the trust between us had grown, allowing for new forms of authentic relating. I had begun to feel for some time that there was growing mutual warmth between us, that the space between us was becoming less charged even though our conflict over the chair had not abated. He sometimes smiled and had begun to enter the room on time instead of stalling outside. For my part, I had moved off the chair as the essential place of inquiry. Our relationship felt less coercive overall, and I became more aware of his other attributes.

I chose to respond to him as honestly as I could. I said, "I was not aware of choosing white pieces, but perhaps it's possible," particularly in that we seemed to be "in some sort of war" most of the time. I added that I wanted us to be closer and was hoping he could trust me enough to help him.

He listened without comment as he played with Legos. I felt he would continue to wait and see if I would be true to my word.

In therapy, like life, race is difficult to discuss in an intimate fashion. There is a gulf of silence between Blacks and whites that affects us both personally and politically. In cross-racial therapeutic encounters, both the participants can be uncomfortable. The patient fears alienating his therapist and undermining his treatment if he talks about race. The therapist may be afraid to stir up difficult feelings or say or do something with racial overtones. And at the same time, it is crucial that we try to have these discussions, even when they are painful and awkward. In therapy, racial differences can be a barrier both to growth and intimacy in the patient's treatment and to the growth of the therapist. In communal life, the harsh division between Blacks and whites underlies deep divisions in policing, education, and law enforcement. These issues are front and center today. But the psychological dynamics that propel these conflicts are largely hidden.

The problem of the chair remained between us. He continued to want exclusive control of this prize. Although I was more open to accepting and embracing my own feelings of helplessness to allow him the power and the throne, I was still hoping he would be more generous with me.

Nevertheless, in the following session, I remarked, "We both know I want my chair back. But my relationship with you is more important. Why don't we just agree that it's your chair to use whenever you want from now on."

He did not respond, but over the next weeks the atmosphere began to change. I had accepted my vulnerability. He, in turn, seemed more open. Once, when he came in, he asked me how I was. Our discussions broadened. We began to talk more about race and about his experiences in school and in his family.

David's treatment lasted two years. I never did get my chair back. But I got something more special and rare in our culture: a closer, more real relationship of equality, love, and healing.

Chapter 18

White Privilege and Its Fissures
A Personal Perspective

Alexandra Woods

If we choose to do so, each of us can find a way of looking through the lens of our personal experiences to consider white privilege and white supremacy and the ways these phenomena are communicated, internalized, and passed on. This is a particularly important task for white people to engage in, for reasons I will address below. It is often not an easy one.

There's privilege, and then there's privilege; I have lived both. While there were periodic economic downturns in my family's life, the baseline was one of great wealth. This wealth came largely from my German-American grandfather on my mother's side. His father was one of a large wave of middle-class German immigrants who moved to the Midwest in search of opportunity. These Germans were considered desirable in their whiteness, Protestantism, and relative prosperity, as opposed to the Jews of Europe, Blacks and Catholic immigrants including the Italians, Irish, Poles.

My father and stepfather (they were related to each other) came from the Anglo-American aristocracy. And while the extraordinary wealth of their forebears had long since been frittered away, they and I, whether I liked it or not, had our illustrious heritage, and all that it implied, to lean on.

There were deep fissures in my family structure that exposed me to the fact that all was not right in the world of wealth and class privilege. This is something I came to consciously feel by about the age of nine, and the lesson was drilled home by the time I was a teenager. The term "white privilege" had not been coined in the 1950s or 1960s, and it would be years before I had the remotest sense of what such a term might possibly mean. Frankenberg states, "'Whiteness' refers to a set of cultural practices that are usually unmarked and unnamed" (as cited in DiAngelo, 2011, p. 56).

Looking back, I see a slew of markers. I was born in an old mining town in Colorado that was on the cusp of change. My grandfather had seen Aspen's possibilities. He promptly moved his family's vacation home there and set to work to transform Aspen into the center for culture and intellectual development it became by the early 1950s. My father had also seen Aspen's potential during World War II, when he trained with the 10th Mountain Division in the nearby town of Leadville. After the war, my father returned to Aspen to set up the ski patrol and develop what was at that time in America a virtually unknown sport. That is where my parents met. My mother's beauty and her access to capital, coupled with my father's lineage and dashing demeanor, served to paper over complicated attractions/fissures.

I have come to study the economics of white supremacy and white privilege in some detail. I have been particularly interested in the ways that most white Northerners have little awareness of the North's deep complicity in slavery and are oblivious to the fact that American capitalism and prosperity are founded on the fruits of slavery. Two prominent contemporary historians, Sven Beckert and Seth Rockman, write that until very recently, historians viewed the institution of slavery as premodern and anti-capitalist (Beckert and Rockman, 2016). Slavery was considered to be "rather like an extended cul-de-sac… ultimately a dead end in the path towards the nation's 'modern' political and economic institutions." But "a new consensus is emerging, one that… treats slavery as the interstate highway system of the American past" (Einhorn, "Slavery," as cited in Beckert and Rockman, 2016, p. 6). It was the northern Anglo-European banks that financed southern banks, which in turn provided plantation owners and westward-bound pioneers with credit (Boodry, 2016). Northern credit financed the "cleansing" of lands of Native peoples; the capture, enslavement, transportation, sale, and purchase of human beings; and the creation, at minimal cost, of the "empire of cotton" (Beckert, 2015, throughout). Northern investment in slavery permitted the accumulation of capital never witnessed previously in history. This accumulation led, in turn, to the building of entire cities in the northern US, the endowment of over forty northern universities (Wilder, 2014), the construction of northern teaching hospitals, and, most dramatically, the dominance by the United States of the economies of the world. Beckert (2015, throughout) calls this entire process "war capitalism." (This research was previously cited in Woods, 2020.).

My maternal grandparents' family was aware of its privilege and believed both in its right to prosperity and also in the importance of giving back. However, I do not believe that anyone on either side of my family considered their white privilege. I doubt that anyone thought that the opportunities available in the nineteenth century to my Anglo-American forebears, and in the nineteenth and twentieth centuries to my German forebears, to accumulate capital, develop networks, build institutions, live in aesthetically pleasing homes, and contribute to shaping the national narrative, had any relation to war capitalism or to the institution of slavery. Nor, of course, would almost any white professional who attended Yale, Harvard, NYU, or Columbia, or trained at McLean Hospital in Boston or Mount Sinai Hospital in New York, recognize that they were the direct beneficiaries of slavery (Wilder, 2014). And yet, to return to my family, the amount of white-owned capital, connection, and access to power that led to my parents' meeting and, more importantly, that led to the transformation of Aspen, Colorado, over the ten-year period from 1950 to1960 is quite mind-boggling. Recently, Kirkland Vaughans stated that blacks in the 1850s owned .05 percent of American capital. In 2018, with all the progress this nation has made, that percentage has risen to 1.5 percent (Vaughans, 2018). Gump (2010, 2014), among other authors (Alexander, 2010; Altman, 2000; Browne, 2008; Gould, 1981; Leary, 2006; Painter, 2010; Vaughans, 2015; Zinn, 1980), and the newer economic historians (Baptist, 2016; Beckert and Rockman, 2016; Boodry, 2016) trenchantly describe the racist practices that have perpetuated such extraordinary socioeconomic disparities to this day.

Gump examines white privilege from a somewhat different vantage point. She speaks of the passport that all white immigrants, no matter how impoverished or traumatized, carried with them: white (unmarked) skin color (Gump, 2014). Gump writes that, in stark contrast, "[W]e (Africans)… arrived in garments more defining and elaborated than those of any immigrant group. What we wore was our color….Thus we arrived *known* to a significant degree, formulated by the colonial discourse" (Gump, 2014, p. 761).

Gump cites Frankenberg who explains that

> this discourse grew out of the colonial expansion of the 16th century, which produced "knowledge" central to the success of colonial rule. These "modes of knowing... that enable[d] and rationalize[d] colonial domination from the standpoint of the West, [also] produced ways of conceiving 'Other' societies and cultures whose legacies endure into the present."
>
> (Gump, 2014, p. 761)

In accordance with Gump's observations, my German forebears shared something else with other white immigrant groups, even those who had experienced much more trauma than they; they shared the experience of hope --"hope that hard work would be rewarded; hope the inequities suffered by their ancestors would be reversed; hope, in this land of meritocracy, that they might thrive" (Gump, 2014). Enslaved Africans in America could hope for something better only in the afterlife (Cone, 2013; Gump, 2014). My German-American forebears were full of hope; fortunes were made, and lost, and made again. They were people who contributed: professors of linguistics, businessmen who did, in fact, create thousands of jobs, patrons of the arts, proponents of progressive thought, a longstanding leader in the US government. They/we were on the side of those who had the power to formulate the colonial discourse.

Divorce was one of the fissures that ran through both my maternal and paternal lines. My parents attempted what in Alcoholics Anonymous is called "the geographic solution" to salvage their marriage; they moved to Bogotá, Colombia. They had connections that enabled my father to start anew; there was always a safety net, and work was not essential. When their marriage failed, my mother and I moved to San Francisco. The woman who had been my nanny in Colombia, Eva P., joined us. I was not quite four. I received the first lesson on race relations that I remember when I was six. On one of Eva's days off, my mother arranged for a babysitter so that she could go out for the evening. I had become an expert at sizing up sitters, and I took an immediate dislike to the stranger who walked through our door. The woman, whose name I don't recall, told me that she would never spend the night at anyone else's house. Uninterested, I asked her why. "Because I wouldn't want to sleep in a bed where an——has slept." When my mother returned, I was awake; I told her what had been said. My memory is that my mother fired this woman before my eyes, telling her that she did not want such ugliness in her presence, nor in the presence of her daughter. It is more likely that my mother told me about what she had done after the fact. That memory, and my attachment to this part of my mother, became an indelible part of me.

However, there were other parts of me that I can trace from my family heritage. For one or two summers, my nanny, Eva, and I would fly to the East Coast so that I could see my father. My grandmother, the daughter of a patrician marriage and divorce, had bought a massive, white-columned Georgian house with the number "1773" etched into its side. "Bowlingly" sat on the Chesapeake Bay in Maryland. Every summer, my grandmother would summon her grandchildren and her children, whose marriages were all falling apart, to stay. We cousins had free run of Bowlingly, racing through its long hallways, sliding down the curving banisters of a double staircase that swooped to the foyer, and racing outdoors to leap into the pool that my grandmother had built for us. I did not understand why some of Bowlingly's outbuildings were called the "Quarters." Such things were not discussed. But I think on some level I had a sense of something very troubling. There were times when the Big House became very full, and Eva and I were sent to stay in the Quarters, a low and humid structure with no air-conditioning. I spent the longest night of my life there, sweat soaking the sheets as I watched the blades of a fan turn endlessly while flies got stuck to hanging yellow strips of flypaper. I wept for my mother, who was very far away.

I sensed that my grandmother did not like Eva, though I did not know why. Now, I conjecture that she resented her connection to my mother; resented that Eva and I spoke Spanish together; resented that she could not control her the way she was used to controlling everyone around her, particularly her Black servants; resented that Eva, a descendant of indigenous peoples, had dark skin. I do not recall how my grandmother conveyed her dislike of Eva, except I do remember my own words.

Upon our return to San Francisco and to my mother at the end of the summer, Eva was putting me to bed one night, something I resented. I informed her, "I don't have to listen to you. You're only a servant." Eva let my mother know what had transpired; my mother reprimanded me severely and made me apologize to Eva. I immediately recognized my mother's rough justice, and I felt deeply ashamed that I could so easily forget who Eva was. One may have sympathy for the child who was shuttled across the country between parents, but I would like to draw attention here to how ideas of superiority and inferiority, ideas about who has the right to order another person around, and ways that the "colonial discourse" can be internalized and communicated. And, buried in there, was the need, and the power, to project a humiliating experience of abjection away from myself onto another: Eva belonged in the Quarters, not I.

Recently, Stoute stated (2018) that the worst thing that a child can experience in navigating the complicated world of racial identification and disidentification is silence. Yet silence, blankness, erasure are central to how whiteness maintains itself (DiAngelo, 2011; Holmes, 2018). And other than my mother's fierce early stands, there was no direct discussion of race in my family.

There is no end point to the unpacking of the knapsack of white privilege (McIntosh, 2002); it must be a process (DiAngelo, 2011; Hart, 2018; Holmes, 2014, 2018; Powell, 2018; Stoute, 2017, 2018). I note my attendance at private girls' schools in which the only person of color over thirteen years of education was a princess from a South Asian country and my entry into an Ivy League school where a family friend knew the college president as more examples of great privilege. At the same time, I believe a growing rage built in me, which put me on a path to want to deconstruct whiteness. That rage was fueled by the loss of my mother. My work represents, in part, an ongoing wish to find her.

When I was eleven, my mother remarried, and we moved to England to live with my American-expatriate stepfather. In retrospect, and after many years of analysis, I believe that I witnessed, up close, the corrosion of a tiny part of the Anglo-American aristocracy. Neither my stepfather nor my father, the two men who participated in my upbringing, were able to adjust to the world of work. Instead they were supported, as if in an Edith Wharton novel, by the inherited wealth of the women in their lives. No endeavor, no work, was good enough to match the achievements of our illustrious forebears. In family systems theory, we know of "family tasks"; how might we conceptualize *class-based* family tasks, and how might we understand the ways these tasks are carried out? For many in my paternal line, the task of the descendants was to recall and mimic what once had been. My stepfather was particularly concerned with social class and ensured that I was indoctrinated. Within a year of moving to England, I was able to identify anyone's social class and region of origin by hearing the person utter a single sentence.

Determined to preserve her marriage, the mother who had once fiercely instilled values in me faded away; she no longer saw herself as someone who could interpret, or help me interpret, social and political relations. She abandoned her bohemian ways, her love of flair and color, and she buried the hard-won common-sense voice that she'd fought for in a psychoanalytic treatment she had undertaken during the San Francisco years. Her efforts to conform to a somewhat strange version of upper-class British life were costly. She became intermittently quite ill. And there were rituals. Each night after cooking elaborate meals in the kitchen, which was in the basement, she would go upstairs to don a floor-length skirt, dressy blouse, and jewelry, and then she would serve us dinner. Each night, my stepfather wore a navy blazer and tie to dine at that kitchen table. The adjoining dark, velveted dining room was reserved for "guests" who were rarely invited. A conversation repeated many times over the ensuing years in the kitchen went this way:

"Table Rock [his grandparents' massive home in Tuxedo Park, New York] had 14 servants even when there was no one there (*sic*)."
"Yes, but you were very unhappy at Table Rock."
"That's not the point!"

Increasingly, my mother deferred to my stepfather's idiosyncratic notions of child-rearing, notions which he had inherited from a world of full-time British governesses, quarterly glimpses of his parents as they travelled the world, and boarding schools where sadism was rampant. Audre Lorde said it best:

It is eas(y)… for white women to believe the dangerous fantasy that if you are good enough, pretty enough, sweet enough, quiet enough, teach the children to behave,… then you will be allowed to coexist with patriarchy in relative peace.

(1984, p.288)

All things American faded away; old friends were no longer welcomed, and my stepfather pronounced that it was good we had left the US. These were the years from 1963 to 1969—the height of the Civil Rights movement and, later, the Vietnam War.

At the socially prominent and not very academic girls' school that I was sent to, there was a brilliant minister, whom I met just before he retired. In his final sermon to us, he spoke of oolites. He described them as tiny crustaceans that build their circular shells progressively from the outside inward. Eventually these creatures suffocated, trapped by their own constructions. For many years, this image haunted me.

Robin DiAngelo, in her 2011 article "White Fragility," describes a constellation of whiteness, white privilege, and white fragility in the following ways: Whites live "in a social environment that protects and insulates them from race-based stress" (p.55). Whiteness is a social location that is "insulated," (p. 55) which expects "racial comfort," (p.61) is "surrounded by protective pillows of resources," "repels gossip and voyeurism," and "demands dignity" (p.55). "White Fragility is a state in which even a minimum amount of racial stress becomes intolerable, triggering a range of defensive moves" (p. 57). The defensive moves include "anger, fear, and guilt, and behaviors such as argumentation, silence, and leaving the stress-inducing situation" (p. 54). To me, the move to England and the lifestyle that we entered represent an ultimate expression of white fragility. More complicated to this day were my own parallel strategies in battling the losses and the extremes of white privilege I was living; my strategies included anger, fear, guilt, argumentation, and silence. White privilege and white fragility are like flypaper.

While I escaped to college in America, it took me many years to really leave. Eventually, I found a remarkable psychoanalyst, Bert Freedman, with whom I worked for a very long time. It became highly relevant that he was a German Jew who had escaped the Anschluss. My own deep ambivalence about my Germanness and my anxieties about the choices I might have made had I been alive in the 1930s, became an ongoing thread through our work. A remarkably resilient and humane man, Bert helped me navigate my fantasies in all their rage and despair and move to a better place.

I have decided to end on an uncomfortable and unresolved note. It echoes the deep internal identifications and alliances that can be seen most starkly in the context of extreme privilege, but which apply to the world of whiteness in general.

While I ended up opposing the Iraq War and participated in what was the largest international protest in history (Kaufman, 2017), I was initially very ambivalent about whether the war was wrong; for some time, I was inclined to believe what was being presented by the administration—that Saddam Hussein had been stockpiling weapons of mass destruction. My ambivalence alienated some of my more political friends, for whom the issues were much clearer. In 2004, in the middle of the Iraq War, my great-uncle died after a long life and a prominent career in the US administration. I am proud to have been related to him. I went to his funeral, which was held at Washington National Cathedral. In the front pew sat Donald Rumsfeld, Dick Cheney, and Paul Wolfowitz. I returned to New York and talked about the experience with one of my dearest friends, a Jewish man whose ancestors had fled pogroms in a province of Russia that no longer exists. I said to him, "What scares me is that my gut reaction is to feel that these men are friends. They look like members of my family." My friend replied, "My gut reaction is to feel afraid." We have discussed this conversation since. Both of us felt ashamed of our reactions. My friend felt ashamed for responding first with fear over rage; I felt ashamed because my reaction had reminded me once again how deep the roots of the colonial discourse run within me.

Dorothy Holmes states in *Black Psychoanalysts Speak* (in Winograd, 2014) that

> more than once I've had a… white clinician say, I don't know if I want to talk to patients about this. 'I like my privilege. I don't know if I want to share my privilege'…. All the isms most probably cannot be cured… That doesn't mean, oh well. It means more like… if you have high blood pressure, once you have it, you can't get rid of it. But you can treat it every day, and you'd better treat it every day.

References

Alexander, M. (2010). *The New Jim Crow*. New York: The New Press.
Altman, N. (2000). Black and white thinking: A psychoanalyst reconsiders race. *Psychoanalytic Dialogues* 10:589–605.

Baptist, E. (2016). Toward a political economy of slave labor: hands, whipping-machines, and modern power. In *Slavery's Capitalism: A New History of American Economic Development*, eds. S. Beckert and S. Rockman. Philadelphia: University of Pennsylvania Press, pp. 31–61.

Beckert, S. (2015). *Empire of Cotton: A Global History*. New York: Vintage Books.

Beckert, S. and Rockman, S., eds. (2016). *Slavery's Capitalism: A New History of American Economic Development*. Philadelphia: University of Pennsylvania Press.

Boodry, K. (2016). August Belmont and the world the slaves made. In *Slavery's Capitalism: A New History of American Economic Development*, eds. S. Beckert and S. Rockman. Philadelphia: University of Pennsylvania Press, pp. 162–178.

Browne, K., dir. (2008). *Traces of the Trade: A Story from the Deep North* (film). PBS: POV.

Cone, J. (2013). *The Cross and the Lynching Tree*. New York: Orbis Books.

DiAngelo, R. (2011). White fragility. *International Journal of Critical Pedagogy* 3(3):54–70.

Gould, S.J. (1981, 1996). *The Mismeasure of Man*. New York: Norton and Co.

Gump, J. (2014). Discovery and repair: Discussion of the article by Lynne Jacobs. *Psychoanalytic Inquiry* 34(7):759–765.

Gump, J.P. (2010). Reality matters: The shadow of trauma on African American subjectivity. *Psychoanalytic Psychology* 27(1):42–54.

Hart, A. (2018, February). The vicissitudes of curiosity in cross-racial dialogue: The case of the Toney-Greenson conversation. In "African Americans and Psychoanalysis: What's Going On (and How Can We Talk about It)?" (panel conducted at the 107th National Meeting of the American Psychoanalytic Association, K. Vaughans, chair).

Holmes, D. (2014). In *Black Psychoanalysts Speak* (film), dir. B. Winograd. PEP Video Grants 1(1).

Holmes, D. (2018, February). Discussion. In "African Americans and Psychoanalysis: What's Going On (and How Can We Talk about It)?" (panel conducted at the 107th National Meeting of the American Psychoanalytic Association, K. Vaughans, chair).

Kaufman, L.A. (2017). *Direct Action: Protest and the Reinvention of American Radicalism*. New York: Verso Books.

Leary, K. (2006). In the eye of the storm. *Psychoanalytic Quarterly* 75(1):345–363.

Lorde, A. (1984). Age, race, class, and sex: Women redefining difference. In *Words of Fire: An Anthology of African-American Feminist Thought*, ed. B. Guy-Sheftall. New York: W.W. Norton & Co., pp. 284–291.

McIntosh, P. (2002). White privilege: Unpacking the invisible knapsack. In *White Privilege*, ed. P. Rothenberg. New York: Worth, pp. 97–102.

Painter, N. (2010). *The History of White People*. New York: W.W. Norton and Co.
Powell, D. (2018, February). Discussion. In "African Americans and Psychoanalysis: What's Going On (and How Can We Talk about It)?" (panel conducted at the 107th National Meeting of the American Psychoanalytic Association, K. Vaughans, chair).
Stoute, B. (2017). Race and racism in psychoanalytic thought: The ghosts in our nursery. *The American Psychoanalyst: Special Section: Conversations on Psychoanalysis and Race* 51(1):10–16.
Stoute, B. (2018, February). Our curiosity about difference and what happens to it: Developmental aspects of race awareness. In "African Americans and Psychoanalysis: What's Going On (and How Can We Talk about It)?" (panel conducted at the 107th National Meeting of the American Psychoanalytic Association, K. Vaughans, chair).
Vaughans, K. (2015). To unchain haunting blood memories: Intergenerational trauma among African-Americans. In *Fragments of Trauma and the Social Production of Suffering: Trauma, History and Memory*, eds. M. O'Loughlin and M. Charles. New York: Rowman & Littlefield, pp. 277–290.
Vaughans, K. (2018, February). Discussion of V. Gay. In "On the Pleasures of Owning Persons: The Hidden Face of American Slavery" (panel conducted at the 107th National Meeting of the American Psychoanalytic Association, A. Hart, chair).
Wilder, C. (2014). *Ebony and Ivy: Race, Slavery and the Troubled History of America's Universities*. New York: Bloomsbury Press.
Winograd, B. (2014). "Black Psychoanalysts Speak," 2014 PEP Documentary (accessible through American Psychoanalytic Association Psychoanalytic Electronic Publishing database) https://www.youtube.com/watch?v=N8-VIi7tb44 (Last accessed July 2, 2022).
Woods, A. (2020). The work before us: Whiteness and the psychoanalytic institute. *Psychoanalysis, Culture & Society* 25(2):230–249.
Zinn, H. (1980). *A People's History of the United States*. New York: Harper Row.

Chapter 19

"It Takes One to Know One"

Matthew von Unwerth

I

"White Like Me," a 1984 *Saturday Night Live* sketch conceived and performed by Eddie Murphy in his protean prime, shows an impastoed Murphy affecting surprise at the rhapsodic, erotic, profligate reception he receives as he makes his way through a tableaux of white America (Murphy 1984). At a newsstand, white Eddie gets the news for free; at a bank white Eddie is shoveled shoeboxes of cash; as the last Black passenger disembarks, the sepulchral silence of an afternoon bus gives way to the raunchy racket of a honky speakeasy. In each of these scenes, whiteness itself is the shibboleth that provides an entry into a welcoming world in which everything is permitted, everything received, *entre nous*.

These scenes were described to me when I was thirteen by my father, whose humor was drawn to repression's scabs, not long after we had relocated from Atlanta to the D.C. suburbs, and from a messy but engaged experience of integrated school and public life where Black and white students not only attended school together, but were *concerned* with one another. In Atlanta, we traded plastic soldiers for broken bits of magnets, each trying to exploit the other in the deal, each emerging victorious. We chased one another on the blacktop, hot pursuit drawing blood from one another's knees; we came to each other's rescue, when the older bullies came for us. We tried out terrible, vicious (yet delicious) language on one another, including the most triggering sorts of racial argot, to which the response was always, annoyingly, reciprocally inevitable: *It takes one to know one.* Give as you get, and in the giving, close up the wound that the insult opened up, suturing it into a shared joke.

DOI: 10.4324/9781003280002-24

In Maryland, the schools were better. There was no appalling legacy of segregation to overcome, no one sent to the principal for occasionally bringing hatred to school, nothing to explain the much more orderly, hushed and altogether less integrated community, where Black and white children haunted the same halls, but hardly knew one another.

My father loved the sketch, much as he loved pricking my selfish conscience with an askew "that's *mighty white* of you" when I gave my sister the rump of the Milky Way bar we were to share, and he offered it to me as preface and recommendation to John Howard Griffin's (1961) bestselling *Black Like Me* (Griffin 1961). Griffin, like my father a religious white southerner who regarded racial injustice as the insistent spiritual challenge of his time, passed himself for a month (with the help of a dermatologist) as a Black man in segregated New Orleans, and returned with a damning account (shocking to no Black reader) of the "hate stares," casual insults, threats of violence and pervasive stigmatization he encountered.

That this work was both a sensation (10 million copies were sold) and acclaimed as authentic revelation of Black experience is itself testament to how authority and trust in discussing race were evaluated by white Americans in its time and ours (for what account of African American life by a Black author would have had its reach and impact?). And yet Griffin's experiment also raised a troubling, even tragic question, as urgent in our time as it was sixty years ago: How can one understand the experience of another, marked by racial stigma as being "other" than oneself, without having shared their worldly road?

I took from these early, undigested experiences troubling news that the world was only fair to the fairer race; that there was safety in sameness, especially if one's sameness were white; and perhaps also that, in order to approach race matters, one would do well to find oneself a ventriloquist.

Or perhaps a psychoanalyst.

My subsequent experiences in education, in professional life, in the prosperous, progressive citified settings in which I traveled, extended and confirmed these early lessons of my sentimental education; but thankfully for me, my work has tugged me, however fitfully, in other directions. Two decades of personal analysis and clinical experience have helped me to start sifting these early intimations of the treachery of race, and hopefully at times to mark twain my efforts to bear witness to the worlds of those marked different—different from my whiteness, different from me.

From my own analyses, I began to understand the roots of my incomprehensibly intense hostility to the familiar figure of the paternalistic "white savior" in my own oedipal concerns. In the post-civil rights South, white saviors were everywhere – men (mostly men), in the disavowed mold of the benevolent plantation owner, whose journey of personal liberalism on race matters illuminates, resolves and redeems the whole world of racism. Certainly we remember *their* names: Huckleberry Finn, Atticus Finch, Viggo Mortenson's benighted chauffeur in *Green Book*, anti-KKK crusader Morris Dees, Presidents Lincoln, Kennedy, and Johnson, even Griffin himself. In the narratives in which these men and many like them figured, each sought justice on behalf of their Black brothers and sisters; and yet, in the process of doing so, they merely reversed the valence of their white power, from overseer to emancipator, foregrounding, as Charles Blow (2021) puts it, the "starring role for white liberal guilt, one that…center[s] their capacity for growth and evolution." It was perhaps an important and necessary step, but one that demanded no embrace, entwine nor yielding to the animating other.

Ruefully, I came also to recognize the roots of my problematic identification with certain marked, oppressed *others* in earlier epochs of my own development. Adolescence in America is often marked by experiences of conflict and longing around connectedness and individuality, and mine was no different. As an adolescent, it was not uncommon to recognize in myself a longing for the tangible *stigmata* of racial, sexual, historical oppression which I conspicuously lacked, I suppose to confirm my nonetheless consuming private hurt.

For me, as for many young Americans steeped in the poetry of the blues and the Gullah tales of Br'er Rabbit, Motown and tap, jazz, hip hop and rap, Black experience was often associated with creativity and authenticity; and its productions, in contrast to white experience, connected with suffering, the fruits of an unrelatable anguish. In this identification I joined a tradition—exemplified by Lou Reed's gruesome identification with Martin Luther King's martyrdom in "I Wanna Be Black" and the rageful rap posturings of the protagonist of Ben Lerner's *The Topeka* School – in which whiteness regards the lived experience of Black oppression as horrific, but at least, in compensatory contrast to the souls of whiteness who emulate them, authentic, legitimate and *real* (Reed 1978).

2

In these accidents of personal experience, I believe I have come to recognize two of the more general features of white race consciousness: *identification* (however conflicted) of one's vulnerabilities with the power and safety of the white, the self-same, the first term; and *projection* (however, ambivalent) of the despised, feared, hated, and impotent or helpless aspects of oneself into the despised "Other."

The notion of the constitutive Other in human relations, ideology, and psychology comes to us from a tradition of Western philosophy epitomized in G.W.F. Hegel's formulation of the *dialectic*, in his fable of the entwined *agon* of "master" and "slave" in *The Phenomenology of Spirit* (Hegel 1807). In Hegel's formulation, master (who seeks to exploit the other as resource) and slave (who seeks to be for himself) call one another into being, depend on one another for consciousness, and, intrinsic to the consuming nature of the struggle between them, cannot exist independent of one another, each being the "other" to its "self." Hegel's philosophical fable is offensive to modern sensibilities, but it was inspired *ab ovo* by the contradictions underlying the white European institution of slavery (Hegel seems to have been guided by the revolution of Haitian slaves in the early nineteenth century). The dialectical tradition, which is the foundation of the contemporary disciplines of critical race theory and post-colonial studies (which give us so much of the language we use today to discuss race matters), emphasizes that what we consider in daily life to be the "self" ironically cannot exist independently of the different others—people, cultures, perceptions—that lie beyond its borders, and which borders indeed are what make a sense of self, safety, belonging, home possible— but which also invite violence towards and erasure of the other in the process of self-definition.[1]

In psychoanalytic thinking, a dialectical conceptualization of the self is central. Winnicott's (1960) remark that "[t]here is no such thing as an infant" (p. 587)—independent of the mother who recognizes, is preoccupied with, and translates the infant to himself—is precisely analogous to the way in which what is proper to the self cannot exist without the other that it defines itself *against*. This dialectical relationship may be said to exist, too, between experiences of whiteness and Blackness, which only have sense in the context of one another. So the infant's generation of entwined senses of self and other (both actual and psychical) that is at the heart of our contemporary psychodynamic notions of child development, intersubjective relations—and thus the workings of transference and therapeutic action within the psychoanalytic field—through its dialectical structure, bears some affinity with the *mutuality* of whiteness and Blackness. But how?

Though still insufficiently theorized in analytic thinking, the advent of race consciousness in child development seems to me to belong to what Sandor Ferenczi called the development of the sense of reality (Ferenczi 1913). For the emerging mind of the child, reality signals the internal movement from a hallucinated, omnipotent control over his environment to a more conditional, dependent autonomy—a rueful acknowledgment that he cannot survive without the world around him. In this new configuration, the infant—once "his majesty the baby," ruler of all he surveyed—now lurches from adoration for the nurturing environment to hateful loathing of what deprives him in his dependence and lies beyond his control. To bridge the untenable divide in his own feeling mind, the infant has to resolve these profoundly opposed attitudes—first experienced towards his parents or immediate caregivers in his environment, and eventually displaced onto the entire world of "objects"—into ambivalence, in which love and hate temper and mediate one other.

This sketch of an ideal of child development within the analytic perspective also presumes ideal conditions for the growth and nurture of the infant's mind. But what if, despite the caregiver's exemplary attunement, the conditions aren't ideal? What if, before infant and mother call each other into being, the world has already interposed itself, despised some of those parents, differentiated and stigmatized some from others, and valued them differently in relation to one another (better and worse, native and foreign, more and less)? When one's parents are already differentiated as white or Black, what does it mean when it comes time for the infant to form his own ambivalent resolution of the elemental love and hate inside him?

3

These gleanings from analytic thinking have oriented me in my work with patients. But the best part of my education has come with my patients themselves, from whom I have learned, sometimes through failure, to bear witness to their individual experiences. From patients whose race marks them as different than me, I have been learning repeatedly how questions regarding whether or not we can be known to one another eventually force themselves to the center of treatment. In some cases, race is front and center from the first word. For some, the need to deny our racial difference, or their difference from whiteness, has precluded any exploration of what lies between us for years. For others, the annihilating threat of being misapprehended, assimilated or erased by my privileged difference has proved too much for the two of us to manage. In every instance, these experiences of difference and sameness, connection and disconnectedness, love and hate, are irreducibly reflective of each person's individual history and psychic development. "Race" is dialectically constituted with each person's psyche, and so is formed by each mind it reaches even as it shapes that mind in turn.

These experiences of race are just as varied for the people who (as James Baldwin and Ta-Nehisi Coates helpfully put it) "believe themselves to be white"; as with people of color, white experiences of being white unfold along a spectrum reflecting the polarities of sameness and difference (Baldwin 1962; Coates 2015. On the one dimension, regarding analyst and patient as indifferent from one another allows for the critical safety of sameness; on another, it offers the complex consolation of differentiation from a despised, despairing, devalued or impotent other, a vessel which can allow for the relocation of hated, feared and weak or passive aspects of one's self.

I have listened to a number of white patients speak of race in ways that seem to me to fit this frame of reference. One man was attracted to women of color, explicitly because of their exotic difference, and in fantasy because of how he imagined their sexuality—in which he imagined femininity and passivity to be closely entwined—would endorse his own assertive and aggressive masculinity, which he felt to be constantly fragile and in doubt.

Another patient was deprived of the capacity to know his own mind because of the emotional unavailability of his parents, epitomized by his abandonment to sexual abuse by a caregiver over an extended period. He had compensated for his experience of annihilating weakness and isolation as a child through fortressing himself in an enormous physique, while making himself the servant of everyone in his world against the annihilating fear of not being useful or wanted. In the days following the 2016 election, he explained to me (he was afraid of my reaction) that he admired and voted for Donald Trump because of Trump's ability to take what he wanted and say what he wanted, to get away with *being himself*, especially with a hated often racial other as a foil—in contrast to his own profound sense of powerlessness and fragility.

Another young man, who had been hospitalized following a manic episode, reported in its aftermath the following dream, in which he described himself as not present, but watching the scene as if from the outside. The scene involved a Black woman, riding on a subway, "being told something that was good"; she then turned to tell this good news to a young white man, who heard it and died. A Black doctor appeared and was trying to help the young man, but there was no hope. The patient associated this powerful dream to his experiences in the hospital and elsewhere, in which he had been convinced that Black staff members who worked with him in hospital were part of a benevolent conspiracy, "an underground railroad" that would help him to escape his confinement.

A woman in her sixties was in the habit of dividing the world into who was "for" or "against" her. The daughter of Holocaust survivors, who couldn't perceive that the threats to her safety came mainly from the pervasive fear of annihilation in her family environment, she routinely despised others who were different from her, Black people in the neighborhood where she worked, Latina women whom she worked with whom she felt were conspiring against her; homeless people who moved into her neighborhood during the pandemic, feeling that they both threatened and degraded her environment and sense of safety.

In another case, a teenage girl, for whom her extraordinary intelligence was both core to her identity and her ability to defend herself from the ubiquitous threats she faced within and without her, referred to the racist rationalizations of *The Bell Curve* (which argued for a racial basis to intelligence), and felt attacked and despairing when she was "cancelled" for her rigid racializing.

In each of these cases, the psychic boundary offered by racial difference facilitates an external repository for aspects of the self that are feared or despised; or alternately, a safe haven for parts of the self that are under attack. At the same time, the analyst's racial sameness offers reassurance and proof against these threatening, feared, despised, helpless parts of the self.

For the white patient and white analyst, the privileged sameness they share may provide a common ground upon which the ruptures and restorations of the therapeutic relationship may take place, along with the fantasies of merger or (as in the case of the psychoanalytic training relationship) inheritance.

This shared basis may well not be assumed in dyads with racial differences. For white and non-white patients alike, the fantasy of connectedness and protection within the analytic dyad is always threatened with rupture. For a white dyad, or even a Black dyad, shared experiences of race may offer a point of identification, an "unobjectionable part of the transference" (Stein), which is never interrogated. For nonwhite patients with a white analyst, it may feel always already ruptured.

Of course, as suggested by the symptomatic nature of the examples I have presented, the apparent safe harbor offered to the dyad by this point of sameness is not really safe, any more than the danger represented by racial difference (or any other essential difference between the pairs of the dyad) need be fundamentally destabilizing to the treatment. What is essential is not to essentialize: Not to assume the meaning of one's whiteness or other privileged sameness (including analytic authority) is stable and immutable, either for oneself or one's patient. Instead, one must try, as analysis has taught us, to be radically open to the difference of the other.

To be clear, I do not believe this use of race as a repository of despised parts of the self is innate or immutable. The mind uses whatever tools are available to it to evolve and defend, and differentiation is core to human mental functioning. Race is a mark of difference, and differences of skin pigmentation and facial feature were marked even before the advent in the Enlightenment of the racial ideology in which we are caught. Just as certainly, racial difference can be disambiguated, from worldview and ideology, and even from the logic of differentiation which is inherent to the mind. But that requires the ability to observe the whole landscape of the self, in which the various aspects of the psyche have out their conflicts. And that requires further analysis.

How to achieve this? One approach to the irreducible problem is suggested by African American psychoanalyst Dorothy Evans Holmes, in her remarks at the second "Black Psychoanalysts Speak Conference, in 2013 (Holmes 2013). At that time, she shared the memory of her first meeting with her training analyst, a southern white man (there were, of course, no Black training analysts).

> *I went in there and scratched my head and said —"I don't know if I can do this." And he asked me to elaborate, and I did, in terms of misgivings about racism and white southern racism… And he said, what was ideal or perfect for me at that time: "If you decide to work with me, I will not try to dissuade you from anything you feel." I think he was saying, "I accept you. You can feel anything towards me you need to feel." It worked out well since I had another five years of analysis. It also helped me to have an open attitude of my own about things racial, things having to do with class and regional origins. Let's see how it plays out in the wash. No preconceived notions—that can't be, of course. But let's do the best we can to be open to whatever may come up. It was important to me, too, to have a Black analyst, I mean I chose my first analyst [who was not at the time a training analyst]. But struggling with these issues with a white southern man was very, very helpful and not always easy, but is possible.*
> (Winograd, 2014, documentary made from the 2013 conference)

Holmes' experience points to the essential promise of the psychoanalytic relationship: that one person can be open, even radically open, to receive the feelings and experience of another, including—especially—those feelings which both, or either, may find alien, threatening, or painful. And in this reception, curiosity and tolerance of the whole range of one's feelings—which is to say the whole range of one's being—and in the survival of the relationship that contains them, lies synthesis, and healing.

But Holmes also clearly derived distinct, complementary benefits from her two analyses, first with a Black analyst and then with a white one. One inference from her remarks is that she had distinct transformative experiences with each of her Black and white analysts, which allowed her to negotiate her internalized, racially marked experiences of same and different, safety and danger, self and other.

Holmes' remarks encapsulate the thesis and antithesis of the analytic dialectic: On the one hand, analysis is an experience of being received by an "other" in all one's difference and different affect. On the other, analysis means being welcomed home, into the bosom of safety and sameness. An urgent question for psychoanalysis is whether a "good enough" analytic experience requires such different analytic experiences for each of us. Or might it be possible to negotiate these borders within any dyad, however racially marked?

4

The poet Arthur Rimbaud wrote: "I is another." Hegel's dialectical thinking has it that master and slave, thesis and antithesis, mutually call and are called by one another into being, eventually collating in a synthesis which then calls new definitional differences into being. Psychoanalysis, too, tells us that we cannot know ourselves except through the intervention of an *Other*. This other calls to us from our borders, the analyst's psychic and actual difference both challenging and securing the boundaries of the self, and this process gives our inner world integrity and resilience, clarifying inside and outside, safety and danger, self and not-self.

It is the challenge of psychoanalysis to address difference where we find it, to help translate ourselves to ourselves, and in the process to help to make the other known to itself, just as infant and mother mutually define one another, and as master and slave bleakly do the same. Winnicott tells us that a mother is there to be left by her infant, that he may define himself anew in his agonistic tensions with the world, by which he will define his sense of self and also his difference from that world. Analysis is a recapitulation of this developmental struggle, and its progressive iteration of differences, analyst and patient discover, again and again, that there are many distinctions between any two people: But a difference need not be a rupture, and a rupture may be repaired.

At the end of "White Like Me" Black Eddie, now returned from his journey into whiteness, is daunted by what he has seen. In the final scene, in the dressing room where he first affected his transformation, he sounds his note of hope, in a bluesy minor key: He has a lot of friends, and a lot of makeup. They too, he suggests, will all make their ventures into whiteness, and, it is implied, leave whiteness changed by their encounters. In order to know oneself, one must also stand at one's borders, and call out to the other. As we used to say on the playground of E. Rivers Elementary in Atlanta, as a taunt, a dare, and an invitation, in the face of an insult hurled with the force of difference: It takes one to know one.

Note

1 Neil Altman (2006) invokes Hegel in a related sense in his essay "Whiteness": When people's images of others are constructed too heavily out of projections, the other's subjectivity as a separate person is denied or occluded. There is not enough room for the otherness of the other person. Slavery, of course, constitutes an effort at complete denial of the subjectivity of the slave—although, as the philosopher Hegel pointed out, the master needs the slave to recognize him or her as master. Thus, the master must erase the subjectivity of the slave while at the same time being dependent on it; otherwise, his recognition is without value (p.65).

References

Altman, N. (2006). Whiteness. *Psychoanalytic Quarterly* 75:45–72.
Baldwin, J. (1962). *The Fire Next Time*. New York: Vintage International
Blow, Charles (2021). We need a second Great Migration. *New York Times*, January 8.
Coates, T. (2015). *Between the World and Me*. New York: Spiegel & Grau.
Ferenczi, S. (1913). Stages in the development of the sense of reality. In *Sex and Psychoanalysis: The Selected Papers of Sandor Ferenczi, M.D.*, transl. E. Jones. New York: Basic Books, 1950, pp. 213–239.
Griffin, J.H. (1961). *Black Like Me*. New York: Houghton Mifflin.
Hegel, G.W.F. (1807). *Phenomenology of Spirit*, trans. A. V. Miller. New York: Oxford University Press, 1977.

Holmes, D. (2013). Unpublished remarks from transcript of second *Black Psychoanalysts Speak* conference, May 11, 2013.

Murphy, E. (1984). White like me. *Saturday Night Live*, television broadcast, December 15.

Reed, L. (1978). I wanna be black. *Street Hassle*. New York: Arista Records.

Winnicott, D.W. (1960). The theory of the parent-infant relationship. *International Journal of Psychoanalysis* 41:585–595.

Winograd, B. (2014). "Black Psychoanalysts Speak," 2014 PEP Documentary (accessible through American Psychoanalytic Association Psychoanalytic Electronic Publishing database) https://www.youtube.com/watch?v=N8-VIi7tb44 (Last accessed July 2, 2022).

# Chapter 20

Psychoanalysis by Surprise

An Ad Hoc Experiment in Community Psychoanalysis on a South African Wine Farm

Mark Solms

Solms-Delta is the name of a wine farm originally granted by the government of the Cape Colony in 1690. It is situated in the region of Franschhoek in South Africa. I became custodian of this farm when I returned to South Africa in 2001, after many years abroad. The farm had fallen on bad times, and it was effectively bankrupt.

Having grown up in South Africa as the scion of an old land-owning family and a beneficiary of the apartheid system, I wanted to make a citizen-sized contribution to the reconstruction and development of the country by fixing the social fabric of just this one farm. I considered it appropriate to think small, as an individual citizen can easily be overwhelmed by the magnitude of the task faced by South Africa as a whole. My task was limited to transforming just a few hectares of the country. However, I was also aware of the symbolic significance of a historic Cape farm. It was, after all, with the granting of these farms that South Africa's troubles began.

Particularly daunting to me was the fact that when one acquires a farm in South Africa; even today, it typically comes with a community of people who live on it. Not to put too fine a point on it, but the farmer inherits the people who live on his land. To describe this situation as feudal is not an exaggeration.

Solms-Delta came with seven large households of people linked in complex ways with each other and with various extended families living on the surrounding farms. Six of the households were located next to the manor house in an old wine fermentation cellar, where they lived in appalling conditions (e.g., without hot water or proper sewerage), and the seventh lived in a semi-derelict cottage nearby. All of this was, and remains, typical of contemporary South African farm life.

DOI: 10.4324/9781003280002-25

I was keen to meet with my newly acquired tenants as soon as possible, as I was told they were anxious about the future of the farm and their place on it. I wanted to reassure them that I would try to create jobs for them and that I had no intention of evicting anyone—which seemed to be the general assumption. I also wanted to explain as quickly as I could that although I looked like my predecessors, the farm would now be run along different lines. I had not worked out the details of how this would be done, but the farm was going to be aligned with the values and aspirations of the newly democratic South Africa.

I set aside one hour for each of my meetings with the families, because I wanted to canvass their views as to how we might go about achieving this. As it happened, most of the meetings lasted barely 20 minutes. This was because we could not talk to each other. As I made my introductions and proposals and posed my questions, the farm people became visibly uncomfortable. They looked at each other sheepishly, or at the floor, shuffling in their seats; it was clear they wanted to get out of my house as quickly as possible. Direct questions received no responses. The atmosphere could be cut with a knife. It was evident not only that we could not talk to each other, but also that we could not even look each other in the eye. It later became apparent why this was the case, but on that day in April 2001, I felt absolutely stumped.

When I actually moved to the farm with my young family later that year, things went from bad to worse. It seemed that the tenant workers, having by then realized that I really meant what I said, had come to the conclusion that I was a fool. They started arriving late for work, knocking off early, skipping Mondays, helping themselves to things here and there. I even noticed that beautiful, mature camphor trees in my forest were being chopped down (in the dead of night) for no obvious reason.

I started to feel scared. Murder of farmers is not uncommon in post-apartheid South Africa. I also started to feel annoyed. Was this any way to respond to my generous gestures? I had thoughts of which I am not proud. I entertained the possibility that what the neighboring (white) farmers had explained to me was true: "Your plan will never work. These people are not like us, they are lazy and untrustworthy. They will take what you give them with one hand and stab you in the back with the other." It seemed the social fabric of the farm was so deeply imprinted with a pattern of abuse that this was the only way things could work. If I, the farmer, did not assume the customary role of abuser, then I would become the one who was abused. I felt I needed to protect myself and my family.

Within a few short months, I was becoming my own worst nightmare. I was thinking and feeling like a typical white South African farmer. In short, I was being put in my place.

My psychoanalytic training then came to my rescue. I recognized that I was in a bad situation, but in my desperation, I remembered the old adage: "Don't just do something; stand there!" So for several months I did nothing, withstanding the urge to act before I properly understood the predicament I found myself in.

When new patients are referred to me and tell me what is ailing them, my first task—like that of any clinician—is to *take a history*. Asking the patient how the symptoms began, when they appeared, in what context they started, and how they developed is how you begin to understand what you are dealing with clinically. It is how you eventually make a diagnosis, which identifies the mechanism underlying the ailment. This tells you what you are up against, what needs to be put right.

Let me clarify: I did not consider myself to be the doctor and the farmworkers the patients in the figurative image I am using. Far from it. The farmers were very much a part of the problem here; in fact, they were the nub of the problem. If farmers are going to assist with the diagnosis, they must look inward.

The "doctors" I asked to help us were academics—mainly historians and archaeologists—from the University of Cape Town. We, the residents of the farm (workers and owner combined), were the patients.

So we stopped farming and spent the next several months digging the place up, in an entirely different manner from what the workers were used to. Under the guidance of the archaeologists and historians, we literally uncovered the past. We already knew about this past in the abstract, but now we discovered it for ourselves.

First, we uncovered evidence of a very long period of pre-colonial occupation of the farm. Early and Middle Stone Age tools littered the fields of Solms-Delta, as they do every farm in this part of the world, the cradle of humankind. But far more impressive to the farmworkers, many of whom show obvious physiognomic features of Khoisan descent, was the discovery of a Later Stone Age settlement site barely 50 meters from the front door of my house. There, 6000 years ago, the ancestors of modern Bushmen had lived. And they had obviously lived there for a very long time. We found, on average, 1300 stone artifacts per cubic meter of soil. And this was not all. We found mystical rock paintings in the mountains around us, with delicate depictions of the long-gone elephants that gave this valley its original name, Olifantshoek (Elephant Quarter), before it became Franschhoek (French Quarter) following the arrival of the Huguenots in the 1680s. We also found shards of Khoi pottery scattered all about.

This gave the archaeologists and the historians an opportunity to teach us about the lifestyle and culture of the hunter-gatherers and nomadic pastoralists who lived on our tract of land before us, and also to explain what became of them and their economy when—one day in 1690—the Dutch East India Company took it upon itself to grant this land to European settlers to produce the fresh meat, vegetables, grain, and wine it needed to supply its trading fleets shuttling around the Cape between Europe and the East. The Bushmen and Khoi-khoin did not recognize the concept of land ownership; how could anyone *own* land, which so obviously served all who lived on it? One can only imagine their incomprehension as they were jailed by the hundreds for "stock theft," or worse, shot on sight by the thousands as vermin. Their timeless occupation of the dramatic watercourses and valleys of this land, my land, ended in genocide. Today, people seem to imagine that Bushmen (those few who survived) prefer to live in deserts, but those were the only parts of the land that the farmers didn't want. The Bushmen and Khoi who remained in my valley had to abandon all they loved and forget all they knew, and apparently, forevermore work in menial capacities for the invading farmers. They no doubt did so with a lingering sense of shock and confusion as to what had become of them, at the catastrophe that had befallen their world. And their descendants are working still for the sons of those settler farmers—people like me—in the same menial capacities.

I am not sure how widely this is known, but Khoisan origins are not considered something to be proud of among the farmworkers of the Cape. To be called *boesman* (San) or *hotnot* (Khoi) is an insult. These are terms of abuse. They imply that you are less than fully human. Yet, as the archaeologists—whom the workers realized had nothing to gain or lose and clearly knew what they were talking about—told us about the Bushmen and Khoi-khoin who lived here as recently as 330 years ago, and explained the tools and the meanings of the paintings and pottery, and gave us a sense of their profound wisdom, so these workers gained a pride in their indigenous origins, which were previously unknown to them. I will never forget the day when one farmworker, Benny Daniels, excitedly looked me in the eye, holding a microlithic tool in his hand that he himself had just excavated from the settlement site, and declared, "You see, Professor, my people were here before yours!"

Moments like that changed everything. His relationship to the land was transformed in a flash. As was his relationship to me. The power dynamics between us could never be the same again. For, implicit in his statement of the obvious fact that his people lived here before mine, was a stark question: "So how come you own it now, and why am I working for you?" I no longer felt as if I were being generous.

The second major thing we uncovered while digging up the history of Solms-Delta (as one would learn at any such farm in South Africa) was the fact that it was built, literally, on the backs of slaves. I had to look at the grand whitewashed gables of my house differently after I was told that their beautiful lines had been molded by someone ripped from the bosom of his family in a faraway Eastern land and forced to work here against his will for the rest of his days without pay—and without the prospect of ever returning home. The same applied to the laying of every brick in every wall of my house, including those in the very bedrooms in which my children slept at night. The same applied also to the planting of the majestic oaks and camphors that surround my homestead and to the construction of the graceful and generously proportioned outbuildings of the *werf* (farmyard) beyond, and so on. My lovely farm was built upon not one, but at least two crimes against humanity.

Slave descent, I learned in this process, was also something the farmworkers were ashamed of. Admitting to slave ancestry (despite, again, the obvious physiognomic evidence) was akin to conceding that your grandfather was a pedophile. The psychological process by which the trauma and abuse of the slaves was twisted back again upon its victims, rather than its perpetrators, to produce such deep self-hatred, is almost too painful to contemplate. But as the historians explained these things to us, so our attitudes changed, until at last it was only me—the owner—who was left feeling ashamed.

When we finally completed our work, we established a museum at Solms-Delta to display what we had found. We took care to install at the heart of the exhibition a wall of granite plaques, with one plaque to remember each slave who gave their life to the establishment and development of this farm, against their will. The enormous amount of research that went into the identification of these almost 200 souls was made possible by the horrific fact that their information was recorded in meticulous detail in the same manner as that of the farmer's other major assets: in his will or tax assessments or mortgage bonds. Farmers borrowed money against their slaves, the value of which was determined by age, gender, occupation, and ethnicity; that is how we recovered this identifying data.

As I absorbed the lessons of the historians, I understood many things about my first encounter with the people living on my farm. They were descended not only from the indigenous Khoisan, but also directly from those slaves—from generations upon generations of real individuals who learned the hard way to give up hope, that it was dangerous to hope and believe that the future might be better than the past. Every parent who loves their children would have passed such lessons down, until nobody even knew anymore why they did so. It seems inevitable that over two centuries of slavery, a culture would develop among the survivors—the farmworkers living here today— that is defined by hopelessness, despair, and fatalism. How can you ask people who have suffered generations of such treatment to envisage a better future? They rightfully do not believe they can shape their futures; the future is something that happens to them, and they must suffer it and just keep their heads down, hoping not to be noticed. In such a culture, it is also not difficult to understand their unenthusiastic attitude toward their jobs. They are not living on my farm by choice. They did not freely decide to sell their labor to people like me at an agreed price. They are more or less compelled to work here, just as their ancestors were, and we, the farmers, since the abolition of apartheid, are compelled to pay them a minimum wage. There is more than a faint echo in this of the resentment felt by the Boers when they were first forced (by the English colonial government when they abolished slavery in 1834) to pay for their labor at all. Both parties know, still today, somewhere deep down that neither of them entered into this arrangement by choice.

And so I understood, bit by bit, why it was impossible for the farmworkers to be enthused about my transformation plans for *my* farm.

Following the abolition of slavery and the introduction of the *dop* system (paying workers by means of wine, whereby hangs another tale, which made enlightening listening for the alcoholics among the farmworkers)—as if the dispossession of the Khoisan and the dislocation of the slaves were not enough—came apartheid, a third crime against humanity. This one is still etched vividly in the memories of those of us who lived through it. We might be forgiven for wanting to believe that it could be miracled away by just one man, Nelson Mandela, who gave 27 years of his life for our sins. But of course it can't. I might nevertheless (perhaps) be forgiven for wanting to believe that I could arrive on an old Cape farm as the new owner, wave a wand that wiped away those memories, and enable everyone—not least, myself—to start again by simply saying, "Although I look like my predecessors, the farm will now be run along different lines." Why would anyone believe that? And why should it be so easy?

The university's historians did not have to teach us about the apartheid period. What they did instead was arrange oral history sessions in which we told them (and each other) our own life stories, which they recorded for posterity. I shall never forget the pain of listening to one farmworker after another tell those stories—stories of grinding poverty, lost childhoods, frozen feet and empty bellies, neglect and abuse of every kind, banal humiliations day by day, and the ever-present, envious awareness of what the white children had. All this was remembered and recounted with quiet dignity instead of rage. How pathetic were the problems of my own privileged life by comparison.

But listening to each other's stories, being listened to and being heard, definitely changed us. We came to know each other and trust each other, and understand something about how we feel toward each other (and about ourselves). I believe, on the basis of this experience, that every white South African of my generation, somewhere in the deep recesses of their minds, knows that they have inherited ill-gotten gains. This makes them ashamed and guilty and fearful, even if they do not consciously know it. What becomes of such feelings if you do not allow yourself to feel them? I have come to the conclusion that the main way we white South Africans (the beneficiaries of this history) defend ourselves against the feelings is by racism. Racism is a rationalization we have constructed in order to avoid looking at the real reasons why things are distributed so unequally. And at why the victims behave toward us as they do.

The alternative—the fundamental ethic of psychoanalysis—is to *face the facts* of what really happened, of what was actually done in our names and is still being done, and then deal with those facts. That is what we did at Solms-Delta. The aim was not to blame anybody. The aim was to *get our minds back*, so that we could think properly again, so that we could think about a new way forward rather than be compelled forever to repeat the mistakes of the past. I believe that we South Africans, as a nation (apart from a very few, exceptional leaders), have severely limited our ability to think clearly about our problems, because we are too scared or guilty or ashamed—or too angry or humiliated or hopeless, as the case may be—to confront the facts of what happened here and what is still happening here. If we do not face up to these facts, we cannot possibly find appropriate solutions, because the very things we cannot think about are the things that we have to put right.

Having faced those facts at Solms-Delta, with the help of our "doctors," we finally had a basis for approaching the task I had envisaged at the outset.

The single most important thing we learned was this: The farm belongs to me today because of this history, and the farmworkers live here today and have to work for me because of this same history. The landowner is always white, and the farmworkers are always black. The white family is always rich and lives in the big house, and the black ones are always poor and live in the outbuildings. And so on. These are the simple facts, but now we had to face them.

This obviously led to the million-dollar question: What are we going to do about these facts? Must I give the farm back?

As I contemplated this question, now actually *feeling* the guilt and *knowing* that our situation was wrong and untenable, the first answers that came to me were, once again, rationalizations. It wasn't *me* who took the land away from the Bushmen; I paid good money for it (my family had to buy out the farm's creditors). The farmworkers who live here today are a mishmash of people, accumulated over hundreds of years. So who am I supposed to give the farm to, a symbolic representative of some long-gone society? Who chooses such a representative? And what good would it achieve anyway? Should we not rather divide the farm up and give an equal little piece to every person living here? But then it wouldn't be a farm anymore. And in any event, you aren't allowed to do that with agricultural land, by law. It would destroy the country's food security. And so on.

Working through all these rationalizations, I eventually came upon a feeling that I knew was real and true: I didn't *want* to give my farm back. I wanted to keep it, and enjoy it, and pass it down to my children. That is what I came back to South Africa for. I came back for selfish reasons. My transformation plans were a sort of excuse, a way that I could come home and live the privileged life that I thought was my due without having to feel bad about it, and without really having to give anything up. Even though I knew the farm came to me and my kind via a process that was wrong and indefensible, still I didn't want to let go of it. I just didn't. And I wouldn't.

That was what I really felt. Now I had to admit that to the farmworkers and discuss it with them.

Actually, such feelings are not so difficult for people to understand. We are few of us saints. Everybody understands self-interest, so long as you are honest about it. And especially, so long as you recognize that others have self-interests, too. Problems with self-interest arise only when it is exclusive. So long as you take cognizance of the self-interest of those around you, there is nothing wrong with looking after your own. Even the scriptures say, "Love your neighbor as yourself," not "Love your neighbor instead of yourself."

So we at Solms-Delta came up with a simple solution: I will keep my farm, but I will also use it as security for a bank loan, made out to the farmworkers, so that they can buy the farm next door to mine (called Deltameer, which came with another 11 families). That way we can all own land, and nobody loses anything.

When my neighbors got wind of this plan, they thought I was mad: "Do you not realize what a risk you are taking? Think of your children!" What they did not seem to appreciate was that the risk is there already. The situation we are living in, whereby the land stays in the hands of the whites, the perpetrators of all those crimes against humanity, and the blacks simply carry on working for them, is untenable. It is completely unsustainable. How can anybody *not* see that? I wasn't taking on a risk, I was acknowledging a risk. Once you acknowledge a risk, you can manage it. And it was precisely because I was "thinking of my children" that I did so.

I believe most South African farmers know these facts and know that the way they are living is untenable. They must know the facts but be too scared (and guilty) to face them. So they live with blinkers on, hoping that the chickens will only come home to roost after they have passed on. But what about their children? And at what psychological cost? It is no exaggeration to say that most farmers live with constant fear—in fact, paranoia—which is not a good way to live.

Having acknowledged the risk, I managed it by sharing skills. Self-interest is a good, realistic motivation for transferring skills. That is, I went into partnership with the farmworkers. We took equal shares in the company Solms-Delta and leased our respective farms to it, and then farmed them as a combined operation. In fact, we were also joined in this by an English friend of mine, Richard Astor, who bought a third neighboring farm, Lübeck-Delta; we now had a three-way partnership, increasing our resources and economies of scale.

How have things turned out for us? The answer is: very well.

It is important to remember that the sustainability of our project depends entirely upon the commercial success of our wine-producing business. We have so far created 130 new full-time jobs directly on the farm. Everyone who lives here or works for us and was disadvantaged under apartheid and their dependents (whether they live here or not), becomes a beneficiary of the trust that owns the farmworkers' shares in the company.

There cannot be a company anywhere with better human resources and labor relationships than ours. We are all on the same side. We also really like each other. This is important, considering that we live together cheek by jowl on the same small piece of land. (Solms-Delta Wine Estate comprises 76 hectares, with 180 residents spread across the three farms.)

Wine is a hand-made product, both in the vineyard and the cellar. If it is made with love and enthusiasm, it shows. As a result, our wine is really good! That is no doubt the main reason why our sales have increased from 30,000 bottles in 2006 to a projected 1,000,000 bottles in 2015.

Wine tourism is another important part of the wine business, because by visiting an estate, customers taste its wines and learn what sets it apart in a very competitive market. The museum on our estate, the Museum van de Caab, which chronicles our social history, attracts 30,000 visitors a year. These visitors taste our wines, and then they become our customers for life.

I was impressed to witness the process by which the beneficiaries of the workers' trust decided to use their new income. Not surprisingly, a good portion of the money was expended on improving their immediate quality of life, including better housing, with satellite television in every home (which may seem like a luxury but is actually an important way to broaden the horizons of such an isolated community). In addition, the trustees employed a full-time social worker to help them decide, objectively and professionally, how the sometimes widely different needs of the beneficiaries could best be met. The social worker also introduced many programs concerning alcohol and drug abuse, child neglect and domestic violence, and so on, addressing the social ills that afflict such farming communities. She also instituted many recreational and sporting programs.

However, by far the greatest proportion of the trust's income was expended, from the first, on the education of the farmworkers' children. This was an investment in the long-term future that everyone seemed willing to make. First, the trust employed teachers to help the children with their homework and to provide after-school lessons and other support, such as internet access. One easily forgets that the farmworkers themselves cannot help their children with their schoolwork, not only because they work such long hours but also because they have had minimal formal education. After two years of trying to bridge the divide in this way, the teachers advised the trustees that the schooling provided locally was simply too weak; it could not be buttressed by after-school support. The children would have to be enrolled in better schools. On the basis of this advice, the trust offered to pay the fees of every child whose parents wished to enroll them in a nearby fee-paying school. Almost every family took up the offer. This required the purchase of a bus and the employment of several assistant teachers (or "facilitators") to work with the children in the classrooms of the new school to help them catch up, because they were very far behind the town's children. As one can imagine, this was a delicate social exercise, as the "backward" farm kids could easily have become an ostracized minority. This danger was forestalled in various ways, not least because we had the enthusiastic support of the staff of the school, which we had almost single-handedly rendered financially viable by introducing such a large contingent (more than 60) of new learners. Lastly, to improve the school-readiness of our children even before they entered this school, we opened a day care at Solms-Delta in 2008, with a large, well-trained staff.

Today, we are seeing the fruits of this multifaceted educational program, not only in the school results but also beyond school, where our children are entering a wide range of tertiary educational programs and taking employment of a kind that their parents could never realistically aspire to.

Also, we have a rich and active cultural life on the estate. Nothing exemplifies this better than our music. Interest in the vernacular music of the Cape flourished among the farmworkers during our historical and archaeological digs. The cultural melting pot of the early Cape gave rise to a rich tapestry of musical styles, from trance dance and Riel to Ghoema and gospel, from Vastrap and Langarm to Cape jazz and Boeremusiek. The explosive revival of interest in this music among the farmworkers was truly "'by popular demand." We provide lessons in strings, brass, percussion, voice, and song-writing to over 200 amateur musicians, drawn not only from our own farm but also from those of our neighbors and even from the townships beyond. We have four musical ensembles (the Delta Optel Band, Valley Entertainers, Langbroeke, and Soetstemme) that have released successful albums and are in heavy demand at local events. The biggest of these events by far is our annual Oesfees (harvest festival), which is attended by well over 5000 people every year—farmworkers (who are given free tickets, to thank them for the harvest), farm owners, and farm managers, all together, dancing and celebrating a shared rural culture. There is nothing on the region's calendar that better promotes a sense of common identity and belonging. Whereas the children and teenagers on many other farms escape their boredom and despair with alcohol, drugs, petty crime, and other antisocial activities, ours are making music together (even with their parents and grandparents) and actually becoming musicians. At the same time, they are learning to value their own unique culture and showcasing it to the world.

What we have achieved at Solms-Delta provides a beacon of hope, which is becoming a springboard for many other things, too, such as the Franschhoek Valley Transformation Charter. We are also seen as a source of information for other farmers who want to learn from our example. For instance, in 2013 we received (by their own initiative) a delegation of more than 60 farmers from a very conservative farming region, who wanted to spend a day with us learning from our experiences. We have also been actively engaged with organized agriculture, and with the government in their important task of developing a new Land Reform policy for South Africa.

I think we can truly say today that Solms-Delta is transformed. The centuries-long cycle of poverty and dependency is broken, and there is a better future for all. Psychoanalysis played an important, if unexpected, role in this success. Of course we are not yet living in paradise, and transformation is always a work in progress, but a transformed *attitude* has taken deep root in this place. That attitude can best be captured in a phrase that the farm children once chanted on a local community radio station: *"Ons help mekaar om ons self te help."* We help each other to help ourselves.

Part V

Interpreting Racism in Jordan Peele's *Get Out*

Chapter 21

Get Out of My Head
Experiencing Cultural Paranoia in Jordan Peele's *Get Out*

Grant Shreve

> Engender in [him] a sense of his inferiority and it will paralyze his aggressiveness and do more to keep him down than a standing army. What we practice ... is racial hypnotism.
> —Sutton Griggs, from *Unfettered* (1902)
>
> A mind is a terrible thing to waste.
> —United Negro College Fund slogan

Numerous studies have demonstrated that African Americans are empirically less likely to seek out psychotherapy than white Americans (Williams, 2011). One of the most important causes of this is what Whaley (2001) calls "cultural mistrust," which has "a significant impact on the attitudes and behaviors of African Americans, especially mental health services use." Cultural mistrust is a mitigated version of "healthy cultural paranoia," which Grier and Cobbs (1968) define as the conviction shared among many African Americans that "every white [person] is a potential enemy unless proved otherwise and every social system is set against [them] unless [they] personally find out differently" (p. 149). In one focus group of African American men and women conducted in 2004, for example, participants expressed concerns that to seek therapy would put them at risk of "misdiagnosis, labeling, and brainwashing" (Thompson and Brazile 2004). Nor are they entirely wrong, since, as Whaley (2001) has shown, adaptive conditions like cultural mistrust are often mistaken for symptoms of schizophrenia, which has resulted in the pathologizing of healthy, rational behavior.

What makes African Americans' cultural paranoia *healthy* (Wilson, 1999), especially in a medical context, is that it is historically justified, since there exists nearly four centuries' worth of evidence documenting the continual medical experimentation upon Black bodies by white physicians. In *Medical Apartheid*, her comprehensive history of medical experimentation on African Americans, Harriet Washington (Washington, 2006) asks readers to remember that the

> experimental exploitation of African Americans is not an issue of the last decade or even the past few decades. Dangerous, involuntary, and nontherapeutic experimentation upon African Americans has been practiced widely and documented extensively at least since the eighteenth century.
>
> (p. 7)

Washington's emphatic claim reminds us that, given the endless parade of traumas that whites have visited upon African Americans, cultural mistrust toward medical—and especially mental health—professionals not only *is* pervasive, but also *should* be.

While focus groups and surveys can give voice to the suspicions African Americans continue to harbor about therapy, these methods will never entirely capture the inside view of cultural paranoia as it is experienced. By necessity, these reports are conducted and packaged so as to be fit for print in the annals of professional colloquia and journals and are thus sanitized in ways that inevitably dilute the visceral skepticism and historical trauma seething beneath African American expressions of cultural mistrust. As such, their capacity to inform professional practice is inherently limited. Art can compensate for this lack. The representational flexibility afforded to novels, films, plays, paintings, and poems enables them to present human subjectivity in all its affective complexity, and few pieces of twenty-first century popular art more intimately and intensely depict African American cultural paranoia than Jordan Peele's 2017 film *Get Out*.

Released to nearly universal acclaim, *Get Out*'s premise sounds at first like Stanley Kramer's *Guess Who's Coming to Dinner* (1967) for the Obama era: Chris Washington and Rose Armitage, a young interracial couple living together in New York, drive upstate for the weekend to visit Rose's white, liberal parents, only Rose hasn't yet told them that her new boyfriend is Black. Once they arrive at the Armitages' palatial country home, however, *Get Out* veers beyond the borders of Kramer's domestic drama into the surreal social horrors of *The Stepford Wives* and *Rosemary's Baby*. Peele, a biracial actor and comedian most famous for co-creating the incisive sketch-comedy show *Key & Peele*, has said in interviews that he wished to capture in the film the sense of "justified paranoia" (Nigatu & Clayton, 2017) many African Americans feel on being the only Black person in a white social setting. As the film progresses, Chris discovers his inklings of paranoia about the Armitages' intentions are indeed justified, for behind the genial racism of this affluent white social world—where residents congratulate themselves for voting for Barack Obama and fawn over Chris's Blackness in the most stereotypical terms—lies an insidious multidecade scheme to kidnap Black men and women, sell them to white people, and replace their brains with those of the highest bidders. This is *Invasion of the Body Snatchers* retold as a story of American race relations. The Armitages enact this scheme by using Rose to lure Black men (and occasionally women) to her family's estate, where they are promptly trotted out at a garden party to be sized up by a group of white elites, sold at a silent auction, and finally, lobotomized. As if this weren't grotesque enough, a mote of each subject's original consciousness persists just beneath the surface of the new host, forced to observe but ultimately unable, except under one strange condition, to act.

Peele has described *Get Out* as a "social thriller," a cinematic genre of his own invention. The clearest sense he has given us regarding how to think about this genre was in the film series he curated for the Brooklyn Academy of Music in February 2017 titled "The Art of the Social Thriller." The diverse crop of films he screened for this series included *Rosemary's Baby, The Stepford Wives, Night of the Living Dead, The People Under the Stairs, Rear Window, The Shining,* and *The 'Burbs*. One of the key features uniting many of these films is their exploitation of the paranoia experienced by marginalized and oppressed groups. These films take quotidian experiences of social anxiety and exaggerate them to monstrous proportions, tracking the cognitive dissonance this escalation induces in their protagonists. In *The Stepford Wives*, for example, familiar uses of patriarchal power intended to dampen women's aspirations toward autonomy and erase their individuality are stretched to almost comical extremes when Joanna Eberhart and her family move—at her husband's bequest—to the insular community of Stepford, a town run by a secretive men's club that literally kills women and replaces them with docile robotic doppelgangers. Similarly, in *Rosemary's Baby*, Rosemary Woodhouse gets pregnant after her husband rapes her and, over the course of her pregnancy, becomes convinced that a cabal of witches is plotting to abduct her child when it's born and sacrifice it; the movie's conclusion toys with the possibility that she may have been right all along. *Get Out*'s structure owes much to these antecedents, mining the struggle waged within the minds of marginalized people as to whether the small acts of violence inflicted upon them are *really* part of a larger conspiracy or whether they've just gone crazy. In a March 2017 interview with the *New York Times*, Peele was asked what scared him the most. He answered, "Human beings. What people can do in conjunction with other people is exponentially worse than what they can do alone. Society is the scariest monster" (Zinoman, 2017). This answer may border on cliché, but it speaks to the psychosocial perspective Peele brings to his understanding of his film's genre, which is grounded first and foremost in the horrors human sociality produces.

Therapy is a crucial element in *Get Out*'s representation of cultural paranoia and racial violence. In fact, it is the narrative catalyst for the ghastly social rituals the film slowly unveils. Missy Armitage, Rose's mother, is a therapist who runs a practice out of her home. Played expertly by Catherine Keener—who has spent her career portraying earnest, well-meaning liberal white women—Missy first offers her services to Chris under the cover of getting him to quit smoking. She promises to do this, however, not through talk therapy but hypnosis, which she assures Chris will relieve him of his nicotine habit without any effort on his part. Chris politely refuses, and the matter is forgotten until later that evening when, after having snuck outside to smoke, he reenters the house to find Missy waiting for him in the living room. Eager to impress the woman who may eventually be his mother-in-law, Chris sits and talks with her, even as Missy's questions become progressively more invasive. With the help of a delicate china teacup that becomes exponentially more menacing over the course of the film, Missy gradually puts Chris into a hypnotic torpor and, once in control, forces him to recount the day his mother died: the central trauma of his childhood. Chris's mother, we discover, had been killed in a hit-and-run while he was watching TV on his bed in the dark waiting for her to come home. In his retelling, Chris implies that he had intuitively known something was wrong but didn't call for help for fear of the wave of pain he saw breaking on the horizon. Had he acted, he imagines, his mother may have lived. Once Missy has extracted this confession from him, she sends Chris's consciousness to what she calls "the Sunken Place," an endless expanse of empty space in which a person's conscious mind watches helplessly as the world passes in front of their eyes. It is as terrifying and vivid a representation of depersonalization as any that has been put on film.

Peele's staging of this scene is done with a deep awareness of African American suspicions toward psychotherapy. He remarked in one particularly candid interview that

> the Black community hasn't exactly embraced therapy as a means to get to where they [can resolve] inner turmoil.... There is this fear that I wanted to play off of here that's like, "I don't know about anybody fucking with my head."
>
> (Nigatu & Clayton, 2017)

In *Get Out*, African American skepticism toward mental health services is accentuated by having Missy Armitage practice hypnosis rather than talk therapy. To the popular mind, hypnosis has long stood as a fecund metaphor for the psychological manipulation of individuals by mental health professionals at its most sinister (Leighton, 2001, p. 117). Little wonder, then, that African American authors have at times employed hypnosis as a figure to represent either the strategies of white supremacy, as in this essay's first epigraph from Sutton Griggs's novel *Unfettered*, or as the only available solution to racism, as in E. G. Bamberg's 1968 short story "The Hypnotist," in which a Black hypnotist passes as white and uses hypnosis to convince white racists that their skin (and favorite color) is brown. For Peele, the danger Missy's invasion of Chris's mind poses is twofold. It deprives him of agency by separating his mind from his body, but it also signals the prelude to the crude, brutal violence of the brain transplants performed by Rose's father and brother, which themselves evoke the long history of medical experimentation on Black bodies.

Therapy in *Get Out* is therefore just the latest iteration of this violent tradition stretching back to the eighteenth century, which is itself—or so the film posits—borne out of an Anglo-European desire for Black bodies without Black minds. (The original motive for the Armitages' horrifying project was Rose's grandfather's loss to Jesse Owens in trials for the 1936 Olympic team.) Chris's childhood trauma had already engendered in him what the literary critic Christopher Freeburg calls "epistemic estrangement," a characteristic feature of Black personhood wherein an individual's deepest desires, attachments, politics, and ideas are withheld from outside knowledge. In Freeburg's account, "epistemic estrangement" often looks like the defiance of white efforts to assert their power over Black bodies through knowledge, and his *exemplum par excellence* of this trait is the famous 1899 photograph of Frank Embree staring sneeringly into a camera right before he was lynched. But for Chris, on the other hand, epistemic estrangement is not how he most wants to relate to others and the world. Throughout the film he is cheerful, compassionate, and gentle, yearning to overcome this estrangement, to know and be known. When Missy Armitage sends Chris's consciousness to the Sunken Place, she exploits the formative trauma of his youth to control his mind, revealing herself definitively as a cog in the gears of a vast racial conspiracy, not a healer.[1]

The late-night hypnosis session is thus emblematic of how *Get Out* represents cultural paranoia on the screen, offering an inside view of what these fears *look like* and, more importantly, *feel like*. Even as the film indulges and validates this feeling, however, it also acknowledges how extreme and irrational such anxieties may appear, and not just to white people. Late in *Get Out*, when Chris's friend Rod approaches a Black female police officer with his—correct—interpretation of the events leading to Chris's disappearance, she gathers her colleagues together to laugh him out of the station. Nevertheless, the film urges its viewers to take its horrifying premise seriously.

Over the course of his psychohistorical journey at the Armitage house, Chris ultimately does resolve the trauma of his mother's sudden death, and this in spite of the fact that every white person in the movie is out to kill him. At the end of the film, after Chris has killed all the Armitage family but Rose, he begins to drive away in Rose's brother's car when he suddenly strikes the Armitages' Black female servant, Georgina, whom the audience has now deduced is Rose's grandmother in the body of a Black woman. Chris hesitates, wondering whether to leave the woman's body on the driveway to die. The moment recalls his own failure to act as a boy to potentially save his mother's life. He knows, too, that some spark of the Black woman whose body was wrenched away from her to preserve the mind of Rose's racist grandmother still lives inside. Earlier, in what is certainly the single most heart-wrenching shot of the film, Chris tries to speak candidly with Georgina about the anxiety he feels being around so many white people. While he speaks, the camera closes in on her face and tears well up in her eyes, as if something in her is struggling to escape but can't. Chris's memory of this instant of humanity rising to the surface of a body whose agency has been stripped through racial violence is what finally compels him to lift Georgina's body into the car. Even though she viciously attacks him the moment she regains consciousness, his decision to assist whatever is left of the woman who once occupied this body enables him to overcome his guilt through an act of compassion. This is clearly a Hollywood version of psychological maturation, but we shouldn't fault the film for this, since its aim is to produce a psychological response in its audience through narrative structure rather than to represent psychological transformation with pinpoint accuracy.

We might go so far as to say that *Get Out* presents itself as a complement, and maybe even an alternative, to therapy insofar as it aspires both to represent the experience of cultural paranoia and to be a homeopathic balm for it. Peele has spoken openly about his hope that the film would function *like* therapy by providing audiences with a communal experience of catharsis. In an interview for *The Guardian* (Anthony, 2017), Peele said that the reason

> why [films] get primal, audible reactions from us is because they allow us to purge our own fears and discomforts in a safe environment. It's like therapy. You deal with deep issues that are uncomfortable with the hope that there is a release.

Peele here appears to propose an Aristotelian form of collective psychotherapy. In the *Poetics*, Aristotle theorized that tragedy's chief aim is catharsis, a purging of pity and terror through the excitement of these same emotions. Although it is now firmly ensconced in the philosophy of art, catharsis was originally a medical term describing a bodily phenomenon. It is a process that affects us at the most fundamental levels of our being, or, to quote the novelist Ralph Ellison (1995), on our "lower frequencies" (p. 581). *Get Out*, Peele clearly hoped, would trigger a collective catharsis in its audiences and thus act as a kind of social therapy. This is not, however, to say that once the pity and terror evoked by this film have been purged viewers will suddenly feel at ease with each other and the world, for terror, as the philosopher Martha Nussbaum (2003) reminds us, "has this good thing about it: it makes us sit up and take notice" (p. 26).

I saw *Get Out* on its opening weekend in Baltimore, Maryland, a city that has been a focal point of the nation's conversation about race in the 2010s. The audience was a true cross section of the city. Men and women, Black and white, teenagers and the over-forty crowd, all crammed together to see a low-budget *Guess Who's Coming to Dinner*-themed horror film directed by a sketch-comedy performer for which only one trailer had been released. That so many people showed up to see this film made the experience of watching it feel electric and rare. From its chilling cold open to its closing credits, a communal bond was forged among this motley group of strangers. When Chris finally wraps his hands around Rose's neck to kill her in the film's closing minutes, there were audible cheers. For this audience to be collectively invested in watching a Black man murder a white woman—however psychopathic she may be—felt unprecedented and, in its way, radical. That *Get Out* achieved such a reaction is a testament to its power as art. It is one of the few movies I've seen in theaters that elicited a feeling that so closely approximated Aristotelian catharsis, where, for a brief moment, the pain and the guilt and the hopelessness surrounding race in the United States could be shared, wept over, and even laughed at collectively.

Although the film's therapeutic catharsis is meant to be a shared experience, it functions differently for Black and white audiences. For the former, it provides a vision of black agency on the screen in a genre where black characters typically exist only to be victimized. In bucking this tradition, *Get Out* intends to invite African American audiences into the world of the film through their identification with the protagonist. Catharsis would then stem from seeing a racial avatar survive a scenario that taps into some of this audience's deepest and most diffuse anxieties. For white audiences, on the other hand, catharsis is achieved by drawing viewers into an empathetic relationship with the film's black protagonist so that they, too, begin to feel, viscerally, his paranoia, fear, and tension along with him. Peele explained his hope for the film's impact on white viewers this way:

> [T]he power of story is a profound thing. Maybe you get white people coming to see this movie and for 90 minutes they're seeing through the eyes of this black protagonist, and they're not being told what that perspective is, they're feeling what that perspective is, they're going through it. And that's the missing part of the conversation, experiences where you can go and feel and empathize, not just be dictated that "this is what it's like."
>
> (Nigatu & Clayton)

Peele puts his faith in narrative's power to compel white audiences to see the world through a black person's eyes, but the film is not so naïve as to think such an identification is either simple or inevitable. Indeed, the film even reflects on this aspiration through the person of Jim Hudson, the failed photographer turned blind art dealer who eventually purchases Chris's body at the silent auction.

Chris first meets Jim Hudson during the garden party. After the barrage of explicit racism unleashed by the other guests, the solitary blind man is a breath of fresh, nonracist air. He can't see Chris's skin, but he knows who Chris is, claiming to have had Chris's photographs described to him by his assistant. He praises the young man's keen artistic eye. "You've got something," he remarks, "The images you capture. So brutal, so melancholic. It's powerful stuff, I think." At first blush, these encomiums seem like a welcome reprieve from the crude compliments the other attendees had made about Chris's body. But are Chris's photographs *really* "brutal" and "melancholic"? It's easy for the first-time viewer to forget that they've seen Chris's photographs before, splashed across the screen in quick succession during the film's opening credits as Childish Gambino's funk track "Redbone" plays beneath them. The three black-and-white photographs we see are naturalistic snapshots of African American urban life: a man walking along an empty sidewalk clinging to a bunch of white balloons, a pregnant woman's exposed belly on a street corner, a Rottweiler in an abandoned lot straining on a leash its owner is struggling to rein in. They are scenes of life, and while they evoke themes of solitude, fecundity, and restraint, there is nothing inherently "brutal" or "melancholic" about them. Jim Hudson may be literally blind and may use that biological reality to present himself as also being race-blind, but his assessment of Chris's photographs reveals a distinctive racial tilt to his thinking, since what he describes to Chris is not the actual content of the pictures but his own internalized projections about the terrible conditions of black life.

If one doubted Jim Hudson's claims to race blindness in his first conversation with Chris, they become even harder to ignore (and stomach) in his second. This brief exchange occurs via teleconference while Chris is bound to a chair in the Armitage's basement, having just learned that his body will soon play host to another mind. Stunned, Chris asks Hudson, "Why us? Why black people?" The art dealer throws up his hands and chuckles.

> Who knows? People want to change. Some people want to be stronger, faster, cooler. But please don't lump me in with that. I could give a shit what color you are. No. What I want is deeper. I want your eye, man. I want those things you see through.

For Hudson, Chris's body holds forth the promise not only of regaining sight but of acquiring an aesthetic gift, too. But this raises the question of whether it is even possible to see beyond race. Chris's photographs, we recall, are all photographs of black life. His artistic eye is already racialized insofar as it is directed towards certain objects and certain themes drawn from a certain kind of historical experience. It is an eye honed by experiences of race. There is no separating race from art, no possibility of color blindness. Hudson will never truly be able to see as Chris sees, because race is so profoundly formative. Chris's aesthetic sensibility is indelibly shaped by his mother's death and by his experience as black person living in a racist society. The very act of deciding what to point his lens at is already, in some sense, racialized. In this final conversation between the two men, we can sense Peele throwing down his own aesthetic gauntlet and declaring that no film, and especially not this one, can be truly race blind. But that, ultimately, is an enabling condition for art. At the same time, however, *Get Out* is also asking its white audience to do precisely what Jim Hudson claims to want to do: see through Chris's eyes. The difference lies in the fact that, unlike Hudson, the film insists we see Chris's experience with the full knowledge that what we are watching is inextricable from the realities of race.

But what lessons can be drawn from *Get Out* for clinicians? Obviously, the film is not didactic, which is to say that its purpose is not to instruct but rather to communicate a form of social experience rarely represented on film. It implores its white viewers, especially, to bear witness to how centuries of racial violence and the Anglo-European desire for black bodies without black minds continue to inform race relations in our own moment. Peele (Zinoman, 2017) was blunt about what he believed was the film's driving force:

> This movie is [...] about how we deal with race. As a black man, sometimes you can't tell if what you're seeing has underlying bigotry, or if it's a normal conversation and you're being paranoid. [...] There are still a lot of people who say, "We don't have a racist bone in our bodies." But we have to face the racism in ourselves.

Peele assiduously works not to give viewers the titillating thrills that the film's white characters desire, of inhabiting Black bodies whose subjectivity has been cast to the back corners of their brains. Instead, he has put on screen not just the physical eye, but a comprehensive experience of the world—an entire complex regime of feeling, interpretation, and appreciation. The film validates and affirms this experience, and, hopefully, enlarges the sympathies of its many audiences, even those—like clinicians and medical professionals—whom the film implicates in its critique.

Note

1 *Get Out*'s paranoid fear of psychological manipulation by mental health professionals is not inherent to the genre of the "social thriller" as Peele has defined it. Indeed, in one of *Get Out*'s most important forerunners, The Stepford Wives, a brief scene of talk therapy that appears toward the end of the film offers one of the few moments of hope and relief in an otherwise crushing film. There the therapist is a woman, and even though she doesn't necessarily believe in the facticity of Joanna's conspiratorial theories nevertheless understands the affective reality beneath them and counsels her accordingly.

Bibliography

Anthony, A. (2017). Jordan Peele on making a hit comedy-horror movie out of America's racial tensions. *The Guardian*, March 4. https://www.theguardian.com/film/2017/mar/04/jordan-peele-interview-get-out-its-about-purging-our-fears-horror-film-daniel-kaluuya. Accessed June 27, 2022.

Bamberg, E.G. (1968). The hypnotist. *Phylon* 29(4):403–409.

Ellison, R. (1995). *Invisible Man*. New York: Vintage.

Grier, W.H., and Cobb, P.M. (1968). *Black Rage*. New York: Bantam Books.

Leighton, M.E. (2001). 'Hypnosis Redivivus': Ernest Hart, 'British Medical Journal,' and the hypnotism controversy. *Victorian Periodicals Review* 34(2):104–127.

Nigatu, H. and Clayton, T., hosts) (2017). *Another Round With Heben and Tracy*, audio podcast, March 1.

Nussbaum, M. (2003). Compassion & terror. *Daedalus*, 132(1):10–26.

Peele, J., director. (2017). *Get Out*. Blumhouse Productions.

Thompson, V.L.S. and Brazile, A. (2004). African Americans' perceptions of psychotherapy and psychotherapists. *Professional Psychology: Research and Practice* 35(1):19–26.

Washington, H. (2006). *Medical Apartheid: The Dark History of Medical Experimentation on Black Americans from Colonial Times to the Present*. New York: Anchor Books.

Whaley, A.L. (2001). Cultural mistrust and mental health services for African Americans: A review and meta-analysis. *The Counseling Psychologist* 29:4.

Williams, M.T. (2011). Why African Americans avoid psychotherapy. *Psychology Today*, November 2. https://www.psychologytoday.com/us/blog/culturally-speaking/201111/why-african-americans-avoid-psychotherapy. Last accessed June 27, 2022.

Wilson, M.D. (1999). Cultural paranoia. In *Key Words in Multicultural Interventions: A Dictionary*. Mio J. S., Trimble J. E., Arredondo P., Cheatham H. E., and Sue D., eds. Westport, Connecticut: Greenwood Press.

Zinoman, J. (2017). Jordan Peele on a truly terrifying monster: racism." *New York Times*, February 16.

Chapter 22

From *Guess Who's Coming to Dinner* to *Get Out*

Attaining Psychic Freedom and Emancipation across the Racial Divide

Dionne R. Powell

Bracketing the expanse of 50 years, the 1967 film *Guess Who's Coming to Dinner* and the 2017 film *Get Out* serve as an intimate window into race relations and the colonization and ongoing attempts at psychic emancipation of Black minds in white spaces. As well, these films represent persistent tensions between liberal whites and Blacks which, as sources of resistance to knowing the other, can hinder a therapeutic encounter. By exploring this 50-year evolution, beginning with the *Loving* Supreme Court decision, and relating these films to the clinical situation, this chapter hopes to further the movement toward psychic emancipation from a complicated racial history that has been difficult to reconcile. Part of the challenge toward reconciliation is that white liberalism and privilege remain too closely aligned with themes of possession/appropriation and dependency on/envy of the psychic freedom of the racial other. Clinical examples will highlight these challenges.

The Lovings

In 1958, a mixed-race couple, Mildred and Richard Loving, were arrested in their home in rural Central Point, Virginia, for living together as a married couple. Married five weeks earlier in Washington, D.C., where interracial marriages were legal, they had returned to their home in Caroline County. The 1924 Virginia State Act to Preserve Racial Integrity prohibited interracial couples from marrying out of state then returning to live as a couple in Virginia, and prohibited miscegenation. Charged under both provisions of the law, in 1959 they pleaded guilty to "cohabiting as man and wife, against the peace and dignity of the Commonwealth." Their one-year

DOI: 10.4324/9781003280002-28

jail sentence was suspended on condition they leave the state and not return together for 25 years. The decision was upheld by the Supreme Court of Virginia.

Mildred, of mixed Native American and African American heritage, and Richard, who was white, grew up in a community in which socializing between the races had existed since the nineteenth century. They met when Richard was in high school and Mildred was 11, attending segregated schools. Friendship became love, they got pregnant when Mildred was 18, and they married. After the decision, adhering to the terms of the court, they reluctantly moved to Washington, D.C. There, socially isolated, having financial difficulties, and unable to visit family together in Virginia, Mildred Loving wrote Attorney General Robert Kennedy seeking redress. He referred her letter to the ACLU, which filed suit to overturn the decision of the Virginia courts.

On June 12, 1967, the Supreme Court of the United States did overturn the Lovings' conviction, struck down the Virginia act, and held that laws banning interracial marriages violated the due process and equal protection clauses of the United States Constitution. The Lovings returned to Virginia.

At the time, 16 states had laws banning interracial marriage. Only in 2000 did Alabama become the final state to repeal its law. Two films, the 1967 *Guess Who's Coming to Dinner* and the 2017 *Get Out,* each sharply focused on an interracial couple, seek to illuminate and explore Black–white relations in the United States. More narrowly, the films engage the evolving awareness of the limitations and horror of upper-middle-class white liberals facing Black people of similar attainment. The racial harmony one might imagine to have been the outcome of the *Loving* decision is shown on the margins by *Guess Who's Coming to Dinner* to have been a facade seeking to magically correct the traumatic racial unrest of the time, providing a type of comfort and safety for white audiences. Fifty years later, during a time of equally pronounced racial unrest, *Get Out* rips the bandage off the racial scab, revealing the horror of white envy and appropriation of Black bodies and culture. For the African American, unrest and injustice had never remained in the past. The disavowal of this psychic reality and its implications for Black and white people and for all Americans who can or cannot fold into whiteness is the focus of this chapter.

The Films: A Psychodynamic Synopsis, with Commentary on 50 Years of Race Relations

Guess Who's Coming to Dinner, directed by Stanley Kramer, was an aspirational utopia for the times. The film portrays America's racial tensions resolved by calm, relatively muted conversations. There is civility at all costs. Love conquers all. In the country at large, the loftiest dreams of racial equality and harmony were on display and in action. Martin Luther King, Jr. gave the speech in which he called forth the future with "I have a dream." It was 1963. In 1964, the Civil Rights Act became law; in 1965, the Voting Rights Act. Thurgood Marshall, who had argued against school segregation before the Supreme Court and won in 1954, became the first Black justice of the Court in 1968. *Rolling Stone* magazine was launched in San Francisco in 1967, epitomizing the most topical issues in entertainment, culture, and politics. John Lennon was on its inaugural cover.

While 1967, the year *Guess Who's Coming to Dinner* was released, was termed the "Summer of Love," the times were hardly idyllic. President John F. Kennedy had been assassinated in 1963, exacerbating racial tensions. The crescendo of the civil rights movement was countered by domestic terror, including, in 1963, the bombing of a Black church in Birmingham, Alabama, killing four young Black girls. Two years later, Malcolm X was assassinated. And on April 4, 1968, Dr. Martin Luther King, Jr. was shot while standing on his motel balcony in Memphis, Tennessee, and killed. King was 39 years old. In contrast to the movie, 1967 America was ablaze with race riots and anti-war protests. Muhammad Ali was stripped of his boxing title for objecting to military service for religious reasons, and over 20,000 were dead from the war in Vietnam.

As an African American and a psychoanalyst, it is impossible to remove the film from the times which surround it.

While *Guess Who's Coming to Dinner* provides a respite from the turbulence of its decade, with enough balm to assuage both sides of the racial divide, the viewer is left through coded language with the lingering feeling that a multitude of tensions lies just below the surface. Although Richard Loving, whose marriage was the subject of a *Life* magazine photo spread in 1966, was a construction worker, with a wife of the same working-class socioeconomic background, by contrast, the Black protagonist of the film is a highly educated member of the professional class. By placing his relationship at a socioeconomic level far removed from the lives of most African Americans, the film seeks to cement as reality a view of racial harmony and the American dream cherished by white liberals. By doing so, it further separates and isolates the white American imagination from the far-less-than-idyllic lives of most African Americans, who often live in abject poverty or marginalized circumstances (Holmes, 2006). They do not have the elevated pedigree of the Black male protagonist of the film.[1] This film concretizes the high, nearly impossible bar African Americans must attain to receive approval from white liberal elites. Simultaneously, it is important to note that there was opposition to the film's creation by Columbia studios. After its creation, the cast and the director received death threats from people opposed to its positive treatment of interracial love. Viewed through this perspective, *Guess Who's Coming to Dinner* was a radical, some would say revolutionary, film in its racial significance.

In the opening scene of *Guess Who's Coming to Dinner,* we observe Joey Drayton (Katharine Houghton) and John Prentice (Sidney Poitier), an interracial couple, blissfully arriving in San Francisco to introduce John to Joey's parents and secure their blessing after a chance meeting in Hawaii turned to love. In the background, Billy Hill's *The Glory of Love,* sung by Jacqueline Fontaine, with the following opening lyrics as the couple walks through the San Francisco airport, provides an air of tranquility.

What the audience captures but the couple is oblivious to as they walk through the airport are the incredulous stares by white adults. All watch with a look of concern except a group of white elementary school children, who are unaffected as, without pause or hesitancy, they share an escalator with the couple. The opening scene reminds us that racial difference and the values, stereotypes, and biases placed on the other are learned and shaped both consciously and unconsciously from familial experiences and teachings dating from childhood (Clark, 1963; Stoute, 2019; 2023). It also suggests that the backdrop for the movie, the 1948 law banning interracial marriage in the state of California, 19 years prior to the 1967 *Loving* decision, could not alone erase racial bias, discrimination, and hatred. The "story of love," especially when biracial, is far more complicated. As a 37-year-old Black man, Sidney Poitier as John is aware of the racial tensions, while for his young fiancée, Joey (played by Katharine Houghton), age 23 and blinded by her love for John, they are a minor factor. Her disavowal of the significance of John's race reflects her liberal, upper-middle-class upbringing and lack of racial exposure, except for the adoring gaze of the Black maid. For John, race is the primary reason he seeks her parents' consent. He knows from experience that while love may be blind, for biracial couples in America, color-consciousness is demanded.

Joey's liberal parents quickly become suspicious and distressed at the prospect that their daughter might marry a Black man. Her father, Matt Drayton (Spencer Tracy), is so unsettled he arranges a background check. The indignity of the additional steps required for acceptance and legitimacy by whites is an ongoing challenge for African Americans (Powell, 2012). The "background" reveals that John is a world-renowned physician and researcher for the World Health Organization, with degrees from Hopkins, Yale, and the London School of Infectious Diseases. By contrast, the audience is not informed of Joey's educational or professional pedigree. We are left to conclude that the color of John's skin necessitates that he be an academic Olympian if he is to be the equal partner to his white fiancée, whose affluent parents have financial means and clout.[2] In 1967 and beyond, African Americans have been judged by the color of their skin and not the content of their character. One doubts Matt Drayton would conduct a similar investigation were his future son-in-law white with half the résumé.

In the 60s, demands of the civil rights movement for equal justice under the law combined with proactive steps to remove barriers to improved jobs, health care, and education. The result was a marked rise of the Black middle class. Increasingly, Blacks interacted with whites in the workplace in roles other than the historical ones of helper, servant, or slave. Simultaneously, the Black Power movement challenged African Americans to unapologetically embrace their cultural heritage, re-narrating their history as one not just of resilience but of equality. In that pressure cooker of opportunity and integration, a recurrent theme in the history of Black people in America again comes to the fore: Should one follow W.E.B. Dubois or Booker T. Washington; Martin Luther King or Malcolm X? In *Guess Who's Coming to Dinner,* the choice of identity and path is manifest intergenerationally. When John's father states his reservations about the marriage, John pushes back, "You think of yourself as a colored man, I think of myself as a man."

The playwright August Wilson (1945–2005), in his generationally themed plays tracing the history of Black people from post-Reconstruction to modern times, writes about the need for Black people to know their song, their cultural place in the world, rooted in an ancestral past and present in the here and now. One's song is a narrative construct that serves as an invaluable place of intrapsychic safety and identity while in the throes of a racist society (Sandler, 1960). Wilson's conceptualization is similar to that of Ruby Sales (personal communication), the civil rights activist and theologian, who asks, "Who are your people...who do you belong to?" As Wilson's plays advance toward modern times, the threat of losing one's song, one's cultural identity, corresponds to attempts at assimilation to the dominant white culture. In contrast, John, by knowing his song well, is able to present himself on an equal footing to his father and to his future father-in-law.

While not able to give sufficient space in this writing to the gender and religious politics of the film, I note that the three characters who most affirm the interracial union are the two mothers (including Beah Richards as Mary Prentice) and the priest (Cecil Kellaway as Monsignor Ryan). Even though they provide support and have some influence, they are not decisive in the direction of the plot. Reflecting the patriarchal society of the times, the final approval and blessing of the marriage are left to Matt Drayton, who ends the film with a long soliloquy. In his closing speech, as he comes to terms with his daughter's decision, Drayton conveys his soft bigotry. Tracy poignantly reveals the complexities of love between the races in this scene, which closes the movie.

Guess Who's Coming to Dinner is an example of the disavowal of African Americans and their experiences by white liberals, especially those of some means. Liberal whites unwittingly and unconsciously neutralize Blackness by demanding that to be accepted, Black people must have academic and professional pedigrees that mirror or exceed those of whites. In this way, Black (retaliatory) aggression and sexuality are mitigated.

In the news, the overtly racist acts and opinions of some American citizens and political leaders are easily available; the racism of white liberals is more challenging to tease apart. It remains hidden, unconscious, behind an understanding facade of empathy with the victims of racism. Michelle Alexander's book *The New Jim Crow* (2010) and Carol Anderson's *White Rage: The Unspoken Truth of Our Racial Divide* (2016) show the benefits institutional racism continues to provide whites at the expense of Blacks, regardless of political leaning. The result: a white nation all too silent about its underpinnings of racial privilege.

Get Out: America's Racial History Revealed

The 2017 movie *Get Out* shattered the fabled pretense of Black–liberal white harmony. From the moment a Black man lost in a white suburban neighborhood is knocked unconscious by a white assailant and stuffed in the trunk of a car, we are entering a nightmarish dystopia. In this dark, tragic thriller, the Black experience isn't neutralized, contained, and controlled as in *Guess Who's Coming to Dinner*. Rather, it is appropriated for its superior attributes. From the perspective of *Get Out*, *Guess Who's Coming to Dinner* is an escapist bromide for society's racial ills. Instead, *Get Out* offers a fantastical illumination, a cultural vivisection, of the structure of current liberal race relations. Written and directed by Jordan Peele, the film chronicles the developing relationship between Chris Washington (Daniel Kaluuya) and Rose Armitage (Allison Williams) as she takes him to meet her parents at their Northeastern estate.[3] All seems mundane—until it's not. Peele's movie unmasks the idea of a conflict-free zone between middle-class Blacks and white, non-Southern, coastal liberals. *Get Out* exposes the ongoing legacy of the acquisition and possession of the Black body, mind, and spirit. As metaphor, *Get Out* imaginatively captures contemporary issues of white privilege, Black emancipation, and the ongoing psychic vestiges of racism in our presumed colorblind society.

In Peele's film, race, white privilege (defined here as the advantages awarded to whites based on the oppression of others, whether consciously or unconsciously derived), and racial tensions between the romantic couple are at first played down, although with unnerving undertones. For instance, while driving to her parents', Rose hits a deer, foreshadowing what the viewer later learns of Chris's traumatic past and the perils he's about to endure. Her open defiance of the state trooper emphasizes the freedom and privilege she possesses to challenge authority, which Chris, due to his Blackness, does not.[4] Every scene of Peele's film holds historical and current significance. Chris's silence is an early harbinger of deeper dissociative processes that Blacks are subject to when confronted with white authority.

Rose is the quintessential body snatcher. She convinces Chris that her liberal parents' being unaware that she's bringing a Black man home won't be a problem.[5] There are hints of what will come: the parents' overly solicitous greeting of Chris, the father's repetitively expressed love for former president Barack Obama, their claims to not being racists, and the soullessness of the estate's gardener and maid, the white grandparents in Black bodies. By the time Chris is hypnotized by Rose's mother, ostensibly for smoking cessation, and led to believe that his mother's death was his responsibility, the acquisition of Chris's body and mind is nearly complete. An ostensibly benign but actually racist afternoon garden party transforms into the backdrop for auctioning off Chris to the highest bidder.

Chris awakens (becomes "woke") when the flash from his camera, his "sensitive eye," awakens the kernel of a Black man still within the white-occupied body of a black partygoer. This man's emotional plea to "Get out!" shocks Chris into recognizing his danger.

To "get out" speaks not only to the physical escape that Chris must make, but also to his struggle to recapture his identity as a Black man. As August Wilson repeatedly portrays, the accumulation of microaggressions that occur on a daily basis has eroded his song. Unlike John Prentice in *Guess Who's Coming to Dinner,* Chris has had to reclaim his identity, his soul, and his song by emancipating himself immediately from Rose's family. Chris has come to the Armitages' while in the "sunken place" of dissociated trauma and guilt at the intersection of personal trauma (related to his emotional paralysis and inaction at the time of his mother's death) and racial trauma (related to the transgenerational experience of post-traumatic slave syndrome) (DeGruy, 2005). When we meet Chris, he is in a dissociated state, lacking in healthy cultural paranoia, unaware of surrounding dangers, and living with the illusion of a post-racial society. Only by escaping the liberal country estate can he reclaim aspects of his racial identity, otherwise threatened with extinction.

The ties Chris has to his Blackness are maintained by his friend, Rod Williams (Lil Rel Howery), who, as the threat emerges, provides the vital connection to a safe psychic space. Rod warns Chris that he risks becoming a "sex slave" and warns Chris not to allow Rose's mother, Missy, a therapist (Catherine Keener), to hypnotize him ("Some people don't want strangers fucking with their heads"). Rod is speaking about Blacks' fear of being manipulated by white mental health clinicians. Thus, Rod becomes Chris's North Star, his Underground Railroad, and his Harriet Tubman, motivating him to fight for his freedom.

At its core, *Get Out* highlights the desire of white people to own and possess the Black mind and body. Envy and the desire to possess run throughout the film. Centrally, Jim Hudson (the blind gallery owner, played by Stephen Root) says of Black people in general and Chris in particular: "You're chosen for your *natural* gift." Chris responds: "Why Blacks?" Hudson answers: "You're stronger...cooler...faster ... I want your eye." Volney Gay, professor of anthropology, religion, and psychiatry at Vanderbilt University, writes compellingly that white Americans' dependence for social and individual identity on owning a person was an outgrowth of defenses of "denial and splitting" developed during slavery.

> For example, many—if not most—cultured Christians of the prewar South could affirm both Jesus' teaching of equality and, at the same time, defend their ownership of persons. What they affirmed on Sunday, they contradicted Monday through Saturday. They managed to live within this contradiction by splitting their minds into separate regions, and their religion and its preachers helped them maintain these splits.
>
> (2016, p. 57)

To cover up this contradiction and justify continued domination, whites emphasized that Black families were dependent on whites, or as Georgina (Betty Gabriel) in *Get Out* states with double irony: "They treat us like family." Being a part of society and yet remaining outside of its normal advantages is the history of the African in America.

Jeremy Armitage (Caleb Landry Jones), Rose's brother, has the role of voicing the overt hostility and envious rage behind the color-blind facade erected by the Armitages. He is the violent wing, the trigger finger, of the Order of the Coagula, who are willing to destroy in their attempt to inhabit and possess. Jeremy also destroys the fantasy that violent racism in America is a Southern problem. Racism, Peele shows, is in white society in every geographic region.

Being Black in white spaces is a constant negotiation between assimilation and identity. Increasingly, with the Civil Rights Era, the Black Lives Matter movement, and the presidency of Barack Obama, the greater freedom African Americans now have to define Blackness within the culture has reduced their urge to abandon the racial self for outward acceptance within the larger society. By being unapologetically Black in every psychic space, younger African Americans actively push back against those who demand allegiance to whiteness as the sole pathway to full acceptance as citizens. Clinically, I have observed a greater willingness of younger African Americans to actively rebut the demands and pressures of a societal racism. Those from the middle and upper-middle classes have witnessed the strain and stress of their parents, who were often the first in their families to go to college or have positions of influence and esteem in the white world. They had to silently absorb racist insults and microaggressions from colleagues and others as they strove to achieve in the workplace.

The Clinical and the Personal: Moving Toward Psychic Emancipation; Working through White Liberal Guilt and Privilege

"Were your ancestors slaves?" a white patient in total sincerity asked me once. Our work together had shown that these questions would reflect his internal struggles with autonomy and agency.

I REPLIED: "Before answering, can you say some more about why you're asking the question?"
PATIENT: "Because, you seem so free!"

This exchange captures the potential for psychic emancipation through the therapeutic endeavor. To free oneself from internal conflicts, relationship mis-attunements, a traumatic childhood and suspended psychic development is the goal of dynamic treatment. My patient was alluding to an ongoing psychic enslavement of his own that could benefit from psychodynamic exploration. While these are universal themes, there are particular—and different—residues for those who historically have had a legacy of enslavement or been the beneficiaries of a racist society. In this seminal moment, my patient was coveting something in me that he lacked. Fully elaborating his envy of my psychic freedom revealed his belief that if my ancestors were slaves I should feel and act from a position of enslavement.

African Americans for 400 years have been resilient in the face of ongoing racial trauma and dehumanization. What we are permitted to do with our minds and bodies has been an ongoing debate since our first arrival on these shores. Peaceful protests, such as the march from Selma to Montgomery and NFL players taking a knee, expose these raw truths regarding ownership and agency for our consideration.

Harry Belafonte, accomplished actor, singer, activist, and humanitarian, was asked on *60 Minutes*—during the height of the civil rights movement—how he withstood the racial taunts, harassment, and daily threats to his life. He replied, "Psychoanalysis." Belafonte's reply supports the premise that attainment of internal psychic freedom mitigates the external blows of racial trauma that are a daily feature for Black and brown people. Working clinically with people of color to achieve psychic liberation, or "getting out" from a psychic racial stranglehold, will be the focus of this section.

Ms. C, a 32-year-old African American woman, was raised in a solidly middle-class home filled with intellectual rigor and standards of decorum. In her position as an executive at an advertising firm, Ms. C was known as a thoughtful contributor able to provide innovative ideas that frequently led to successful ad campaigns. During her third year at the firm, her husband, a white man, found a position at a lower level within the same agency. Simultaneously and inexplicably, the advancement that Ms. C had previously anticipated, supported by consistent positive year-end reviews, became more tenuous. She worried that her co-workers and superiors, the majority of whom were white, single, and female, were jealous of her marriage to a white man. Tensions arose in her marriage as her husband's career advanced while Ms. C's stagnated.

In sessions, Ms. C found herself unable to assert herself when others seized her ideas, claiming them as their own. She began to question whether she had originated these ideas. Ms. C spoke of rising guilt, feeling undeserving of the career she'd built. While before, she and her husband had spoken openly about racial matters that made the news, she now found herself unable to speak with him of her fears, doubt, suspicions, and hurt that became a daily part of her work experience. She feared that any attempt to assert herself at work would have her being labeled as an "angry Black woman." Her parents told her to not rock the boat, that she still had a job, encouraging her to toe the line. Therapy became her only sounding board.

A younger, less experienced white woman was promoted to the position Ms. C coveted. In the next session, she described her devastation at the promotion party. Everyone, including her husband—who had been promoted—attended. Most disturbing to her sense of reality was the expectation that she smile and show "gratitude," while her husband, obliviously unaware, chatted jovially with colleagues. As time went on, Ms. C felt increasingly abandoned, marginalized, and embarrassed. She feared she would lose her mind. She had fallen into the "sunken place," living the pre-auction *Get Out* garden-party scene.

This example highlights the multiple tensions confronting African Americans, especially the younger generation who became adults during the Obama presidency. Although her parents had been passed over by less qualified whites in their professional lives, these racial discriminations were held privately by her parents. Simultaneously, Ms. C had been raised with an abiding faith in meritocracy, reinforced by the presidency of Barack Obama. She felt blindsided by the racial discrimination suddenly arising at her job. The advice from her parents confused her more, as they had always said to speak out against injustice. Their admonition to not speak out and settle for her current position felt like a betrayal of their teachings and her upbringing. Only later, with direct confrontation, did her parents convey the extent of racial injustice they had experienced in their professional lives.

DeGruy writes that African Americans have had the trauma of slavery transmitted intergenerationally within their community (2005). Safety within a hostile, racist environment is often privileged over psychic freedom. Accordingly, many African Americans are persuaded to "color within the lines," sacrificing agency in order to survive. Ms. C's parents' advice, along with Ms. C's discomfort at expressing appropriate anger, promoted a false self in her efforts for professional success that ultimately compromised her agency

(Winnicott, 1969). Focusing and working through these internal tensions, especially as revealed in the transference, allowed Ms. C to separate from her parental inhibitory teachings, allowing her to openly explore her racial trauma. She could express her anger, and she began to take risks. Her agency increased. In time, she secured a new position at a different firm that emphasized the burgeoning market of advertising for diverse populations.

Ms. C's treatment also focused on her relationship with her husband. She became more attuned to the greater freedom and opportunity her husband experienced in their workplace given his white privilege. As Ms. C. became more assertive, articulating her feelings with decreased fear of her anger, her husband also came to recognize his privilege and the depths of racialization from childhood that falsely had him believe that all people were treated equally, except in those gross racial injustices that make the news. Through his wife's experiences and her directly sharing the subtle racial microaggressions, he recognized that the playing field was far from even. With the "browning of America," the oddity of the romantic couple in *Guess Who's Coming to Dinner* is becoming the commonplace of Rose and Chris in *Get Out*. Societal norms and expectations are changing, but the psychic challenges confronting biracial couples as they reconcile their relationships intrapersonally and to the society at large will, by necessity of our racist past, be complicated and at times arduous.

Final Remarks

The intimate racial relationships that both films portray present conflicts in which reparative steps seem elusive. In my clinical practice, African American patients have described feeling "Rosed" by their white romantic partners: placed in predominantly white spaces and expected to abrogate significant Black cultural identifiers, including language, intonation, style of dressing and dancing, and means of expression through behaviors sanctioned by their community. In this regard, both films reveal ongoing white domination of Black minds and bodies, even within the most liberal of white spaces.

The vital question for analysts and therapists, who are sought out to help untangle difficult questions of love, betrayal, kinship, and conflict, is whether we will be tribalistic in our work at this moment of unenlightenment. Will we be ruled by the disavowal of race and difference portrayed in *Guess Who's Coming to Dinner*? There, Matt Drayton is discombobulated when confronted by an African American suitor for his daughter who is highly accomplished. His racism lingers. Will we live in a society with a level of sociopathy in which, as in *Get Out*, there is an absence of guilt, shame, or empathy? The latter, a true horror story, appears in the current political climate to be uncomfortably close for many African Americans and other people of color.

Although raw and overt at the time of this writing, after the murder of George Floyd, after the presidency of Donald Trump, it would be mistaken to attribute today's racial conflict to that murder and that presidency. The opening scene of *Get Out*, when an unidentified Black man walking in a suburban neighborhood is hit on the head and stuffed in a car trunk to then vanish, is about as probable as that a white man (George Zimmerman) who murders an unarmed Black teenager (Trayvon Martin) walking back home from a convenience store might proffer a defense that he was "standing his ground" and be acquitted by a jury in Florida. How can Black parents allow their sons and daughters the freedom that the rest of society takes for granted if these incidents are warped into narrative distortions that cloak the truth? When the narrative of events becomes distorted time and time again by such outcomes, society loses its moral center.

Monsignor Ryan provides a moral inflection to *Guess Who's Coming to Dinner*. He says to Matt Drayton, as the father confronts his own racism, "You're angry with yourself; you've been thrown off balance." Later, describing Matt's discomfort, he rips into Matt's facade to expose rot: "To see a broken-down, phony liberal come face to face with his principles—of course I always believed that within that biting liberal facade there must be a reactionary bigot trying to get out." It is an attack on a representative man who fails to live up to his liberal principles. Fifty years later, *Get Out* blows the cover off liberalism itself.

Ryan speaks to the psychic cost of defensively denying our bigotry and racism, the results of which our current societal abyss shows to be disastrous. And by doing so, he offers hope.

That the soft bigotry of liberal whites carries a covert insistence that Blacks neutralize their cultural selves in order to be accepted within white liberal circles is an ongoing adaptive challenge for whites as African Americans insist on being acknowledged fully on their own terms with their own minds (Leary, 2007; 2012). Put another way by Claudia Rankine (Kellaway, 2015), "Blackness in the white imagination has nothing to do with Black people." Jordan Peele has provided us through *Get Out* a searing exposé, a psychological deep dive, into the difference between the real and the imagined (LaFarge, 2004). Only when whites challenge themselves on what's imagined, experience a different consciousness, and become less entrenched in fantasy, less blind to their own minds, will they and we all begin to engage in the real, especially in consideration of the racial other (Irving, 2014; Coates, 2015; DiAngelo, 2018; Cushman, 2000). Jordan Peele in *Get Out* delivers us collectively to this place of enlightenment.

The dynamic question is whether we, as therapists and analysts, can become curious and less defensive to our racist states of mind (Keval, 2016). Just as whites must confront the soft bigotry by which the racist structures of society require Blacks to neutralize their cultural selves, I have had to acknowledge that in my analysis, at moments of optimal defensiveness, I had accused my analyst of "talking like a white woman," claiming that she could never understand me due to her whiteness. I came to appreciate that I could better tolerate my accusations than confront and work through my rage and destructiveness and, on an even deeper level, speak of my fears and anxieties. These were much harder for me to acknowledge and accept.

Albert Einstein stated, "No problem can be solved from the same consciousness that created it." As therapists, we are charged to understand the racism we each harbor to the same degree that we understand our sexual and aggressive impulses. Only then can we help patients explore these aspects of themselves. Our ability as analysts and therapists to reclaim conversation, to lean into uncomfortable truths in order to seek psychic reconciliation and psychic emancipation in the face of racial trauma, can be beneficial to all our patients as our young country struggles with its past, present, and future as a multicultural, multiracial nation.

Notes

1 In 1968, whites living below the poverty line (defined as $25,000 a year for a family of four by 2016 standards) represented 10 percent, while Blacks represented 35 percent. Fast forward to 2016, and 9 percent of whites continued to live below the poverty line, while 22 percent of

Blacks remained below the poverty line. Thus the Lovings' economic circumstances were far closer to those experienced by most African Americans than to the upper middle class circumstances of the protagonists of the films being discussed.

2 With the momentous shift for women in the 1960s—controlling their reproduction, entering the workforce in record numbers, increased access to higher education—a separate chapter could be written on the marginalized role of women in this film.

3 Multiple companies throughout the United States were intimately involved in the slave trade, including major insurance companies, train lines, and banks, predominantly north of the Mason-Dixon Line. Thus slavery was a major revenue source, privileging whites throughout the country.

4 The increase of racial incidents occurring as African Americans attempt to live their lives has been distilled into memes representing the multiple daily ways Blacks put their lives in danger: driving while Black, shopping while Black, learning while Black, playing in the park while Black, and commuting while Black...to name a few. We recall Sandra Bland in 2015, anticipating working for her alma mater, Prairie View A&M University, in less than three weeks, being pulled over by a white Texas state trooper for not signaling a lane change. Three days later, Bland was discovered dead in jail from an apparent "suicide." These unprovoked incidents confirm the oft-stated belief that Blacks aren't as free to live in society as whites are.

5 Note the similarities and contrasts in the roles of the female protagonists, Joey Drayton and Rose Armitage, over the course of 50 years. Both claim that there is "no problem" in bringing their Black boyfriend/fiancé home to meet their parents, although we're soon aware of the differences in intent. Joey Drayton is quiet and relatively ill-defined compared to the three other lead protagonists, while Rose Armitage is sharp-edged, no-nonsense, totally in control. After the trooper stop when, continuing the drive, Rose states, "(I'm) not going to let anyone fuck with my man," the aggressive possessiveness is thinly veiled.

6 U.S. Census Bureau statistics found that in 2010 a record 15.1 percent of all new marriages in the United States were between spouses of different race or ethnicity compared with 8.4 percent of all current marriages.

References

Alexander, M. (2010). *The New Jim Crow: Mass Incarceration in the Age of Colorblindness*. New York: The New Press.

Anderson, C. (2016). *White Rage: The Unspoken Truth of Our Racial Divide*. New York: Bloomsbury.

Clark, K.B. (1963). *Prejudice and Your Child*. Boston: Beacon Press.
Coates, T.-N. (2015). *Between the World and Me*. New York: Penguin Random House.
Cushman, P. (2000). White guilt, political activity, and the analyst. Commentary on paper by Neil Altman. *Psychoanalytic Dialogues* 10(4):607–618.
DeGruy, J. (2005). *Post Traumatic Slave Syndrome: America's Legacy of Enduring Injury and Healing*. Milwaukie, OR: Uptone Press.
DiAngelo, R. (2018). *White Fragility: Why It's So Hard for White People to Talk About Racism*. Boston: Beacon Press.
Gay, V. (2016). *On the Pleasures of Owning Persons: The Hidden Face of American Slavery*. New York: International Psychoanalytic Books.
Holmes, D. (2006). The wrecking effects of race and class. *Psychoanalytic Quarterly* 75:215–235.
Irving, D. (2014). *Waking Up White, and Finding Myself in the Story of Race*. Cambridge, MA: Elephant Room Press.
Kellaway, K. (2015). *The Guardian*, December 27, 2015.
Keval, N. (2016). *Racist States of Mind: Understanding the Perversion of Curiosity and Concern*. London: Karnac.
LaFarge, L. (2004). The imaginer and the imagined. *Psychoanalytic Quarterly* 73(3):591–625.
Leary, K. (2007). Racial insult and repair. *Psychoanalytic Dialogues* 17:539–549.
Leary, K. (2012). Race as an adaptive challenge: Working with diversity in the clinical consulting room. *Psychoanalytic Psychology* 29:279–291.
Powell, D.R. (2018). Race, African Americans, and psychoanalysis: Collective silence in the therapeutic situation. *Journal of the American Psychoanalytic Association* 66(6):1021–1049.
Sandler, J. (1960). The background of safety. *International Journal of Psychoanalysis* 41:352–356.
Stoute, B.J. (2019). Racial Socialization and Thwarted Mentalization: Psychoanalytic Reflections from the Lived Experience of James Baldwin's America. *American Imago* 76(3), Fall 2019, pp. 335–357.
Stoute, B.J. (2023). How our mind becomes racialized: Implications for the therapeutic encounter. In *Textbook of Psychotherapeutic Treatments*, 2d ed., eds. H. Crisp and G.O. Gabbard. Washington, DC: American Psychiatric Association Publishing (in press).
Winnicott, D.W. (1969). The use of an object. *International Journal of Psychoanalysis* 50:711–716.

Index

Note: Page numbers in *italics* indicate figures. Numbers followed by n indicate notes.

abandonment: fear of, 98, 232; in urban ER, 258–59
abhayahasta (fearless hand), 210–13
Abney, Veronica, 24–25, 32n3
Abrams, Stacey, 169
Abul-Jamal, Mumia, 152
abuse, sexual, 145–46
accommodations, 259–60
achievement gaps, 284
Achilles, 167
acute racially discriminatory trauma, 116–20; *see also* race and racism
Adams, Joan, 32n3
adolescents: police violence against Black boys, 282; racial socialization of, 226–27, 229–35, 301; under slavery's legacy, 75–79; struggles to individuate, 131
Adorno, Theodor, 20
adultification of Black girls, 150
affective neuroscience, 182
African American (term), 65n2
African Americans, 1; adolescent boys, 229–35, 282; anti-Black oppression of, 204–5; awareness of white privilege, 283–87; Black children, 75–79, 137–58, 283–87; Black Rage, 159–91; boys, 75–79, 229–35, 282–87; case examples, 230–35; and Child Protective Services (CPS), 263–67; children, 137–58, 283–87; Covid-19 cases, 163–64; cultural paranoia, 327–38; daily life of, 80–88; defense against psychic intrusions, 93–95; denial of dependency of, 97; depressive anxiety, 100–103; distrust of mental health care, 254; domination of, 96–97; double consciousness, 86; emasculation of, 97; encounters with the system, 262–68; enslavement of, 15–17, 22, 43–44, 48–49, 65n1, 140–54, 167, 177–81, 261, 277; fear of abandonment, 98; fear of domination, 98; fear of not being able to understand, 98; fear of not being understood, 98; fear of police, 85–87; fear of rejection, 98; forced migration of, 154; identity formation, 139; as invisible, 55–56; mental illness among, 261; mistreatment of, 45–52; as objects of projection, 92–94; ownership of capital, 290; police violence against unarmed Black men, 1–2, 9–10, 77, 84, 86–87, 168, 221, 236; post-traumatic reactions to racial trauma, 105–15; prejudice against, 25–26; prison population, 152; in psychoanalysis, 42–71, 65n3; psychoanalysts, 23–26, 32n2–3, 44, 49, 65n3, 276; racism toward, 28–29, 43 (*see also* race and racism); suspicions toward psychotherapy, 331; theoretical conceptions of, 17–23; urban life, 259–62, 335–36; views of white therapists, 259–62; violence against, 46–47, 83–85; white indifference toward, 155n2; women, 80–88
African nations, 21
age distortion, 76–77

Akhtar, Salman, 25–26, 62
Alabama: Civil Rights movement, 279; interracial marriage, 340
alcohol, 267–68
Alexander, Lisa, 215n9
Alexander, Michelle, 345
Ali, Muhammad, 341
Allport, Gordon, 19
Altman, Neil, 309n1
American Civil Liberties Union (ACLU), 340
American Psychoanalytic Association (ApsaA), 23–24, 33n4, 187n8; discriminatory and exclusionary practices, 187n8; membership, 24, 44; training and education, 27–28
American Psychoanalytic (ApsaA) Institute, 24
Anagwelem, Patricia, 33n3
anal theory of racism, 22
Anderson, Carol, 345
anger and rage, 96; berserk rage, 167; Black Rage, 159–91; indignant rage, 167; post-traumatic reactions, 114–15, 118–19; RAGE/Anger system, 182–83, 185; in self-discovery, 125–27
Ann Arbor, Michigan: housing discrimination, 21
Ansley, Frances Lee: definition of white supremacy, 214n2
anthropology, racist, 28
anti-Semitism: in Europe, 29–30, 43; Freud's lived experience of, 16, 102, 160–61, 171–72, 187n6; Holocaust, 29, 43–44, 139, 177; lived experiences of, 273–75; in psychoanalysis, 19–20, 27
Antonelli, Mildred, 167
anxiety: clinical vignettes, 224–25; confusional, 98, 101; depressive, 98, 100–103; FEAR/Anxiety system, 182; persecutory, 98, 101
APA Handbook of Trauma Psychology, 138
apartheid, 317
archaeology, 313–14
Aristotle, 333
Armenians, 155n3
articulation: power of, 110
Asians, 224
assimilation, 62
Astor, Richard, 320
Atlanta, Georgia, 299, 309
attitude, 323

awareness: of racial difference, 222–26; of racism, 125–27; of white privilege, 271–323

Baldwin, James, 62, 159, 179–80, 304; James Baldwin's America, 221–24, 235–40
Ballard, Bruce, 32n3
Baltimore, Maryland, 334
Bamberg, E. G., 331
Barca, Hamilcar, 187n6
Beckert, Sven, 289–90
behavior: defiant, 283–84; shaping, 125–36
Belafonte, Harry, 349
Bennet, Janice, 33n3, 278
Bennett, Janice, 280
Bennett, Neomi, 101–2
Berlin, Germany: 2007 IPA Congress ("Trauma: New Developments in Psychoanalysis"), 42
Berlin, Ira, 137
Bernard, Viola, 23–24, 32n2, 49
Bernays, Martha, 51
Bernstein, Neil, 151, 154
berserk rage, 167
bias: implicit, 45, 50; racial, 49
Biassey, Earl, 32n3
Bibbs, Henry, 144–45
bicultural competence, 228; *see also* multicultural competence
Bion, Wilfred, 98
Bird, Brian, 19–20
Black (term), 65n2
Black children: adolescent boys, 229–35, 282; adultification of girls, 150; awareness of white privilege, 283–87; boys, 75–79, 229–35, 282–87; case examples, 230–35; and Child Protective Services (CPS), 263–67; development of, 137–58; enslaved girls, 145–46; identity development, 227; incarceration of girls of color, 149–51; police violence against, 282; school-to-prison pipeline, 146–53; special education students, 151; "the talk" with, 237; in urban ER, 253–54, 258–59, 263–67
Black Codes, 152–53, 178
Black is Beautiful movement, 25
Black Lives Matter movement, 1, 9–10, 76, 165–66, 168, 182–83, 348

Black Lives Matter Plaza (Washington, D.C.), 170, *170*
Black men: emasculation of, 97; police violence against, 1–2, 9–10, 77, 84, 86–87, 168, 221, 236
Blackness, 353; theoretical conceptions of, 17–23; in urban ER, 257–59; a white therapist's response to, 257–59
Black Other, 174–76
Black Power movement, 76, 172, 343–44
Black Pride, 97
Black Psychoanalysts Speak, 276, 278, 282
Black Psychoanalysts Speak (PEP-Web), 244, 278, 280
Black Rage, 159–91; as adaptive defense, 173–77, 181–82; clinical extensions, 181–82; during Covid-19, 162–66; as emotional drive, 182–83; examples, 169–70, *170*; Freud's secret Black Rage, 171–72; as functional, 173–77; as mental construct, 172–73; as mobilizing, 169, 174–75; as trans-generational, 177–81
Blacks, *see* African Americans
Black Sambo, 24–25
Blackwell, Jerry, 186n3
Bland, Sandra, 84, 354n4
Blands, Irma, 32n3
Blanton, Smiley, 16
Blow, Charles, 237, 301
Blyew v. United States, 196
Bobo, Lawrence, 49–50
Boers, 316–17
boesman (San), 314–15
Bollas, Christopher, 45
Bonilla-Silva, Eduardo, 49–50
Bonner, Frances, 32n3
Booth, Martin, 32n3
Bottoms, Keisha Lance, 163, *164*
Bowser, Muriel, 170
boys: adolescent, 229–35, 282; African American, 75–79, 229–35, 282–87; police violence against Black boys, 282; *see also* children
Brickman, Celia, 28
British Psychoanalytical Society, 161
Brooklyn Academy of Music, 329
Brown, James, 93
Brown, Michael, 47
Brown v. Board of Education of Topeka, Kansas, 13, 147, 223

Brummit, Houston, 33n3
The 'Burbs, 329
Bureau of Indian Affairs (BIA), 279
Burris, Arthur, 33n3
Bushmen, 314–15
Butts, Hugh, 23–24, 32n2, 33n3

California: interracial marriage, 342
Campbell, Dan, 275–76
cancel culture, 210, 306
Canino, I.A., 24
capitalism, war, 289–90
CARE/Nurturing system, 182
case examples, 106–15, 230–35
case vignettes, 127–35, 224–26
Celia (enslaved girl), 146
Chakrabortty, Aditya, 94
Chauvin, Derek, 164–65, 186n3
checker games, 285–86
Cheney, Dick, 296
Chicago, Illinois: Chicago Police Department, 86–87; Red Summer (July 27, 1919), 186n4
Child Protective Services (CPS), 263–67
children: African American, 75–79, 137–58, 283–87; awareness of racial difference, 222–26; awareness of white privilege, 283–87; Black boys, 75–79, 229–35, 282–87; Black child development in America, 137–58; child development theory, 303–4; curiosity about racial difference, 222–26; enslaved, 142–46; identity development, 227; incarceration of, 154; investment in, 321–22; in urban ER, 253–54, 258–59, 263–67; vignettes, 224–26
choice, 210
chosen trauma, 178
Christmas, June, 24, 33n3
chronic racially discriminatory trauma, 116–20; *see also* race and racism
Civil Rights Act, 13, 341
Civil Rights movement, 21, 82–83, 187n5, 279, 295, 343–44, 348–49
Clark, Kenneth, 92, 148, 223, 227
Clark, Mamie, 92, 223, 227
Clark University Psychology Conference Group (1909), 46–47, *47*
class differences: in urban ER, 251–69
clinical vignettes, 224–26
Clinton, Hillary, 151

Coates, Ta-Nehisi, 51, 221, 236, 276, 304
Cobbs, Price, 172
cocaine, 267–68
collective trauma, 178
colonial discourse, 292–93
colonialism, 21, 187n5
color-blind racism, 50; case example, 113
Columbia University, 24, 32n2, 49, 61, 290
Comer, James, 98
Communism, 43
community mental health movement, 23
community psychoanalysis, 311–23
Confederate statues, 138
confusional anxiety, 98, 101
Congress of Racial Equality (CORE), 279
Connecticut: history of slavery, 142
conspiracy of silence, 275–77
conversations: "the talk," 237, 276–77; therapeutic, 52–60, 122–23, 286–87, 306–7
conversion therapy, 187n8
convict leasing, 153
cool pose, 229
Cooper, Amy, 165, 215n9
Cooper, Christian, 165
countertransference, 135–36; case vignettes, 127–35
Covid-19, 2, 162–66
criminalization, 148, 151
critical race theory, 302
critical theory, 249
Cross, William, Jr., 227
cultural assimilation, 62
cultural identity, 98, 227
cultural introjects, 140
cultural life, 322–23
cultural memory, 177
cultural paranoia, 327–38
curiosity about racial difference, 125–35, 222–26
Curtis, James, 33n3

daily life, 80–88
daily racism, 89–104
Dalal, Farhad, 25–26
Daniels, Benny, 315
Danto, Elizabeth, 23, 32n1, 281
Davids, Fakhry, 92
Davis, Angela, 147
day care, 322
Declaration of Independence, 15
Dees, Morris, 301

defending against psychic intrusions, 93–95
defiant behavior, 283–84
Deleon, Charles, 33n3
Deltameer, 319
Delta Optel Band, 322
delusions of omnipotence (case example), 113–14
denial: of dependency, 97; of difference, 206–8; of racism, 103
dependency: denial of, 97
depressive anxiety, 98, 100–103
despair, 316
Detroit, 237
Detroit, Michigan: race riots, 20, 237
Devereux, George, 279
Diagnostic and Statistical Manual of Mental Disorders III (DSM III), 231
Diagnostic and Statistical Manual of Mental Disorders IV (DSM IV), 231
Diagnostic and Statistical Manual of Mental Disorders V (DSM V), 121, 123–24, 138–39, 231
dialectics, 302, 304
dialog: therapeutic conversations, 52–60, 122–23, 286–87, 306–7; unformulated, 246–50
DiAngelo, Robin, 295
Dido (Elissa), 187n6
difference, 91–92; awareness of, 225–26; denial of, 206–8; preoccupations about, 135–36; *see also* class differences; ethnic differences; racial differences
dignity, 27, 295; definition of, 238–39; indignant rage, 167; maintaining, 237–38; making space for, 255
Dinebeiina Nahilnabe Agaditahe, 279
disavowal, 204–7
discrimination: case examples, 106–15; against LGBQT community, 187n8; racial, 104–24 (*see also* race and racism)
discriminatory gestures, 105, 201–2; case example I, 106–11; case example II, 112–15; defensive life of, 202–4; vs open hand gestures, 212–13; psychological phenomena associated with, 116–20, 123–24; secondary, 208–10
disruptive mood dysregulation disorder, 225
dissociative forgetfulness, 202

distortions, 97, 99–100
Django Unchained, 78
Dollard, John, 18
doll test, 92
domination, 96–97; fear of, 98
dop system, 317
double consciousness, 86
Douglass, Frederick, 166–68
drapetomania, 48
Duane, Anne Mae, 154n1
DuBois, W.E.B., 47, 86, 137, 343
DuCille, Ann, 151
Dunlap, Constance, 33n3
Dutch East India Company, 314

Eddo-Lodge, Reni, 95, 97
education, 321–22; *Brown v. Board of Education of Topeka, Kansas,* 13, 147, 223; school life, 283–87, 299–300, 309; school segregation, 147; school-to-prison pipeline, 146–53; special education students, 151
educational policy, 149
Edwards, Henry, 33n3
Einstein, Albert, 353
Elissa (Dido), 187n6
Ellison, Ralph, 55–56, 155n2, 334
emancipation, psychic, 175–76, 339–55
emasculation, 97
emergency room (ER): alliance in, 253–57; psychoanalysis in, 251–59; racial differences in, 257–62; urban, 251–69
emotional action systems, 182
epistemic justice, 213–14
epithets, *see* slurs
Erikson, Erik, 162
Eros, 159, 185
essential workers, 163–64, 261
ethical asymmetry, 211
ethnic differences: preoccupations about, 135–36; racial-ethnic-cultural (REC) identity, 227
Evarts, A.M., 17
everyday life: of African American women, 80–88; racism, 89–104
evocative gestures, 125–36
exclusions, 96
expropriation, 97
Eyerman, Ron, 139

"Facing the Pain" (2013 IPA Prague Congress), 42–43

family history: fear of family breakup, 143; intergenerational trauma, 138–42; lost, 81–83
family values, 139
Fanon, Frantz, 21, 154, 174
fantasy(-ies), 22–23; Freud's fantasy about Hannibal, 160–61, 171–72; post-traumatic reactions, 114–15; revenge, 114–15; unconscious, 93, 177; of violence, 199
farm life: American, 292; South African, 311–23
fatalism, 316
fear: of abandonment, 98, 232; of annihilation, 305; of domination, 98; of family breakup, 143; of loss or being sold away, 143; of not being able to understand, 98; of not being understood, 98; of police, 84–87, 262–63; post-traumatic reactions, 114–15, 318–19; racism as based on, 237–38; of rejection, 98; of self, 130; *see also* paranoia
FEAR/Anxiety system, 182
fearless hand *(abhayahasta),* 210–13
Ferenczi, Sandor, 21, 303
field theory, 249
film: *Get Out,* 327–40, 345–48, 351–54; *Guess Who's Coming to Dinner,* 339–45, 351–53; social thrillers, 329–30, 337n1
Finch, Atticus, 301
Fine, Michelle, 149
Finn, Huckleberry, 301
fire: case vignette, 132–35
Florida, 352
Floyd, George, 1, 10, 33n4, 100, 164–65, 168, 182–83, 186n3, 352
Fonagy, Peter, 284
Fontaine, Jacqueline, 342
forgetfulness, dissociative, 202
foster care, 263–67
Fraiberg, Selma, 25
Franklin, A.J., 284
Franschhoek (French Quarter), 314
Franschhoek Valley Transformation Charter, 323
Frazier, Darnella, 164–65
Freedman, Bert, 295
Free Speech Movement, 279
Frenkel-Brunswik, Else, 20
Freud, Sigmund: conceptual framework, 17–18, 28, 95, 97, 185; definition

of disavowal, 206–7; fantasy of Hannibal, 160–61, 171–72; and Fuller, 46–47; lived experience of racism, 16, 102, 160–61, 171–72, 187n6; *Nachträglichkeit*, 199–200; neglect of race and racism, 160–62, 171–72; secret Black Rage, 171–72; theory of cultural memory, 177; theory of universal mind, 159–60; views on dignity, 238; views on race, 29–30, *31*, 51
Freud-Jung lectures, Clark University (1909), 46–47, *47*
frustration, 97
Fuller, Ruth, 24, 33n3
Fuller, Solomon Carter, 46–47, *47*

Gabriel, Betty, 347
Gambino, Childish, 335
Gandhi, Mahatma, 188n10
Gardner, Richard, 25
Garner, Eric, 138
gay (term), 215n10
Gay, Peter, 32n1, 160
Gay, Volney, 141, 347
gender-based violence, 145–46, 155n4
generational transmission of trauma, 45, 139, 221–24, 235–40
generational trauma, 52–60, 138–39
genocide, 64n1
Georgia: Black Rage, 169; Civil Rights movement, 279; Covid-19 cases, 163
Germany: 2007 IPA Berlin Congress ("Trauma: New Developments in Psychoanalysis"), 42; Nazi, 29
gestures of the open hand, 210–13
Get Out, 339–40, 351–53; cultural paranoia in, 327–38; female protagonists, 353–54; psychodynamic synopsis and commentary on, 345–48
Gilman, Sander, 16, 160
girls: adultification of Black girls, 150; enslaved, 145–46; incarceration of girls of color, 149–51; special education students, 151; *see also* children
Giroux, Henry, 148
Goldberger, Marianne, 58
Goodman, Mary Ellen, 222–23
Gourguechon, Prudence, 153
graffiti, racist, 125
Gray, Arthur, 33n3
Green Book, 301
Greenson, Ralph, 14, 61

Grier, William, 172
Griffin, John Howard, 300–301
Griggs, Sutton, 327, 331
group affiliations, 226–27
group identity, 227
group psychology, 19–20
Guantanamo, 277
Guess Who's Coming to Dinner, 339–40, 351–53; female protagonists, 353–54; psychodynamic synopsis and commentary on, 341–45

Haitian slaves, 302
Hall, G. Stanley, 46
Hamilton, James, 21
Hannibal, 160–61, 171–72, 187n6
Harrison-Ross, Phyllis, 25
Hart, Anton, 28, 33n3, 278
Harvard University, 290
hate and hatred, 27; post-traumatic reactions, 118–19; racial, 119; shifts between curiosity and, 125–35
Head Start, 112–13
health equity, 7–12
Hegel, G.W.F., 302, 309n1
helplessness, learned, 101
Henry's restaurant (New York City, NY), 278, 282
Herman, Judith, 145, 155n4
hermeneutical injustice, 214
hermeneutics, 249
heroin, 267–68
Hicks, Donna, 239
Hill, Billy, 342
Hill, Robert, 33n3
Hindus, 225–26
Hispanics, 149, 151
historical context, 45–52, 63–64; America's history of slavery, 15–17, 22, 43–44, 138, 140–54, 354n3; America's racial history, 345–48; Civil War, 260; epidemics, 163; Freud's history as a Jew, 16, 102, 160–61, 171–72, 187n6; history taking, 313; lost family history, 81–83; oral history, 317–18; South African history of slavery, 315–17
historically Black colleges, 180–81
historical perspectives, 5–71
historical self, 179
Holiday, Billie, 46
Hollar, Milton, 33n3

Holmes, Dorothy Evans, 14, 26, 28, 33n3, 57, 171, 237–38, 278, 296, 307–8
Holmes Commission on Racial Equality, 33n4
Holocaust, 43
Holocaust survivors, 29, 139, 177
Homer, 167
homophobic slurs, 207
honesty, 285
Hong, Grace Kyungwon, 195
hopelessness, 316
Horowitz, Eugene and Ruth, 227
hotnot (Khoi), 314–15
Houghton, Katharine, 342–43
housing discrimination, 21
Houston, Sam, 260
Howery, Lil Rel, 347
Huckleberry Finn (Twain), 197, 301
Huguenots, 314
humor, 299–300
Hunter, Caroline, 144
Hurricane Katrina, 148–49
hypercriminalization, 151
hypervigilance, 116
hypnosis, 330–31

idealizations, 97
identity: cultural, 98; group, 227; large group, 227; personal, 227; post-traumatic reactions, 116; racial, 223, 293
identity development, 227
identity formation, 139
identity trouble, 205–6; disintegration, 116
Illinois: history of slavery, 142
immigrants, white, 290–91
Implicit Association Tests, 48
implicit bias, 45, 50
incarceration: of children, 154; of girls of color, 149–51; prison-industrial complex, 152; school-to-prison pipeline, 146–53; youth, 151
India, 21
indigenous origins, 314–15
injustice: hermeneutical, 214; testimonial, 213–14
Institute for Psychoanalytic Training and Research (IPTAR), 278
institutional racism, 275
integration, 299–300
intergenerational trauma: and Black child development in America, 137–58; in family and nation, 138–42

internalization, adolescent, 227
internal racism, 92
International Psychoanalytical Association (IPA): 2007 Berlin Congress ("Trauma: New Developments in Psychoanalysis"), 42; 2013 Prague Congress ("Facing the Pain"), 42–43
interpretation-in-action, 212
interracial marriage, 339–40, 342, 354n5
intersectionality, 27
isolation: post-traumatic reactions, 116; in urban ER, 258–59

Jacobs, Harriet, 144
Jamestown, Virginia, 142
Japanese Americans, 277
Jefferson, Thomas, 143, 145
Jenkins, Lee, 33n3
Jennings, Pamela, 33n3
Jews: anti-Semitism, 16, 19–20, 27, 29–30, 43–44, 102, 160–61, 171–72, 273–75; clinical vignettes, 224; Holocaust survivors, 29, 139, 177; racial trauma, 16, 19–20, 28–30, 102
Johns Hopkins University, 261
Johnson, Charles, 154
Johnson, Lyndon Baines, 301
Johnson, William, 33n3
jokes, racist, 29–30, *31*
Jones, Annie Lee, 33n3, 96, 278, 282
Jones, Arnold, 33n3
Jones, Caleb Landry, 347–48
Jones, Enrico, 33n3
Jones, Ernst, 29
justice: epistemic, 213–14; juvenile, 147; social, 165

Kalinkowitz, Bernie, 276
Kaluuya, Daniel, 345
Kardiner, Abram, 18–19, 49, 66n6, 76
Keener, Catherine, 330, 347
Kellaway, Cecil, 344
Kemp, Brian, 163
Kendrick, Curtis, 33n3
Kennedy, John F., Jr., 301, 341
Kennedy, Robert, 340
Khoi-khoin, 314–15
Khoisan people, 314–16
King, Martin Luther, Jr., 64, 170, 188n10, 239, 301, 341, 343
Kirby, Edward, 33n3

Kleinian theory, 15–16
Kliger, Paula, 33n3
Kovel, Jovel, 20–22, 102
Kozol, Jonathan, 147
Kramer, Stanley, 328, 341
Kristof, Nicholas, 155n2
Kubie, Lawrence, 21
Kuriloff, Emily, 28–29, 62
Kurosawa, Akira, 162

La Barre, Weston, 279
Lafargue clinic (Harlem, NY), 23
laissez-faire racism, 50
The Lancet, 9, 168
land, relationships with, 315
Langbroeke, 322
language: distortions of, 97; n-word use, 192–218, 292
Later Stone Age, 314
law enforcement, 147, 287; *see also* police
Lawrence, Margaret Morgan, 23–24, 33n3, 49, 61, 66n6
learned helplessness, 101
learning and re-learning race, 219–69
Leary, Joy DeGruy, 137
Leary, Kimberlyn, 14, 26, 33n3
Leeming, David, 237
legal socialization, 228
Lennon, John, 341
Lerner, Ben, 301
lesbian, gay, bisexual, and transgender (LGBT) youth, 150
Levine, Susan, 238
LGBQT community: discrimination against, 187n8; LGBT youth, 150
liberalism, 352; white, 352–53; white liberal guilt, 301, 348–51
Lightfoot, Orlando, 33n3
Lincoln, Abraham, 301
Lind, John, 17
linking capacity, 176
listening: suggested dimension of, 135–36; in urban ER, 253; *see also* therapeutic conversations
Lorde, Audre, 215n5, 294
Los Angeles Institute and Society for Psychoanalytic Studies, 14, 61
loss: of connection, 99; of family history, 81–83
love, 180
Loving, Mildred and Richard, 339–41, 354n1

Lübeck-Delta, 320
LUST/sexuality system, 182
lynchings, 46–47, 153

Maafa, 142
Maasai, 137
MacDonald, Marjorie, 24–25
Maine: history of slavery, 142
Mallory, George, 33n3
Mandela, Nelson, 221, 317
mapping racism, 27
Marcovitz, Eli, 238
marginalization: post-traumatic reactions to, 116–20; of women, 354n2; *see also* race and racism
marijuana, 267–68
marriage, interracial, 339–40, 342, 354n5
Marshall, Thurgood, 341
Martin, Marilyn, 33n3
Martin, Trayvon, 43, 83–84, 221, 352
Maryland, 300
Massachusetts: history of slavery, 142
McCurtis, Henry, 33n3
McIntosh, Peggy, 278, 280
McKay, Claude, 165
McLean Hospital (Boston), 290
media, 229
medical experimentation, 261, 328
Meeropol, Abel, 46
memory, cultural, 177
mental health care, 7, 9–10, 261; African American community distrust toward, 254; community, 23; *see also* psychotherapy; therapeutic conversations
mentalization, 229; case example, 230–35; in school, 284
mental representations, 177–81
mental stress, 97–98
meritocracy, 350
meta-racism, 102
MetroCards, 150
microaggressions, 49, 78, 226, 280–81
microassaults, 280
Middle Passage, 142; Second Middle Passage, 154; third, 154
Miles, Carlotta, 33n3
mistrust: cultural paranoia, 327–38; post-traumatic reactions, 116
Mitchell, Regina, 33n3
modeling, 64
Moore, Evan, 33n3

moral injury, 166–71
Morgan, Margaret, 32n2
Morgan, Michelle, 33n3
Morris, Dolores, 33n3, 278
Morrison, Toni, 57
Moskowitz, Michael, 278
Moss, Donald, 48, 215n8
Mount Sinai Hospital (New York), 290
multicultural competence, 244–50; bicultural competence, 228
multiculturalism, 59–60
multicultural training, 244–45
Murphy, Eddie, 299, 309
Museum van de Caab, 316, 321
music, 322–23
Myrdal, Gunnar, 21

Nachträglichkeit, 199–200, 205, 212, 214
narcissistic perversion, 209
National Association for Research and Therapy of Homosexuality (NARTH), 187n8
Native Americans, 64–65n1, 167, 277, 279, 289
Navajo people, 279
Nazism, 28–29, 43
Negroes: Jews as Negroes of Vienna, 16; theoretical conceptions of, 17–23
neo-Nazis, 48
neuroscience, affective, 182
neuroticism, 27
New Hampshire: history of slavery, 142
New Jersey: history of slavery, 142
Newsom, Robert, 146
Newton, Huey P., 162
New York: history of slavery, 142
New York University (NYU), 276, 290
Night of the Living Dead, 329
Numa, Sharon, 92
Nussbaum, Martha, 334
n-word use, 192–218, 292; case vignettes, 207–8; violent world of, 196–99

Obama, Barack, 13, 32, 236, 329, 348
Obama, Michelle, 169
Obendorf, Clarence, 25
Obourn, Megan, 81
Obserländer, Adolf, *31*
Oedipal theory, 14, 16, 19–20, 22–25, 140, 171
Oesfees (harvest festival), 322
Office of Economic Opportunity, 279

Olifantshoek (Elephant Quarter), 314
omnipotence: delusions of, 113–14
oolites, 295
open hand gestures, 210–13
openness, radical, 28, 246
oppression: anti-Black, 204–5; narratives of, 32
oppression trauma, 174; definition of, 178–79; psychic adaptation to, 159–91; transgenerational mental representations of, 177–81
oral history, 317–18
othering, 27
Otherness, 175, 299–310; African American, 15–17; assumptions of, 89–90; projection into, 302–4; psychoanalytic engagement of, 244–50; racial, 174–76; theoretical formulation of, 173–74
Ovesey, Lionel, 18–19, 66n6, 76

PANIC/Sadness system, 182
paranoia, 14, 248; cultural, 327–38; post-traumatic reactions, 116
parents, 102–3
Parker, Milford, 33n3
patriarchal attitudes, 143–44, 294
Peele, Jordan, 329–30, 333, 337; *Get Out,* 327–40, 345–48, 351–53
Pennsylvania: history of slavery, 142
The People Under the Stairs, 329
persecutory anxiety, 98, 101
personal identity, 227
personal meaning, 116
personal perspectives, 288–310
Peters, Mercedes, 33n3
Pinderhughes, Charles, Sr., 33n3
PLAY/Social Joy system, 182
Poitier, Sidney, 342–43
police: fear of, 84–87, 262–63; "the talk" about, 237, 276–77; violence against unarmed Black men by, 1–2, 9–10, 77, 84, 86–87, 168, 221, 236, 282
Polite, Craig, 33n3, 278
Port Jervis, New York, 274
post-colonial studies, 302
post-racial society, 147
post-traumatic reactions, 105–24; case example I, 106–11; case example II, 112–15; psychological phenomena, 116–20
post-traumatic slave syndrome, 50–51
poverty, 354n1

Powell, Dionne, 25–26, 33n3, 175–76, 278
Prague, Czech Republic: "Facing the Pain" (2013 IPA Prague Congress), 42–43
Prater, Vivian, 279
pre-awareness, 227
prejudice, 105, 248; against African Americans, 25–26; consolidation of, 226–27; post-traumatic reactions, 117; in psychoanalysis, 25–26; theory of, 17–23; *see also* race and racism
prisons: prison-industrial complex, 152; school-to-prison pipeline, 146–53
The Progressive, 221
projection, 91–92; being objects of, 92–94; into Other, 302–4; post-traumatic reactions, 118–19
provocative gestures, 125–36
pseudoscience, 48
psychic adaptation to oppression, 159–91
psychic emancipation, 175–76, 339–40, 348–51
psychic enslavement, 175–76
psychic intrusions: defending against, 93–95
psychoanalysis, 13–71, 308–9; African American psychoanalysts, 23–26, 32n2–3, 44, 49, 65n3, 276, 282; benefits of, 349; Black Psychoanalysts Speak, 276, 278, 282; *Black Psychoanalysts Speak* (PEP-Web), 244, 278, 280; citizen psychoanalysts, 153; community, 311–23; engagement of otherness, 244–50; failure to address racism's trauma, 122–23; Freud's neglect of race and racism in, 160–62; fundamental ethic of, 318; identity trouble, 205–6; of racism, 172; racism in, 23–28, 276; reflections from lived experience of James Baldwin's America, 221–24, 235–40; self-examination, 28–30; by surprise, 311–23; theoretical, 17–28; therapeutic conversations, 52–60, 122–23, 286–87, 306–7; therapeutic silence, 42–71, 153–54; in urban ER, 251–69; white psychoanalysts, 281–82; a white therapist's response to Blackness, 257–59
psychoanalytically oriented psychotherapy, 122–23; *see also* psychotherapy

Psychoanalytic Electronic Publishing (PEP-Web): *Black Psychoanalysts Speak,* 244, 278, 280
Psychoanalytic Review, 17
Psychodynamic Diagnostic Manual-2 (PDM-2), 138–39
psychodynamic psychotherapy, 64; *see also* psychotherapy
psychologic effects, 89–104
psychotherapy, 9–11; African American suspicions toward, 331; case examples, 106–15; case vignettes, 127–35; failure to address racism's trauma, 122–23; in *Get Out,* 331–32; psychoanalytically oriented, 122–23; psychodynamic, 64; suggested dimension of listening for, 135–36; *see also* therapeutic conversations

queer (term), 215n10
queer theory, 249

race and racism: acknowledgement of, 127–32; as adaptive challenge, 27; toward African Americans, 28–29, 43; in anthropology, 28; anti-Semitism, 16, 19–20, 27, 29–30, 43–44, 102, 160–61, 171–72, 187n6, 273–75; awareness of, 125–27, 222–26; James Baldwin's America, 221–24, 235–40; case examples, 106–15; case vignettes, 127–35; color-blind, 50, 113; as constructed rationalization, 318; during Covid-19, 162–66, *164*; as culturally imposed trauma, 28; defending against, 93–95; denial of, 103; destiny of, 125–36; dialectical constitution, 304; discriminatory gestures, 105; everyday, 89–104; evolution of, 49–50; Freud's neglect of, 160–62, 171; Freud's secret Black Rage, 171–72; Freud's views on, 29–30, *31*, 51; and health equity, 7–12; institutional, 275; intergenerational trauma of, 137–58; internal, 92; internalization of, 123; internalized, 171–72; interracial marriage, 339–40; laissez-faire, 50; learning and re-learning, 219–69; living with, 73–218; meta-racism, 102; microaggressions, 49, 78; perpetuation of, 146–53, 290; persistence of, 23–28, 147; personal experiences of, 304–8;

post-traumatic reactions to, 105–24; preoccupations with, 135–36; as projection, 91–94; in psychoanalysis, 13–71, 276; psychological effects of, 89–104; psychological phenomena associated with, 116–20; recognition of, 125–27; self-discovery of, 125–32; shaping behavior, 125–36; stereotypes, 78–79; structural, 147, 268–69; systemic, 237, 268–69, 354n4; theoretical framework for, 17–23; in theory and training, 23–28; trauma of, 1–4; unconscious, 7–8; unspoken, 269; in urban ER, 251–69; white indifference, 155n2; white reflections on, 278–82

race relations: in *Get Out*, 345–48; in *Guess Who's Coming to Dinner*, 341–45; interracial marriage, 339–40, 354n5

race riots, 341; Detroit, Michigan, 20, 237; Red Summer (Chicago), 186n4

racial differences: awareness of, 222–26; curiosity about, 125–35, 222–24; learning about, 223; in therapy, 286–87, 306–7; in urban ER, 257–62

racial discrimination, 104–5, 120–24; acute trauma, 116–20; case example I, 106–11; case example II, 112–15; chronic trauma, 116–20; *see also* race and racism

racial-ethnic-cultural (REC) identity, 227
racial hatred, 119
racial identity, 223, 293
racialization, 26–27, 306
racial melancholia, 27
racial Otherness, 174–76
racial slurs, 192–218
racial socialization, 221–43
racial stress, 95–99
racial trauma: intergenerational, 137–58; post-traumatic reactions, 105–24; psychological phenomena associated with, 116–20; signs and symptoms of, 181–82; silent response to, 42–71

racist graffiti, 125
radical openness, 28, 246
Radó, Sándor, 49
rage, *see* anger and rage
RAGE/Anger system, 182–83, 185
Rankine, Claudia, 56, 83, 353
rape, 153

Reagan, Ronald, 141
reality: assault on one's sense of, 99–100; definition of, 162; distortions of, 97, 99–100; as ongoing threat, 100–103

Rear Window, 329
Reconstruction, 146
recovery from substances, 267–68
Red Summer (Chicago, 1919), 186n4
Reed, Lou, 301
Reichbart, Richard, 25
rejection: fear of, 98
relational gaps, 284
re-learning race, 219–69
resilience: trans-generational transmission of, 237; in urban ER, 255
respect, 259–60
revenge fantasy, 114
revolution, 187n5
revolutionary counterviolence, 187n5
Rhode Island: history of slavery, 142
Richards, Beah, 344
Rimbaud, Arthur, 308
Roberts, Carolyn, 8
Roberts, Dorothy, 7
Robinson, Jacqueline, 33n3
Rockman, Seth, 289
Rodgers, Terry, 20
Roheim, Geza, 279
Rolling Stone, 341
Root, Stephen, 347
Rose, Tricia, 49–50
Rosemary's Baby, 330
Ross, Robert, 33n3
Rucker, Naomi, 33n3
rumination: post-traumatic reactions, 115; retaliatory, 115
Rumsfeld, Donald, 296

sadism, sexual, 209
sadness, 181
sadomasochism, 209
Sales, Ruby, 62, 344
Sandler, Joseph and Anne-Marie, 93
Saturday Night Live, 299
Schachter, Judith, 24
school life, 283–87; integration, 299–300, 309; segregation, 147
school-to-prison pipeline, 146–53
Scott, Hannah, 144
Second Middle Passage, 154
SEEKING/Expectancy system, 182

Segal, Hanna, 92
segregation, 178; checker games, 285–86; school, 147
self-concept, 207, 227
self-determination: case example I, 110–11; historical self, 179
self-disclosure, 64
self-discovery, 125–27; case vignettes, 127–35
self-esteem, 111; post-traumatic reactions, 116
self-examination, 28–30
self-hatred, 315–16
self-image, 229–30
self-medication, 267–68
self-worth, 237–38
sense of reality: assault on, 99–100; as ongoing threat, 100–103
Sentencing Project, 152
sexual abuse, 145–46
sexuality, 181
sexual minorities, 153
sexual sadism, 209
Shay, Jonathan, 167
Shengold, Leonard, 237
The Shining, 329
Shipp, Thomas, 46
Siegel, Nathaniel, 23
silence: between Blacks and white, 286–87; conspiracy of, 275–77, 292–93; in response to racialized trauma, 42–71; therapeutic, 42–71, 153–54
Sims, James Marion, 261
slavery: American history of, 15–17, 22, 43–44, 138, 140–54, 188n9, 277, 289, 354n3; fear of family breakup, 143; fear of loss or being sold away, 143; Haitian, 302; Hegel on, 302, 309n1; horrors of, 142–45; institutions of, 146–53; legacy of, 48, 75–79, 172, 261; perpetuation of, 146–53; post-traumatic slave syndrome, 50–51; psychic enslavement, 175–76; psychic impact of, 43–44; South African history of, 315–17; Southern apologists for, 202; trauma of, 138, 140–45, 350–51
slave trade, 354n3
slurs, racial, 192–218; advocacy for, 206; case vignettes, 207–8; as defensive response, 208–10; disavowal of, 204–5; history of, 196–99; homophobic, 207; malign power of, 197; perceptual defense of, 202–4; reclamation of, 215n10; unseen harm of, 194–96
Smaller, Mark, 33n3
smallpox epidemic (1860s), 163
Smith, Abram, 46
Smith, Charles, 33n3
Smith, Lillian, 18–20
Socarides, Charles, 187n8
socialization: legal, 228; PLAY/Social Joy system, 182; racial, 221–43
social justice, 165
social networks, 228
social thrillers, 329–30, 337n1
Soetstemme, 322
Solms-Delta Wine Estate (Franschhoek, South Africa), 311–23
South Africa, 187n5; community psychoanalysis in, 311–23; *dop* system, 317; farm life, 311–23; Franschhoek (French Quarter), 314; history of slavery, 315–17; Land Reform, 323; Olifantshoek (Elephant Quarter), 314; Truth and Reconciliation Council, 45
Southern apologists, 202
Southern Christian Leadership Conference, 279
Southerntown, Mississippi, 18
Spanish flu pandemic (1918), 163
special education students, 151
Spielberg, Warren, 229
Spock, Benjamin, 49
Spurlock, Jeanne, 24, 33n3
The Stepford Wives, 329–30, 337n1
Sterba, Richard, 20
stereotypes: about Black females, 150–51; racial, 48–49, 78–79
Stevens, Rutherford, 33n3
Stoute, Argyle, 33n3
Stoute, Beverly J., 33n3, 278
"Strange Fruit" (Meeropol), 46
stress: mental, 97–98; post-traumatic reactions, 119–21; racial, 95–99
structural racism, 147
substance abuse: recovery from, 267–68
substitution test, 90–91
survivors, 29, 139, 155n3, 177
suspicion: post-traumatic reactions, 116
systemic racism, 237

"the talk," 237, 276–77
talk therapy, *see* therapeutic conversations

Tarantino, Quentin, 78
Tate, Claudia, 29, 33n3
terminology, 26, 65n2; racial slurs, 192–218
testimonial injustice, 213–14
Thanatos, 159
theory: anal theory of racism, 22; child development theory, 303–4; critical race theory, 302; critical theory, 249; field theory, 249; Freud's neglect of race and racism in, 160–62; Freud's theory of cultural memory, 177; Freud's theory of universal mind, 159–60; Kleinian, 15–16; Oedipal, 14, 16, 19–20, 22–25, 140, 171; persistence of racism in, 23–28; of prejudice, 17–23; psychoanalytic, 17–28, 160–62; queer, 249; racism in theory and training, 23–28
therapeutic conversations, 122–23, 306–7; examples, 52–60; silence in, 286–87
Thompson, Cheryl, 33n3, 278
threat, ongoing, 100–103
Time magazine, 222
Toney, Ellis, 14, 24, 33n3, 61
Tracy, Spencer, 343
training: multicultural, 244–45; persistence of racism in, 23–28; psychoanalytic, 23–28
transgenerational Black Rage, 177–81
transgenerational model, 140
transgenerational transmission of trauma, 45, 139, 221–24, 235–40
trauma: chosen, 178; collective, 178; collective therapeutic silent response to, 42–71; cultural introjects of, 140; culturally imposed, 28–29; deposited representations of, 140; discriminatory, 116–17; facing and accepting, 257; "Facing the Pain" (2013 IPA Prague Congress), 42–43; intergenerational, 137–58; moral injury, 166–71; oppression, 159–91; in post-racial society, 147; post-traumatic reactions, 105–24; post-traumatic slave syndrome, 50–51; psychic adaptation to, 159–91; psychological phenomena associated with, 116–20; psychological response to, 28–29, 43–44; racial, 105–24, 181–82; racialized, 42–71; of racism, 1–4; of slavery, 138, 140–45, 350–51; social aspects of, 140; transgenerational mental representations of, 177–81; transgenerational transmission of, 45, 139, 221–24, 235–40; two-stage model of, 200; unresolved, 138; unseen harm, 194–96
"Trauma: New Developments in Psychoanalysis" (2007 IPA Berlin Congress), 42
tribalism, 50
Trout, Bobbye, 33n3
Trump, Donald, 305, 352
Trussel, Elizabeth, 33n3
Truth, Sojourner, 143
Truth and Reconciliation Council (South Africa), 45
Turkey, 155n3
Tuskegee syphilis study, 261
Twitter, 83–84

uncertainty, 97
unconscious fantasy, 93, 177
understanding: fear of not being able to, 98; fear of not being understood, 98
United Nations, 21
United Negro College Fund, 327
United States: African American population, 146; James Baldwin's America, 221–24, 235–40; Black child development, 137–58; Black codes, 152–53; Civil Rights movement, 21, 82–83, 187n5; Covid-19 pandemic, 162–66; educational policy, 149; founding fathers, 15; health care system, 262–68; historical context, 45–52, 63–64, 260; history of epidemics, 163; history of slavery, 15–17, 22, 43–44, 138, 140–54, 188n9, 277, 289, 354n3; intergenerational trauma, 138–42; legacy of racism, 161; legacy of slavery, 48, 75–79, 261; mistreatment of Blacks, 28–29, 45–52; post-racial society, 147; poverty, 354n1; prison population, 152; prisons, 146–53; racial history, 345–48; Reconstruction, 146; schools, 146–53; societal system, 262–68; unresolved trauma, 138
United States Constitution, 15, 146–47
universal mind: Freud's theory of, 159–60
University of California, 279
University of Cape Town, 313

unseen harm, 194–96
urban ER, 251–69
urban life, 335–36

Valley Entertainers, 322
Vaughans, Kirkland, 33n3, 229, 278, 290
verbalization: power of, 110, 233–34; *see also* therapeutic conversations
Vermont: history of slavery, 142
Vietnam Vet Center (West Haven, Connecticut), 275
violence: assault on one's sense of reality, 99–100; fantasies of, 199; fresh acts of, 83–85; gender-based, 155n4; lynchings, 46–47, 153; police against unarmed Black men, 1–2, 9–10, 77, 84, 86–87, 168, 221, 236; revolutionary counterviolence, 187n5; sexual abuse, 145–46
Virginia: history of slavery, 142; interracial marriage, 340; State Act to Preserve Racial Integrity, 339–40
Volkan, Vamik, 177–78, 187n8, 227
Voting Rights Act, 13, 341

Wadas, B. Lois, 33n3
Walker, David, 50–51
Walker, Sandra, 33n3
war capitalism, 289–90
Washington, Booker T., 343
Washington, D.C., 257–58, 339; Black Lives Matter Plaza, 170, *170*
Washington, Harriet, 8, 328
Weaver, Fred III, 33n3
West Haven VA (Connecticut), 275
White, Cleonie, 33n3, 278
White, Kathy Pogue, 33n3, 278, 280
white fragility, 295
white gaze, 96
Whitehead, Colson, 46
white immigrants, 290–91
white liberal guilt, 301, 348–51
white liberalism, 352–53
whiteness, 27, 288–89, 295–96
white privilege, 27, 45, 61–62, 260; awareness of, 271–323; daily effects of, 280; definition of, 345; indifference toward Blacks, 155n2; personal perspective on, 288–310; shades, 276–77; understanding, 273–77; white reflections on, 278–82; working through, 348–51
white psychoanalysts, 281–82
white race consciousness, 302–4
white saviors, 301
white supremacist violence, 47–48
white supremacy, 214n2
white therapists, 257–59, 281–82
Wilkerson, Isabel, 15, 100
Wilkes, Quentin, 33n3
Williams, Allison, 345
Williams, David, 9, 168
Williams, Patricia, 96
Williams, Serena, 56
Wilson, August, 344, 346
wine, 320
Winnicott, D. W., 161, 308
Winograd, Basia, 244, 307
Wolfowitz, Paul, 296
women: African American, 80–88, 145–46; denial of dependency of, 97; enslaved, 145–46; everyday lives of, 80–88; fear of police, 85–87; female protagonists in *Get Out* vs *Guess Who's Coming to Dinner*, 353–54; marginalization of, 354n2; stereotypes about Black females, 150–51
women's liberation, 153
Woods, Alexandra, 278
World War I, 155n3
World War II, 161
Wright, Richard, 23
Wyche, Samuel, 33n3
Wyden, Barbara, 25

X, Malcolm, 78, 275, 341, 343

Yale University, 290
yellow fever epidemic (1793), 163
Young-Bruehl, Elisabeth, 21
youth: incarcerated, 151; juvenile justice, 147; lesbian, gay, bisexual, and transgender (LGBT), 150

Zilboorg, Gregory, 19
Zimmerman, George, 43, 52, 84, 352

For Product Safety Concerns and Information please contact our EU
representative GPSR@taylorandfrancis.com
Taylor & Francis Verlag GmbH, Kaufingerstraße 24, 80331 München, Germany

www.ingramcontent.com/pod-product-compliance
Lightning Source LLC
Chambersburg PA
CBHW050526300426
44113CB00012B/1971